The field of psychological anthropology has changed a great deal since the 1940s and 1950s, when it was often known as "Culture and Personality Studies." Rooted in psychoanalytic psychology, its early practitioners sought to extend that psychology through the study of cross-cultural variation in personality and childrearing practices. Psychological anthropology has since developed in a number of new directions. Tensions between individual experience and collective meanings remain as central to the field as they were fifty years ago, but, alongside fresh versions of the psychoanalytic approach, other approaches to the study of cognition, emotion, the body, and the very nature of subjectivity have been introduced. And in the place of an earlier tendency to treat a "culture" as an undifferentiated whole, psychological anthropology now recognizes the complex internal structure of cultures.

The contributors to this state-of-the-art collection are all leading figures in contemporary psychological anthropology, and they write about recent developments in the field. Sections of the book discuss cognition, developmental psychology, biology, psychiatry, and psychoanalysis, areas that have always been integral to psychological anthropology but which are now being transformed by new perspectives on the body, meaning, agency, and communicative practice.

Publications of the Society for Psychological Anthopology 3

New directions in psychological anthropology

Publications of the Society for Psychological Anthropology

Publications of the Society for Psychological Anthropology is a joint initiative of Cambridge University Press and the Society for Psychological Anthropology, a unit of the American Anthropological Association. The series has been established to publish books in psychological anthropology and related fields of cognitive anthropology, ethnopsychology, and cultural psychology. It will include works of original theory, empirical research, and edited collections that address current issues. The creation of this series reflects a renewed interest among culture theorists in ideas about the self, mind–body interaction, social cognition, mental models, processes of cultural acquisition, motivation and agency, gender, and emotion. The books will appeal to an international readership of scholars, students, and professionals in the social sciences.

1. Roy d'Andrade and Claudia Strauss (eds.) *Human motives and cultural models*
2. Nancy Rosenberger (ed.) *Japanese Sense of Sey*

New directions in psychological anthropology

Edited by

Theodore Schwartz

Department of Anthropology
University of California, San Diego

Geoffrey M. White

Institute of Culture and Communication
East–West Center

Catherine A. Lutz

Department of Anthropology
University of North Carolina, Chapel Hill

Published by the Press Syndicate of the University of Cambridge
The Pitt Building, Trumpington Street, Cambridge CB2 1RP
40 West 20th Street, New York, NY 10011–4211, USA
10 Stamford Road, Oakleigh, Victoria 3166, Australia

First published 1992

Printed in Great Britain at the University Press, Cambridge

A catalogue record for this book is available from the British Library
Library of Congress cataloguing in publication data applied for

ISBN 0 521 41592 6 hardback
ISBN 0 521 42609 X paperback

Contents

Contributors

JAMES S. CHISHOLM Department of Applied Behavioral Sciences, University of California, Davis

BERTRAM J. COHLER Committee on Human Development, University of Chicago

VINCENT CRAPANZANO Department of Comparative Literature, City University of New York Graduate Center

ROY G. D'ANDRADE Department of Anthropology, University of California, San Diego

KATHERINE P. EWING Department of Anthropology, Duke University

BYRON J. GOOD Department of Social Medicine, Harvard University

SARA HARKNESS Department of Individual and Family Studies, Pennsylvania State University

DOROTHY HOLLAND Department of Anthropology, University of North Carolina, Chapel Hill

LISA HOOGSTRA Committee on Human Development, University of Chicago

JANET DIXON KELLER Department of Anthropology, University of Illinois, Urbana

ROBERT I. LEVY Department of Anthropology, University of California, San Diego and University of North Carolina, Chapel Hill

CATHERINE A. LUTZ Department of Anthropology, University of North Carolina, Chapel Hill

PEGGY J. MILLER Department of Speech Communication and Department of Psychology, University of Illinois, Urbana

NANCY SCHEPER-HUGHES Department of Anthropology, University of California, Berkeley

THEODORE SCHWARTZ Department of Anthropology, University of California, San Diego

GEORGE W. STOCKING, JR. Department of Anthropology, University of Chicago

GEOFFREY M. WHITE Institute of Culture and Communication, East–West Center

CAROL M. WORTHMAN Department of Anthropology, Emory University

Introduction

Geoffrey M. White and Catherine A. Lutz

While once almost synonymous with American cultural anthropology, psychological anthropology remains one of the largest subdisciplines of the field. It also remains the field most centrally concerned with putting people and experience into theories of culture and society. Increasingly more diverse in their approaches and interests, psychological anthropologists have been energized by a series of recent debates and by historical and institutional factors contributing to a renewed interest in the field. The chapters in this book, which emerged out of several years of organized reassessment of the field, reflect on an ongoing revitalization indexed by numerous recent collections focusing on the intersection of culture and psychology (e.g. Lee 1982; Marsella, DeVos, and Hsu 1985; Shweder and LeVine 1984; Stigler, Shweder, and Herdt 1990; White and Kirkpatrick 1985).

These theoretical and institutional changes have together facilitated more dialogue within the subdiscipline as well as with other kinds of anthropologists. The short history of these changes could be written in many ways but would include the development of interpretive approaches to culture compatible with (and challenging to) clinical and Freudian perspectives; the reflexive turn in methodology which has raised the question of how North American ideologies of self and person might structure our thinking as a discipline and as enculturated human beings doing fieldwork; the breakdown of monolithic views of culture which has encouraged person-centered ethnographic approaches (e.g. LeVine 1982); and narrative experimentation in ethnographic presentation, some of the earliest examples of which dealt with classical issues in psychological anthropology (e.g., Briggs 1970; Crapanzano 1980; Riesman 1977; Shostak 1981). These and other factors will be briefly considered in this introduction.

Institutionally, the growth in the 1970s and 1980s of important new university centers of work in psychological anthropology at the University of California at San Diego and Emory University as well as the continued vitality of work at places such as the interdisciplinary centers at

Chicago, Harvard, and University of California, Los Angeles has also been crucial to the renaissance in the field. Also important – at least for such areas as human development or psychiatric anthropology – has been the strong growth of the cognate fields of psychology and psychiatry. The ubiquity and strength of the psychological paradigm – both in popular culture and in academic circles – must in large part be a function of the resonances of that discipline's individualistic perspective with American conceptions of person. The cultural and social conditions that helped create this state of affairs include such things as the medicalization of psychiatry (see Good and Scheper-Hughes, this book) and the American cultural obsession with self-awareness. However challenging the anthropological perspective on the self can be to the universalizing claims of psychology, some of the same cultural foundations underlie the vitality of both fields.

A more immediate prompt to this book was the efforts of Theodore Schwartz who promoted a stock-taking of the field, or what he called "appraisal and prospectus." He, together with Catherine Lutz and Susan Abbott, organized three years of such comprehensive sessions at the annual meetings of the American Anthropological Association in 1986, 1987, and 1988. The chapters in this book are the outgrowth of the first two of those years of sessions, meetings which were heavily attended and rife with the excitement of a watershed period of new questions and research directions and renewed collegial dialogue. The contributors to those sessions – all central figures to their respective fields – were asked *not* to review recent work comprehensively or dispassionately, but to give their vision of where research has been and where it ought to go. They were asked to stimulate discussion and debate rather than to attempt closure or balanced overview.

The present set of chapters emerged from this charge.[1] In this introduction, we do not attempt any kind of heroic synthesis or statement of fundamental principles. In fact, such an effort would misrepresent the diversity and debates that characterize this book. Mindful of these differences, we offer a reflection on themes that emerge in these papers and their significance for research directions. Whereas the recent collection edited by Stigler, Shweder, and Herdt (1990) has articulated the theoretical bases for an emerging interdisciplinary field of "cultural psychology," the authors in this book orient their discussions toward problems that characterize psychological anthropology (historically and at present) – whether cognitive, developmental, biological, psychoanalytic, or psychiatric, to name some of the areas addressed. Out of this mix emerges a broad spectrum of overlapping approaches that nonetheless share anthropology's root concerns with problems of meaning, cultural analysis, and the study of persons in society. Offering neither reports on ongoing research nor sweeping reviews of the literature, the papers in this book rather seek to raise issues and offer assessments of promising directions for future research.

Through the postwar years, a number of books have intermittently appeared which attempt to survey the field (e.g., Bourguignon 1979; Spindler 1978). In each, current philosophies of science can be seen structuring the notion of what this or any other "field" is. The present mood is reflected in these chapters, many of which are concerned with charting the terrain of the shifting psychocultural borderlands between mind, culture, and society – a terrain which is increasingly seen as reflecting the cultural and social context of its inhabitants rather than merely an intellectual history of questions which follow naturally from previous questions.

It then also seems useful to draw attention to the similarities between the constitution of psychological anthropology as "a field" and processes of group identity generally. Ethnic, gender, or class identities and symbolizations are most evident at their peripheries, where contacts with others evoke articulations and dramatizations of the self. In this view of identity as emergent, culturally constructed, and context dependent, psychological anthropology may be seen not as a set of essential definitions but as what individual psychological anthropologists do or have historically done. The contributors to this book are all concerned in some way with boundary issues, with questions that arise at the interstices of anthropology and related fields. In often new and creative ways, many contributors critique the dualisms and boundaries presented by received theoretical categories of mind and body, psyche and society (see also Lutz 1988). In thus drawing attention to the social and cultural processes involved in academic work in psychological anthropology, these analysts have begun to find new paths through and around old terms of debate (see also Scheper-Hughes and Lock 1987).

Periods of intellectual fragmentation have the effect of calling into question definitional assumptions that are relegated to the background during periods of "normal science." Developments inside and outside anthropology in recent decades have posed problems and opportunities for psychological anthropology – not the least of which is the definition of the niche within which the subdiscipline locates itself theoretically. During the heyday of culture and personality studies in the 1940s and 1950s, the Parsonian division of the world into personality systems, cultural systems, and social systems provided a clear agenda for research on relations between personality variables and culture. As framed by many practitioners, the objective of "culture and personality" studies was to apply the theories and insights of personality theory (with Freudian psychoanalytic theory being the modal type) to analyzing the meaning and motivating force of cultural forms for individuals. The theoretical niche occupied by culture and personality became much less secure, however, with a variety of movements elsewhere in social science and society. These included (1) the development of interpretive and praxis theories which expanded the role of symbolic and institutional forces in accounting for social action; (2) the challenge to the utility of the psychoanalytic focus on personality and affective hydraulics by revitalized cognitive, language-based, and biological perspectives on the person; (3) renewed emphasis upon intracultural variation that has made problematic any simplistic splitting of culture as collective and personality as individual; and (4), more generally, by a postmodern, poststructuralist suspicion of depth models of human experience that not only questions the pre-eminence of the private individual in explanatory models, but seeks to deconstruct the very notion of a human psyche beneath history and culture. While these changes at first appeared to signal the end of a psychological anthropology, their challenge has resulted in some important reformulations of the problem of the individual. These new antidualistic approaches have shifted and opened up the boundaries between "psychological" and other kinds of anthropologies.

More specifically, numerous responses to these developments might be traced in the work of psychological anthropologists since the 1960s, with some continuing to apply and adapt psychoanalytic theory during an era of interpretive social science, and others pursuing cognitive, linguistic, and semiotic approaches to self and experience. Overall, however, psychological anthropology since the 1960s has been characterized by increasingly diverse methodologies focused on more narrowly drawn problems. Previous interest in global assessments of personality or character has largely given way to investigations of particular psychocultural processes and strategies of adaptation. These developments are reflected in the organization of the book *The Making of Psychological Anthropology* into two sections labeled sparsely "Part I" and "Part II" with the latter including topics of symbolism, consciousness, and cognition that, according to the editor George Spindler, had "only recently emerged as primary concerns of psychological anthropology" (1978: 2). This change was an effect both of specialization occurring everywhere in an increasingly populated academy and of a relative downturn of interest in global universalizing theories rooted in depth psychology. The "return of grand theory" (Skinner 1985), particularly in the last decade, has only slowly and recently come to psychological anthropology.

It may seem ironic or contradictory that the initial decline of interest in culture and personality and psychological anthropology more generally since the 1950s has occurred despite a simultaneous explosion of interest in and resources devoted to academic, popular, and clinical psychology. Some of these reasons have to do with the lack of interest in other people's psychology, as well as the therapeutic and applied bent of much of psychology in contrast with anthropology's version. Whereas psychology may appear to the society at large to be about helping one's self, anthropology, less enticingly, appears to be about explaining an other. Calls for communication across disciplinary boundaries (between anthropology and psychology, anthropology and biology, and psychological anthropology and sociocultural anthropology proper) may ring hollow and/or fail if the kinds of institutional, cultural, and historical factors influencing formation of the field in the first place are ignored.

The present collection further extrapolates the ongoing transformation of psychological anthropology and its relations with other subdisciplines and social sciences. While we offer no unified definition of psychological anthropology, the chapters included define a loosely integrated field of investigation by outlining a series of overlapping foci for current research. The fact that these focal areas shade into the work of other disciplines is evident in the extent to which each chapter draws from the perspectives and methods of other fields. Without exception, each contributor to this volume addresses the possibilities for interdisciplinary communication and exchange as a basis for enriching the work of anthropology and neighboring disciplines. Consider the range of modifiers of "anthropology" that appear in the table of contents for this volume: "psychoanalytic," "biological," "psychiatric," and "cognitive" – all designating some facet of that subspecies referred to here as "psychological anthropology." Whereas prewar culture and personality studies largely relied upon a theory of mind derived from psychoanalysis, contemporary psychological anthropology is engaged in a broader range of dialogues with other human sciences. While psychoanalysis continues to be a major influence – as articulated in the chapters by Katherine Ewing, Bertram Cohler, and Vincent Crapanzano – we now find that biology, psychiatry, developmental psychology, linguistics, discourse analysis, praxis theories, and cognitive science are having a greater impact than was evident in earlier decades.

The view of culture as emergent, contested, and temporal (Clifford 1988) – a view itself emergent, contested, and temporal – has had a significant impact on the field of anthropology as a whole. This movement is important to the field covered in this book for two reasons. It is influencing theory building in psychological anthropology, where recent developments suggest a more social, less essentializing model for conceptualizing psychocultural processes. In addition, this view of culture leaves new room for the reinsertion of the person as agent, for models of consciousness and motivation to which psychological anthropologists have something significant to contribute (Shweder and Sullivan in press). Renewed interest in performance has also encouraged description and theorization of the social enactment of psychological process, that is, of psyche's social life.

To varying degrees, the bridgework in these chapters addresses deep divisions in our conceptual apparatus – divisions between mind and body, reason and emotion – that have not only guided theory building in the social sciences, but underlie the social organization of knowledge into disciplinary spheres of biology, psychology, and sociology (or between general medicine and psychiatry, or social and psychological brands of anthropology, among others). The force of these divisions is continually replayed in our attempts to specify a framework for comparative work. For example, in a recent article on "Concepts of Individual, Self, and Person in Description and Analysis" Grace Harris defines three terms that have been key words in psychological anthropology (individual, self, and person) as grounded in "biologistic, psychologistic, and sociologistic modes of conceptualizing human beings" (1989: 599). The chapters in this book are, in general, far less prepared to enshrine these divisions as bedrock concepts from which to begin comparative investigations. Each chapter suggests strategies for exploring these domains as mutually intertwined and contingent regions of experience.

One of the anthropological challenges to social-scientific assumptions about personality derives from a series of studies by Shweder and D'Andrade showing that much of the consistency in personality assessment results from cultural or semantic associations that systematically skew social perception and memory (Shweder and D'Andrade 1980). While there is by no means universal agreement about the significance of these findings, acknowledgment of the importance of cultural constructs in dynamically shaping understanding and experience is directing a considerable amount of work towards the interrelation of linguistic, cognitive, and communicative processes in constituting personal and social realities. As White discusses in his chapter, anthropologists have recently begun to pay close attention to ethnopsychological understandings – of self, emotion, person, and the like – as one way of doing justice to the complexity and variety of the culturally constituted subjectivities in which people live their lives. The traffic between symbolic, cultural approaches and work on psychological issues has become heavy, marked particularly by the upsurge of anthropological studies of emotion in social life (e.g., Abu-Lughod 1986; Lutz 1988; Myers 1979; Rosaldo 1980; see Lutz and

White 1986 for a review). It is here more than at the biology/culture boundary that discussions have actually and intensively taken place. The contributions of ethnopsychological investigation, however, have yet to have these kinds of reverberation in other areas of the field of psychological anthropology (with the exception of human development research, see below).

Cognitive anthropology is discussed in this book by D'Andrade, Holland, and Keller. In the original symposium D'Andrade's paper was discussed by both Keller and Holland. Because their presentations complemented one another closely, the papers are presented here as a trilogy of chapters that make up a three-way conversation about the field. Proceeding from the view that human experience necessarily entails the thinking of active, aware, and interested agents, cognitive anthropologists have taken the problem of human understanding (conscious and otherwise) as a primary domain of investigation. The rapid growth of interest in studying cognition follows from the recognition that thought and understanding are amenable to analysis through language and other semiotic systems applied in social interaction.

As cognitive theories were developing in psychology and linguistics in the 1950s as a challenge to the dominant behaviorist paradigms, Anthony Wallace (1961) noted that their formulations were consistent with anthropological views of culture organized in terms of "schemata" and "mazeways" that mediate the responses of social actors. It was not long, however, before anthropologists in the sociocultural mainstream found the narrowly linguistic and terminological approach of the "new ethnography" or "ethnoscience" to be misdirected for the purposes of broader social and cultural analysis. One of the early salvos fired by symbolic anthropology in its efforts to differentiate itself from ethnoscience or ethnosemantics was Geertz's (1973: 11–12) assertion that meaning could not be discovered in people's heads, but rather needed to be studied as emergent in the public marketplace of interactively produced ideas and institutions. It now seems as if such proclamations contributed to an overly textual and homogeneous conception of culture, cut off from, among other things, the micropolitics of personal experience and cognition. Ironically, perhaps, the role of social and situational factors in structuring understanding is now a major area of research in cognitive anthropology (see Lave 1988; Holland 1988, this book). Additionally, some of the most exciting work on problems of intracultural diversity and the social distribution of knowledge and belief has come from psychological and cognitive anthropology (Romney, Weller, and Batchelder 1986; Schwartz 1976; Wallace 1961).

The discussions of cognitive anthropology in this book show that "schema theory" has developed considerably in the intervening thirty years since Wallace wrote about schemas and mazeways. The papers here discuss strategies for investigating conceptual processes and their relations with such things as metaphor and narrative as well as social processes (see Casson 1983; Holland and Quinn 1987; Luhrmann 1989). One of the central theoretical tensions that emerges from the conversation between D'Andrade, Holland, and Keller concerns the degree to which cognitive models attempt to incorporate contextual factors associated with the variation and flexibility inherent in cultural understanding (see also Strauss 1990). Holland's argument for attending to the social and situational factors that organize and shape cognitive processes resonates with the emphasis on communicative practices evident in much of the current research on language acquisition and socialization.

In her chapter dealing with the role of language in child development and the process of enculturation, Miller outlines issues that have fueled the rediscovery of Vygotsky's pragmatic theories of language and learning by psychologists, linguists, and anthropologists working on developmental issues (Holland and Valsiner 1988; Wertsch 1985). The Vygotskian emphasis upon the communicative processes that mediate human thought views technologies and social activities as integral extensions of cognitive process, and so challenges the often dichotomized oppositions of inner/outer and ideational/material. And it is these dichotomies that have tended to locate culture either "inside" the head in cognition or "outside" in public symbols, producing often fruitless debates about whether the locus of culture is in the minds of individuals or the signs and activities of daily life. By going beyond these dichotomies, this and other perspectives discussed in this book are provoking a rethinking of the ways we conceptualize relations between mind, self, and society.

Another source of challenges to individuated theories of personality comes from correlational studies of child behavior. The review by Sara Harkness of cross-cultural research on human development describes a history of interdisciplinary work focused to a large extent on testing the generalizability of theories of developmental processes or stages (whether about personality, cognitive abilities, language, or moral reasoning). Beyond the largely descriptive role of "cataloguing similarities and differences," Harkness argues that comparative research at its best aims "to reformulate existing psychological theories of development and to elaborate new perspectives." She mentions several areas of recent anthropological work, including studies of child language socialization as well as cognitive and emotional development, as contributing to the emergence of new perspectives on old problems addressed in psychological theories.

The resulting overview suggests a broad shift in emphasis in anthropological studies of child development from research on socialization conceived as personality formation to greater concern with processes of enculturation (see Schwartz 1981).

One example in particular noted by Harkness (and one which shows links between developmental and cognitive research in psychological anthropology) is reflected in Shweder's (1979a, b) interpretation of the accumulated findings of cross-cultural research on child social behavior done by John and Beatrice Whiting and their colleagues over a period of many years. Shweder argues, among other things, that the concept of personality as the central, organizing link between early experiences and patterns of adult behavior does not hold up under scrutiny (see also Riesman 1983). His critique and others have had broad repercussions for social scientific models of the person, including reexamination of the concept of motivation and its relation to culture (D'Andrade and Strauss 1992).

Biological factors have been an everpresent component of psychological anthropology's agenda, although usually in the background as "givens" rather than in the foreground among the topics and variables to be examined in research. The common framework of human physical capacities, needs, and their ontogenesis has been invoked repeatedly as the basis for the psychic unity of humanity – a framework within which to conduct comparative examinations of variations in the perceptual, conceptual, and emotional life of peoples around the world (Spiro 1986). The theoretical dilemmas posed by such a project – emblazoned in familiar dualisms of universalist/relativist, positivist/interpretivist, materialist/idealist, and the like – are even more problematic today than they were earlier in the century when Margaret Mead and others set off to use the "laboratory" of human cultural variation to dislodge the natural status ascribed to concepts of race, gender, and developmental stage. However, the chapters in this collection indicate that, even if these dualisms remain problematic, approaches being tried on a variety of fronts hold the possibility of novel solutions and integrations.

The two chapters in this book that deal directly with relations between biological and psychological research, by James Chisholm and Carol Worthman, challenge dichotomous conceptions of mind and body that regard biology as a source of fixed, determinant features in human experience. As Worthman writes, "Over a century of progress in life sciences has blurred [this] dichotomy by abundantly demonstrating that biology, too, is emergent in life histories." Ironically, the conception of biology as a domain of invariant and universal processes which has given biological variables a privileged position in Western theories of human development has also had the effect of removing physiological factors from serious consideration in research on psychocultural variation. The privileged position of biology also meant that few researchers in either discipline seriously expected that anthropological techniques developed for the study of culture would be useful for research on biological processes. In contrast, Chisholm and Worthman both argue that certain biological problems require detailed studies of the cognitive, perceptual, and socioemotional processes that structure subjective experience – that is, the primary subject matter of psychological anthropology. They identify a number of topics that have long been subjects of anthropological research as promising areas for collaboration between biological and psychological anthropologists. Prominent among these are comparative studies of child development (such as those discussed in this book by Sara Harkness) and anthropological studies that incorporate biophysical factors (such as Scheper-Hughes' studies of the psychological and social responses to hunger and to high infant mortality rates in Brazil: this book and 1985). On the biological side of this relationship, these authors point to the emerging field of "life-history theory" as an area of research that stands to benefit from greater "investigative syncretism" (Worthman's term). The biological notion of "life-history" views culturally mediating devices (such as strategies and ethnotheories of parenting) and psychological changes as necessary, interactive processes in human phenotypic variation.

The chapters in this book that examine relations between the biological and the psychocultural may be seen as working at one of the "edges" of psychological anthropology where concerns with subjectivity and consciousness shade into psychological research. Differences between the types of problems and methods that characterize biological and psychological anthropology reflect more than simply the methodological preferences of two subdisciplines. These contrasts reflect differences between two varieties of science – varieties that proceed from quite different assumptions about the sorts of generalizations and truths they seek to derive. To use terms employed by D'Andrade (1986), biology, a "natural science," deals in contingent generalizations about complex adaptive machine-like systems while cultural anthropology, a "semiotic science," pursues contingent generalizations about the creation of intersubjective realities that shape, guide, and constrain social action. As Richard Shweder has observed (*Anthropology Newsletter* 1989: 19), psychological anthropology is "some kind of hybrid form" – a semiotic natural science. As a result, ambiguities and disagreements about the types of methods and truths that ought to characterize this hybrid field have been abundant.

The conceptual tensions evident in the interplay of biological and psychocultural approaches also run through several other chapters in this volume, particularly those by Good on psychiatric anthropology and Cohler on psychoanalytic anthropology. Since both psychiatry and psychoanalysis have their own traditions of defining and studying mind–body relations, anthropological entrepreneurs in these areas have had to reckon with issues similar to those articulated by Worthman and Chisholm.

As Byron Good outlines in his chapter, communication with modern psychiatry requires a confrontation with biologically driven models of behavior disorder. The history of psychiatry in the twentieth century has been one of progressive differentiation of diagnostic categories around clusters of observable symptoms that may be shown to respond to drug treatments. Good notes what he calls an "extraordinary paradigm shift" in psychiatric discourse during the last twenty years from the psychoanalytic to the biological. Striving to establish its own legitimacy within modern medicine where the prototypic illness is one with a clear physiological etiology and treatment strategy, psychiatric research has focused its resources on syndromes such as schizophrenia in which physiological mechanisms responsive to pharmacological treatment have been identified. Good here points to the phenomena of medicalization in psychiatry that Scheper-Hughes in her chapter identifies as a social process involved in class conflict in Brazil, encouraging the (mis)definition of psychosocial distress in biological terms.

Good illustrates the sociology of contemporary psychiatric knowledge in his discussion of the ongoing redefinition of anxiety disorders through their assimilation to a model of panic disorder defined as discrete, unprovoked, and physiologically triggered. In making panic disorder the prototypic case, psychiatry expresses its preference for illness categories that are less *contingent* on a socially constructed subjective reality, conscious or unconscious. On the one hand, this shift in the orientation of psychiatric knowledge and practice diminishes the opportunities for collaboration with anthropological colleagues who work in the sphere of "semiotic science." On the other hand, it calls for anthropological research critiquing the validity of psychiatric categories, both with Western cultures and focused comparatively. Good suggests a variety of strategies that anthropology may pursue to broaden and deepen the generalizations sought by modern psychiatry by elaborating the interpreted and experiential dimensions of disorder located within social–historical contexts. And, as Robert Levy argues in his chapter, this task should not be overly constrained by the vicissitudes of Western psychiatry and its obsessions at a particular moment in history. Levy raises the problem of how anthropologists may define their tasks and contributions as distinct from the categories and institutions of psychiatry, built as they are upon the pervasive social, political, and economic power of Western medicine. For Good, one of the potentially productive responses is to make the premises and practices of psychiatry an object of ethnographic investigation.

Given the significance of biological factors for psychoanalytic theory, it is not surprising to find that the conceptual tensions inherent in formulations of mind–body relations are also discussed by Ewing, Cohler, and Crapanzano in their papers on psychoanalytic anthropology. Cohler notes that psychoanalysis and anthropology not only share an interest in the study of subjectivity (see, e.g., Obeysekere 1981), but that both encompass internal tensions regarding the place of a natural science approach to the study of matters such as "wish and intent." He suggests that confusion between "natural and human science" perspectives in both fields has clouded our ability to articulate an experience-based approach to the study of meaning. Much of the language that continues to be used by psychoanalytic anthropologists concerned with interpreting subjective experience – terms such as primary process and infantile fixation – derive from Freud's "scientific world view" that reflects his earlier concerns with physiology, as distinct from constructs that emerged from his clinical work concerned with the "empathic study of lives over time."

The chapters by Ewing, Cohler, and Crapanzano view psychoanalysis, and hence its relevance for anthropology, from somewhat different angles. Ewing begins with a most basic question: "Is psychoanalysis relevant for anthropology?" and proceeds to answer in the affirmative by exploring the extensive (and as yet still uncharted) overlap between interpretive and psychoanalytic investigations of symbols and their relation to experience. Cohler pursues related issues by asking what aspects of Freudian theory may contribute to the study of culturally constituted subjectivities, and focusing particularly on that centerpiece of Freudian thought – the Oedipal complex – that has been an endless source of anthropological debate. Crapanzano provides a provocative reflection about the "theological" structure of psychoanalysis that derives from privileging Freud's writings as a primary corpus of texts. Even though anthropology and psychology have acknowledged some degree of shared subject matter almost since their inception, their relationship has continued to shift as historical changes have taken place in each. Crapanzano notes that in recent years both disciplines have experienced what he calls an "interpretive turn." His view is consistent with Ewing's and Cohler's assessments that the study of the experience of self in relation to others is given greater weight in psychoanalysis by a shift from a natural-science perspective to a human-science perspective. This shift entails greater attention to the interpretive and dialogic processes that have been central to anthropological theory, as reflected in the focus on the self and interpersonal relations in the psychology of Heinz Kohut (1977), in the emphasis on clinical experience as symbolic interaction in ego psychology (e.g., Klein 1976; Schafer 1976), and in the structural and semiological perspective of French poststructuralism (e.g., Lacan 1968; see also Trawick 1990).

The interest in interpretive processes in psychoanalytic anthropology, although itself variable and contested, reflects the degree to which the subdiscipline situates itself squarely within the domain of "semiotic science" (and hence vulnerable to exile from biologically oriented modern psychiatry). Whereas psychoanalytic theories increasingly find the "surfaces" of language, thought, and semiotic practice to be relevant to their interest in plumbing the "depths" of experience and motivation (Ewing, this book), other strands of investigation in psychological anthropology take problems of understanding, communication, and meaningful activity as primary for the understanding of self and emotion (e.g., Lutz and Abu-Lughod 1900; White 1991). In this regard, Peggy Miller and Lisa Hoogstra's chapter on language and the acquisition of culture, as well as the chapter on ethnopsychology by Geoffrey White and those on cognitive anthropology by Roy D'Andrade, Janet Keller, and Dorothy Holland, discuss anthropological approaches to language and cognition that have developed along with a broad "cognitive revolution" in postwar psychology and linguistics.

Historically, psychological anthropologists have drawn far more from psychoanalytic and clinical approaches than from academic psychology. Until recently, the domination of the latter by behaviorist theories and experimental methods drove a wedge between the discourse of psychologists and that of anthropologists accustomed to describing social action in terms of meaning, value, and experience. But the cognitive turn evident in contemporary psychology during the last three decades has produced a broad spectrum of interest in language and conceptual processes that is compatible, at least in broad outline, with the anthropological view of culture as a primary force in shaping human behavior. However, as Theodore Schwartz notes in his chapter, the potential for developing an exchange relationship between anthropology and psychology has so far gone "unrequited." In their symposium discussion of Schwartz's paper, Erika Bourguignon and Linda Hartranft observed that anthropological research has been either absent or only minimally cited in the major textbooks and journals of contemporary psychology. (This might suggest that the psychologists whom some anthropologists think of as the prototype for psychological anthropology's communicative partners are of the order of "imaginary" friends.) To the extent that a relationship is developing, it is discussed here in the chapters dealing with cognition and with child development.[2]

Each variety of psychological anthropology discussed in this book approaches problems of mind, culture, and experience from a vantage point that identifies a certain class of problems as significant and certain types of methods as most likely to be valid and fruitful. Another way of saying this, to borrow phrasing used by Crapanzano, is to note that from one approach to another methods differ in the manner in which they decontextualize the complex exchanges of everyday life and then recontextualize them in conventionalized forms of analysis. Which contingencies within the matrix of social, cultural, and personal forces that shape social reality is the investigator willing to "hold even" or place in the background? In terms of the broad objective of psychological anthropology to develop a set of approaches capable of representing persons as embodied, meaning-making agents, the diversity of approaches represented in this book is a distinct asset. As the lines of research described here are pursued, we may hope that each will provide accounts of certain "contingent truths" that qualify or amplify the truths of other approaches and disciplines, giving a more complex and satisfying understanding of social experience than has been produced by single-minded theories bent on reproducing a natural science of the individual.

NOTES

1 We would like to acknowledge others who presented papers and discussions at those occasions. The present book has benefited substantially from their contributions. In addition to the authors included here, Philip Bock, Erika Bourguignon, Ellen Corin, Linda Hartranft, Gilbert Herdt, Solomon Katz, Lewis Langness, Benjamin Lee, Robert LeVine, Robert Paul, James Peacock, Paul Riesman, and Beatrice Whiting all participated in the formal program of the two symposia.

2 One can ask why the study of child development has been exceptional in this regard. One factor has surely been the strong influence of John and Beatrice Whiting on this field; their strong interdisciplinary focus and charisma has influenced the large number of practitioners who continue to talk to people in the fields both of psychology and anthropology (such as Sara Harkness, Richard Shweder, Tom Weisner, and numerous others).

REFERENCES

Abu-Lughod, Lila. 1986. *Veiled Sentiments: Honor and Poetry in a Bedouin Society*. Berkeley: University of California Press

Bourguignon, Erika. 1979. *Psychological Anthropology*. New York: Holt, Rinehart, and Winston

Briggs, Jean. 1970. *Never in Anger: Portrait of an Eskimo Family*. Cambridge, MA: Harvard University Press

Casson, Ron W. 1983. Schemata in Cognitive Anthropology. *Annual Review of Anthropology* 12: 429–462

Clifford, James. 1988. *The Predicament of Culture: Twentieth Century Ethnography, Literature and Art*. Cambridge, MA: Harvard University Press

Crapanzano, Vincent. 1980. *Tuhami: Portrait of a Moroccan*. Chicago: University of Chicago Press

D'Andrade, Roy. 1986. Three Scientific World Views and the Covering Law Model. In D. W. Fiske and R. A. Shweder, eds., *Metatheory in Social Science: Pluralisms and Subjectivities*. Chicago: University of Chicago Press

D'Andrade, Roy E. and Claudia Strauss, eds. 1992. *Human Motives and Cultural Models*. Cambridge: Cambridge University Press

Gardner, Howard. 1985. *The Mind's New Science*. New York: Basic Books

Geertz, Clifford. 1973. Thick Description: Toward an Interpretive Theory of Culture. In *The Interpretation of Cultures*. New York: Basic Books

Harris, Grace Gredys. 1989. Concepts of Individual, Self, and Person in Description and Analysis. *American Anthropologist* 91: 599–612

Holland, Dorothy. 1988. In the Voice of In the Image of: Cognitive Presentations of Attractiveness. *International Pragmatics Association Papers in Pragmatics* 2(1/2): 106–135

Holland, Dorothy and Naomi Quinn, eds. 1987. *Cultural Models in Language and Thought*. Cambridge: Cambridge University Press

Holland, Dorothy and Jaan Valsiner. 1988. Cognition, Symbols and Vygotsky's Developmental Psychology. *Ethos* 16: 247–272

Klein, George F. 1976. *Psychoanalytic Theory: An Exploration of Essentials*. New York: International Universities Press

Kohut, Heinz. 1977. *The Restoration of the Self*. New York: International Universities Press

Lacan, Jacques. 1968. *The Language of the Self: The Function of Language in Psychoanalysis*, trans. Anthony Wilden. Baltimore: Johns Hopkins Press

Lave, Jean. 1988. *Cognition in Practice*. Cambridge: Cambridge University Press

Lee, Benjamin, ed. 1982. *Psychosocial Theories of the Self*. New York: Plenum Press

LeVine, Robert. 1982. *Culture, Behavior and Personality*. Rev. edn. Chicago: Aldine

Luhrmann, T. M. 1989. *Persuasions of the Witch's Craft: Ritual Magic in Contemporary England*. Cambridge, MA: Harvard University Press

Lutz, Catherine A. 1988. *Unnatural Emotions: Everyday Sentiments on a Micronesian Atoll and Their Challenge to Western Theory*. Chicago: University of Chicago Press

Lutz, Catherine A. and Lila Abu-Lughod, eds. 1990. *Language and the Politics of Emotion*. Cambridge: Cambridge University Press

Lutz, Catherine A. and Geoffrey M. White. 1986. The Anthropology of Emotions. *Annual Review of Anthropology* 15: 405–436

Marsella, Anthony, George DeVos, and Francis Hsu, eds. 1985. *Culture and Self: Asian Perspectives*. London: Tavistock

Murdock, G. P. 1950. *Outline of Cultural Materials*, 3rd edn. New Haven: Yale University Press

Myers, Fred. 1979. Emotions and the Self: A Theory of Personhood and Political Order Among Pintupi Aborigines. *Ethos* 7: 343–370

Obeyesekere, Gananath. 1981. *Medusa's Hair: An Essay on Personal Symbols and Religious Experience*. Chicago: University of Chicago Press

Riesman, Paul. 1977. *Freedom in Fulani Social Life: An Introspective Ethnography*. Chicago: University of Chicago Press

1983. On the Irrelevance of Child Rearing Methods for the Formation of Personality. *Culture, Medicine and Psychiatry* 7: 103–129

Romney, A. Kimball, Susan C. Weller, and William H. Batchelder. 1986. Culture as Consensus: A Theory of Culture and Informant Accuracy. *American Anthropologist* 88: 313–338

Rosaldo, Michelle. 1980. *Knowledge and Passion: Ilongot Notions of Self and Social Life*. Cambridge: Cambridge University Press

Schafer, Roy. 1976. *A New Language for Psychoanalysis*. New Haven: Yale University Press

Scheper-Hughes, Nancy. 1985. Culture, Scarcity and Maternal Thinking: Maternal Detachment and Infant Survival in a Brazilian Shantytown. *Ethos* 13: 291–317

Scheper-Hughes, Nancy and Margaret Lock. 1987. The Mindful Body: A Prolegomenon to Future Work in Medical Anthropology. *Medical Anthropology Quarterly* 1: 6–41

Schwartz, Theodore. 1976. Where is the Culture? In G. Spindler, ed., *The Making of Psychological Anthropology*. Berkeley: University of California Press

1981. The Acquisition of Culture. *Ethos* 9(1): 4–17

Shostak, Marjorie. 1981. *Nisa: The Life and Words of a !Kung Woman*. Cambridge, MA: Harvard University Press

Shweder, Richard A. 1979a. Rethinking Culture and Personality Theory Part I: A Critical Examination of Two Classical Postulates. *Ethos* 7: 255–278

1979b. Rethinking Culture and Personality Theory Part II: A Critical Examination of Two More Classical Postulates. *Ethos* 7: 279–311

1989. The Future of "Cultural Psychology." *Anthropology Newsletter* 30 (7): 19

Shweder, Richard and Roy D'Andrade. 1980. The Systematic Distortion Hypothesis. In R. Shweder, ed., *Fallible Judgment in Behavioral Research*. San Francisco: Jossey-Bass

Shweder, Richard and R. LeVine, eds. 1984. *Culture Theory: Essays on Mind, Self and Emotion*. Cambridge: Cambridge University Press

Shweder, Richard and Maria Sullivan. In press. The Semiotic Subject of Cultural Psychology. In L. Pervin, ed. *Handbook of Personality Theory and Research*. New York: Guilford Publications

Skinner, Quentin, ed. 1985. *The Return of Grand Theory in the Human Sciences*. Cambridge: Cambridge University Press

Spindler, George D., ed. 1978. *The Making of Psychological Anthropology*. Berkeley: University of California Press

Spiro, Melford. 1986. Cultural Relativism and the Future of Anthropology. *Cultural Anthropology* 1: 259–286

Stigler, James, Richard Shweder, and Gilbert Herdt, eds. 1990. *Cultural Psychology: Essays on Comparative Human Development*. Cambridge: Cambridge University Press

Strauss, Claudia. 1990. Who Gets Ahead? Cognitive Responses to Heteroglossia in American Political Culture. *American Ethnologist* 17: 312–328

Trawick, Margaret. 1990. *Notes on Love in a Tamil Family*. Berkeley: University of California Press

Wallace, Anthony F. C. 1961. Culture and Cognition. In *Culture and Personality*. New York: Random House

Wertsch, James, ed. 1985. *Culture, Communication and Cognition: Vygotskian Perspectives*. Cambridge: Cambridge University Press

White, Geoffrey M. 1991. *Identity Through History: Living Stories in a Solomon Islands Society*. Cambridge: Cambridge University Press

White, Geoffrey M. and John Kirkpatrick, eds. 1985. *Person, Self and Experience: Exploring Pacific Ethnopsychologies*. Berkeley: University of California Press

Part I

Cognition and social selves

1 Ethnopsychology

Geoffrey M. White

In his article "The Self and Its Behavioral Environment" A. I. Hallowell writing in 1954 observed that aspects of self-awareness were at that time generally excluded from theorizing about the basic constituents of culture. Those who compiled inventories or lists of pan-cultural constructs might include reference to concepts of "soul" but rarely mentioned reflexive elements of experience, of the "self." Hallowell did, however, note stirrings of interest in this area, and commented approvingly that,

> now, in contrast with earlier editions, the *Outline of Cultural Materials* includes an item called "Ethnopsychology" under which we find "concepts of self, of human nature, of motivation, of personality," so that, in the future, we should have more detailed inquiries into such topics. (1967: 79)

On the one hand, the recent rise of interest in "ethnopsychology" makes Hallowell's speculations seem prophetic (see Levy 1973; Lutz 1988; M. Rosaldo 1980; Straus 1977; Wellenkamp 1988; and White and Kirkpatrick 1985 for examples of work that fit loosely under this rubric). But, on the other hand, increased attention to ethnopsychologies, to indigenous modes of constituting persons, selves and experience, has raised a host of complications not foreseen in Hallowell's optimistic assessment. In particular, ethnopsychological investigations are producing a critique of taken-for-granted assumptions about the domain of the "psychological." In this chapter I discuss this critique in relation to two constructs that lie at the heartland of the psychological: emotion and personality. In so doing I suggest that definitional debates in these areas hold the seeds of a reconceptualization of culture and self that may reconnect experience and motivation with cultural understanding.

In this discussion, I raise problems of "translation" that point to more basic issues of language and representation that are now the focus of attention in writings on discourse in all its varieties. In particular, the renewed emphasis on pragmatics in theories of language and thought challenges concepts of culture that assume an a-priori separation of emotion and cognition, and that dichotomize (private) individual experience and (public) collective representation.

When listed as one item of cultural knowledge among others (for example, as item 828 in the 1950 *Outline of Cultural Materials*), "ethnopsychology" acquires a somewhat narrow reading as an essentially cognitive object of study – simply another domain of local theorizing that may be bracketed by the frames of "ethno-" or "folk." Shweder gives just this reading to the term "ethnopsychology" when he writes, "ethnopsychology is a subdiscipline of ethnosemantics or ethnoscience. It is primarily concerned with the investigation of mind, self, body, and emotion as topics (along with, for example, botany or kinship) in the ethnographic study of folk beliefs" (1990: 16). In this light, Shweder rightly concludes that a narrow focus on ethnopsychology would seem to be less concerned with "the actual psychological functioning and subjective life of persons" than such things as "doctrines about mind," "representations of emotions," and "formal texts about the self." However, one of the major thrusts of recent studies of ethnopsychology is that this division between "actual psychological functioning" and "doctrines," "representations," and "texts" is in fact untenable, based on a false analogy between abstract formal theories and ordinary understandings as used in everyday life (see, e.g., Lutz 1985, 1988; M. Rosaldo 1980; White 1985). Ironically, perhaps, some of the best evidence indicating the limitations of strictly cognitive approaches to ethnopsychology derives from studies of meaning and conceptualization. Current work in cognitive anthropology is showing that the coherence and force of cultural discourse is as much a matter of social pragmatics as ideation ("doctrines," "texts," "theories") (see chapters by D'Andrade, Keller, and Holland, this book).

Nonetheless, we are left with the observation that people nearly everywhere think and talk a great deal about persons, feelings, motivation, and the like. The fact that such talk occurs widely in diverse societies suggests that ethnopsychological discourse is relevant to a broad range of issues. Asking what this sort of talk is all about, what it does for people, and how it shapes social realities are unavoidable questions for anyone interested in the nature of local subjectivities and, I would argue, social institutions.

One of the byproducts of ethnopsychological research has been a greater awareness of the culture-bound quality of categories and models that drive our own theory building. As a focus for comparative research, an interest in ethnopsychology immediately problematizes the domain of "psychology." Hallowell's gloss of ethnopsychology presumes that terms such as "motivation" and "personality" are common denominators of folk psychology everywhere. But it is increasingly clear that these carry distinct cultural baggage, and that beginning a study of ethnopsychology by looking for native theories of personality may skew the results toward models that resemble Western conceptions of the individual. Such an approach leaves unexamined more basic parameters of personhood such as the purposes and contexts in which individuals emerge as salient and forceful constructs. These issues are taken up in the second section of this chapter to unpackage some of the assumptions bound up in the notion of personality.

"Anger," 'anger' and *anger*

Conventions for representing emotions and emotion words in ethnographic writing belie unacknowledged problems of translation. At least three distinct usages of emotion words such as "anger" may be distinguished: (1) as analytical construct, (2) as a gloss of native terms, and (3) as an English-language emotion word. In most ethnographic writing, the distinction between usages (1) and (3) is blurred, and the problems of equating (2) and (3) minimized. In this chapter the word "anger" is placed in quotes ("anger") to indicate reference to analytical usage, in single quotes ('anger') to indicate a gloss, and in italics (*anger*) when referring to the English-language term. The distinction draws attention to certain differences between social scientific and commonsense "theories" of anger. In particular, the former rely on definitions that highlight biological and/or psychological dimensions of "anger" while leaving the social and moral meanings of *anger* implicit.

Certain emotions in non-English-speaking (and non-Western) societies are routinely labeled "anger" as if the meanings of the term were both transparent and culture neutral. This blurring is implicitly justified by theories of emotion that postulate a number of universal, biologically based core effects presumed to occur in every culture. Given these assumptions, basic English terms are valid and convenient labels for processes that should also be represented in many other languages. However, this apparent transparency rests upon a view of ordinary emotion words as labels for motivational feeling states (and possibly hard-wired expressions in behavior), without regard to the extensive conceptual, social, and moral processes that also shape their significance. As a result, the manner in which English speakers (including ethnographers) conceptualize emotions has only recently been a subject of ethnographic interest (see Lutz 1988).[1]

Even though *anger* may be the most salient and frequently used English-language word, and a top candidate for universality, some of the sharpest debates about the emotional life of non-Western peoples have focused upon interpretations of "anger" and its place in culture and society. For example, the controversy surrounding divergent portraits of Samoan life offered by Margaret Mead (1928) and Derek Freeman (1983) turns on the significance of "anger" and related forms of aggression in that society. In this now notorious case of ethnographic disagreement, two contradictory, global assessments of ethos are derived from different orders of psychological data, neither of which gives serious attention to local Samoan formulations of experience. The varied examples of "aggressive" behavior that Freeman notes from historical, survey, and observational data cannot even be related to (much less contradict) the largely idealized portrait that Mead presents without a detailed analysis of Samoan models of emotion and violence that give those data socio-cultural significance, that is, without an account of Samoan ethnopsychology (but see Gerber 1985). I now turn to another ethnographic controversy that parallels the Samoan case in that it too centers on "anger" and violence in a non-Western society.

In her book *Knowledge and Passion: Ilongot Notions of Self and Social Life* (1980) Michelle Rosaldo presents a rich ethnographic account of emotions among the Ilongot of the Philippines (see also Briggs 1970; Gerber 1975; Lutz 1988). In that book and subsequent writings she approached the problem of interpreting Ilongot emotional experience as a process of translation. However, hers is not so much a translation of language as one of modes of thought and feeling inferred from social contexts and institutions. Language is an access point to worlds of understanding and experience, not an independent system of abstract meanings. The goal of explicating key words and patterns of language use is not to produce a semantic accounting, but to render cultural emotions intelligible.

By focusing on problems of translation or, more broadly, interpretation, Rosaldo emphasizes points of divergence between Western and Ilongot emotions, noting that the use of English terms such as *anger* for purposes of ethnography may produce distorted descriptions skewed toward presumed universal elements of affective experience. She argues that the Ilongot not only think about emotions differently than Westerners, but that "in important ways their feelings and the ways their feelings work must differ from our own" (M. Rosaldo 1984: 144). In an epilogue to the volume in which Rosaldo published the article cited above, Spiro (1984) challenges her claim to have documented variant modes of feeling, and uses her own data to do so. He reevaluates Rosaldo's account of Ilongot emotions to argue that, far from contradicting Western theories of "anger," the Ilongot data are consistent with the very sort of psychodynamic model that she is at pains to refute.

How is such disagreement possible? What are the implications for current anthropological approaches to cross-cultural psychological interpretation?

The disagreement here concerns the interpretation of "anger" in Ilongot society and its relation to both Ilongot and Western discourses of emotion. Related to the problem of deciding about the role of "anger" in Ilongot experience is its relation to an indigenous emotion designated by the term *liget*. The Ilongot, with their history of headhunting, have cultivated violent practices associated with *liget*, an emotion which Rosaldo says overlaps with, but is distinct from, the English-language concept of *anger* (1984: 145). Since Western understandings (both commonsense and scientific) posit a connection between underlying "anger" and overt violence, application of the hydraulic model of frustration–anger–aggression to understand the practice of headhunting seems compelling. However, the Ilongot themselves evince no such ideology to account for violence as an expression of frustration and hostility. According to Rosaldo, they do not "see in violent actions the expression of a history of frustrations buried in a fertile but unconscious mind" (1984: 144). To illustrate differences in the cultural patterning of *liget* and "anger," Rosaldo recounts an incident from her fieldwork in which a man who had every reason to be frustrated with his brother's lack of cooperation got drunk and attacked his sibling. Whereas Rosaldo at first ascribed the fight to "disruptive feelings hitherto repressed" (1984: 144), the Ilongot did not; and neither did they show any interest in "containing" such dysfunctional energies. For them the perpetrator had simply gotten drunk and "forgotten" the sibling bonds which should have restrained his actions.

Rosaldo regards this incident as evidence that the Ilongot emotion of *liget* is fundamentally different from that designated by "anger." In contrast, Spiro (for whom the meanings of *liget* are not a primary issue) finds in this case, and in the ethnographic details of Ilongot headhunting generally (R. Rosaldo 1980), clear evidence for the operation of "anger" as defined in (Western) psychological theory. While M. Rosaldo offers the case in support of the proposition that "affects, whatever their similarities, are no more similar than the societies in which we live" (1984: 145), Spiro's reading of the case leads him to conclude that, "their anger and ours seem to work in similar ways" (1984: 334). It is instructive to ask how such diametrically opposed interpretations are derived. The answer shows how different theoretical orientations may give the "same" beliefs and practices differing behavioral and explanatory significance.

At the most general level, Rosaldo regards indigenous concepts and practices as constitutive of social reality, whereas Spiro finds the behavioral significance of those same concepts and practices in less visible psychodynamic processes specified by certain psychological principles. The psychoanalytic theory of anger and aggression postulates *unconscious* processes that link expressions of violence with underlying anger. Specifically, by appealing to mechanisms of denial and displacement, the practice of headhunting may be linked to unrecognized emotions that derive from frustrations with one's fellows. Spiro hypothesizes that these unconscious processes account for the fact that anger-like resentments and hostilities are neither recognized nor observed in the context of in-group conflicts.

The hypothesized denial and displacement explain why Ilongot do not attribute "anger" in contexts where it is disapproved, as in the fight between brothers. However, beyond this motivated (mis)perception remains the fact that neither do the Ilongot recognize "anger" in contexts where it is, presumably, permitted, such as headhunting. This is because, according to Rosaldo, the Ilongot have no model of "anger" as conceptualized by English speakers (and represented in the English term *anger*). The absence of *anger*-like concepts in Ilongot understandings raises the question, is "anger" still "anger" without *anger* – the (conscious) subjective interpretations used to interpret evocative events and feelings, thereby creating its social significance? If the ethnographic data suggest that nowhere in a society are socio-emotional responses conceptualized in terms that correspond with a particular theoretical construct (such as the Western model of "anger"), in what sense does *that* emotion operate? And what type of data could be brought to bear to test for the presence or absence of such thoroughly invisible processes?

The primary difference between the biopsychological and the ethnopsychological view of emotion lies in the degree to which biological processes are privileged in the definition of what counts as a specific emotion. Once psychological mechanisms are defined as the ultimate arbiter of what constitutes "anger," cultural models are relegated to a secondary role as "filters," "screens," or "veneers" that transform "basic" or "core" emotions into their surface expressions. Solomon's (1984) critique of physiological theories of emotion focuses precisely upon this point, arguing that particular emotions do not adhere solely in biopsychological feeling-states and facial expressions, but rather consist of socially embedded responses that take on significance within a field of culturally interpreted person–person and person–situation relations. So, for example, the American model of prototypic *anger* may be represented as a scenario in which the perception of an offending action produces a wish to harm the offending other (Lakoff and Kövecses 1987; see also Averill 1982). Incorporating cultural models and interactive processes in the *definition* of emotion implies that ethnopsychological constructs are constitutive elements of emotional experience.

The use of English-language terms to interpret non-Western emotions readily confounds ordinary and scientific language – a practice common, and to some degree unavoidable, in ethnographic writing. Many anthropological works that deal explicitly with the cultural patterning of emotion make use of English terms as if their meanings were transparent or unproblematic. (As mentioned earlier, this may reflect the common-sense view that emotion terms are denotative labels for biologically based feelings or behaviors.)

Both Spiro and M. Rosaldo use the English term *anger* to describe the dynamics of Ilongot emotion, but do not specify which aspects of the term's complex meaning(s) are being invoked. For example, Rosaldo writes, "Ilongot discourse about 'anger' overlaps with, but is different from, our own. The same things can be said about the ways Ilongot feel" (1984: 145). She does not, however, articulate which aspects of experience lie at the intersection of *anger* and *liget*. In recent writings on the interpretation of emotion words and concepts in a variety of languages, Wierzbicka (1986 and in press) has questioned the soundness of ethnographic models that use undefined English-language terms as the focal point for representation. She argues for a "semantic metalanguage" that could be used to represent and compare the propositional meanings of emotion words across cultures. Taking up the disagreement between Rosaldo and Spiro about the place of "anger" in Ilongot society, she examines the semantics of *anger* and *liget* and concludes that "the two words embody two entirely different (though overlapping) concepts" (n.d.: 230–231).

Wierzbicka's analysis is helpful in specifying which aspects of the conceptual model of *anger* are most pertinent to Ilongot emotion. Specifically, she represents the meaning of *anger* as a set of interrelated propositions, one of which stipulates the desire to harm an offending other (n.d.: 231):

(a) X thinks this: Y did something bad to me
(b) I don't want such things to happen
(c) X feels something bad toward Y because of that
(d) X wants to do something bad to Y because of that

Even though this is a highly rarefied representation of a complex concept (see Lakoff and Kövecses 1987), it captures minimal elements of common-sense *anger* in terms of a scenario of offense–anger–retribution. This model also suggests a resemblance between social scientific and ordinary conceptualizations insofar as the psychobiological idiom of "frustration–anger–aggression" is paralleled by the moral scenario of "offense–anger–retribution" implicit in ordinary language. In contrast, *liget* codes no such retributive element, but rather pertains primarily to competitive strivings, with elements of "ambition" and "envy" that may lead the subject to harm others, but not necessarily out of an intention to hurt or punish.

Although Spiro notes that the psychological data that would be required to test the psychoanalytic thesis are not at hand, he does enumerate elements of M. Rosaldo's data that are consistent with that thesis. The central issue for the psychoanalytic formulation is also the focal element in Wierzbicka's semantic model of English *anger*: the wish to harm an offending ("frustrating") other. However, when Spiro lists a series of features of Ilongot headhunting that he regards as consistent with the psychoanalytic theory (1984: 333–334), none of the items mentioned directly express this facet of "anger."[2] Instead of bearing out the symbolic link between victim and "frustrating fellows" called for by the displacement hypothesis, the listed features of headhunting emphasize the experience of emotional catharsis, with only a secondary (and not even necessary) role for hostility directed at an offending or hated other.[3]

Asking whether a particular element of "anger" (such as "the wish to harm an offending other") is part of Ilongot emotional discourse allows a wider range of comparative questions than simply whether Ilongot do or do not experience "anger." Even Spiro's formulation of Ilongot "anger" appears to be less tightly linked to the image of a frustrating other and the desire to harm (1984: 334). It is possible, then, to hypothesize an alternative model of motivating emotion that resembles "anger" in certain respects, but that could also be spelled out in terms of culturally constituted goals and events. The fuller account of *liget* given by M. Rosaldo (1980) suggests that cultural goals connected with male identity, strength, courage, and competitive rivalry could, in themselves, constitute a motivational basis for violent practices without drawing inferences about displaced hostility. This is not to say that such an account of headhunting must equate motivation with conscious intention, but only that Ilongot emotional discourse need not be represented in terms constrained by the conceptual framework of English-language emotions.

Because Rosaldo's approach directs ethnography toward indigenous understandings and practices, it produces an accounting of processes that shape self-awareness and conscious action. In contrast, Spiro concentrates on searching out connections between (public, collective) cultural structures and the often unconscious (private, personal) forces assumed to move people to feel and act in the way they do. Since he is less concerned with representing local emotions, the motivational properties of *liget* as a culturally recognized and socially constituted emotion are underplayed. This has the effect of amplifying the explanatory niche occupied by unrecognized, private "anger."

The problem of deciding between these contrastive positions is exacerbated by inadequate representations of the meanings and behavioral force of both *anger* and *liget*. Minimizing the behavioral significance of ethnopsychological formulations skews the ethnographic base from which any theorist, psychoanalytic or symbolic, would wish to make inferences about the dynamics of emotion and social life. Thus, Spiro may appeal to the operation of unconscious processes to make the case for similarity, but the conceptual organization and motivational role of Ilongot models of experience remain secondary. Rosaldo for her part argues ideological difference, but does not specify points of similarity and difference in an explicit or systematic form that could be used to draw further comparisons or to identify unrecognized motivational structures.

Noting the implicit semantics of English emotion terms raises the larger issue of our (Western, academic) conceptions of emotion itself, formulated in relation to other, basic understandings of person and action (see Lutz 1988). Those who argue for the universality of emotions labeled by English terms such as *anger* and *fear* usually do so on the basis of a referential theory of language in which the core meanings of such terms are seen to derive from their function in labeling psychobiological states, facial expressions, or (culturally modulated) ethological sequences (e.g., Ekman 1984: Izard 1977). In each case, emotional meaning is found in denotative referents that presume a separation between precultural emotion and cultural ideology. In contrast, constructivist theories of emotion tend to collapse that separation and include cultural models, rhetorical practices, and social institutions among the primary definitional components of emotional experience.

A more ethnographic approach to emotions would frame the parameters of comparative research in terms of "a set of problems of social relationship or existential meaning that cultural systems often appear to present in emotional terms" (Lutz and White 1986: 427) rather than in terms of a given set of psychobiological universals. So, instead of beginning with a concept of "anger" as a response to frustration or as the English-speaking scenario of offense and simmering retribution, we might postulate a generalized model of the problem of real or symbolic violation of cultural codes, and then examine the manner in which the problem is articulated in idioms of emotion, that is, as an event interpreted or experienced as compelling personal response. Such an approach applied to the Ilongot would examine *liget* and the motivational basis of headhunting in terms of the personal and interpersonal dilemmas posed by culturally constituted challenges to the self, rather than an a-priori model of displaced "anger." Ethnopsychological research indicates that prototypic event schemas underlie emotional understanding across cultures

(Quinn and Holland 1987; Lakoff and Kövecses 1987; Lutz 1987; White 1990a), and that in some cases these articulate with "core emotions" posited in psychobiological theories. At the same time, however, this research is showing that such convergences cannot be predicted solely on the basis of presupposed Western models.

Discourse-oriented approaches offer a range of methods for analyzing emotions along the lines suggested. Whether focusing on the cognitive organization of emotional understanding (Lutz 1987), the pragmatics of emotion talk (Crapanzano 1990; White 1990b), or the role of emotions in sustaining social relations (Abu-Lughod 1986), culturally framed emotional discourses situate meaning within a field of action where its semiotic and practical significance can be more directly examined (see Watson-Gegeo and White 1990; Lutz and Abu-Lughod 1990). As a result, such approaches face less formidable problems linking emotion with ideology and institutions than do theories that separate personal experience from public culture, and so must rely upon longer chains of psychological inference to reconnect them.

From personality to person

The contrast between *anger* and *liget* goes beyond cognitive differences in folk models to broader issues pertaining to relations between ideology, experience, and action. At issue is the manner in which ideational models and experience sustain institutionalized patterns of relation and interaction. The problem of motivation, of why people value and do the things they do, traditionally falls squarely within the province of psychology where individual motives and behavior are often subsumed under the concept of "personality." Concepts of motivation and personality make up two of the four top-level items listed under "ethnopsychology" in the 1951 *Outline of Cultural Materials* mentioned at the outset of this chapter. But whereas that view of ethnopsychology saw these concepts as bedrock pancultural constructs found in most societies, more recent research is turning the definitional spotlight on these constructs themselves.

The concept of "personality," traditionally on a par with concepts of "culture" and "social structure," is a master explanatory concept that organizes much of ordinary and social science theorizing about social behavior. Most theories of personality turn upon the notion of the autonomous individual as the primary locus of organization in behavior. Concepts of personality inevitably refer to individual thought and behavior, looking within the individual to find distillations of experience that underlie observable patterns of belief and action. The notion of personality conjoins individual differences with inner, psychological processes presumed to underlie those differences. While schools of academic psychology have differed over the relative utility of focusing on outer behavior or inner motivation, nearly all have predicated their theories upon the individual mind or personality as the basic unit of analysis. In so doing, the domain of individual psychology is opposed to that of collective culture, setting boundaries that define problems to be studied and the disciplines to study them. (How many departments offer courses on psychological anthropology which, if not labeled "culture and personality," are called "the individual and society"?) But these boundaries are themselves culturally constructed, and so ought to be viewed with greater suspicion as a basis for setting scientific agendas. It is increasingly clear that our conceptualization of personality, with its implicit equation of person and individual (as opposed to collective culture) has constrained the kinds of questions we ask.

The fact that our understandings of "personality" are deeply embedded in language and culture is evident in the extensive vocabularies of personality type found in all European languages. Words such as "extroverted" or "cooperative" code cultural understandings about persons that presume consistencies in individual behavior through time and across situations. In one of the clearest acknowledgments of the similarity between folk models and academic theories, a tradition of research in social psychology has attempted to systematize categories of personality type from the analysis of personality terms in English and other languages. During the 1940s and 1950s, Raymond Cattell, a leader in developing personality-measurement techniques, undertook an inductive review of English personality terms with the assumption that, "all aspects of human personality which are or have been of importance, interest, or utility have already become recorded in the substance of language" (1943: 483). This assumption – one that essentially argues for the behavioral validity of ethnopsychology in the narrow sense – has been shared by repeated social psychological studies of English-language terms and concepts for personality (e.g., Goldberg 1981; Schneider 1973; Wiggins 1979). It is ironic, however, that this line of research, which argues for the predictive utility of essentially *cultural* constructs, has been challenged by the findings of anthropological research showing that ordinary language terms and categories tend to signify cognitive consistencies more than behavioral ones (see D'Andrade 1974; and Shweder and D'Andrade 1980 for studies of the "systematic distortion" inherent in folk models of personality). In the domain of personality, as already noted for emotion, our tendency to view language referentially turns personality trait words into labels for personal essences lodged within individuals (albeit essences presumed to represent a history of experience, see Crapanzano 1990).

But, personality theorists respond, evidence of the lack of validity in folk models of personality does not necessarily imply that scientific models of personality are incapable of rendering valid assessments. Obviously, this question continues to be an area of vigorous research in fields of personality and social psychology, with large industries devoted to rendering formal and quantitative measurements of personality for clinical and commercial purposes. Critical assessments of the reliability and validity of standard measurement techniques such as rating scales and projective instruments have exposed unimpressive correlations. The work of Walter Mischel (1968) marked a turning point in the development of personality theory, signalling a move away from developing finer and finer actuarial methods for measuring individual variation toward the reconceptualization of personality itself in ways that incorporate cognitive, interpersonal, and situational variables.

At about the same time that this self-examination was gaining momentum in personality psychology, a similar rethinking was emerging in psychological anthropology. In an influential review of explanatory assumptions in the field of "culture and personality" Shweder (1979a,b), citing the findings of Mischel and others on personality measures, argued that the problems of personality assessment within Western traditions are further compounded in cross-cultural studies. In particular, he suggested that decades of cross-cultural research with observational and projective techniques have failed to demonstrate either the within-culture consistency or the between-culture variation called for in global characterizations of "basic personality" or "national character." It is apparent that much of the persuasiveness of reports of cultural differences in personality relies upon the implicit semantics of English trait words. As in the case of emotion, terms for ordinary language are applied to the interpretation of behavior in other cultures without regard to the relevance or irrelevance of the conceptual models that underlie them. The same simplifying and essentializing functions of trait words that produce cognitive consistency in characterizations of individual personalities also contribute to the coherence of "personality writ large" assessments of whole societies.[4]

The assumptions behind the view that Western concepts of personality are universally relevant for the tasks of personality assessment have contributed to the relative neglect of indigenous models and problems of translation. The stance typical of early personality and culture studies is summarized by Caughey (1980: 175):

> there is little tendency to see the meaning of personality terms as a problem. Where the subjects' terms are reported at all they are often described simply by equating the local label with an English gloss whose meaning is taken to be obvious in itself and approximately equivalent to that of the subjects' term. This

tendency is itself linked to the assumption, often quite explicit, that a single universal mode of personality appraisal underlies different ethnopsychologies.

Once we view local discourses of person (including talk of "personality") as having directive force in shaping psychosocial reality, the constituents of those discourses assume a more central role in theories of person, action, and society. Talk of selves and persons everywhere constitutes a moral rhetoric – a way of explaining and evaluating everyday actions and events. Investigating the conceptual and institutional forces that sustain such talk and make it socially consequential requires a more broad study of discourse than has typically been pursued in individual-centered studies of cultural psychology. Since the social and emotional significance of human interaction is contingent upon cultural models of person, an account that applies English-language terms without reference to local concepts is incapable of representing the moral and political dimensions of social action. The fix for these deficiencies, however, will require more than simply improving translations for local terms representing something called "personality."

Some of the issues that arise when studying concepts of person in non-Western societies are illustrated by my research in a Solomon Islands society (White 1980, 1985). That research began with just such a translation project as its primary agenda. Working with a largely unwritten language, the A'ara or Cheke Holo language of Santa Isabel, I compiled an inventory of terms and phrases used to characterize persons, and then explored their meanings with a variety of lexical techniques. Examining the general themes that emerged from clusters or dimensions of similar terms, the findings at first indicated a surprising convergence between the thematic structure of local concepts and those derived from similar studies in other languages, especially numerous analyses of English-language personality terms (White 1980). However, looking more closely at the A'ara language revealed an unanticipated result: "personality" descriptors in that language pertain almost entirely to concepts of *inter*personal behavior.[5] Noting that the language of person description is almost exclusively forged in the crucible of communal life and interpersonal relations opened up the more fundamental problem of the relevance of the concept of personality itself. Only after pondering the interpersonal embeddedness of these conceptualizations of person did my assumptions about "personality," and their influence on my interpretations of A'ara language and culture begin to become apparent.[6]

The results of the lexical study reflect the fact that A'ara talk about persons usually concerns actions embedded in particular social contexts, structured by known identities and relations. This is a familiar theme in the now substantial literature on non-Western ethnopsychologies. This more relational and contextualized mode of thinking about persons may be characteristic of small face-to-face communities in which social discourse does not *begin* with the individual as an autonomous system of organization that may be transplanted from one situation to another, interacting in various ways with a separate "social environment." Local interpretations of social behavior are more often predicated upon persons-in-relations than upon the individual. The interpersonal and relational character of A'ara ethnopsychology is consistent with the broad thrust of innumerable studies of personhood in non-Western societies (see Markus and Kitayama 1991), especially in Oceania where the primacy of interpersonal relations and contextualized identities emerges strongly in many accounts (e.g., Read 1955; Shore 1982; White and Kirkpatrick, 1985). Many other studies in diverse culture areas have produced similar conclusions, such as Dumont's (1970) critique of the misapplication of the ideology of the Western individual to the analysis of Indian social systems (see also Shweder and Bourne 1982).

When placed in comparative perspective, these repeated findings of contrast between non-Western person constructs and the Western concept of the individual are perhaps too easily construed as an argument for the uniqueness of the latter. Furthermore, when framed in dichotomous terms such as "individual" versus "collective" orientations, such categories risk becoming totalizing typologies with the same sort of cognitive distortions evident in personality stereotypes. Such exclusionary schemes do not do justice to the varied range of either Western or non-Western psychologies, any one of which may utilize diverse modes of conceptualizing persons in a range of institutional settings.

In A'ara society where the language of personality is built upon concepts of interpersonal relations, people also notice and talk about individual differences. For the most part, however, talk of individual differences is not generalized, but rather is grounded in particular contexts and institutions, especially those involving aspiring "big-men" or political leaders (White 1991). It is such big-men who are the most visible actors in public situations, who enact and represent collective identities, and who become the object of talk that reformulates and evaluates their actions in an idiom of personal character. A substantial proportion of the words compiled in my inventory of personality descriptors was in fact abstracted from contexts of leadership in which they are otherwise embedded. Reflecting this, one of two primary dimensions to emerge from the lexical study was that of "dominance," a dimension anchored in a cluster of words that includes terms glossed as 'strong' (*hneta*) and 'commanding' (*checheke koba*, literally, 'always talks') (White 1980). The prototypic meanings of these terms derive from scenes of traditional leadership activity such as raiding, making speeches and directing collective work.

I interpret these Solomon Islands findings to indicate that "individuals" are neither brute natural facts nor generalized cultural ones. Personal differences become relevant or operative in distinct social and cultural arenas. It is also apparent that whole societies differ in the degree to which personal differences are enshrined in cultural categories and social institutions. In the A'ara case, personal differences become ideological operators in specific institutionalized contexts. It is in the arenas of competitive leadership that personal differences are the basis for individual reputations that carry significant sociopolitical weight. Instead of asking what personality traits characterize successful big-men (as have a great many ethnographic studies in Melanesia), or even glossing native terms and asking what *indigenous* traits are attributed to them, we might ask, "In what contexts do culturally constructed individuals emerge?", and "What is the significance of this mode of personhood for social and political institutions in this society?" (see Kirkpatrick 1985). These questions call for a social ecology of ethnopsychological formulations, as they are distributed within a community, and as they are used in socially organized situations (Black 1985; Lutz 1988: 86). By implication, the anthropological study of person concepts is widened from the symbolic focus on variable cultural models to include the contexts and activities in which those models may be seen to have social and political force. Ethnopsychological research may help to unpack our abstract concepts of "self" and "person" by exploring the specific linguistic, ideological, emotional, and institutional structures through which particular types of subjectivity and personal experience are constructed.

The study of personality in culture has entailed a range of individual-centered methods aimed at probing personal experience (with the aim of then relating the analysis back to collective cultural forms). One of the stock-in-trade methods employed for such ethnographic probing is the life history. However, both the "life" and the "history" components of the term articulate closely with Western notions of individuality and personality, and so merit critical examination when applied in cross-cultural contexts (Peacock and Holland 1988).

The life-history method (actually a plurality of methods) has been used for a variety of purposes within anthropology, but usually presumes a model of the person in which a "life" consists of personal experiences that accumulate through time, shaping individual identity and personality. Early experiences with significant others are typically regarded as particularly salient. The individual in this view is a repository of experience that may be tapped with the appropriate elicitation techniques. "Doing life histories" is one such technique which, along with the observation of socialization practices, is aimed at uncovering past experiences that have had a formative influence upon present attitudes and actions – a kind of archaeology of the individual. Life histories are often talked about as if they were objects or texts that might be elicited through a straightforward, even mechanical, procedure: "collected" like kin terminologies or botanical specimens. Following the rationale behind much psychological inquiry, life-history material is typically elicited in interview situations created by the investigator and removed from ordinary contexts of self (re)presentation. The strategy is deliberate, but not without its methodological side-effects.

The method as usually practiced does not examine local modes of self representation, that is, those culturally constituted practices in which identities are created and propagated within socially organized contexts of everyday life (Crapanzano 1977; Peacock and Holland 1988). Given that the situation in which self-reports are typically elicited is usually defined and structured by the investigator, the method does not shed much light on the question of whether, and to what extent, personal lives are normally constructed as culturally constituted "histories" – in narratives that portray lives as a chronological sequence of contingent events that accumulate in the form of an individual career or life path (Clifford 1976). As in the case of emotions, the cultural relevance of such narrative forms may not be at issue for a research perspective that defines its objective in terms of "underlying" motivational structures rather than "surface" forms of representation. But the presumption of such a separation overlooks the constitutive role of communicative practices in everyday life. Assumptions about individual lives and the performative means available for representing them (such as narratives of personal experience) constrain the kinds of ethnographic questions that might be posed about alternative modes of self construction.

Since social experience is not passively recorded in human memory, but actively interpreted and negotiated in local forms of talk and action, specifying the significance of key events and interactions for the acting subject requires analysis of cultural discourses of the self, particularly modes of narrating personal experience and the institutions that support them. It is through institutionalized modes of remembering and representing events that past experience may become collectively or politically salient (White 1991). So, for example, rather than investigating personal experience solely through the framework of life histories and individual careers shaped by early socialization, we might ask the prior ethnographic questions, "How are lives fashioned out of experience, and with what consequences for selves and social structures?", and "How are distinct forms of self-representation related to various forms of personhood on the one hand, and to institutionalized patterns of power and emotionality on the other?" (see, e.g., Abu-Lughod 1986).

The orientation toward eliciting life histories from individuals has resulted in relatively little attention being given to collective and interactive modes of representing shared experience. Research on the narration of personal experience indicates that moral narratives are not produced as disembodied texts waiting for an exegesis, but rather as interactively produced performances that engage audience and co-narrators in an activity that is itself an instantiation of social relations (Miller, Potts, Fung, Hoogstra, and Mintz 1990). Investigating the self as a socially organized process places relations between conceptual, semiotic, and sociopolitical structures at the center of ethnographic attention rather than at the end of a deductive process.

The ethnography of ordinary forms of self construction is not a replacement for investigator-initiated interviews. But it does offer a vantage point from which to examine the articulation of personal experience with structures of community and polity. Instead of assuming that cultural constructs become personally salient through a process of *internalization*, and then probing and eliciting from individuals, we may also discover emotional salience and power through attention to the *externalization* of cultural forms in situated activities where they are put to use shaping identity, evoking feelings and moving people to action. In their well-known formulation of symbolic interactionist theory Berger and Luckmann (1966) conceived of "internalization" and "externalization" as two moments in an ongoing dialectical process. Despite these insights, many psychological theorists discuss internalization in isolation, as a one-way process that brings the outside inside, giving public signs personal significance, but analytically divorced from the mediating practices that externalize and validate social meaning. The result is that motivational forces are lodged in an inner world of the individual and the outer, social world becomes a somewhat homogenous universe of collective norms and institutions. This individuation of emotion and motivation has directed the psychological anthropologist's attention inside the individual to mental processes, personal associations, memories, dreams, and the like, and away from the activities and institutions where such personal constructs obtain pragmatic force. In this paper I am suggesting that a more productive approach to motivation and emotional meaning, at least for the purposes of ethnography, would focus on discourse processes (conceptual, communicative, and institutional) that link personal experience and sociopolitical structures in contingent relations.

The weight of individual-centered methods has created a significant blank spot in our knowledge of the experience of people living in societies characterized by less individuated forms of personhood, such as many of the small-scale *gemeinschaft* communities so often studied in anthropological research. Given the overriding salience of local definitions of community for personal identity in these "traditional" societies, discourses of collective history are at least as important as life histories for the dynamics of identity and self. But we still understand very little about the problems created by colonialism and nationalism for culturally constituted selves in such communities because the "psychological" issues have been framed as if they pertained solely to individuals rather than persons-embedded-in-collectivities or polities (see Scheper-Hughes, this volume). Issues of political dominance and dependency have often been framed in terms of individual "adjustment," "stress," "loss," or "deprivation," without regard to the local idioms that embed personal experience in intergroup relations and community organization. It is apparent that many small communities have worked out subtle and complex practices for dealing with dominant others and the problematics of subordination (e.g., Taussig 1980; White 1991). But rather than deconstructing monolithic relations of dominance in terms of local models and their implementation in situations of encounter, studies of the self have tended to invoke the essentializing language of individual psychology and pursue strategies that give primacy to projective data (myths, dreams, thematic apperception tests [TATs], and the like) as a source of psychological insight. As a result, we have spent little time listening to naturally occurring discourses of remembrance such as narrations of collective history that might suggest alternative ways of construing the problems of self and experience.

Conclusion

This chapter began by noting differences between narrow and broad approaches to ethnopsychology. In the narrow definition, exemplified in the work of A. I. Hallowell (1967), ethnopsychology is identified with the study of conceptual models – specifically, of indigenous understandings of "self," "personality," "motivation," and the like. Broader approaches focus upon discourse processes through which social and emotional realities are constituted in ordinary talk and interaction. Here the ambiguities of the word "discourse" signal a common interest in language and communicative practices that cuts across current research on cultural schemas, social routines, and institutionalized regimes of knowledge and power. Discourse-centered approaches have the methodological consequence of directing ethnography of the self or person toward relations among cognitive, communicative, and social-institutional forces rather than discrete "concepts" or "symbols". By way of conclusion, I want to discuss briefly these contrastive approaches in terms of more basic differences grounded in assumptions about language, thought, and culture.

With the rise of interpretive perspectives in anthropology and social science generally, the work of psychological anthropology has been distinguished by its concern with inner worlds of individual experience, in contrast with the more semiotic and sociological problems addressed by the "mainstream." Despite common agreement about the importance of problems of meaning for the study of culture, the contrast between psychological and more strictly cultural orientations reflects persistent dualisms in Western theorizing about self and society: private–public, inner–outer, emotion–reason, individual–society. To some extent, these contrasts are reflected in anthropological usages of the terms "person" and "self," with the former characteristic of the Durkheimian focus upon collective representations and ideology (e.g., Mauss 1938; Dumond 1970; Fortes 1973; Fajans 1985), and the latter indicative of psychological interests in reflexive forms of subjectivity (e.g., Hallowell 1967; Straus 1977; LeVine 1982; see also Lee 1982). M. Rosaldo (1980: 262), for example, comments on this cultural loading of the person–self opposition in justifying her decision to use the two terms interchangeably.

In a theoretically unified world, the different concerns and methods of psychological and interpretive anthropology would represent a division of labor in which each worked on distinct but related facets of human experience. But this is not the case. More often, these approaches embody incommensurable assumptions about "where the action is," about how culture obtains behavioral force. Where does one look to find the factors that shape (if not determine) social thought and behavior? For Clifford Geertz, who has best articulated the interpretive view of culture as "webs of significance," the study of person and self involves "searching out and analyzing symbolic forms – words, images, institutions, behaviors – in terms of which, in each place, people actually represented themselves to themselves and to one another" (1983: 58). In this view, questions of precultural or supracultural determinants of experience are secondary to the ethnography of symbolic forms, offered as a phenomenological model of social reality. Compare this with the psychological perspective that behaviorally significant meanings are lodged "inside" the individual, "in the (private) mental representations of social actors, rather than in the (public) collective representations of their group" (Spiro 1984: 325). Furthermore, in the psychoanalytic view, the most powerful meanings may also be out of the awareness of the acting subject, located in the unconscious mind best approached through the analysis of projective and other sorts of psychological data.

Despite their differences in theorizing about the forces that constrain and direct human action, these interpretive and psychological orientations share a view of culture as essentially public and collective, to be distinguished from what goes on in the hearts and minds of men and women. Whereas Geertz takes pains to refute the "cognitivist fallacy" (that culture consists of mental phenomena) in order to underscore the public and collective nature of culture as "socially established structures of meaning" (1973: 12), Spiro asserts that, "as culture is a public system, thoughts no less than emotions are, by definition, excluded from 'culture'" (1984: 325). For both schools of thought, the analytic separation of culture from thought and emotion is built upon a social theory that dichotomizes individual experience and public meaning, and a semiotic theory that finds meaning in abstract signs, symbols, and propositions (see Ewing, this book).

But language is not simply representational; it is also ideological and pragmatic – consisting of processes put to use in creating and transforming social reality. The move away from representational models of language in anthropology and psychology is evident in discourse-oriented theories that approach cognition as socially mediated activity (see Holland, this book). The emphasis upon praxis in recent theories of culture is paralleled in cognitive and developmental psychology by renewed interest in Vygotsky (Wertsch 1985; Holland and Valsiner 1988) and activity theory (Lave 1988). These approaches challenge the a-priori separation of culture and thought (as well as emotion) that has effectively internalized or psychologized the problem of motivation in anthropological theory.

Two moves in this direction merit brief mention. The first is evident in research exploring the motivational properties of cultural models (D'Andrade and Strauss 1991). This work offers a more complex account of the notion of "motive" as more structured by cultural understanding and social situations than has been indicated in psychological accounts of "drives," "needs," "wishes," and the like. For example, D'Andrade (1991) discusses the manner in which conceptual schemata may exhibit motivational properties insofar as they encode goals embedded in larger frames of understanding. He suggests that ethnographic studies focusing on the "organized complexity" of cultural models are capable of identifying "the way in which various goals are organized and activated" and that "One of the important potentials of treating motivation as schemas with embedded goals is that such an account not only connects cognition with behavior, it also shows how goals are organized" (1991: 14).

The other move that is challenging the separation of culture and motivation focuses on emotion in discourse (Lutz and Abu-Lughod 1990; Watson-Gegeo and White 1990). The increasing number of anthropological studies of emotion reflects the realization that emotion is probably a universal topic of talk and understanding embedded in the same "socially established structures of meaning" that have always been the subject of ethnographic inquiry (cf. Myers 198). A substantial literature is growing up dealing with local emotions constituted in everyday social life (Lutz and White 1986). This work is not about ideas about emotions, so much as the creation of emotional experience in discourse. Here the term "discourse" calls attention to the dialectic relation between culture and performance, between model and practice, such that emotion language is seen to exert its own force in defining social relations and directing practical action. Moving away from referential theories of language and meaning that ask what concepts are coded in emotion terms and statements, a discourse-centered approach attends to the social uses of emotion as an idiom capable of transforming social reality in interaction. For example, A'ara talk of emotion in certain well-defined situations uses emotions glossed as 'anger' and 'sadness' to transform conflict in interpersonal relations (White 1990a, 1990b). Furthermore, it is in the process of talking about emotions that experience is collectively validated and potentially transformed according to culturally available "scripts" for conflict resolution. In symbolic interactionist terms, these emotions become forceful when they are "externalized" in social contexts where they instantiate powerful models of personal and collective reality. Research on local discourses of emotion suggests that their motivational force may be assessed not just in terms of what gets internalized, but also what is externalized in forms that are evocative and socially persuasive. Instead of regarding emotions as primarily inner and private, we might begin to think in terms of the socially organized "emotive institutions" that constitute this dialectic between cultural subjectivity and socially validated understanding.

Finally, the formulation of ethnopsychology outlined here has certain consequences for the relation of ethnography to theory building. In the narrow view, the study of ethnopsychology is essentially a descriptive task focused on cultural conceptions of the self and the social environment. There is nothing in this sort of formulation to imply that the structure of variant, non-Western psychologies should affect the premises of social science theories. Limited to the realm of ideation, there is no indication that attention to ethnopsychological constructs would provide direct access to either the motivational or sociopolitical processes that ultimately instigate, direct, and constrain social action. In contrast, the study of ethnopsychology as discourse constitutive of self and social life implies that our theoretical constructs may need to be reshaped in the light of comparative findings. By implication, the study of ethnopsychology may contribute to the broader agenda of psychological anthropology by building a more general comparative framework within which to assess human (including our own) experience.

NOTES

I am grateful to Theodore Schwartz for the impetus to write this paper, and to Catherine Lutz for insightful comments on an earlier version.

1 Recently several linguists (rather than anthropologists) have offered detailed studies of the conceptualizations underlying the meanings of English-language emotion words such as *anger* (Lakoff and Kövecses 1987; Kövecses 1990; Wierzbicka n.d.).

2 Of course, the psychoanalytic theorist would argue that the symbolic associations at issue are best found in clinical or projective material: "as an inference from clinically oriented interviews, dreams, projective tests, and culturally constituted projective systems such as myths, folklore, and the like" (Spiro 1984: 324).

3 Spiro lists ten items extracted from R. Rosaldo's *Ilongot Headhunting* (1980). The first item notes that headhunting expeditions are often occasioned by "insults or wrongs," but that these may be quite trivial, even undertaken "without any recognizable motive at all." But "recognizable motive" here apparently does not include the point (in item 4) that the source of their desire is "above all envy of their peers and elders, those men who . . . have taken a head" (R. Rosaldo 1980: 140, cited in Spiro 1984: 333).

4 One of the consequences of using readymade Western models of personality to interpret non-Western persons and cultures is that comparison easily takes the form of inferring a lack or deficit in the non-Western culture for which a particular type of behavior or character structure is found to be absent. It is then only one step to convert difference into deficiency. For example, studies of achievement motivation find repeatedly that various non-Western cultures are lacking in personality capacities such as "future-orientation," "inner-direction," or some other feature of the Western model of achievement. Findings such as these are then easily extended to explain the "failure" of non-Western societies to modernize (e.g., Inkeles 1976). For other examples of the potential excesses of personality attribution written on a societal scale, see Dower's (1986: ch. 6) account of the mobilization of culture-and-personality analysts for studies of Japanese national character during World War II (see also Yans-McLaughlin 1986).

5 While it is the case that many English personality terms are also, in some sense, about interacting with others, these are only a subset of the broader field of personal attribution. Various analysts such as Leary (1955) or Wiggins (1979) have noted the importance of focusing specifically on these interpersonal dimensions of personality.

6 Simply collecting a corpus of terms presupposes the existence of a coherent

"domain" of terminology and types; and then applying lexical procedures derived from the study of referential semantics further reinforces the interpretation that the words under review are primarily used to label or discriminate among individuals.

REFERENCES

Abu-Lughod, Lila. 1986. *Veiled Sentiments: Honor and Poetry in a Bedouin Society*. Berkeley: University of California Press

Averill, J. 1980. A Constructivist View of Emotion. In R. Plutchik and H. Kellerman, eds., *Emotion: Theory, Research and Experience*. New York: Academic Press

1982. *Anger and Aggression: An Essay on Emotion*. New York: Springer-Verlag

Berger, P. and T. Luckmann. 1966. *The Social Construction of Reality*. New York: Doubleday

Black, Peter. 1985. Ghosts, Gossip and Suicide: Meaning and Action in a Tobian Folk Psychology. In G. White and J. Kirkpatrick, eds., *Person, Self and Experience: Exploring Pacific Ethnopsychologies*. Berkeley: University of California Press

Briggs, Jean L. 1970. *Never in Anger: Portrait of an Eskimo Family*. Cambridge, MA: Harvard University Press

Cattell, Raymond B. 1943. The Description of Personality: Basic Traits Resolved Into Clusters. *Journal of Abnormal and Social Psychology* 38: 476–506

Caughey, John L. 1980. Personal Identity and Social Organization. *Ethos* 8: 173–203

Clifford, James. 1976. "Hanging Up Looking Glasses at Odd Corners": Ethnobiographical Prospects. In F. Reynolds and D. Capps, eds., *The Biographical Process*. The Hague: Mouton

Crapanzano, Vincent. 1977. The Life History in Anthropological Fieldwork. *Anthropology and Humanism Quarterly* 2(2–3): 3–7

1990. On Self Characterization. In J. Stigler, R. Shweder, and G. Herdt, eds., *Cultural Psychology: Essays on Comparative Human Development*. Cambridge: Cambridge University Press

D'Andrade, Roy G. 1974. Memory and the Assessment of Behavior. In T. Blalock, ed., *Measurement in the Social Sciences*. Chicago: Aldine

1987. A Folk Model of the Mind. In D. Holland and N. Quinn, eds., *Cultural Models in Language and Thought*. Cambridge: Cambridge University Press

1992. Schemas and Motivation. In R. D'Andrade and Claudia Strauss, eds., *Human Motives and Cultural Models*. Cambridge: Cambridge University Press

D'Andrade, Roy G. and Claudia Strauss, eds. 1992. *Human Motives and Cultural Models*. Cambridge: Cambridge University Press

Dower, John. 1986. *War Without Mercy: Race and Power in the Pacific War*. New York: Pantheon

Dumont, Louis. 1970. *Homo Hierarchicus*. Trans. Mark Sainsbury. Chicago: University of Chicago Press (originally published 1966).

Ekman, Paul. 1984. Expression and the Nature of Emotion. In K. Scherer and P. Ekman, eds., *Approaches to Emotion*. Hillsdale, NJ: Lawrence Erlbaum

Fajans, Jane. 1985. The Person in Social Context: The Social Character of Baining "Psychology". In G. White and J. Kirkpatrick, eds., *Person, Self and Experience: Exploring Pacific Ethnopsychologies*. Berkeley: University of California Press

Fortes, Meyer. 1973. On the Concept of the Person Among the Tallensi. In Germaine Dieterlen, ed., *La Notion de personne en Afrique noire*. Paris: Editions du Centre National de la Recherche Scientifique

Freeman, Derek. 1983. *Margaret Mead and Samoa: The Making and Unmaking of an Anthropological Myth*. Cambridge, MA: Harvard University Press

Geertz, Clifford. 1973. Thick Description: Toward an Interpretive Theory of Culture. In *The Interpretation of Cultures*. New York: Basic Books

1983. "From the Native's Point of View": On the Nature of Anthropological Understanding. In *Local Knowledge: Further Essays in Interpretive Anthropology*. New York: Basic Books

Gerber, Eleanor. 1975. The Cultural Patterning of Emotions in Samoa. Unpublished Ph.D. dissertation. University of California, San Diego

1985. Rage and Obligation: Samoan Emotions in Conflict. In G. White and J. Kirkpatrick, eds., *Person, Self and Experience: Exploring Pacific Ethnopsychologies*. Berkeley: University of California Press

Goldberg, Lewis. 1981. Language and Individual Differences: The Search for Universals in Personality Lexicons. In L. Wheeler, ed., *Review of Personality and Social Psychology*. Beverly Hills: Sage Publications

Hallowell, A. I. 1967. The Self and Its Behavioral Environment. In *Culture and Experience*. New York: Schocken Books (originally published in 1954)

Holland, Dorothy and Naomi Quinn, eds. 1987. *Cultural Models in Language and Thought*. Cambridge: Cambridge University Press

Holland, Dorothy and Jaan Valsiner. 1988. Cognition, Symbols and Vygotsky's Developmental Psychology. *Ethos* 16: 247–272

Inkeles, Alex. 1976. The Modernizing Personality. In Theodore Schwartz, ed., *Socialization as Communication*. Berkeley: University of California Press

Izard, Carroll E. 1977. *Human Emotions*. New York: Plenum

Kirkpatrick, John. 1985. How Personal Differences Can Make a Difference. In K. Gergen and K. Davis, eds., *The Social Construction of the Person*. New York: Springer-Verlag

Kövecses, Zoltan. 1990. *Emotion Concepts*. Berlin: Springer-Verlag

Lakoff, George and Zoltan Kövecses. 1987. The Cognitive Model of Anger Inherent in American English. In D. Holland and N. Quinn, eds., *Cultural Models in Language and Thought*. Cambridge: Cambridge University Press

Lave, Jean. 1988. *Cognition in Practice*. Cambridge: Cambridge University Press

Leary, Timothy. 1955. Interpersonal Diagnosis: Some Problems of Methodology and Validation. *Journal of Abnormal and Social Psychology* 50: 110–124

Lee, Benjamin, ed. 1982. *Psychosocial Theories of the Self*. New York: Plenum

LeVine, Robert. 1982. The Self in Culture. In *Culture, Behavior and Personality*. Rev. edn. Chicago: Aldine

Levy, Robert. 1973. *The Tahitians: Mind and Experience in the Society Islands*. Chicago: University of Chicago Press

Lutz, Catherine. 1985. Ethnopsychology Compared to What? Explaining Behavior and Consciousness Among the Ifaluk. In G. White and J. Kirkpatrick, eds., *Person, Self and Experience: Exploring Pacific Ethnopsychologies*. Berkeley: University of California Press

1987. Goals, Events and Understanding in Ifaluk Emotion theory. In D. Holland and N. Quinn, eds., *Cultural Models in Language and Thought*. Cambridge: Cambridge University Press

1988. *Unnatural Emotions: Everyday Sentiments on a Micronesian Atoll and Their Challenge to Western Theory*. Chicago: University of Chicago Press

Lutz, Catherine A. and Lila Abu-Lughod, eds. 1990. *Language and the Politics of Emotion*. Cambridge: Cambridge University Press

Lutz, Catherine A. and Geoffrey M. White. 1986. The Anthropology of Emotions. *Annual Review of Anthropology* 15: 405–436

Markus, Hazel and Shinobu Kitayama. 1991. Culture and the Self: Implications for Cognition, Emotion and Motivation. *Psychological Review* 98: 224–253

Mauss, Marcel. 1938. Une Catégorie de l'esprit humain: la notion de personne, celle de "moi". *Journal of the Royal Anthropological Institute* 68L: 263–281

Mead, Margaret. 1928. *Coming of Age in Samoa*. New York: Morrow

Miller, P. J., R. Potts, H. Fung, L. Hoogstra, J. Mintz. 1990. Narrative Practices and the Social Construction of Self in Childhood. *American Ethnologist* 17: 292–311

Mischel, Walter. 1968. *Personality and Assessment*. New York: Wiley

Myers, Fred R. 1988. The Logic and Meaning of Anger Among Pintupi Aborigines. *Man (N.S.)* 23: 589–610

Peacock, James and Dorothy Holland. 1988. The Narrated Self: Life Stories and Self Construction. Paper read at meeting of the American Anthropological Association. Phoenix, AZ

Quinn, Naomi and Dorothy Holland. 1987. Culture and Cognition. In D. Holland and N. Quinn, eds., *Cultural Models in Language and Thought*. Cambridge: Cambridge University Press

Read, Kenneth. 1955. Morality and the Concept of the Person Among the Gahuku-Gama. *Oceania* 25: 233–282

Rosaldo, Michelle Z. 1980. *Knowledge and Passion: Ilongot Notions of Self and Social Life*. Cambridge: Cambridge University Press

1984. Toward an Anthropology of Self and Feeling. In R. Shweder and R. LeVine, eds., *Culture Theory: Essays on Mind, Self and Emotion*. Cambridge: Cambridge University Press

Rosaldo, Renato. 1980. *Ilongot Headhunting*. Stanford: Stanford University Press

Schneider, D. J. 1973. Implicit Personality Theory: A Review. *Psychological Bulletin* 79: 294–309

Shore, Bradd. 1982. *Sala'ilua: A Samoan Mystery*. New York: Columbia University Press

Shweder, Richard. 1979a. Rethinking Culture and Personality Theory Part I: A Critical Examination of Two Classical Postulates. *Ethos* 7: 255–278

1979b. Rethinking Culture and Personality Theory Part II: A Critical Examination of Two More Classical Postulates. *Ethos* 7: 279–311

1990. Cultural Psychology: What Is It? In J. Stigler, R. Shweder, and G. Herdt, eds., *Cultural Psychology: Essays on Comparative Human Development*. Cambridge: Cambridge University Press

Shweder, Richard and Edmund Bourne. 1982. Does the Concept of the Person

Vary Cross-Culturally? In A. J. Marsella and G. M. White, eds., *Cultural Conceptions of Mental Health and Therapy*. Boston: D. Reidel

Shweder, Richard and Roy G. D'Andrade. 1980. The Systematic Distortion Hypothesis. In R. Shweder, ed., *Fallible Judgment in Behavioral Research*. San Francisco: Jossey-Basss

Solomon, Robert C. 1984. Getting Angry: The Jamesian Theory of Emotion in Anthropology. In R. Shweder and R. LeVine, eds., *Culture Theory: Essays on Mind, Self and Emotion*. Cambridge: Cambridge University Press

Spiro, Melford E. 1984. Some Reflections on Cultural Determinism and Relativism with Special Reference to Emotions and Reason. In R. Shweder and R. LeVine, eds., *Culture Theory: Essays on Mind, Self, and Emotion*. Cambridge: Cambridge University Press

Straus, Anne S. 1977. Northern Cheyenne Ethnopsychology. *Ethos* 5: 326–357

Taussig, Michael T. 1980. *The Devil and Commodity Fetishism in South America*. Chapel Hill: University of North Carolina Press

Watson-Gegeo, Karen A. and Geoffrey M. White, eds. 1990. *Disentangling: Conflict Discourse in Pacific Societies*. Stanford: Stanford University Press

Wellenkamp, Jane. 1988. Notions of Grief and Catharsis Among the Toraja. *American Ethnologist* 15: 486–500

Wertsch, James, ed. 1985. *Culture, Communication and Cognition: Vygotskian Perspectives*. Cambridge: Cambridge University Press

White, Geoffrey M. 1980. Conceptual Universals in Interpersonal Language. *American Anthropologist* 82: 759–781

1985. Premises and Purposes in a Solomon Islands Ethnopsychology. In G. White and J. Kirkpatrick, eds., *Person, Self and Experience: Exploring Pacific Ethnopsychologies*. Berkeley: University of California Press

1990a. Moral Discourse and the Rhetoric of Emotions. In C. Lutz and L. Abu-Lughod, eds., *Language and the Politics of Emotion*. Cambridge: Cambridge University Press

1990b. Emotion Talk and Social Inference: Disentangling in a Solomon Islands Society. In K. Watson-Gegeo and G. White, eds., *Disentangling: Conflict Discourse in Pacific Societies*. Stanford: Stanford University Press

1991. *Identity Through History: Living Stories in a Solomon Islands Society*. Cambridge: Cambridge University Press

White, Geoffrey M. and John Kirkpatrick, eds. 1985. *Person, Self and Experience: Exploring Pacific Ethnopsychologies*. Berkeley: University of California Press

Wierzbicka, Anna. 1986. Human Emotions: Universal or Culture-Specific? *American Anthropologist* 88: 584–594

In Press. *Semantics, Culture and Cognition*. New York: Oxford University Press

Wiggins, J. S. 1979. A Psychological Taxonomy of Trait-Descriptive Terms: The Interpersonal Domain. *Journal of Personality and Social Psychology* 37: 395–412

Yans-Mclaughlin, Virginia. 1986. Science, Democracy, and Ethnics: Mobilizing Culture and Personality for World War II. In G. Stocking, ed., *Malinowski, Rivers, Benedict and Others: Essays on Culture and Personality*. Madison: University of Wisconsin

2 Cognitive anthropology

Roy G. D'Andrade

In the past decade there has been a convergence in cognitive anthropology toward the use of *schema theory*. Work in a variety of fields – in lexicology, in folk theories, in folk taxonomies, and in the study of the relationship between culture and inference – has moved towards the general conclusion that adequate description of cultural symbols from the word level to the level of large knowledge systems requires explication of the basic cognitive schemas which underlie these symbols. This does not mean that schema theory alone will account for all the phenomena studied by cognitive anthropologists, but rather that schemas form basic building blocks for more complex kinds of organization.

There is a large body of work which supports this conclusion (Casson, 1983). For example, in the field of lexical analysis, Fillmore (1975, 1977) has made the case that definitions based on a feature checklist, such as the definition of a *bachelor* as an "unmarried man," are seriously inadequate. Fillmore argues that understanding of the meaning of a term requires understanding the *simplified world* on which a term is predicated. One piece of evidence for this view is that when a term is used in a context which does not fit this simplified world, the result is a semantic anomaly. Fillmore says:

> How old does an unmarried man have to be before you can call him a bachelor? Is someone who is professionally committed to the single life properly considered a bachelor? (Is it correct to say of Pope John XXIII that he died a bachelor?) If so, is bachelorhood a state one can enter? That is, if a man leaves the priesthood in middle life, can we say that he became a bachelor at age 47? When we say of a divorced man or a widower that he is a bachelor, are we speaking literally or metaphorically? How can we tell? Would you call a woman a widow who murdered her husband? Would you call a woman a widow whose divorce became final on the day of her husband's death? Would you call a woman a widow if one of her three husbands died but she had two living ones left?
>
> . . . According to the prototype theory of meaning, these concepts are defined in the context of a simple world in which men typically marry around a certain age, they marry once, they marry exclusively, they stay married until one partner dies. Men who are unmarried at the time they could be married are called bachelors. Women whose husbands have died are called widows. (Fillmore 1975: 128–129)

This type of *simplified world* can be called a schema – a simplified interpretative framework used to understand events. Fillmore (1977) has pointed out that whole sets of terms are often based on a single underlying schema. In English a large set of terms is based on the schema of a *commercial event*. This schema, which is a basic part of Western culture, contains a *buyer* who gives *money* to a *seller* to *purchase* the *ownership* of some *object*. Some of the great variety of English words which presuppose understanding this schema include terms like *buy*, *sale*, *loan*, *rent*, *lease*, *purchase*, *charge*, *bid*, *tip*, *ransom*, *refund*, *tuition*, *salary*, etc. Interesting analyses of how the meaning of words depends on understanding implicit cultural schemas have been presented by Eve Sweetser (1987) for the word *lie*, by Paul Kay (1987) on linguistic hedges such as *loosely speaking* and *strictly speaking*, by Janet Dougherty Keller and Charles Keller (Dougherty and Keller 1982) on the understanding of terms for tools used by blacksmiths, by Dorothy Holland and Debra Skinner (1987) on the understandings of gender terms in the United States, by Naomi Quinn (1982) on the meaning of the term *commitment* in marriage, and by Lakoff and Kövecses (1987) on the word *anger*.

Research on the relationship between culture and inference has also found cognitive schemas to be of basic importance. Work by Edwin Hutchins on reasoning among Trobriand Islanders (1980) showed that Trobrianders' discourse in legal disputes contained numerous inferences which were logically correct – correct in the sense that these inferences follow the *forms* of logical inference such as *modus ponens* and *modus tollens*. Trobriand reasoning about the transfer of *dala* rights – lineage rights – turned out to be quite complex and intricate. Understanding the transfer of *dala* rights is a basic part of Trobriand culture – a set of schemas which are frequently used and which are highly shared. The ability of Trobrianders to reason so well, Hutchins concluded, was based on the availability of these well-understood schemas.

Work I have done on reasoning among US undergraduates reinforces this conclusion (D'Andrade 1989). I have found that college undergraduates cannot do simple *modus tollens* syllogisms with *arbitrary content*, but that they can do *modus tollens* syllogisms when they are constructed out of well-formed cultural schemas. *Modus tollens* has the form:

1. *If p then q.*
2. *Not q.*
3. *Therefore, not p.*

A *modus tollens* logic problem using a well-formed cultural schema (the cultural schema here is the relation between cities and states – the understanding that a city is a geographic area *contained within* the larger area of a state) is illustrated below:

1. *Given*: If Tom was born in San Diego then Tom is a native Californian.
2. *Suppose*: Tom is *not* a native Californian.
3. *Then*:

(a) It must be the case that Tom was born in San Diego.
(b) Maybe Tom was born in San Diego or maybe he wasn't.
(c) It must be the case Tom was not born in San Diego.

Eighty-six percent of University of California, San Diego (UCSD) undergraduates select the correct answer – that it must be the case that Tom was not born in San Diego.

A *modus tollens* problem using arbitrary content is exemplified below:

1. *Given*: If Tom is drinking a Pepsi then Peter is sitting down.
2. *Suppose*: Peter is not sitting down.
3. *Then*:

(a) It must be the case that Tom is drinking a Pepsi.
(b) Maybe Tom is drinking a Pepsi or maybe he isn't.
(c) It must be the case that Tom is not drinking a Pepsi.

Only 53 percent of UCSD undergraduates selected the correct answer – that Tom is not drinking a Pepsi. This result is not strikingly above chance.

I think these results are remarkable. The ability to do a relatively simple type of inference depends almost entirely on the content of the problem. The reasoner's ability to see that some conclusion is true or false depends on being able to construct a schematic representation or mental model of the first premise, and then to be able to construct what happens when the state of affairs described by the second premise is added to model. When arbitrary relations are presented, the typical respondent does not seem to integrate the state of affairs described by the second premise with the state of affairs described by the first. Respondents say about the second problem "So what if *Peter* is not sitting down. That doesn't have anything to do with *Tom's* drinking a Pepsi."

This, of course is just plain wrong – they have just been told that Peter's sitting down *does* have something to do with Tom's drinking a Pepsi – that is, *if* Tom is drinking a Pepsi then Peter is sitting down – which has to mean that if Peter is *not* sitting down then Tom is *not* drinking a Pepsi because if Tom *were* drinking a Pepsi then, of course, Peter *would* be sitting down. What using a well-formed cultural schema seems to do for the reasoner is to make it possible to create a mental model and *integrate* the situations described by the premises so that the final integrated situation can be checked against the situation described by the conclusion.

I should mention that there are *some* syllogistic forms which undergraduates can do with quite arbitrary content. Given the *modus ponens* form, which goes:

1. *If p then q.*
2. *p.*
3. *Therefore, q.*

Ninety percent of UCSD undergraduates select the right answer for the following problem, even though the content is arbitrary:

1. *Given*: If Tom is drinking a Pepsi then Peter is sitting down.
2. *Suppose*: Tom is drinking a Pepsi.
3. *Then*:

(a) It must be the case that Peter is sitting down.
(b) Maybe Peter is sitting down or maybe he isn't.
(c) It must be the case that Peter is not sitting down.

My explanation of why it is that undergraduates can do *modus ponens* but not *modus tollens* with arbitrary content is that the integration of the first and the second premises is much harder in *tollens* because the respondent must both negate a part of the situation and reverse the conditional relationship. The model that respondents build when they hear that "If Tom is drinking a Pepsi then Peter is sitting down" appears to be too fragile to support the combined operations of negation and reversal when there is no "sense" to the relationship. So, in sum, it looks as if people can do very simple reasoning without relying on well-formed schemas, but cannot do complex reasoning.

There are some clear implications of such findings for our understanding of what it is to be *smart*. The Western folk model of intelligence treats being able to figure things out as an ability which is content free – geniuses, it is thought, can figure out anything faster than other people because of their great ability. And someone who can't figure out something that other people can figure out is considered *dumb*. But the results just described show that in order to figure things out, one must have a well-formed schema about the things to be figured out, and that even smart people like college undergraduates cannot figure things out when they do not have well-formed schemas with which to operate.

No doubt there are individual differences in how quickly and effectively individuals can form schemas, and individual differences in reasoning with already well-formed schemas, but what we have found is that these differences do not account for the largest amount of the variability in performance on reasoning tasks – the largest amount of the variability in reasoning tasks appears to be accounted for by the degree to which an individual has well-organized cognitive structures for the material being used in the task.

Another implication of these findings is that there should be very large *cultural* influences on the ability to reason on almost any topic. That is, given that cultures and subcultures differ in the areas of experience for which culturally learned and shared schemas are provided, one would predict that individuals from different cultures would vary greatly in what they can reason effectively about. The quest for a *culture-fair* test of reasoning – something some people have given considerable time and effort to – becomes the search for a domain about which people in every culture have equally well-formed schemas – a difficult quest.

Another research result which has led anthropologists to turn to the use of the schema concept is the realization that an alternative approach to describing cultural knowledge systems, the *semantic network* approach, has serious inadequacies. The semantic network approach attempts to represent cultural knowledge systems as a network of interrelated concepts in which sets of *objects* have various *relationships* with other objects. One example of such a system is a *taxonomy*. The objects here might be *plants* or *animals* or *diseases*, and the relationship between the objects is *class inclusion*. Major problems with this approach have been discussed by Hunn (1985), Randall (1976), Dougherty (1978), Wierzbicka (1984), and others in a series of papers and monographs over the past decade.

While a full critique of taxonomic model is beyond the scope of this chapter, it seems clear that the taxonomic model *per se* does not do justice to the very *different* amounts of information people know about objects at the various taxonomic levels. Generally people know a great deal about mid-level taxonomic objects, the so-called *generics* such as *oak* and *horse*; they know so much in fact that an attempt to elicit a definition of a term like *dog* brings forth an encyclopedic amount of material, while the top-level terms – the *unique beginners* and *life-form* terms like *plant* and *grass* – are so bare of characteristics that they seem to consist of nothing but an imposed abstraction. Often taxonomies seem to be something created by the elicitation techniques of the anthropologist, rather than something which corresponds to some well-formed structure that the informant frequently and naturally uses to understand the world. It is as if in looking for taxonomies the anthropologist was trying to find a format for holding knowledge which corresponds to a format used in the anthropologist's *scientific culture*, rather than discovering the form of *knowledge organization* used by the informant.

The argument here is that the increasing use of the concept of a cognitive schema is not just the result of a fad or adoption of high-tech terms from other disciplines. The discovery that the meanings of lexical items presuppose schematically simplified worlds, and the finding that people can do complex inference only when using material utilizing well-formed schemas, and the conclusion that alternative models of knowledge representation – such as taxonomies and other kinds of semantic nets – do not yield adequate descriptions of the way knowledge is organized by informants, has given considerable impetus in cognitive studies in anthropology to the use of the schema concept. Casson's 1983 *Annual Review* paper gives more than 200 citations of work in anthropology and related fields involving the schema concept. Detailed examples of complex cultural models, such as the Western folk model of the mind (D'Andrade 1987), the American cultural model of marriage (Quinn 1987), the Trobriand mythic model of spirits of the dead (Hutchins 1987), the Ifaluk model of emotion (Lutz 1987), the American models of how heat thermostats work (Kempton 1987), models of common sense and proverbs (White 1987), and various folk models of evaporation (Collins and Gentner 1987) have been presented using the schema concept. Quinn and Holland (1987) have reviewed generally the problems and prospects of the cognitive schema approach to the issue of how cultural knowledge is organized.

What then, precisely, is a schema? First, it should be said that a schema is not a picture in the mind. It is a cognitive structure through which interpretations about the world are made. One simple example is the schema we have all learned for recognizing the letter *A*. A lot of very different kinds of physical stimuli – black print, wood blocks, flashing lights, etc. – can all yield the interpretation that one has encountered yet again the letter *A*.

An important characteristic of schemas is that they permit a range of possibilities, like flexible templates. Thus there is great variety in the kinds of lines and relations among the lines which will still yield the interpretation that something is an *A*. Another important characteristic of schemas is that they use what are called *default* values – that is, things which will be *filled in* even if they are not perceived or not present in the actual stimuli. One can erase part of an *A* and still recognize what it is. Rarely does one perceive a whole battleship – both sides, top and bottom, inside and out; most of the battleship one understands to be there is filled in by default values.

Another characteristic of schemas is that they can be constructed out of other schemas; for example, the complex schema of a commercial event, mentioned above, is made out of the schemas which interpret that someone is a *buyer*, someone else a *seller*, that something is the *price*, and that there has been an *exchange* of *goods* for *money*.

It should be stressed that when one interprets something to be a particular letter *A*, or a particular battleship, this perception is *not* the schema – it is what is *produced* by the schema. A *prototypic* battleship is *not* the schema for a battleship; it is rather one instantiation of the battleship schema – an instantiation which corresponds to often-used default values – that is, what one expects if one knows nothing about what is there except that it is a battleship. Schemas are the procedural devices one *uses* to make an interpretation; they are not any one interpretation, even the most typical or most common.

Another point to be made about schemas is that they are not just recognition devices. The battleship schema, for example, consists of all the elements that are normally *activated* for someone by the interpretation that something is a battleship. These might include anticipations of disasters which may be created by modern technological war machines, personal memories of being in the military, images of waves parted by the bow of a ship, faint desires to ride on a battleship, etc. Not all parts of the total schema would be likely to produce conscious interpretations at any one time, but all would have the potential of doing so under the right conditions.

One of the important recent developments in cognitive psychology is the construction of a new model of the mind: the *parallel distributed processing model*. Using this model, it is possible to create very simple physical devices which act very much the way schemas have been hypothesized to act (Rumelhart and McClelland 1986). Basically, this model treats mental processes as the action of a network of partially interconnected elements. One can think of these elements as brain neurons with dendrites which activate or inhibit the activation of other neurons. A network of these elements can be constructed using several hundred elements, each connected to twenty or so other elements in the cluster, which has the capacity to do things like recognize the letters of the alphabet or learn regular and irregular verb endings. The device learns by discovering which connections should be activated when certain inputs are presented so that certain special output elements are triggered. The algorithm by which the device learns is relatively simple, involving continuous readjustment of the strength of the various connections.

David Rumelhart, using some American data I collected on the properties of various animals, has taught such a device to list the correct properties of whatever animal one presents to it. Thus if you type in the word *monkey*, it types back *lives in trees*, *is very intelligent*, *does not have hooves*, etc. The network consists of relatively few elements, and is able to hold so much information because it is able to find patterns in the data, and use these patterns in giving its answers. The device has some interesting problems, however, when some animals do not fit the patterns it has discovered – for example, it has real difficulty learning that people eat bears.

Beside their simplicity and the direct analogy they provide to the physical structure of the brain, these PDP – parallel distributed processing – models have other attractive properties. One of these is the fact that a PDP model, when it learns something, acts as if it were following rules, but the rules do not exist as anything the device explicitly codes or correspond to anything the device was explicitly taught. This sounds very much like the way it is with most *cultural* learning – the output behavior *looks* rule governed, but often the person cannot *state* the rule. Another attractive property of a PDP model is that it is quite sensitive to context – a PDP model, like a human, can recognize a letter faster if it is embedded in a word than if it stands alone.

More can be said about physical models of schemas and their implications, but hopefully this should be enough to give an idea of what kind of thing a schema is supposed to be. The next question is this: outside of its use as a means of representing cultural knowledge, of what interest might the schema concept be to other areas of psychological anthropology?

An application of the schema concept to the study of personality is presented in *Human Motives and Cultural Models* (D'Andrade and Strauss 1992). It has been observed that certain general cultural schemas act like *motives* in the sense that these schemas appear to direct behavior (D'Andrade 1984). Consider, for example, the general American cultural schema (or cultural model) of *marriage* which Naomi Quinn (1987) has been studying using interview material from a sample of husbands and wives in North Carolina. In analyzing the metaphors, key words, and inferential structures to be found in the discourse of her informants, Quinn has found a series of basic propositions which characterize the kind of joint relationship which people understand as *marriage*. Among these propositions are:

MARRIAGE IS LASTING
MARRIAGE IS SHARED
MARRIAGE IS MUTUALLY BENEFICIAL
MARRIAGE IS DIFFICULT
MARRIAGE IS EFFORTFUL
MARRIAGE MAY SUCCEED OR FAIL
MARRIAGE IS RISKY

What one finds is that these understandings about the marriage relationship organize *goals* for the individual spouses – goals such as trying to maintain the benefits already existing in the marriage, or trying to insure that the benefits will be truly mutual. The understanding that marriage is difficult and effortful *directs* one to give effort even when it is difficult – otherwise one is not acting in truly married fashion.

Treating marriage as a motive is neither the usual folk analysis nor the standard psychological analysis of what goes on when people marry. The usual analysis is that the marriage is the *object* of desire, not the *creator* of desire. That is, the standard analysis holds that people enter a marriage to satisfy certain desires – desires for companionship, sex, support, etc., and maintain the marriage in order to maintain the satisfaction of these desires.

This standard analysis is all right as far as it goes, but ignores certain facts and sweeps others under the rug. What the standard analysis ignores is that what is *organizing* the desires for companionship, sex, and support is a *marriage*, not something else which might organize these desires differently. If one turned to drinking friends for companionship, to affairs for sex, and to individual retirement accounts for support, one might satisfy the same desires, but one's behavior would be organized very differently. Second, the standard analysis ignores the fact that the marriage schema creates some goals of its *own* – the goal of making benefits *mutual*, for example, or the goal of having an *enduring* relationship in spite of difficulties, goals that might not exist otherwise.

What the standard analysis sweeps under the rug is the fact that the so-called *desires* for companionship, sex, support, and so on are *not* simple things in themselves, some kind of *pure wish* or *motive* independent of culture, but are the conscious interpretations of goals activated by other cultural schemas. *Companionship*, *sex*, or *support* are learned structures of interpretation and understanding, which, like marriage, contain goals which, when activated, direct action, and produce the conscious experience of *wanting* companionship, sex, or support.

What is right about the standard analysis is that it points to the fact that idiosyncratic and cultural schemas are organized in complex hierarchies. For each person certain cultural and idiosyncratic schemas sit at the top of their interpretative system. These top-level schemas give the most general interpretations of what is going on, and they typically contain the most general sets of goals. These schemas might be called a person's *master motives* – for Americans, things like *love*, *success*, *security*, and *fun*.

Further down the hierarchy are things like *marriage*, *my job*, *surfing*, etc., which one might call *middle-level* motives. Such schemas typically require other higher-level schemas to generate some of their goals, but also contain some goals which they generate on their own. (Of course, some people can get "grabbed" by a schema like *surfing* so strongly that it becomes a *master motive* in their life.) Near the bottom of the hierarchy would be things like *dirt*, *memos*, and *birthdays* – schemas that only generate goals when other higher-level schemas intersect with them – the goal of *cleaning up dirt*, for example, generally is triggered only when schemas having to do with *ownership*, *health*, *beauty*, etc., are also invoked.

At this point it is not clear how helpful the directive-force notion will ultimately be. If it is to be more than just a re-labeling procedure, in which the same old data are described in different words, it must have some hooks into the real world. One potential use of the directive-force concept is in psychological ethnography – it would be informative to attempt a psychological description of a people by organizing the data around those cultural schemas which have greatest directive force. In the late fifties and sixties there were similar attempts to organize ethnographic data around the concept of *values*, but the values approach had trouble developing techniques of emic analysis, and in distinguishing between surface prescriptions and what might be called *deep* values. However, at its best, this work gave a vivid picture of the way people see their worlds, and how these interpretative systems constrain and direct them (Vogt, 1955). Research on both motives and values could, I believe, be much refined and deepened by using a schema-based approach.

Another empirical issue concerns the factors that cause cultural schemas to be *internalized*. The general question here, which has been posed by Spiro (1987), is what causes some parts of a culture to become internalized so that they do have emotional and directive force, while other parts of a culture are adopted only as *clichés*, and have no emotional or directive properties? The same question can be asked on an individual level – why does the cultural schema for *surfing* grab some individuals and not others who have been equally exposed to it? Part of the answer, I suspect, will be that it is because some individuals had already learned other schemas which reinforced and supported the new schema.

I have recently been working with short-term psychotherapy transcripts (D'Andrade 1991). In these transcripts it is usually the case that patients want to act and feel in a certain way, but strong emotions or inhibitions prevent them from doing so. Often the course of therapy involves the patients learning that they have certain idiosyncratic schemas which create certain interpretations of the world and themselves which are unrealistic, and which occasion the unwanted and inappropriate feelings. An important part of therapy seems to be learning to become aware of these problem-creating schemas and learning to undo or redo them. The point here is that in some cases people learn schemas – often early in life – which do not support, but rather interfere with the operation of more adult and culturally shared schemas. Each individual's life history can be viewed as the building of new schematic organizations through processes of accommodating to experience and assimilating these experiences to previous schematic organizations. The final result is a complex layering and interpenetration of cultural and idiosyncratic schemas which always contains some degree of conflict.

In summary, I have been describing a trend in cognitive anthropology which has strong relevance to the traditional interests of psychological anthropologists. The schema concept provides a direct way to connect cultural and psychological processes. Since culture is one of the major sources of human schemas, and since schemas play a central role in most psychological processes, schemas provide a way to link culture to other psychological processes which more or less directly influence human action. Examples of these connections have been illustrated here, such as the effect of cultural schemas on inference and the effect of cultural schemas on motivation and values.

REFERENCES

Casson, R. W. 1983. Schemata in Cognitive Anthropology. *Annual Review of Anthropology* 12: 429–462

Collins, A. and D. Gentner. 1987. How People Construct Mental Models. In D. Holland and N. Quinn, eds., *Cultural Models in Language and Thought* (pp. 243–265). Cambridge: Cambridge University Press

D'Andrade, R. G. 1984. Cultural Meaning Systems. In R. Shweder and R. LeVine, eds., *Culture Theory: Essays on Mind, Self, and Emotion* (pp. 88–119). Cambridge: Cambridge University Press

1987. A Folk Model of the Mind. In D. Holland and N. Quinn, eds., *Cultural Models in Language and Thought* (pp. 112–148). Cambridge: Cambridge University Press

1989. Culturally Based Reasoning. In A. R. H. Gellatly, D. Rogers, and J. A. Sloboda, eds., *Cognition and Social Worlds* (pp. 132–143). Oxford: Clarendon Press

1991. The Identification of Schemas in Naturalistic Data. In M. Horowitz, ed., *Person Schemas and Maladaptive Interpersonal Behavior Patterns* (pp. 279–301). Chicago: University of Chicago Press

D'Andrade, R. G. and C. Strauss, eds. 1992. *Human Motives and Cultural Models.* Cambridge: Cambridge University Press

Dougherty, J. W. D. 1978. Salience and Relativity in Classification. *American Ethnologist* 5: 66–80

Dougherty, J. W. D. and C. M. Keller. 1982. Taskonomy: A Practical Approach to Knowledge Structures. *American Ethnologist* 9: 763–774

Fillmore, C. 1975. An Alternative to Checklist Theories of Meaning. In C. Cogen, H. Thompson, G. Thurgood, K. Whilsteler, and J. Wright, eds., *Proceedings of the First Annual Meeting of the Berkeley Linguistics Society* (pp. 123–131). Berkeley: Berkeley Linguistics Society

1977. Topics in Lexical Semantics. In R. Cole, ed., *Current Issues in Linguistic Theory* (pp. 76–138). Bloomington: Indiana University Press

Holland, D. and D. Skinner. 1987. Prestige and Intimacy: The Cultural Models Behind Americans' Talk About Gender Types. In D. Holland and N. Quinn, eds., *Cultural Models in Language and Thought* (pp. 78–111). Cambridge: Cambridge University Press

Hunn, E. 1985. The Utilitarian Factor in Folk Biological Classification. In

J. Dougherty, ed., *Directions in Cognitive Anthropology* (pp. 117–140). Urbana: University of Illinois Press

Hutchins, E. 1980. *Culture and Inference: A Trobriand Case Study*. Cambridge, MA: Harvard University Press

1987. Myth and Experience in the Trobriand Islands. In D. Holland and N. Quinn, eds., *Cultural Models in Language and Thought* (pp. 269–289). Cambridge: Cambridge University Press

Kay, P. 1987. Linguistic Competence and Folk Theories of Language. In D. Holland and N. Quinn, eds., *Cultural Models in Language and Thought* (pp. 67–77). Cambridge: Cambridge University Press

Kempton, W. 1987. Two Theories of Home Heat Control. In D. Holland and N. Quinn, eds., *Cultural Models in Language and Thought* (pp. 222–242). Cambridge: Cambridge University Press

Lakoff, G. and Z. Kövecses. 1987. The Cognitive Model of Anger Inherent in American English. In D. Holland and N. Quinn, eds., *Cultural Models in Language and Thought* (pp. 195–221). Cambridge: Cambridge University Press

Lutz, C. A. 1987. Goals, Events, and Understanding in Ifaluk Emotion Theory. In D. Holland and N. Quinn, eds., *Cultural Models in Language and Thought* (pp. 290–312). Cambridge: Cambridge University Press

Quinn, N. 1982. "Commitment" in American Marriage: A Cultural Analysis. *American Ethnologist* 9(4): 775–798

1987. Convergent Evidence for a Cultural Model of American Marriage. In D. Holland and N. Quinn, eds., *Cultural Models in Language and Thought* (pp. 173–192). Cambridge: Cambridge University Press

Quinn, N. and D. Holland. 1987. Culture and Cognition. In D. Holland and N. Quinn, eds., *Cultural Models in Language and Thought* (pp. 3–40). Cambridge: Cambridge University Press

Randall, R. 1976. How Tall is a Taxonomic Tree? Some Evidence for Dwarfism. *American Ethnologist* 3: 543–553

Rumelhart, D. and J. McClelland. 1986. *Parallel Distributed Processing: Explorations in the Microstructure of Cognition*. Volume I: *Foundations*. Cambridge, MA: MIT Press

Spiro, M. E. 1987. Collective Representations and Mental Representations. In B. Kilborne and L. L. Langness, eds., *Culture and Human Nature: Theoretical Papers of Melford E. Spiro* (pp. 161–184). Chicago: University of Chicago Press

Sweetser, E. E. 1987. The Definition of *Lie*: An Examination of the Folk Models Underlying a Semantic Prototype. In D. Holland and N. Quinn, eds., *Cultural Models in Language and Thought* (pp. 43–66). Cambridge: Cambridge University Press

Vogt, E. Z. 1955. *Modern Homesteaders: The Life of a Twentieth-Century Frontier Community*. Cambridge, MA: Harvard University Press

White, G. M. 1987. Proverbs and Cultural Models: An American Psychology of Problem Solving. In D. Holland and N. Quinn, eds., *Cultural Models in Language and Thought* (pp. 152–172). Cambridge: Cambridge University Press

Wierzbicka, A. 1984. Apples are not a "Kind of Fruit": The Semantics of Human Categorization. *American Ethnologist* 11: 313–328

3 Schemes for schemata

Janet Dixon Keller

Anthropologists have contributed to the study of mind throughout this century. Yet as the discipline has developed, approaches to the study of mind have diversified and communication among scholars with disparate approaches has become increasingly difficult. It is useful at this point in our history to reinstate the more inclusive vision of an earlier time and reopen lines of communication. Ultimately we all focus on some central questions. What are the formal and substantive properties of mind? What metaphysical assumptions must we make to account for particular hypothesized states of mind? To what extent are we dealing with a modular system?

With these questions in view cognitive anthropologists focus on knowledge representation and inference. The key term is *schema.* It replaces the blank slate and the black box, accounting for order, inference, and directive force. Yet the concept of schema has introduced at least as many problems as it has helped resolve. Schema: what is it? D'Andrade, building on Fillmore's (1975) research, argues that a schema is an organization of knowledge which constitutes a *simplified world* used to reason with. To elaborate just a little, schemata are culturally derived, knowledge-generated structures which facilitate comprehension and inferencing (Hutchins 1980; Nuckolls 1986). What constitutes a well-formed schema either formally or substantively? At this point we can't answer this question. The classic cognitive perspective in anthropology thought it could. Knowledge structures early in the history of cognitive anthropology were thought to consist of paradigms and taxonomies which in turn consisted of conceptual nodes defined by etic features in emic combinations. At least one feature was shared by all conceptual nodes thus constituting the integrity of the domain of analysis. Conceptual nodes were internally related by the universal relations of contrast and inclusion. Today, as D'Andrade points out, we are no longer satisfied with limiting our simplified worlds to these structures and the properties of schemata are therefore at issue.

Comparative schematology is likely to be a predominant research direction in cognition throughout this decade. It is only through comparative study that we can explore the class of possible knowledge structures and document universal properties and features for which a general theory of cognition and particular theories of culture must account. At present the general notion of schema seems to have three defining properties. Such structures are organizations of knowledge which (1) simplify experience, (2) facilitate inference, and (3) are potentially invoked by and constitutive of goals. However, this tells us little about the formal or substantive properties which might suggest a principled guide for abstracting particular schemata. Language is frequently used as a key in the identification and description of schematic forms but privileging the relationship between language and cognition in this way insures that our success in describing knowledge structures will be greatest in those areas where language plays a structuring role and weaker elsewhere (Dougherty 1985). In addition presupposing a privileged relationship between language and cognition more generally precludes analyses of the interactive relations among cognitive modes. Such relational analyses have been particularly useful in language-acquisition studies and may also prove fruitful for the study of adult knowledge.

Comparative schematology should provide rich analyses of particular organizations of knowledge and at the same time provide the data for scientific generalization. Studies in cognition have already identified a variety of different organizations of knowledge which satisfy the general definition of schema. Classificatory paradigms and taxonomies are schemata. Recently some scholars have rejected these structures as truly representative of the organization of folk knowledge primarily because such structures appear to lack directive force. Elicitation removed from the context of everyday behavior and the construction of minimal feature definitions, both crucial steps in early research in cognitive anthropology, rendered an account of the relations between taxonomies/paradigms and experience or action problematic. However, taxonomies and classificatory schemata do constitute formulations of order which simplify experience. They facilitate inferencing with respect to the relations among concepts (although see Randall 1976 and Werner 1985). And these schemata potentially constitute goals with respect to identification and naming. In fact such structures were postulated initially in the context of a search for the organizing principles which underlie naming behavior (Tyler 1969). Quinn's (1982) work has demonstrated that word definitions constitute schemata as well. Semantic networks also share the three defining properties. Scripts, mental models, folk theories, and metaphors are other candidates (Schank and Abelson 1977, Brewer 1984, Casson 1983, Gentner and Stevens 1983, Lakoff 1987). We intuitively expect that these structures constitute unique types, yet we are unable to specify adequately the distinguishing properties of each. More adequate typologies of schemata may ultimately emerge, but for the present we have every reason to assume the coexistence of multiple organizational forms within a knowledge hierarchy (Keesing 1979) and to pursue research which will document these structures and specify the nature of their interaction.

At the risk of adding to the present confusion I would like to report an observation made in the process of initiating research on folk conceptions of the American family. Schematic knowledge structures not infrequently stand in contradictory relations with one another. This observation calls up discussions of conflict from psychodynamic studies yet the conflicting schemata appear to coexist at a single level of cognition. These are comparable or alternative knowledge structures with contradictory dimensions (White 1987). D'Andrade reports that Quinn (1986) has found four propositions which characterize marriage for Americans. Marriage is enduring, mutually beneficial, difficult, and effortful. But *love* is a premise upon which many American marriages are based. *Love* constitutes a schema in terms of which these other propositions can be understood. And, at least for many Americans, *love and marriage go together like a horse and carriage*. Yet many Americans believe love just happens. "People do not have control over it – it happens to them" (Bean 1981:63). Here we have contradictory principles which constitute order, organize reasoning, and play a role in the establishment of goals within the same realm of experience. Questions of motivation or directedness, inference, and order are considerably more complex when such variety of structures is possible. It is not at all clear that we can explain away these contradictions as distinctions between perceptions of ideal and real behavior. Which of the above propositions concern real behavior and which exclusively represent ideals? Such a distinction is neither obvious nor, perhaps, relevant.

In 1985 and 1986 I interviewed twenty Americans in a pilot study focusing on concepts of the family. These interviews suggest that such structures of opposition (for lack of a better term) characterize folk knowledge at some level in this domain. Informant interviews and the literature provide evidence for a series of contradictory positions relevant to a cultural model of the American family.

Family members should strive for the good of the whole (Girdner 1983; Schneider 1980).

Family as a group is secondary to each individual (Wahlstrom 1979).

Family is permanent.

Family is always in transition.

Family is a refuge (Wahlstrom 1979).
Family is a place to prepare and rehearse public roles (Laslett 1979).
Family is nurturant.
Family is smothering.
Family is oppressive and divisive, a cauldron of interpersonal tension and domination (Denzin 1984; Orr 1979; Rubin 1976).
Family is an opportunity for open relations, vulnerability, mutual support, unity, and warmth (Tufte and Myerhoff 1979).

Such premises generate particular propositions, and govern the interpretation of experience for individuals. However, the ubiquity of contradiction among these premises raises a number of questions. At what level do these contradictions arise? Do such contradictions arise only as an artifact of analysis directed toward consensual cultural models or are they characteristic of individuals' folk theories? Is there a deeper level at which a folk theory of the American family is internally consistent? At present we have no principled basis for deciding whether such propositions derive from one schema or multiple schemata of the family. Nor has it been possible to specify more abstract structures which would generate the above range of propositions. Perhaps the concept *family* itself is complex, derived from other more basic schemata (Keller and Lehman 1991). In addition the issue of process, how such principles figure in action, is problematic as Holland's description of "messy situations" so well illustrates (this book).

A second dimension of comparative schematology is individual variation. Variation has been accounted for in terms of situational selection, subjective evaluation of normative standards, approximations to a consensual model correlated with age and expertise, and alternative cognitive models (Bricker 1975; Boster 1985; Garro 1986; Romney, Weller, and Batchelder 1986). I found my pilot interviews on the family demonstrated each of these forms of variation. Particularly intriguing is the last. Informant interviews and an American autobiography illustrate some distinctive constructions of the family.

"Family is a place to sleep when there's no place else to go."
"Family is learning to live responsibly in the contemporary world and being a resource from whom others can learn." (Mead 1972)
"Family is being friends."
"Family is two parents, two kids, a dog, a cat and a car."

These propositions are clearly encapsulated descriptions. In some cases they may be only clichés (D'Andrade, this book). In other cases, however, they may constitute premises in a theory of the family. Interviews and extended discussion in the autobiography cited above suggest that these tenets constrain the respective individual's interpretations, inferencing, and goal formation. As with innovation in "messy situations" (Holland, this book), such variability is not presently accounted for by schema theory. Yet, at some level, there seem to be commonalities in informants' knowledge about the family which may be schematically represented. For example, most of the key elements identified by Schneider (1980) in his study of American kinship including parent–child roles, love, and enduring diffuse solidarity are present in each individual's understandings of the American family. Yet the structures in which these symbols are embedded are remarkably divergent and internally complex.

This proliferation of schematic form and substance raises a crucial question for cognitive anthropology: what is the relationship between particular knowledge structures and their conceptual and situational contexts? This question mandates at least two equally important areas for research: acquisition and practice.

To the extent that we are replacing a blank-slate model of the mind with a more structured organ, we need to balance attention traditionally paid to the effect of a system on the individual with attention to the individual acquisition or construction of a system and the processes of relating new to old knowledge (Brewer 1984). Toward this end a reconsideration of sign theory which structures contemporary understanding of the relationship between symbol and meaning is useful. In the work of scholars such as Morris (1938), Pierce (1931), and de Saussure (1959) the relation between signifier and signified (to use de Saussure's terminology) constitutes an absolute bond. De Saussure (1959), for example, argues that the two elements of the linguistic sign are inseparable. He compares language with "a sheet of paper: thought is the front and sound the back" (1959:113). We need to break this tyrannical bond between symbolic form and conceptual image in order to ask by what principles individuals identify symbols and construct meanings.

D'Andrade has argued that "adequate description of cultural symbols from the word level to the level of large knowledge systems requires explication of the basic cognitive schemas which underlie these symbols" (this book). Ultimately I think we will be forced to relinquish the classic picture of a building-block architecture of cognition where belief systems are constructed from propositions which are in turn built from independent concepts defined by features. Instead we are being forced to work back and forth in what appear to be mutually constitutive realms (Murphy and Medin 1985). In fact, recent work in parallel distributed processing noted by D'Andrade suggests that this is exactly what we should be doing. Symbols must be identified with features of relevance from particular experiential settings. As the occasions for use of a symbol arise, previously established "defining" features may be modified (Giddens 1976). However, the process of abstraction away from related conceptualized knowledge and practical experience proceeds only so far (Medin and Ross 1989). This problem is particularly crucial in light of D'Andrade's demonstration that logical inferencing is highly dependent upon previously represented schematic knowledge.

The second research mandate, not unrelated to the first, is the development of a theory of context or practice. Theories of practice have pervaded anthropology in recent years, yet with a few notable exceptions (Lave 1988, Lave and Rogoff 1984), cognitive anthropologists have only recently begun to address the issues raised – and with good reason. As we begin to focus on the relations between knowledge structures and context or practice, we find ourselves again in a constantly shifting set of mutually constitutive figures and grounds. The meaning of particular signs and symbols is inferred from context and context can be inferred from the interpretation given to particular meaningful elements. D'Andrade points out that it is easier to recognize an instance of the letter *A* when the symbol is embedded in a word. Likewise recognition of particular letters is crucial to the identification of a given word. I am reminded of the process of describing an unwritten language encountered in my own fieldwork. Having been trained to treat distinctively the systems of phonology, morphology, and syntax, I found quickly that analysis of any one of these structural levels requires frequent reference to the other two in spite of their theoretical independence. D'Andrade reminds us of the relevance of such shifting for substantive phenomena as well. *Commercial event* constitutes a schema for Americans and incorporates the concepts *buy*, *sell*, and *money* among others. These concepts are only fully understood by reference to the embodying schema. Simultaneously the schema itself is only fully understood by reference to its constitutive concepts. Quinn (1982) has demonstrated the mutual dependence of word meaning and syntactic form in her example of the key word, *commitment*, and its relevance for models of marriage. And research on blacksmithing (Dougherty and Keller 1985) has shown the mutually constitutive relationship between a sense of problem and procedure, referred to as task, and conceptions of incorporated elements such as tools.

At this point we need an holistic theory of cognition, one which will account for the complex dynamics of mental and muscular activity, conceptual and material realms. Perhaps cooperation among scholars of diverse intellectual backgrounds, as is becoming increasingly more common in cognitive-science endeavors, will provide the perspective and insight we need to advance our knowledge. It is clear that we have not simplified our world by introducing the multidisciplinary concept of schema. We have, however, made our project more interesting.

NOTES

Special thanks to F. K. Lehman for useful discussion of this material.

REFERENCES

Bean, Susan S. 1981. Soap Operas: Sagas of American Kinship. In Susan P. Montague and W. Arens, eds., *The American Dimension*, 2nd edn (pp. 61–71). Sherman Oaks, CA: Alfred Publishing Co.

Boster, James Shilts. 1985. "Requiem for the Omniscient Informant": There's Life in the Old Girl Yet. In Janet W. D. Dougherty, ed., *Directions in Cognitive Anthropology* (pp. 177–198). Urbana: University of Illinois Press

Brewer, William. 1984. The Nature and Function of Schemas. In Robert S. Wyer, Jr. and Thomas K. Srull, eds., *Handbook of Social Cognition* (pp. 119–160). Hillsdale, NJ: Lawrence Erlbaum

Bricker, Victoria Reifler, ed. 1975. Intra-Cultural Variation. *American Ethnologist* 2 (1):1–206

Casson, Ron. 1983. Schemata in Cognitive Anthropology. *Annual Review of Anthropology* 12:429–462

Denzin, Norman. 1984. *On Understanding Emotion*. San Francisco: Jossey-Bass

Dougherty, Janet W. D., ed. 1985. *Directions in Cognitive Anthropology*. Urbana: University of Illinois Press

Dougherty, Janet W. D. and Charles Keller. 1985. Taskonomy: A Practical Approach to Knowledge Structures. In Janet W. D. Dougherty, ed., *Directions in Cognitive Anthropology* (pp. 161–174). Urbana: University of Illinois Press

Fillmore, Charles. 1975. An Alternative to Checklist Theories of Meaning. In C. Cogen, H. Thompson, G. Thurgood, K. Whilsteler, and J. Wright, eds., *Proceedings of the First Annual Meeting of the Berkeley Linguistics Society* (pp. 123–131). Berkeley: Berkeley Linguistics Society

Garro, Linda C. 1986. Intracultural Variation in Folk Medical Knowledge: A Comparison between Curers and Noncurers. *American Anthropologist* 88 (2): 351–370

Gentner, Dedre and Albert L. Stevens, eds. 1983. *Mental Models*. Hillsdale, NJ: Lawrence Erlbaum

Giddens, Anthony. 1976. *New Rules of Sociological Method*. New York: Basic Books

Girdner, Linda. 1983. Contested Child Custody Cases: An Examination of Custom and Family Law in an American Court. *Dissertation Abstracts International* 43 (8): 2,718A

Hutchins, Edwin. 1980. *Culture and Inference*. Cambridge, MA: Harvard University Press

Keesing, Roger. 1979. Linguistic Knowledge and Cultural Knowledge: Some Doubts and Speculations. *American Anthropology* 81 (1): 14–36

Keller, J. D. and F. K. Lehman. 1991. Complex Concepts. *Cognitive Science* 15 (2): 271–292

Lakoff, George. 1987. *Women, Fire and Dangerous Things*. Chicago: University of Chicago Press

Laslett, Barbara. 1979. The Significance of Family Membership. In Virginia Tufte and Barbara Myerhoff, eds., *Changing Images of the Family* (pp. 231–250). New Haven: Yale University Press

Lave, Jean. 1988. *Cognition in Practice*. Cambridge: Cambridge University Press

Lave, Jean and Barbara Rogoff, eds. 1984. *Everyday Cognition*. Cambridge, MA: Harvard University Press

Mead, Margaret. 1972. *Blackberry Winter: My Earlier Years*. New York: William Morrow

Medin, Douglas L. and Brian H. Ross 1989. The Specific Character of Abstract Thought: Categorization, Problem Solving, and Induction. In R. J. Sternberg, ed., *Advances in the Psychology of Human Intelligence*, vol. V. Hillsdale, NJ: Lawrence Erlbaum

Morris, Charles. 1938. *Foundations Toward a Theory of Signs*. Chicago: University of Chicago Press

Murphy, Gregory L. and Douglas L. Medin. 1985. The Role of Theories in Conceptual Coherence. *Psychological Review* 92 (3): 289–316

Nuckolls, Charles. 1986. Culture and Causal Thinking: Diagnosis and Prediction in Jalari Culture. Unpublished doctoral dissertation, University of Chicago

Orr, John B. 1979. The Changing Family: A Social Ethical Perspective. In Virginia Tufte and Barbara Myerhoff, eds., *Changing Images of the Family* (pp. 377–388). New Haven: Yale University Press

Pierce, Charles Sanders. 1931. *Collected Papers of Charles Sanders Pierce*, vols. I and II. Cambridge, MA: The Belknap Press of Harvard University Press

Quinn, Naomi. 1982. "Commitment" in American Marriage: A Cultural Analysis. *American Ethnologist* 9: 775–798

1987. Convergent Evidence for a Cultural Model of American Marriage. In Dorothy Holland and Naomi Quinn, eds., *Cultural Models in Language and Thought*. Cambridge: Cambridge University Press

Randall, Robert. 1976. How Tall is a Taxonomic Tree? Some Evidence for Dwarfism. *American Ethnologist* 3: 543–553

1985. Steps Toward an Ethnosemantics of Verbs. In Janet W. D. Dougherty, ed., *Directions in Cognitive Anthropology* (pp. 249–269). Urbana: University of Illinois Press

Romney, A. Kimball, Susan C. Weller, and William H. Batchelder. 1986. Culture As Consensus: A Theory of Culture and Informant Accuracy. *American Anthropologist* 88: 2: 313–338

Rubin, Lillian Breslow. 1976. *Worlds of Pain*. New York: Basic Books

Saussure, Ferdinand de. 1959. *Course in General Linguistics*. New York: McGraw-Hill

Schank, R. and R. Abelson. 1977. *Scripts, Plans, Goals and Understanding*. Hillsdale, NJ: Lawrence Erlbaum

Schneider, David M. 1980. *American Kinship: A Cultural Account*. 2nd edn. Chicago: University of Chicago Press

Tufte, Virginia and Barbara Myerhoff. 1979. Introduction. In Virginia Tufte and

Barbara Myerhoff, eds., *Changing Images of the Family* (pp. 1–25). New Haven: Yale University Press

Tyler, Stephen A. ed. 1969. *Cognitive Anthropology*. New York: Holt, Rinehart, and Winston

Wahlstrom, Billie Joyce. 1979. Images of the Family in the Mass Media: An American Iconography. In Virginia Tufte and Barbara Myerhoff, eds., *Changing Images of the Family*. New Haven: Yale University Press

Werner, Oswald. 1985. Folk Knowledge Without Fuzz. In Janet W. D. Dougherty, ed., *Directions in Cognitive Anthropology* (pp. 73–90). Urbana: University of Illinois Press

White, Geoffrey. 1987. Proverbs and Cultural Models: An American Psychology of Problem Solving. In Dorothy Holland and Naomi Quinn, eds., *Cultural Models in Language and Thought* (pp. 151–172). Cambridge: Cambridge University Press

4 The woman who climbed up the house: some limitations of schema theory

Dorothy Holland

In the late 1950s and early 1960s, cognitive anthropologists looked for cultural knowledge in the lexicon and analyzed semantic features as the key to the cognitive organization of this knowledge. The goal was to account for cultural competence much as the linguists of the day sought to account for linguistic competence. Over the ensuing three decades, the cognitivist position has been formulated and reformulated many times. Today, cultural genres and discourse have taken the place of the lexicon in theorists' concern and cultural schemas have replaced semantic features as the presumed mainstay of cognitive organization. Instead of theorizing cultural competence, the goal is to theorize the ways in which collectively interpreted experience comes to constitute the foundation of the individual's thoughts and feelings. In the spirit of contributing to the ongoing theoretical reformulation, I here consider some limitations of schema theory, especially those limitations that obscure the relevance of cultural schemas to social theory and to depth psychologies.[1] First, I will describe the concept of schema.

A schema is a complicated knowledge structure – a schematized interpretive framework (see D'Andrade, this book). It is a living mental precipitate of past experiences, a precipitate that forms a sort of mental lens. Schemas are significant because they channel experience of the present, inform anticipation of the future, and play an important role in the (re)construction of memories of the past. To the extent that these schemas arise from experiences interpreted according to a collective history and tradition, they are powerful cultural phenomena as well as psychological ones. In more mundane terms, these cultural schemas or cultural models are complexes of assumptions or expectations that individuals have learned, in the company of others, to make about the world or some portion of it. These expectations guide attention, the drawing of inferences about a situation, the evaluation of experience, and the reformulation of memories. They supply interpretations of present situations and often embed goals and impetuses to action.[2] Clearly schema theory encompasses many more areas of human activity than naming theories based on semantic features could. Nonetheless, it too is limited in ways that needlessly restrict its utility in other areas of anthropology.

Some problems with schema theory

In the interest of highlighting the limitations of schema theory, I will caricature humans as schema driven. These caricatured humans have learned sets of simplifying interpretive frameworks that they *exclusively* rely upon to understand events and situations. Furthermore, they reliably feel the feelings, pursue the goals, and engage in the actions encoded by the schemas.

Schema-driven humans actually could do quite a lot; they would not be simple creatures. Their schemas would give them a sensitive purchase both on the world and on themselves and their feelings. To give a hypothetical example inspired by, but not at all capturing the depth of, Hutchins' (1987) account of a Trobriand schema:[3] such a human would be driven by a schema for understanding noises in the night as made by a spirit (*kosi*) that is temporarily hanging around in the land of the living. The schema would supply an interpretive connection between the noises, other annoyances, and frightening encounters happening around the village and the recent death of a disliked old man. Our schema-driven human would not only be able to make an interpretation of the events and their causes, s/he also would have feelings of fear and anxiety about the situation and s/he would have at hand plans of action for responding to the *kosi*. In contrast, with the early ethnosemantic theories of the 1950s, s/he would have been limited to correctly labeling the kind of spirit that was causing the problems. A schema-driven human can clearly do a lot more than supply semantically acceptable labels. However, it is worthwhile to ask how much a schema-driven human would be limited. While there are many situations for which schema theory is adequate (see, for example, those D'Andrade describes in his paper in this book), there are others in which it falls short. There are at least two types of situations – both of which seem important – that are not illuminated by our current view of cultural schemas. One set of circumstances can be dubbed "the messy situation"; the other, "sites of censorship." I will describe an incident that made me vividly aware of these possibilities.

The woman who climbed up the house

Debra Skinner and I were interviewing people in a rural hill community in west-central Nepal. Debra was finishing up her doctoral research and had been in the community for about a year and a half. I had recently joined her so that we could carry out a small joint project.

The community is composed of people of different castes. Since we wanted to interview people from a range of castes we asked women and men from Bahuns to Damai (from the highest to the lowest castes represented in the community) to come to Debra's house to participate in the interviews. For at least one of the people who agreed to be interviewed, as it turned out, our request created a problematic situation.

In the community, lower-caste people are prohibited entry into the houses of higher-caste people. Food and cooking are considered to be especially vulnerable to pollution and, since the only entrance to the houses is on the first floor where the hearth is, people of lower castes are kept away. Under normal circumstances, lower-caste people would have expected to be barred from Debra's house. She was viewed as analogous to a higher-caste person and, in addition, her landlord, a Bahun, lived next door. Debra, however, had during her fieldwork insisted that lower-caste people come into the house to talk and people all around had come to know of her unusual practice.

That day, we were interviewing on the balcony of the second floor of the three-story house. We were in the process of interviewing a woman of the Sunar – the goldsmith caste, considered untouchable – who was becoming uncomfortable. We guessed that her discomfort was due to the proximity of the next person to be interviewed, a Chetri – higher-caste – woman, who was sitting around the corner of the balcony.

About that time another person arrived at the house to be interviewed. The new arrival, whom I will refer to as Gyanumaya, was also of the Sunar caste. Debra called down to Gyanumaya that we wanted to talk to her on the balcony and got up to go down to greet her and bring her through the kitchen and up the stairs. However, while Debra was on her way downstairs, Gyanumaya – a woman in her late fifties – scaled the outside of the house. She somehow crawled up the vertical, outside wall, sidled around the balcony to an opening in the railing, came through and sat down. Gyanumaya knew that Debra did not observe the practice of prohibiting lower-caste people entry to her kitchen or any part of her house. Nonetheless Gyanumaya decided not to enter the house. Instead of climbing the internal stairs, she chose to reach the second floor by scaling the outside of the house. She managed to get to the place of our interview and at the same time avoid going through the house.

The messy situation

Later, I questioned Debra closely about her knowledge of the community that she had gained from a year and a half of ethnographic research. Do people in the community normally climb up the outside of houses to get to the second floor? Had she ever noticed lower-caste people getting around the prohibition against their entry into higher-caste houses in a similar manner? What about Gyanumaya in particular? Was she accustomed to entering houses in this way?

As far as I could discern, Gyanumaya did not have a schema that entailed getting to the second story of a house by climbing up the outside of it. Instead she had come up with a novel solution to a messy situation. The house was in her eyes an upper-caste person's house that she – at least in the usual circumstances of community life – was not allowed to enter. Yet she needed to get to the second-floor balcony. She came up with the solution of climbing up the outside of the house.

The situation was messy in that Gyanumaya probably had a number of different schemas for interpreting and responding to the situation, none of which fitted exactly and some of which were conflicting. She probably had several expectations about multi-storied houses and how one gets to the second floor. She also had an interpretive framework for understanding the houses of upper-caste people and the prohibitions against her entry. As Michael Arbib (1985), a brain theorist and noted proponent of schema theory, has commented in reference to problems like Gyanumaya's, we have many schemas but only one body to commit to action.

Unfortunately for schema theory as presently applied, the world does not seem to be laid out so that only one schema or only one package of schemas nicely applies, without discord, in every case. This vulnerability to imperfect fit and multiple interpretations is amply evident in cases where more than one person gives an interpretation of a situation. Lutz (1987), for example, describes a protracted incident among the Ifaluk in which a set of kinspeople interpreted their social obligations according to different schemas. The differences were serious and the task of reconciling and accommodating their interpretations took a great deal of time and anguish. We are not surprised when different members of a group have different interpretations of the same situation. Nor do we find it unusual if the sequel to disputed interpretations is effort toward negotiating and reconciling the differences. Is it surprising then that the same occurs for individuals? Is it surprising that situations yield themselves to different interpretations that must be reconciled?

Perhaps, the reader might argue: individuals do encounter awkward situations, but these situations are unusual and infrequent. They result from unfortunate coincidences such as those that occur when untoward actors like anthropologists are about. Further, the reader might add: "Messy situations" like the one Gyanumaya encountered are aberrations of little moment. Because they are circumscribed in time and space, they are of little consequence no matter how they are handled.

Gyanumaya's solution seems radical enough, to me anyway, to suggest that she, at least, considered the situation to be important. However, there is no need to debate her case. Other cases show multiple interpretations in clearly non-trivial situations. Quinn (1992), for example, describes women who were facing far-reaching decisions about work and childrearing. Her informants clearly interpreted their situations according to two or more cultural models. From one model they saw their lives in terms of self-fulfillment; from another, in terms of the goals of marriage and their obligations as wives and mothers. The interpretations given by these models were not always compatible. As did Gyanumaya, Quinn's informants faced messy situations that could not be clearly interpreted by any one schema (see also Keller, this book, and Estroff and Price, in preparation).

Schema theory can probably account for each possible interpretation, but as presently formulated, it cannot account for the reconciliation of multiple interpretations. It cannot explain the Ifaluk solution to the case Lutz describes. Neither the Ifaluk's original disagreement, nor their ensuing efforts to accommodate different interpretations, are neatly encompassed by already existing schemas. Nor can we account for Gyanumaya's solution as schema driven. If these messy situations are frequent – and I think they are – then our schema-driven human is sadly at a loss in many circumstances. In order to handle the messy situations, we have to theorize about the ways multiple interpretations of the same situation are negotiated. We have to ask: what puts the schemas together? How are these often novel reconciliations of multiple interpretations arrived at?

In cognitive research our usual goal is to illuminate a given cultural schema or model. We work to ascertain the background or taken-for-granted knowledge about a given domain. Thus we segregate *one* topic of discourse. To the extent we are successful, the method results inadvertently in editing out messy situations. In the practice of the research, it is *as though* we assume that orderly environments are the rule. To the extent that the environment is not orderly, to the extent that people face situations like that of Gyanumaya's, schema theory as presently developed is limited.[4]

To be fair it must be pointed out that schemas are conceptualized as continually changing and always subject to modification by incorporation of the unexpected turn of event as an exception. In my and Skinner's research on cultural models of romance, for example, we found an ever-expanding vocabulary of names for types of men and women who cause the taken-for-granted progress of romantic relationships to go awry (Holland and Skinner 1987). Cultural models are clearly extended to new situations, ones that heretofore were messy. Nonetheless, notwithstanding this capability, schema theory leaves the social and psychological processes of extension and negotiation untheorized. And, in turn, conflicts – social and/or psychological – with their attendant cognitive and emotional "residues" remain absent from the theoretical world of the schema-driven human. The consequences of these limitations become even clearer when we consider another aspect of the case of Gyanumaya.

Sites of censorship

Schemas and cultural models often are described as providing interpretations of situations – as filling in, fleshing out, and as guiding doing. The ubiquitous example of the restaurant script, for instance, is used to demonstrate the manner in which schemas aid interpretation. A story is told about someone in a restaurant. Then the reader or listener is questioned about what happened. As it turns out, the listener or reader can answer many questions about the story, such as what the customer was paying for at the cash register, no matter whether the information is explicitly included. Because of shared schemas about restaurants and what goes on in them, many details can simply go unremarked. The example is used to illustrate that the story is *filled in* or *fleshed out* by the schemas.

But what about the material that is *edited out* of the story or *censored*? Schema theory explains what is not included in the story either as material that is irrelevant or that is taken-for-granted so that it does not have to be included. The act of *not* doing or *not* saying is usually ignored as a problematic issue. Action is to be explained, not inaction. Production is to be accounted for, not non-production or censorship.

I certainly do not know what Gyanumaya, the Sunar woman, thought about as she faced the task of getting up to the second floor of our house, but my guess is that she thought about going through the house and up the stairs. My guess is that she had to censor that idea or keep herself from carrying it out. Debra had worked closely with the children of the community. The lower-caste children had told her of scoldings they had received for getting near the doorway of upper-caste people's houses. They had told her how badly those experiences had made them feel (see also Skinner 1990). Perhaps Gyanumaya did not think about going into the house and up the stairs, but she probably had thought of such a thing earlier in her life and she had had to learn to repress or censor that possibility.

Schema theory can easily incorporate the idea of avoiding behavior. It is not difficult to imagine that a child comes to have a schema of fire that includes keeping his or her body out of the flames. However, censorship can be effected in a number of different ways besides simple avoidance behavior. A useful example is provided by Hochschild (1983) in her account of the management and censorship of emotion by Delta stewardesses.

While in training, the stewardesses are taught to control their anger at obnoxious passengers. They learn to picture the irritating passenger as having recently undergone a traumatic event or to tell themselves that he is behaving childishly because he fears flying. From her study of this process, Hochschild remarks that eventually the stewardesses neither feel anger toward the irritating passengers nor are they aware of imaging the passenger as a child. They have edited out their anger and their means of controlling the anger not only from the passenger's awareness, but also from their own. Hochschild concludes that this historical moment in their development of emotional control has serious consequences (see also Holland and Valsiner 1988). The stewardesses come to have trouble sensing their emotions off the job as well as on the job. Their emotions, Hochschild argues, have been alienated to the service of Delta airlines.

Again the reader may pose the question of the pervasiveness and/or significance of cases of self-censorship. Perhaps Gyanumaya's learned avoidances are few in number, pertaining only to upper-caste houses and the like. Perhaps the way in which she learned to keep herself from approaching such houses has no implications for other aspects of her life and no psychic costs. I would respond that we must, at least, entertain such questions. Does she prevent herself from going near the forbidden doorways because of her assessment of the asymmetries of power between herself and upper-caste people? Do lower-caste adults continue to feel the hurt and anger that Debra's young informants conveyed to her? Perhaps adults have reconciled themselves by embracing the Hindu cosmology and its justification of the social hierarchy. What does schema theory miss by ignoring how these self-controls are achieved?

If we consult Bourdieu's discussion of "habitus" – a concept not altogether dissimilar from schema, especially schemas conceptualized in connectionist terms (see Strauss 1990 and Holland and Strauss forthcoming) – we see a strong argument to the effect that self-censorship is extremely important. Especially in his article on language habitus (1977:655), Bourdieu is clear that self-control must be a central subject of inquiry and that it is closely tied to power relations in the society:

At the basis of self-censorship is the sense of the acceptable – one dimension of that sense of limits which is the internalization of class position – which makes it possible to evaluate the degree of formality of situations and to decide whether it is appropriate to speak and what sort of language to speak on a social occasion at a determinate point on the scale of formality. People do not learn on the one hand grammar and on the other hand the art of the opportune moment. The system of selective reinforcements has constituted in each of us a sort of sense of linguistic usages which defines the degree of constraint that a given field brings to bear on our speech (so that, in a given situation, some will be reduced to silence, others to hyper-controlled language, whereas still others will feel able to use free, relaxed language).

Perhaps schema theory can accommodate censorship. Psychoanalysis and other non-cognitive psychologies treat repression of emotions as their standard fare and cognitive anthropologists certainly recognize the possibility of censorship (e.g., D'Andrade, this book; Lutz 1987; Quinn and Holland 1987). Hutchins (1987), in fact, has presented a case that he concludes to be a type of psychological defense or censorship. He analyzes a Trobriand woman's use of a myth to make sense of the *kosi*, the spirit of the dead man, described above. By using the terms of the myth, Hutchins argues, the woman transformed the psychologically troubling situation, that is, the guilt-ridden feelings of ill will toward the old man before he died, into a less psychically evocative one. Because the myth paralleled the underlying unacceptable feelings but in disguised form, the woman was able to use it to both puzzle out the situation and to keep herself from fully recognizing her culturally unacceptable feelings. Unfortunately, however, Hutchins' application of schema theory is unusual. The research mostly has been oriented toward cases of production not cases of censorship or inhibition. Again, because of the practice of the research – not the explicit tenets of the theory – situations of censorship have been under studied. The result is that humans are depicted as having learned schemas that they simply apply and act out. They are depicted, in effect, *as though* they never chafe against social constraints and never encounter psychic turmoil.

Conclusions

Schema theory is powerful, but is not now helpful for understanding action in messy situations or for understanding the complicated pathways to censorship and inaction. At this point in its development, schema theory is best at accounting for culturally informed interpretations of experience. It is good for depicting how humans use yesterday's experiences to make sense of the situations in which they find themselves today. It is not as good in accounting for the actions and inactions that humans take in these situations.

The problem is not that the interpretations supplied by cultural schemas are irrelevant to action. As contributors to D'Andrade and Strauss (1992), among others, have taken pains to point out, schemas are not dull lifeless "cognitive maps" which, like the official state roadmaps of North Carolina, for example, are stripped of affect and implications for action. Cultural models entail goals and imply action. If one interprets a situation according to the cultural model of anger described by Lakoff and Kövecses (1987), for example, then one expects and prepares for vengeful action. The problem brought out here is not that schemas entail no action or that people fail to act on the interpretations supplied by the schemas, but rather that people often face situations that yield to more than one interpretation. Schema theory is important for helping to understand how people bring cultural knowledge to bear in creating each of a variety of possible interpretations of a given situation, but schema theory does not tell us how people negotiate these varied interpretations and put them together into action. It does not answer, in Arbib's (1985) words, the many-schemas-one-body problem. Nor does it direct us to pay attention to the pragmatics of interpretations, the importance of interpretations in constituting collective situations, or the attendant issues of whose interpretation will prevail.[5] Our caricatured schema-driven human is strangely unable to attend to the social and political relationships between herself/himself and those with whom s/he interacts; s/he is oddly untouched by social constraints and struggles; s/he is peculiarly immune to psychic distress. As argued above, because of the tendency to study cultural productions instead of what is censored – either knowingly or unknowingly – schema theory cannot yet shed light on the internalization of social controls, a topic of considerable importance to other subfields of anthropology. Nor is it relevant to issues of the psychic costs of such controls.

If schema theory is developed to handle only situations that are free of power asymmetries, for example, or "psychic" strife, then it will continue to be of limited interest or relevance to anthropologists outside cognitive anthropology, especially to those concerned with psychodynamic perspectives and emotive issues and to those engaged by social theory and the issues of conflict and control in human life.

Over the three decades of its history, cognitive anthropology has continually outgrown its limited formulations as researchers paid attention to unexpected study results. No doubt the same will occur with the current formulation of schema theory. It will be interesting to see how far schema theory can be pushed before it is necessary to import other theories – perhaps from psychodynamic formulations, from developmental theories, or from other areas of psychological anthropology – to account for the management and interrelation of schemas that make up individuals' cultural knowledge and to accommodate the ways in which social controls are internalized.

NOTES

An earlier draft of this paper was presented in the symposium, "Psychological Anthropology: Appraisal and prospectus," organized by Theodore Schwartz for the 1986 Anthropological Association Meetings held in Philadelphia, Pennsylvania. My thanks to Geoff White, Catherine Lutz, Ted Schwartz, and William Lachicotte for their helpful comments on the draft and to Debra Skinner who has been a close consultant on the case described.

1 Since D'Andrade (this book) lucidly details the positive points of schema theory, I am able here to assume the role of the critic without fear that readers unfamiliar with schema theory will go away with the idea that it is useless. It is not. My objective is not to discard schema theory, but rather to discuss the simplifying assumptions of schema theory as it is being applied and the limitations that these simplifying assumptions impose.
2 D'Andrade (this book) should be consulted for a more thorough discussion of how schemas function as knowledge structures and for references to important work on the topic. See also Quinn and Holland (1987) and Casson (1983).
3 Hutchins' (1987) article is an analysis of a mythic schema, not the one alluded to here. Further he addresses one of the limitations – censorship – that I discuss below.
4 There are exceptions. In explicating the narrative accounts of illness that Ecuadorians exchange with one another, Price (1987), for example, details a range of different cultural schemas that inform the stories. Agar (1980:224), who like Price was examining narratives, calls for "a qualitative Fourier analysis." He likens the life-history interview he is analyzing to a complicated, irregular-appearing wave pattern that can be understood as the simultaneous occurrence of several wave patterns. He analyzes the life history as a product of a number of different schemas operating more-or-less simultaneously. See also Strauss (1988, 1990) who explores recently formulated models of schemas – referred to as "connectionist" models – and their ability to accommodate "messy situations" (see also Holland and Strauss, forthcoming). D'Andrade (this book) and Keller (this book) also point to the possible improvements to be expected from connectionist and parallel distributive processing models.
5 Although cognitive anthropology has gone beyond ethnosemantics, it should be clear from the above discussion that schema theory bears traces of notions of person, language, and culture implicit in the conceptualization of ethnoscience and the goal of theorizing cultural competence. Early cognitive anthropologists treated language and other cultural knowledge as though it were devoted to the competent description of the world in cultural terms. For a more thorough discussion of the need to go beyond these concepts than was possible in this paper, see White (this book). He points out the kind of adjustments that must be made to reorient from an emphasis on language as a means of *representing* to an emphasis on language as a means of *constituting* the world. Bourdieu's (1977) discussion of language habitus, mentioned above, is also useful. He addresses

the limitations inherent in treating language as an instrument of representation rather than an instrument of action and power.

REFERENCES

Agar, M. 1980. Stories, Background Knowledge and Themes: Problems in the Analysis of Life History Narrative. *American Ethnologist* 7(2): 223–239

Arbib, M. 1985. *In Search of the Person: Philosophical Explorations in Cognitive Science*. Amherst, MA: The University of Massachusetts Press

Bourdieu, P. 1977. The Economics of Linguistic Exchanges. *Social Science Information* 16(6): 645–668

Casson, R. N. 1983. Schemata in Cognitive Anthropology. *Annual Review of Anthropology* 12: 429–62

D'Andrade, R. 1984. Cultural Meaning Systems. In R. Shweder and R. LeVine, eds., *Culture Theory: Essays on Mind, Self, and Emotion* (pp. 88–119). Cambridge: Cambridge University Press

D'Andrade, R. G. and C. Strauss, eds. 1992. *Human Motives and Cultural Models*. Cambridge: Cambridge University Press

Estroff, S. E. and M. L. Price. In preparation. My Daughter, The Other Woman: A Cultural Analysis of American Father–Daughter Incest. Unpublished manuscript, University of North Carolina, Chapel Hill

Hochschild, A. 1983. *The Managed Heart: Commercialization of Human Feeling*. Berkeley: University of California Press

Holland, D. and N. Quinn, eds. 1987. *Cultural Models in Language and Thought*. Cambridge: Cambridge University Press

Holland, D. and D. Skinner. 1987. Prestige and Intimacy: The Cultural Models Behind Americans' Talk about Gender Types. In D. Holland and N. Quinn, eds., *Cultural Models in Language and Thought* (pp. 78–111). Cambridge: Cambridge University Press

Holland, D. and C. Strauss. Forthcoming. *Mind in Society/Society in Mind*. Boulder, CO: Westview Press

Holland, D. and J. Valsiner. 1988. Cognition, Symbols and Vygotsky's Developmental Psychology. *Ethos* 16(3): 247–272

Hutchins, E. 1987. Myth and Experience in the Trobriand Islands. In D. Holland and N. Quinn, eds., *Cultural Models in Language and Thought* (pp. 269–289). Cambridge: Cambridge University Press

Lakoff, G. and Z. Kövecses. 1987. The Cognitive Model of Anger Inherent in American English. In D. Holland and N. Quinn, eds., *Cultural Models in Language and Thought* (pp. 195–221). Cambridge: Cambridge University Press

Lutz, C. A. 1987. Goals, Events, and Understanding in Ifaluk Emotion Theory. In D. Holland and N. Quinn, eds., *Cultural Models in Language and Thought* (pp. 290–312). Cambridge: Cambridge University Press

Price, L. 1987. Ecuadorian Illness Stories: Cultural Knowledge in Natural Discourse. In D. Holland and N. Quinn, eds., *Cultural Models in Language and Thought* (pp. 313–342). Cambridge: Cambridge University Press

Quinn, N. 1992. The Directive Force of Self Understanding: Evidence from Wives' Inner Conflicts. In R. D'Andrade and C. Strauss, eds., *Human Motives and Cultural Models*. Cambridge: Cambridge University Press

Quinn, N. and D. Holland. 1987. Culture and Cognition. In D. Holland and N. Quinn, eds., *Cultural Models in Language and Thought* (pp. 3–40). Cambridge: Cambridge University Press

Skinner, D. 1990. Nepalese Children's Understanding of Self and the Social World. Unpublished doctoral dissertation, University of North Carolina, Chapel Hill

Strauss, C. 1988. Culture, Discourse, and Cognition: Forms of Belief in some Rhode Island Working Men's Talk about Success. Unpublished doctoral dissertation, Harvard University

1990. Who Gets Ahead? Cognitive Responses to Heteroglossia in American Political Culture. *American Ethnologist* 17(2): 312–328

Part II

Learning to be human

5 Language as tool in the socialization and apprehension of cultural meanings

Peggy J. Miller and Lisa Hoogstra

Within anthropology there has been a long history of interest in language and communication as they relate to the processes by which children become full and competent participants in their culture. In his classic essay on language, for example, Sapir (1933/1949) asserted, "Language is a great force of socialization, perhaps the greatest that exists" (p. 15). Mead and Macgregor (1951) sought "those sequences in child–other behavior which carry the greatest communication weight and so are crucial for the development of each culturally regular character structure" (p. 27). H. Geertz (1959) conceived of emotional socialization as a communicative process whereby affective and interpersonal messages are transmitted to the child via verbal and nonverbal channels. Language and communication were thus seen as fundamental to the socialization process.

In recent years language has re-emerged as an important locus of inquiry in a number of anthropological enterprises – e.g., ethnopsychology (White, this book), the cross-cultural study of human development (Harkness, this book), cultural psychology (Shweder 1990) – that have an interest in childhood socialization. Part of the appeal has been that language, as both a publicly shared and privately utilized symbol system, crosscuts the internal/external dichotomy that has plagued discussions of culture. The ascendancy of language in socialization studies is perhaps most evident in the creation of a new field of study, language socialization, that is explicitly and focally concerned with language as tool and outcome of socialization, and in the revival of interest in Vygotskian theory, which defines socialization in terms of the joint participation of caregiver and novice in semiotically mediated routine practices. Drawing upon insights from these and other intellectual currents, this chapter asks, how does language figure into the socialization and apprehension of cultural meanings? We address this question primarily with respect to children and secondarily with respect to ethnographers. These two categories of nonmember face rather different tasks: the task for the child is to find ways of understanding and participating in his or her native culture, bringing to bear immature interpretive capabilities, whereas the task for the ethnographer – already equipped with native interpretive frameworks – is to make sense of a new culture. Yet, for both, language is a crucial tool in the apprehension of cultural meanings.

Language as tool in childhood socialization and acquisition

Recent work on language socialization assumes a very broad notion of what language is. Language is not equated with grammar nor even with the linguistic system itself. Instead, terms such as speech, talk, and communication are used roughly synonymously with language to denote the socially appropriate uses of speech, to encompass levels of organization beyond the sentence, and to acknowledge the interconnectedness of verbal, nonverbal, and paralinguistic channels.

Although cultures differ in the extent to which they privilege talk as a defining property of social life, it is probably safe to assume that talk is a pervasive, orderly, and culturally organized feature of social life in every culture (Goodwin 1982; Gumperz and Hymes 1972; Hymes 1967; Sacks 1965–1971/1984). It follows from this premise that becoming culturally competent entails becoming a competent speaker. Because talk comes packaged with nontalk, several aspects of nontalk must be acquired along the way toward full participation in society. That is, children have to learn how to interweave nonverbal systems such as gesture, gaze, and paralanguage with the verbal. They have to learn when not to talk and how and when to listen. Also, and critically important, they need to learn to detect and interpret the unspoken assumptions that lie behind talk, requiring complex processes of social inferencing (Garvey 1986; Rosaldo 1986; Shweder and Much 1987).

This claim, then, seems self-evident and noncontroversial: in order to be a competent member of a culture a person has to be able to talk like a member. It is worth noting, however, that it is only relatively recently that ethnographies of communication have been pursued in any serious way. If we assume that culture, as a shared set of practices and meaning systems, has some coherence and is manifest in multiple ways, then language is at least as good as any other domain (e.g., religion, sex roles, kinship) as a point of entry. For example, if we enter a culture with a question about the ways in which caregivers socialize children into local norms of speaking, that question becomes a locus from which other questions radiate, questions about cultural definitions of children and adults (Schieffelin 1979; Ochs and Schieffelin 1984), local models of childrearing and mental health (Miller and Sperry 1987), status hierarchies (Ochs 1982), codes of respect (LeVine 1990), and basic issues of folk epistemology such as the nature of intentions and interpretations (Ochs 1982).

However, language is not only a domain to be mastered along with many other domains, it is also a tool for socializing novices into the multiplicity of domains. Here the work on language socialization can be read to make a stronger claim, namely that language plays a privileged role in the socialization process, that there is something especially efficient or powerful about language as a socializing tool for transmitting messages. There are several general properties of language that equip it for a privileged role. First, given its propositional nature, language is particularly well suited for conveying explicit messages, for example, how to feel, when to act, what to say. The use of explicit instruction to socialize young children has been reported in a wide variety of cultures (e.g., Blount 1977; Bruner 1983; Demuth 1986; Heath 1983; Miller 1982; Ochs 1982; Schieffelin 1979, 1990; Watson-Gegeo and Gegeo 1986a).

Second, since language has the capability of representing the non-here-and-now, it can be used by caregivers to remind children of events that occurred in the past, to anticipate events that have not yet occurred, to envision what might have been, and to make connections across these various possible worlds. In our study of an American urban working-class community, for example, we found that mothers and other caregivers habitually told one another stories of their past experiences of anger and aggression, thereby providing an implicit socializing context for young children (Miller and Sperry 1987). These narrations were a rich source of messages about the nature and prevalence of these affective experiences and especially about the necessity for justifying anger and aggression by reference to an instigating transgression. Another example is provided by Watson-Gegeo and Gegeo (1986b), who report that Kwara'ae caregivers hold "counseling" sessions in which they review the young child's misdeeds and draw if–then links between misbehavior and its consequences.

In addition to these properties of language as a representational or symbolic system, there is still another way in which language might play a privileged role, and this has to do with the indexicality of language, the ability of linguistic signs to index features of their linguistic and non-linguistic contexts (Silverstein 1976, 1985a, 1985b; Ochs 1990). Speech is not only pervasive, but it co-varies with social context. That is, speech provides a "map" to the social terrain in that it indexes socially constituted categories (e.g., roles, statuses, situations, and events) through the choice of linguistic options. For example, in the Western middle class, a particular configuration of features – short sentence length, high pitch, exaggerated intonation pattern, high rate of imperatives, high rate of repetition – indexes speech to young children in contrast to speech to adults (e.g., Snow and Ferguson 1977). Any one of these features, for example, high rate of imperatives, may co-vary with a different set of features to index a different contrast, for example, boys' versus girls' speech during pretend play (Sachs 1983).

The indexical property of language thus provides a link to models of socialization that emphasize the powerful socializing impact of tacit organizations of time and space, with their associated routines and distributions of persons (Goodnow 1990; Harkness and Super 1983; Super and Harkness 1986; Whiting 1980). To the extent that language forms and functions are distributed contrastively across the various settings to which the child is habitually assigned, they help to define the "cast of characters, activities, and standing rules of the setting[s]" (Whiting 1980: 106). In this way language contributes to the implicit, unintentional delivery of socializing messages.[1]

Of course, language can only index such contrasts as exist in a culture. If the ecology of childrearing is such that mother and child are never alone, then language cannot index the dyadic situation in contrast to the multiparty situation. The multiparty situation, then, represents a pervasive and fundamental cultural ordering of the sort that feels most deeply natural to the native and is least likely to be reflected upon. Such orderings may be noticeable only from the vantage point of another culture, where social configurations are arranged differently.

Indeed, the assumption prevalent in psycholinguistic quarters, that speech to the child is the only relevant verbal environment for language learning seems to reflect, in part, the cultural orderings characteristic of traditional family life in the Western middle class. A "paradox of familiarity" obscures the fact that the Western middle-class version of caregiver speech – sustained dyadic conversation – is embedded in a culture-specific set of spatially structured social arrangements, for example, nuclear families isolated in separate households, small number of children per family, mother as primary caregiver (Ochs and Schieffelin 1984). In addition, family time is organized in such a way as to permit the parent to spend "quality time" alone with each child (Harkness and Super 1989). Recent cross-cultural research on language socialization reveals that these patterns are not necessarily replicated in other cultures. Instead cultures – and subcultures within the United States – differ widely in the extent to which caregivers address speech to young childen versus to other persons in the presence of young children, reflecting variation in spatial, temporal, and social configurations (Heath 1983; LeVine 1990; Miller and Moore 1989; Ochs 1988; Schieffelin 1990; Ward 1971; Watson-Gegeo and Gegeo 1986a). Children who grow up in extended families or who are raised collectively by the community tend to experience heavy exposure to talk addressed to other persons.[2]

In sum, we have considered several general properties of language – propositionality, representational capability, and indexicality – that equip it for a privileged role in the socialization process, that is, in the intentional and unintentional delivery of messages. There is a parallel question regarding acquisition. Does language play a privileged role in the apprehension of cultural meanings by the child once he or she is launched into the linguistic system, and if so, how early in development does this effect occur?

One possibility is a Whorfian (1956) one, namely that the structure of the language constrains the kinds of concepts that are learned. According to this hypothesis, if language A and language B systematically classify experience in different ways, then speakers of these languages will habitually think in ways that reflect the differences between the two languages. Although Whorf's proposal has attracted considerable interest and generated numerous critiques, there have been few theoretical or empirical investigations of his hypothesis. Lutz's (1985a) investigation of the linguistic encoding of emotion and its effects on thinking is one recent example of work on this problem. Unlike Whorf, however, Lutz emphasizes lexical rather than grammatical effects. Lucy's (1987) review and evaluation of work on this hypothesis is the most comprehensive assessment to date, and provides the best statement of the work that remains to be done in adequately addressing both the linguistic and cognitive components of Whorf's theory.

Another way in which language might play a privileged role derives from what Hymes (1966) and, more recently, Lucy (1985) have called functional, as distinguished from structural, versions of the linguistic relativity hypothesis. Vygotskian theory is one example of a functional account, emphasizing the uses of language and their implications for the development of higher mental processes (Vygotsky 1934/1987, 1978; Wertsch 1985). According to this theory, certain kinds of thought, that is, scientific concepts, develop only in cultures in which children encounter the specialized discourse associated with formal schooling. Several recent efforts have been made to expand Vygotskian theory in an affective direction, encompassing the formation of social identity (Holland and Valsiner 1988), the development of the self-analytic function in psychoanalytic treatment (Nye 1988), and the emergence of self expression and understanding (Miller, Potts, Fung, Hoogstra, and Mintz 1990; Miller, Mintz, Hoogstra, Fung, and Potts 1992). These approaches suggest that culturally specific affective meanings are acquired through using language for particular purposes in socially defined activities.

If these proposals are correct, then we would expect that recurrent uses of specialized kinds of discourse would yield predictable configurations of emotional meaning. Consider, for example, teasing as practiced in South Baltimore (Miller 1986; Miller and Sperry 1987), as compared with teasing among the Utku Eskimos (Briggs 1970, 1975). The ability to assert oneself and to speak up in anger are highly valued in South Baltimore, and young children routinely participate in teasing interactions in which caregivers playfully provoke them into defending themselves. The Utku strongly disapprove of negative feelings and encourage children to respond to similar teasing affronts by ignoring them or by laughing. We would expect these groups of children to develop different inter- and intra-personal strategies for coping with felt injury to the self, with the South Baltimore children relying more on tools of retaliation, the Utku children more on tools for maintaining equanimity.

As yet, however, little is known about the social and psychological consequences for the child of habitual participation in these and other culturally organized forms of discourse. This is clearly one area in which more work is needed. We need more detailed ethnographic and micro-level description of how various types of discourse are practiced cross-culturally and of how these verbal practices are organized *vis-à-vis* children. Note that it is not enough to know how the adult genre is defined without also knowing how children are included in or exposed to the various types of discourse. We need to know more about how children participate in and make use of these practices at various ages: what are the conditions under which children acquiesce to, misunderstand, get confused by, playfully transform, or resist socializing messages? We also need to find ways of assessing the integrated impact of the different types of discourse on the child. For example, what is the integrated impact on young children of routine exposure to messages about the importance of being strong and self assertive, when these messages come variously packaged in teasing, explicit instruction, and personal storytelling (Miller and Sperry 1987)? Some messages are redundant across these various types of discourse, some are unique to a particular discourse type, and in any given hour message follows hard upon message, as talk shifts from one to another of these discourse types.

Toward more dynamic conceptions of socialization, culture, and language

This shifting from one to another discourse type, and even from one to another language-created context within a given discourse, is one of the insights that has led students of language socialization to more dynamic conceptions of socialization (Schieffelin 1990). This insight, we believe, followed, in part, from the kind of empirical inquiry that has characterized recent language socialization research, and that distinguishes it from earlier studies of socialization: namely, ethnographic investigation grounded in the meticulous documentation of actual interactions between members and novices as they unfold in particular cultural contexts. A related insight concerns the negotiated nature of interactions even when the power relations between participants are asymmetrical, as in the case of adult–child interactions (Rogoff 1990). (From this standpoint, the "packaging" metaphor that we have used to characterize types of discourse conveys too static a connotation.) Ochs (1988) has argued, in a similar vein, for a model of socialization that accounts not only for the impact that adults have on the child's developing system, but for the impact that children have on the adult's system. When adult and novice come together in recurring communicative contexts, adults too risk transformations to their understanding. Gaskins and Lucy (1987) have suggested how this might happen: when adults routinely interact with children, whose mastery of communicative resources is incomplete, and who, furthermore, occupy a special status by virtue of being children, they are forced to adapt in various ways that affect their own cultural practices. Children are thereby revealed as producers of culture, not just acquirers of culture.

These non-deterministic and negotiated views of socialization that accord a substantial role to the child participant jibe with recent reconceptions of socialization from other disciplinary frames. Wentworth (1980), for example, critiqued sociological theories of socialization and proposed a socialization-as-interaction model that acknowledges that "society cannot replicate itself precisely within the novice, because at the least the novice's own frame of reference plays upon the meaning of the interaction" (p. 84). One of the goals of his model is to render problematic the outcome of socialization, allowing for mistakes, failures, misunderstandings, personal preference, active and eager learning, balking, or simple refusal to learn. Goodnow (1990) arrived at a similar vision via an examination of theories of cognitive development. She advocates a model of socialization that can account not only for bidirectional influences but for "the individuals who resist the information, the skill, or the worldview held out to them" (Goodnow 1990: 280).

In sum, these theoretical advances from both within and outside of language socialization converge on a dynamic model of socialization that regards the shifting varieties of language-engendered contexts as a crucial resource for the culture-acquiring child; that acknowledges the negotiated nature of interaction even with young children; and that accords to the child participant the kind of psychological complexity that yields inevitable individual variation in the apprehension of cultural meanings. Not surprisingly, the emergence of this dynamic model of socialization coincides with similar trends in conceptions of culture and language.

Within symbolic anthropology an interest in discourse and semiotically mediated practices has emerged as part of a general attempt to arrive at more dynamic conceptions of culture. Briggs (1986), for example, notes "a move away from viewing culture as monolithic and static toward analyzing the way in which cultural systems are instantiated in individual events by concrete persons" (p. 112). This development has been fueled, in part, by theoretical advances in allied disciplines, advances that focus on the routine practices of everyday life (Bourdieu 1977; Goffman 1959, 1974; Garfinkel 1967; Sacks 1965–1971/1984, 1972; Vygotsky 1934, 1978/1987).

This trend is also tied to debate about the nature of cultural interpretation. Those who locate interpretation within the interaction of ethnographer and informant see neither culture nor context as given. Culture is dialogic or negotiated (Crapanzano 1980; Clifford 1986; Herdt and Stoller 1990; Kracke 1987), and context is established by discourse (Briggs 1986). From this perspective, Geertz's (1973c) conception of culture as text and of interpretation as description, however "thick," does not go far enough, for it fails to attend sufficiently to the immediate context of interaction – what *specifically* is said, the way it is said, and to whom. What is lost is the fluid situatedness of culture.

Paralleling these developments within cultural anthropology has been the development of more dynamic theories of language within anthropological linguistics. The move has been away from a view of language as an abstract propositional system toward an analysis of the contextualized uses of language, or in Mertz's (1985) terms, away from symbolic toward semiotic conceptions of language. Following Peirce (1974), Mertz (1985) argues that "the symbol is only one kind of sign and the collapsing of 'semiotic' into 'symbolic' fails to do justice to the complicated system by which signs carry and constitute cultural meanings" (p. 1). Central to this theoretical shift has been an appreciation of the pragmatic or indexical capabilities of language – the ability of linguistic signs to index features of their linguistic and nonlinguistic contexts.

In this view of language, reference-and-predication is but one of many functions of language, and indexical signs participate in a number of functional systems simultaneously (Silverstein 1985b, 1987). For example, they can be used for reference and predication and for a variety of pragmatic ends – e.g., requesting, ordering, expressing emotion. This view of language, then, significantly complicates the problem of delineating the socializing implications for the child of habitual participation in particular, culturally constituted forms of talk. How does the child discover how to read indexical signs? How does he or she determine which function is dominant within a given stretch of discourse? Although the propositional function is dominant in certain adult situations of language use, Silverstein (1985b) has cautioned against assuming the same for children, as functional values may change across developmental time (p. 214). Given that language is plurifunctional, and is frequently ambiguous with respect to which of its functions is dominant within a given speech situation, Silverstein (1985b) argues that functional overlaps can "play a significant, and indeed determining role" in language development (p. 216). Such overlaps, he indicates, provide foci for functional differentiation and enrichment. Children's use of reported speech is significant in this regard, and deserves more research attention, since it offers a number of possibilities for functional differentiation (Hickmann 1985; Miller and Hoogstra 1989).[3]

In sum, discourse and situated communicative practices loom large in these revised conceptions of socialization, culture, and language. The fluidity of communicative situations thereby emerges as a resource for the cultural novice while at the same time posing formidable problems of interpretation. How is it possible to make sense of so much flux, particularly for young children whose meaning-making capabilities are immature? It is important to note that these dynamic conceptions do not deny that there are relatively stable symbols and meanings that endure across contexts and over time (Yanagisako and Collier 1987). They recognize, however, that since core meanings are realized through practice, they are never static. Consequently, an understanding of dynamic meanings requires an examination of the contexts in which they acquire significance for particular children.

Consider, for example, the very young child's initial entrée into a particular native genre. Although the genre may have an explicit name associated with it, the name is, of course, of little help to the preverbal child. Instead, affectively tinged regularities in the verbal environment that co-vary with and index communicative function (Silverstein's [1985b, 1987] pragmatic function$_2$) may aid the child in sorting out and understanding different types of discourse. The developmental psychological literature indicates that the prosodic characteristics of speech (e.g., intonation, stress, voice quality) are particularly salient to infants and young children (Andersen 1977; Fernald 1984), and Ochs (1986) reported that Samoan children learned affectively marked linguistic forms prior to affectively neutral forms. Even before the child can fully understand the spoken language in teasing, for example, s/he may pay attention to the paralinguistic and nonverbal features that are abundantly available – the rhythmic contour of the tease; the loud, rapid delivery with shifting stress and provocative and angry tones of voice; and the accompanying threatening gestures, mock angry and smiling facial expressions, and rapid postural changes (Miller 1986). Repeated exposure to such configurations of features may provide children with their first clues that a particular verbal activity is different from other verbal activity and may guide them towards initial affective apprehensions on which future interpretations will be built. From this standpoint, study of the acquisition of cultural meanings is necessary to a full understanding of adult culture, for it helps to explain the non-referential, affectively charged dimensions of meaning.

Language as tool for the ethnographer

Learning to interpret discourse and situated practices poses problems not only for the child but for the ethnographer as well. One problem follows from the fact that the ethnographer, unlike the child, has already "learned" a culture. The ethnographer thereby incurs the inevitable risk of confusing his or her own interpretive framework with the native framework. Ethnographers are not simply objective observers who have no effect on the data they collect and interpret. Because interpretation is inherently dialectical and reflexive (Ricoeur 1971/1979), the interpreter is always implicated in the process of interpretation. A second difficulty concerns the issue of implicit knowledge. A considerable amount of the systematicity underlying native practices is not available to native adult awareness (Geertz 1976/1979; Silverstein 1981; Lutz 1985b). If members of a culture know more than they can tell, how can the ethnographer gain access to and construct a valid account of their knowledge?

One solution to these problems of interpretive validity is provided by Geertz (1973a), who argues that cultural forms provide their own interpretations if one can only figure out how to gain access to them. In "Person, Time, and Conduct in Bali" (1973b), he examines those symbolic forms that serve basic, "generically human," orientational requirements. Geertz includes among these pervasive orientational requirements cultural conceptions of personal identity, temporal order, and behavioral style. The strength of Geertz's approach is its recognition of the need for a framework for cross-cultural comparison. Its weakness is its failure to specify a formal, and cross-culturally valid, means for accomplishing this goal. The selection of cultural data remains theoretically unmotivated in Geertz's account. He provides no principled criteria for selecting and comparing symbolic forms across cultures.

Another strategy is similar but takes a different cultural system, namely language itself, as its focus. This strategy builds on work in anthropological linguistics that exploits the reflexive property of language, that is, the fact that language, unlike other symbol systems, can refer to and predicate about itself. It treats metalanguage, especially metapragmatic usage, as a window into native ideologies of language (Silverstein 1985a). For example, when a narrator quotes what someone said, he or she is using language (in the event of narration) to describe how language was used (in the narrated event). In such cases, language provides its own guide to culture, that is, to people's ideology about how communication works.

Implicit in this characterization of metapragmatics is the suggestion that narrative provides a privileged focus for examining the culture of language. As representations of past events, including past communicative events, narratives often provide a rich source of metacommunicative information. Bauman (1986) suggests that an understanding of the way acts of speaking are overtly contextualized within narrative "can enhance our understanding of how speaking operates and is understood to operate in social life" (p. 54). Silverstein (1985a) outlines a formal method for discovering the relationships between particular metapragmatic constructions and the indexical relations they encode. In contrast to Geertz's (1973b) proposal, this formulation is grounded in observations of diverse languages, all of which have forms – for example, pronominal forms such as *I* and *you* – that describe the relationship between linguistic signs and their contexts of use. In thus linking components of the prototypical speech situation to formal elements of language, Silverstein (1985a) attempts to provide a reliable formal locus for examining metapragmatic constructions across languages. Because reported speech links metapragmatic descriptors (e.g., *say*, *tell*, *exclaim*) with specific examples of the forms they characterize, a systematic analysis of reported speech can provide access to the metapragmatic system that underlies speakers' ability to interpret indexicals. A distributional analysis of metapragmatic forms within narrative allows one to get a sense of the patterning that natives themselves use in understanding discourse. Lucy's (in press) distributional analysis of the quotative *ki-* within a Yucatec narrative illustrates this point. Locally this form signals a direct quote. Within the narrative as a whole, however, it signals what is significant or worthy of comment – the crucial elements of plot and key metapragmatic themes. This in turn leads outside the narrative to what is being commented on: the presuppositions and entailments of speaking in certain kinds of situations – for example, the consequences of publicly insulting someone.

Work on metapragmatic usage has implications not only for how narrative discourse is interpreted but for how data are collected in the first place. Briggs (1986) has argued persuasively that learning how to ask questions that yield interpretable responses from informants requires an analysis of the metacommunicative features of discourse so that the interview context can be located relative to native communicative contexts. The same applies, we maintain, when the data collection context is the observation session, rather than the interview, as in research on language socialization. The goal in such studies is to obtain an ecologically and culturally valid sample of young children's talk, a sample that preserves the integrity of naturally occurring communicative events (Watson-Gegeo 1988). The researcher must be able to communicate well enough with the child's caregivers to gain access to the privileged home context. Moreover, interpretation of recorded observations of the child's participation requires metacommunicative analysis of the observation context relative to other contexts, with a dual focus on child and caregiver. If the ethnographer's talk in the observation session is at odds with the caregiver's communicative norms, the caregiver's confusion or discomfort may affect the child, evoking uninterpretable responses. For example, our initial efforts in a white working-class community in Chicago deliberately to avoid introducing or eliciting narrative talk, in fact seemed to strain the social situation and focus undue attention on whether the child was talking or not, leading to silence or self display on the part of the child. This "communicative blunder" led us to understand that the reciprocal flow of narrative talk is normative when adults from this group visit one another and to alter our procedures accordingly so as to capture more accurately the child's narrative participation.

Because of its potential for revealing native cultures of language, work on metapragmatic usage also has important implications for understanding the verbal genres on which anthropologists depend. A recurring theme in recent discussions of ethnographic description is that ethnography is, in large measure, a narrative enterprise. Ethnographers not only construct stories about the cultures they study (Bruner 1986; Hymes 1982) but they learn about cultural patterns by listening to the stories that people tell about themselves (Goodwin 1982; Gwaltney 1980; Rosaldo 1986; Watson 1973). These narrative tasks pose problems for the cultural analyst: how to interpret native narratives, how to translate native narratives into ethnographic narratives, and how to compare and evaluate ethnographic narratives. These issues are reminiscent of the problem that Bateson and Mead faced in 1942: how to communicate precisely about another culture. They wrote in the introduction to *Balinese Character*, "Most serious of all, we know this about the relationship between culture and verbal concepts – that the words which one culture has invested with meaning are by the very accuracy of their cultural fit, singularly inappropriate as vehicles for precise comment upon another culture" (Bateson and Mead 1942: xi). Their solution was to avoid the verbal medium in favor of a photographic analysis of culture. By contrast, the current solution has been to present transcripts of talk – either in lieu of standard narrative ethnography or incorporated into narrative description – a rhetorical and methodological move that reflects the dynamic concepts of culture discussed earlier. While inclusion of meticuously detailed transcript material is essential for precise description of situated discourse, the problem remains as to how to compare transcribed talk. Work on metapragmatic usage speaks to this problem in that it furnishes a principled means for analyzing discourse cross-culturally.

In sum, for the ethnographer, as for the child, language provides a crucial tool in the apprehension of cultural meanings. Patterns of language use provide the ethnographer with an entrée into cultural systems – a key to interpreting native ideologies of language – and a guide to the collection of interpretable samples of discourse. In addition, metapragmatic analysis of particular verbal genres, especially the narrative genres central to anthropological discourse, may help to generate a principled basis for comparing ethnographic descriptions. From this standpoint, the socialization and acquisition of narrative emerges as an especially significant problem for cultural anthropology. How are narrative practices organized *vis-à-vis* children? In what ways do stories serve as a resource for the culture-acquiring child? Can we, pursuing Sapir's (1934/1949) point, gain a fresh perspective on the adult genre by examining children's efforts to make sense of stories and caregivers' responses to those efforts? Answers to these kinds of questions would help us to understand better not only childhood socialization but the ethnographic study of cultures as well.

NOTES

This work was supported by a grant from the Spencer Foundation awarded to the first author. We wish to thank John Lucy for extensive comments on earlier drafts.

1 Regularities of language use provide both analysts and participants with a basis for interpreting what is said and done in particular contexts of interaction. However, this should not be taken to mean that the relationship between language and context is static, and that interpretation consists only or merely in discovering fixed relationships between linguistic forms and their contexts of use. Linguistic forms *can* presuppose features of their contexts and often do so in predictable ways. Spatial and temporal deictics, for example, contextually anchor discourse and serve as orienting devices for conversational participants. Forms which function in this way thus help to ground interpretation (Silverstein 1987). As Silverstein (1976, 1985a, 1985b) and others (Briggs 1986; Goffman 1976; Ochs 1988) have noted, however, language also functions creatively: the choice of linguistic forms themselves can create or change the

context of interaction. A shift from formal to familiar modes of address, for example, can have consequences for the nature of the interaction and the relationship of participants within it. This recognition of the creative functions of language speaks to the dynamic and situated nature of social discourse and interaction, a conceptualization which we discuss in greater detail later in the chapter.

2 One question that is sometimes raised in relation to cross-cultural variation in children's verbal environments is the following: if verbal environments differ widely and yet children proceed through the same course of language development, does this argue for an innatist position? There are several difficulties that arise in addressing this question, given our lack of knowledge about the cultural organization of verbal practices to which children are exposed. First, how are we to compare children's verbal environments? In order to assess the course or rate of syntactic development, for example, it is necessary to know whether children from different cultures receive equivalent amounts of exposure to a particular structure. (Note that equivalent frequency of occurrence in adult-to-adult speech does not necessarily imply equivalence in the *child's* verbal environment.) We also need to know how to interpret the absence of a particular linguistic form in the speech of children in one culture when that form is present in the speech of their counterparts in another culture. Does absence mean that the child has not yet acquired the form or that the child knows that the norms of appropriate speech preclude its use? (Note that comprehension data are needed to disentangle these possibilities.) Still another problem concerns how to characterize verbal practices cross-culturally. Harkness (1988) has drawn attention to possible functional equivalents of semantic contingency. For example, caregiver expansions of the child's utterance, in which the caregiver pays attention to and interprets the child's intention, and elicited imitation, in which the child is directed to pay attention to what the caregiver is expressing, are alternate ways of achieving shared attention. However, a search for functional equivalents cannot proceed very far until we know much more about the cultural organization of verbal practices involving children, and especially about properties of speech around the child.

3 Hickmann (1985) offers the following possibilities for differentiation within reported speech situations in an analysis of English-speaking children: (1) distinguishing between narrated and narrative speech, i.e., using framing verbs to set quoted speech apart from narrative speech; (2) use of specific metapragmatic verbs to characterize a speech event vs. use of less specific framing verbs; (3) use of indirect vs. direct speech; (4) establishing an orientation to the narrative event, e.g., systematically introducing dialogue participants when more than one speaker is quoted, or otherwise including additional components of the speech situation; and (5) providing a focus for the narrated speech event, e.g., elaborating on the speaker by attributing to him or her certain intentions or desires, or elaborating on the hearer's reaction to what a speaker has said.

REFERENCES

Andersen, E. S. 1977. Learning to Speak with Style: A Study of the Sociolinguistic Skills of Children. Unpublished doctoral dissertation, Stanford University

Bateson, G. and M. Mead. 1942. *Balinese Character: A Photographic Analysis.* New York: The New York Academy of Sciences

Bauman, R. 1986. "Hell, Yes, but not That Young": Reported Speech as Comic Corrective. In R. Bauman, *Story, Performance, and Event: Contextual Studies of Oral Narrative.* Cambridge: Cambridge University Press

Blount, B. G. 1977. Ethnography and Caretaker–Child Interaction. In C. E. Snow and C. A. Ferguson, eds., *Talking to Children: Language Input and Acquisition.* Cambridge: Cambridge University Press

Bourdieu, P. 1977. *Outline of a Theory of Practice.* Cambridge: Cambridge University Press

Briggs, C. L. 1986. *Learning How to Ask: A Sociolinguistic Appraisal of the Role of the Interview in Social Science Research.* Cambridge: Cambridge University Press

Briggs, J. L. 1970. *Never in Anger: Portrait of an Eskimo Family.* Cambridge, MA: Harvard University Press

1975. The Origins of Nonviolence: Aggression in Two Canadian Eskimo Groups. In W. Muensterberger, ed., *Psychoanalytic Study of Society.* vol. VI. New York: International Universities Press

Bruner, E. M. 1986. Ethnography as Narrative. In V. Turner and E. M. Bruner, eds., *The Anthropology of Experience.* Champaign, IL: The University of Illinois Press

Bruner, J. 1983. *Child's Talk.* New York: Norton

Clifford, J. 1986. Introduction: Partial Truths. In J. Clifford and G. E. Marcus, eds., *Writing Culture: The Poetics and Politics of Ethnography.* Berkeley: University of California Press

Crapanzano, V. 1980. *Tuhami: Portrait of a Moroccan.* Chicago: University of Chicago Press

Demuth, K. 1986. Prompting Routines in the Language Socialization of Basotho Children. In B. B. Schieffelin and E. Ochs, eds., *Language Socialization across Cultures.* Cambridge: Cambridge University Press

Fernald, A. 1984. The Perceptual and Affective Salience of Mothers' Speech to Infants. In L. Feagans, C. Garvey, and R. Golinkoff, eds., *The Origins and Growth of Communication.* Norwood, NJ: Ablex

Garfinkel, H. 1967. *Studies in Ethnomethodology.* Englewood Cliffs, NJ: Prentice-Hall

Garvey, C. 1986. Discourse Analysis. Colloquium presented to the Psychology Department, Wayne State University, Detroit, Michigan, April

Gaskins, S. and J. A. Lucy. 1987. The Role of Children in the Production of Adult Culture: A Yucatec Case. Paper presented at the annual meeting of the American Ethnological Society held jointly with the Society for Psychological Anthropology, New Orleans

Geertz, C. 1973a. Deep Play: Notes on the Balinese Cockfight. In *The Interpretation of Cultures.* New York: Basic Books

1973b. Person, Time, and Conduct in Bali. In *The Interpretation of Cultures.* New York: Basic Books

1973c. Thick Description: Toward an Interpretive Theory of Culture. In *The Interpretation of Cultures.* New York: Basic Books

1976/1979. "From the Native's Point of View": On the Nature of Anthropological Understanding. In P. Rabinow and W. M. Sullivan, eds., *Interpretive Social Science: A Reader*. Berkeley: University of California Press

Geertz, H. 1959. The Vocabulary of Emotion. *Psychiatry* 22: 225–237

Goffman, E. 1959. *The Presentation of Self in Everyday Life*. New York: Doubleday Anchor Books

1974. *Frame Analysis: An Essay on the Organization of Experience*. Cambridge, MA: Harvard University Press

1976. Replies and Responses. *Language in Society* 5: 257–313

Goodnow, J. J. 1990. The Socialization of Cognition: What's Involved? In J. W. Stigler, R. A. Shweder, and G. Herdt, eds., *Cultural Psychology: Essays on Comparative Human Development*. Cambridge: Cambridge University Press

Goodwin, M. H. 1982. "Instigating": Storytelling as Social Process. *American Ethnologist* 9: 799–819

Gumperz, J. and D. Hymes, eds. 1972. *Directions in Sociolinguistics: The Ethnography of Communication*. New York: Holt, Rinehart, and Winston

Gwaltney, J. L. 1980. *Drylongso: A Self-portrait of Black America*. New York: Random House

Harkness, S. 1988. The Cultural Construction of Semantic Contingency in Mother–Child Speech. In B. G. Blount, guest ed., Current Topics in Child Language Acquisition. *Language Sciences* 10: 53–67

Harkness, S. and C. M. Super. 1983. The Cultural Construction of Child Development: A Framework for the Socialization of Affect. *Ethos* 11: 221–231

1989. Constructing the Social Environment and the Self Through Language: "Special Time" in American Families. Paper presented at the annual meeting of the American Anthropological Association, Washington, DC, November 16

Heath, S. B. 1983. *Ways with Words: Language, Life and Work in Communities and Classrooms*. Cambridge: Cambridge University Press

Herdt, G. H. and R. J. Stoller. 1990. *Intimate Communications: Erotics and the Study of Culture*. New York: Columbia University Press

Hickmann, M. 1985. Metapragmatics in Child Language. In E. Mertz and R. J. Parmentier, eds., *Semiotic Mediation: Sociocultural and Psychological Perspectives*. Orlando, FL: Academic Press

Holland, D. C. and J. Valsiner. 1988. Cognition, Symbols, and Vygotsky's Developmental Psychology. *Ethos* 16: 247–272

Hymes, D. 1966. Two Types of Linguistic Relativity (with Examples from Amerindian Ethnography). In W. Bright, ed., *Sociolinguistics: Proceedings of the UCLA Sociolinguistics Conference, 1964*. The Hague: Mouton

1967. Models of the Interaction of Language and Social Setting. *Journal of Social Issues* 23: 8–28

1982. What is Ethnography? In P. Gilmore and A. A. Glatthorn, eds., *Children In and Out of School*. Washington, DC: Center for Applied Linguistics

Kracke, W. 1987. Encounter with Other Cultures: Psychological and Epistemological Aspects. *Ethos* 15: 58–81

LeVine, R. 1990. Infant Environments in Psychoanalysis: A Cross-cultural View. In J. W. Stigler, R. A. Shweder, and G. Herdt, eds., *Cultural Psychology: Essays on Comparative Human Development*. Cambridge: Cambridge University Press

Lucy, J. A. 1985. The Historical Relativity of the Linguistic Relativity Hypothesis. *The Quarterly Newsletter of the Laboratory of Comparative Human Cognition* 7: 103–108

1987. Grammatical Categories and Cognitive Processes: An Historical, Theoretical, and Empirical Re-evaluation of the Linguistic Relativity Hypothesis. Unpublished doctoral dissertation, University of Chicago

In press. Metapragmatic Presentationals: Reporting Speech with Quotatives in Yucatec Maya. In J. A. Lucy, ed., *Reflexive Language: Reported Speech and Metapragmatics*. Cambridge: Cambridge University Press

Lutz, C. A. 1985a. Cultural Patterns and Individual Differences in the Child's Emotional Meaning System. In M. Lewis and C. Saarni, eds., *The Socialization of Emotions*. New York: Plenum Press

1985b. Ethnopsychology Compared to What? Explaining Behavior and Consciousness among the Ifaluk. In G. M. White and J. Kirkpatrick, eds., *Person, Self and Experience: Exploring Pacific Ethnopsychologies*. Berkeley: University of California Press

Mead, M. and F. C. Macgregor. 1951. *Growth and Culture: A Photographic Study of Balinese Childhood*. New York: Putnam

Mertz, E. 1985. Beyond Symbolic Anthropology: Introducing Semiotic Mediation. In E. Mertz and R. J. Parmentier, eds., *Semiotic Mediation: Sociocultural and Psychological Perspectives*. Orlando, FL: Academic Press

Miller, P. J. 1982. *Amy, Wendy, and Beth: Learning Language in South Baltimore*. Austin: University of Texas Press

1986. Teasing as Language Socialization and Verbal Play in a White, Working-class Community. In B. B. Schieffelin and E. Ochs, eds., *Language Socialization Across Cultures*. Cambridge: Cambridge University Press

Miller, P. J. and L. Hoogstra. 1989. How to Represent the Native Child's Point of View: Methodological Problems in Language Socialization. Paper presented at the annual meeting of the American Anthropological Association, Washington, DC, November 16

Miller, P. J., J. Mintz, L. Hoogstra, H. Fung, and R. Potts. 1992. The Narrated Self: Young Children's Construction of Self in Relation to Others in Conversational Stories of Personal Experience. *Merrill-Palmer Quarterly* 38:45–67

Miller, P. J. and B. B. Moore. 1989. Narrative Conjunctions of Caregiver and Child: A Comparative Perspective on Socialization through Stories. *Ethos* 17: 428–449

Miller, P. J., R. Potts, H. Fung, L. Hoogstra, and J. Mintz. 1990. Narrative Practices and the Social Construction of Self in Childhood. *American Ethnologist* 17: 292–311

Miller, P. J. and L. L. Sperry. 1987. The Socialization of Anger and Aggression. *Merrill-Palmer Quarterly* 33: 1–31

Nye, C. H. 1988. Psychoanalytic Narratives: The Formulation of Meaning. Unpublished doctoral dissertation, University of Chicago

Ochs, E. 1982. Talking to Children in Western Samoa. *Language in Society* 11: 77–104

1986. From Feelings to Grammar: A Samoan Case Study. In B. B. Schieffelin and E. Ochs, eds., *Language Socialization across Cultures*. Cambridge: Cambridge University Press

1988. *Culture and Language Development: Language Acquisition and Language Socialization in a Samoan Village*. Cambridge: Cambridge University Press

1990. Indexicality and Socialization. In J. W. Stigler, R. A. Shweder, and G. Herdt, eds., *Cultural Psychology: Essays on Comparative Human Development*. Cambridge: Cambridge University Press

Ochs, E. and B. Schieffelin. 1984. Language Acquisition and Socialization: Three Developmental Stories and Their Implications. In R. A. Shweder and R. A. LeVine, eds., *Culture Theory: Essays on Mind, Self, and Emotion*. Cambridge: Cambridge University Press

Peirce, C. S. 1974. *Collected Papers*, vols. I and II. C. Hartshorne and P. Weiss, eds. Cambridge, MA: Harvard University Press

Ricoeur, P. 1971/1979. The Model of the Text: Meaningful Action Considered as a Text. In P. Rabinow and W. M. Sullivan, eds., *Interpretive Social Science: A Reader*. Berkeley: University of California Press

Rogoff, B. 1990. The Joint Socialization of Development by Young Children and Adults. In M. Lewis and S. Feinman, eds., *Social Influences and Socialization in Infancy*. New York: Plenum

Rosaldo, R. 1986. Ilongot Hunting as Story and Experience. In V. Turner and E. Bruner, eds., *The Anthropology of Experience*. Champaign, IL: University of Illinois Press

Sachs, J. 1983. Similarities and Differences in Preschool Boys' and Girls' Language Use in a Pretend Play Setting. Paper presented at a conference on Sex Differences in Language, Tucson, AZ, January

Sacks, H. 1965–1971/1984. Notes on Methodology. In J. M. Atkinson and J. Heritage, eds., *Structures of Social Action*. Cambridge: Cambridge University Press

1972. An Initial Investigation of the Usability of Conversational Data for Doing Sociology. In D. Sudnow, ed., *Studies in Social Interaction*. New York: The Free Press

Sapir, E. 1933/1949. Language. In D. G. Mandelbaum, ed., *Selected Writings of Edward Sapir in Language, Culture, and Personality*. Berkeley: University of California Press

1934/1949. The Emergence of the Concept of Personality in a Study of Cultures. In D. G. Mandelbaum, ed., *Selected Writings of Edward Sapir in Language, Culture, and Personality*. Berkeley: University of California Press

Schieffelin, B. B. 1979. Getting it Together: An Ethnographic Approach to the Study of the Development of Communicative Competence. In E. Ochs and B. B. Schieffelin, eds., *Developmental Pragmatics*. New York: Academic Press

1990. *The Give and Take of Everyday Life: Language Socialization of Kaluli Children*. Cambridge: Cambridge University Press

Shweder, R. A. 1990. Cultural Psychology: What is It? In J. W. Stigler, R. A. Shweder, and G. Herdt, eds., *Cultural Psychology: Essays on Comparative Human Development*. Cambridge: Cambridge University Press

Shweder, R. A. and N. C. Much. 1987. Determinations of Meaning: Discourse and Moral Socialization. In W. M. Kurtines and J. L. Gewirth, eds., *Moral Development through Social Interaction*. New York: Wiley

Silverstein, M. 1976. Shifters, Linguistic Categories, and Cultural Description. In

K. Basso and H. Selby, eds., *Meaning in Anthropology*. Albuquerque, NM: University of New Mexico Press

1981. The Limits of Awareness. *Working Papers in Sociolinguistics* 84: 1–21. Austin, TX: Southwest Educational Development Laboratory

1985a. The Culture of Language in Chinookan Narrative Texts; or, On Saying that . . . in Chinook. In J. Nichols and A. C. Woodbury, eds., *Grammar Inside and Outside the Clause: Some Approaches to Theory from the Field*. Cambridge: Cambridge University Press

1985b. The Functional Stratification of Language and Ontogenesis. In J. V. Wertsch, ed., *Culture, Communication, and Cognition: Vygotskian Perspectives*. Cambridge: Cambridge University Press

1987. The Three Faces of "Function": Preliminaries to a Psychology of Language. In M. Hickmann, ed., *Social and Functional Approaches to Language and Thought*. Orlando, FL: Academic Press

Snow, C. E. and C. A. Ferguson, eds. 1977. *Talking to Children: Language Input and Acquisition*. Cambridge: Cambridge University Press

Super, C. M. and S. Harkness. 1986. The Developmental Niche: A Conceptualization at the Interface of Child and Culture. *International Journal of Behavioral Development* 9: 545–569

Vygotsky, L. 1934/1987. *Thinking and Speech*. Translated by N. Minick. New York: Plenum

1978. *Mind in Society*. Cambridge, MA: Harvard University Press

Ward, M. 1971. *Them Children*. New York: Holt, Rinehart, and Winston

Watson, K. A. 1973. A Rhetorical and Sociolinguistic Model for the Analysis of Narrative. *American Anthropologist* 75: 243–264

Watson-Gegeo, K. A. 1988. Response to Schieffelin and Ochs' Paper on Language Socialization. Paper presented at the American Anthropological Association Meeting, November 16

Watson-Gegeo, K. A. and D. W. Gegeo. 1986a. Calling Out and Repeating Routines in Kwara'ae Children's Language Socialization. In B. B. Schieffelin and E. Ochs, eds., *Language Socialization across Cultures*. Cambridge: Cambridge University Press

1986b. The Social World of Kwara'ae Children: Acquisition of Language and Values. In J. Cook-Gumperz, W. Corsaro, and J. Streeck, eds., *Children's Words and Children's Language*. Berlin: Mouton

Wentworth, W. M. 1980. *Context and Understanding: An Inquiry into Socialization Theory*. New York: Elsevier

Wertsch, J. V. 1985. *Vygotsky and the Social Formation of Mind*. Cambridge, MA: Harvard University Press

Whiting, B. B. 1980. Culture and Social Behavior: A Model for the Development of Social Behavior. *Ethos* 8: 95–116

Whorf, B. L. 1956. *Language, Thought, and Reality: Selected Writings of Benjamin Lee Whorf*, ed. J. B. Carroll. Cambridge, MA: MIT Press

Yanagisako, S. J. and J. F. Collier. 1987. Toward a Unified Analysis of Gender and Kinship. In J. F. Collier and S. J. Yanagisako, eds., *Gender and Kinship: Toward a Unified Analysis*. Stanford: Stanford University Press

6 Human development in psychological anthropology

Sara Harkness

Interest in how children are reared and how they develop in other cultures is probably as old as cross-cultural observation itself, but this chapter's retrospective and prospective reflections are based on a genealogical framework that starts with Franz Boas, the founder of modern American cultural anthropology, as the intellectual great-grandfather of present-day thinking about human development in psychological anthropology. As we develop more of the genealogy and look ahead to future possibilities, this chapter will address the fundamental question of why anthropologists have been interested in human development. I will suggest that within the field of psychological anthropology, interest in human development has been motivated by two main concerns. One is a reluctance to let psychologists define the parameters of normal psychological development on the basis of a highly selected population – that is, the children (mostly white and middle class) of industrialized Western civilization. The second, more central concern that has motivated psychological anthropologists to study human development has been to advance our understanding of culture – what it is, where it resides, and how it gets there. In order to see how this second concern has been expressed, we must look beyond our own ancestors to consider more general intellectual trends in scientific inquiry and its methods. These trends have intersected with psychological anthropologists' research on human development to influence the ways in which we construe culture and the role of human development in cultural processes. I will argue that it is now time to reexamine some of the consequences of these intersecting trends for theory and methods in our field.

The ancestors: Boas and Mead

The retrospective view of human development in psychological anthropology begins with its most important ancestors – Franz Boas and Margaret Mead. In reviewing their contributions to the field, however, one is drawn immediately to contemporaneous developments in psychology. Thus, this history takes us first to Wundt's experimental laboratory in Leipzig, in the late nineteenth century, where academic psychology locates its beginnings as a science. As described by the Laboratory of Comparative Human Cognition (LCHC) (1983: 297), Wundt's goal was "to focus on the 'raw,' 'initial' response evoked by very well-specified physical stimuli. It was crucial that the subject not allow any interpretation to intervene between stimulus and response, which was duly recorded in very precise terms – usually reaction time." Boas, whose initial training was in physics, geography, and mathematics, spent a short time at Wundt's laboratory, but came away convinced that "even 'elementary' sensations were influenced by their contexts of occurrence" (LCHC 1983: 297). His first field research among the Eskimos sought to establish the effects of physical environment on behavior; this experience, however, led him to conclude that although geographical conditions were "relevant in limiting and modifying existing cultures," they were not very significant as "creative elements in cultural life" (Boas 1948, in Harris, 1968: 266). Eventually, as Harris (1968: 280) has described, Boas came to believe that "the structure of the human mind accounted for whatever regularities were manifest in cultural phenomena," and therefore "anthropology could no longer remain aloof from the study of the relationship between the individual psyche and the forms of culture." In contrast to anthropology's previous interest in the historical reconstruction of cultures, Boas now recommended a greater focus on "a penetrating study of the individual under the stress of the culture in which he lives" (Boas 1930, in Harris 1968: 281).

Looking back, it seems both ironic and fitting that anthropology's recognition of the influence of context on human thinking and behavior was contemporaneous with the emergence of the experimental paradigm in psychology. Boas' observations on the human subjects in Wundt's laboratory foreshadowed recent research on the effects of testing situations on behavior (Cole, Gay, Glick, and Sharp 1971; Rogoff 1982), as psychologists have sought to explain human responses beyond the confines of the laboratory. In the meantime, though, Boas had set the stage for the anthropological study of how people's experience over the lifespan is shaped by "the stress of the culture" in which they live.

As is well known, Boas' interest in how culture shaped human development was instrumental in shaping the first fieldwork of his most famous student, Margaret Mead. The goal of Mead's research on adolescent Samoan girls was straightforward: as Mead described it later, "It was a simple – a very simple – point to which our materials were organized in the 1920s, merely the documentation over and over of the fact that human nature is not rigid and unyielding" (Mead 1939, in Harris

1968: 409). The stormy emotional upheavals of American teenage girls, which contemporary opinion attributed to biological changes, might instead be due to the way that society structured girls' lives.

Mead's influence on the ways that Americans thought about human development (as well as her influence on the visibility of anthropology in the public mind) has been widely recognized. An aspect of *Coming of Age in Samoa* (1928) that has not generally attracted attention, however, is that it was stimulated by contemporaneous folk theories of adolescence more than by any particular scientific theories. Boas' interest in the topic came from his own personal observations, as he wrote to Mead in a letter during the summer of 1925 when she was about to sail for Samoa:

> One question that interests me very much is how the young girls react to the restraints of custom. We find very often among ourselves during the period of adolescence a strong rebellious spirit that may be expressed in sullenness or in sudden outbursts. In other individuals there is a weak submission which is accompanied, however, by a suppressed rebellion that may make itself felt in peculiar ways, perhaps a desire for solitude which is really an expression of desire for freedom, or otherwise in forced participation in social affairs in order to drown the mental troubles. I am not at all clear in my mind in how far similar conditions may occur in primitive society and in how far the desire for independence may be simply due to our modern conditions and to a more strongly developed individualism. (Mead 1972:38)

Mead herself referred to a book on adolescence by the psychologist G. Stanley Hall, as well as ideas widely disseminated in textbooks, as the source of the biological interpretation of adolescent behavior. But as she wrote in the introduction to *Coming of Age in Samoa*, this view was not accepted by the more scholarly members of the psychological professions:

> The careful child psychologist who relied upon experiment for his conclusions did not subscribe to these theories. He said, "We have no data. We know only a little about the first few months of a child's life. We are only just learning when a baby's eyes will first follow a light. How can we give definite answers to questions of how a developed personality, about which we know nothing, will respond to religion?" But the negative cautions of science are never popular. If the experimentalist would not commit himself, the social philosopher, the preacher and the pedagogue tried the harder to give a short-cut answer. They observed the behavior of adolescents in our society, noted down the omnipresent and obvious symptoms of unrest, and announced these as characteristics of the period. (Mead 1968: 18)

Thus, Margaret Mead subtitled her book "A Psychological Study of Primitive Youth for Western Civilization." Both the target of her theoretical critique and the audience intended to read it were the larger American public rather than the "experimental psychologists" with whose careful observations she seemed to ally herself. In contrast, Mead drew from her training in psychology for the development and application of systematic research methods to use in combination with the ethnographic approaches she had absorbed in her anthropological training. As a result, her data on the Samoan girls she studied included demographic information on their families, their own personal histories, psychological tests, and many observations of behavior over a period of months, as well as general cultural information (Mead 1968).

Mead's work has drawn criticism as well as praise (Brady 1983; Levy 1984), but it was of great significance for later developments in psychological anthropology in at least three ways. First, the work of Mead and some of her contemporaries such as Malinowski set the stage for investigations over the next forty years into the relationships among cultural environments, childrearing practices, and adult behavior. Both the configurationist and functionalist approaches developed in this early work asserted that there were regularities, which could be discerned through systematic study, in the relationships between culture and human development. These ideas have shaped cross-cultural research on children's environments and development to the present.

Second, this early work provided the first scientific evidence on variability in children's environments and behavior. Although it may be hard to remember now, it is only fairly recently that students of human development have assumed the kind of wide difference that Mead's work documented. Cross-cultural variation in adult behavior had of course previously been noted, but the developmental processes leading to these differences had not been accorded serious attention. In conjunction with a lack of direct observational evidence, earlier theories in anthropology (as well as popular opinion) had labelled "primitive" peoples as childlike in their thought processes – a suggestion that the process of development in non-Western cultures was not really different, just inferior.

Third, Mead's work was important from a methodological point of view. Although her research was not quantitative for the most part, it was systematic. Most important for future research development was the attention she gave to collecting many kinds of information on particular individuals. The use of multiple methods to validate the findings of any one investigation has since been formalized in psychology (e.g. Campbell and Fiske 1959), and this approach remains an important contribution to the study of human behavior in general.

A developmental approach to the understanding of culture: the Whitings

Although the configurationist and functionalist schools had suggested systematic relationships among various aspects of a culture, they could not explain just how various childrearing patterns were related to customs, beliefs, and values of the culture as a whole. The Whiting model for psychocultural research, in contrast, proposed a set of relationships between parts of the culture which were designated as "antecedents" and parts that were seen as "consequents," with childrearing and the development of personality as the crucial connecting links. In a recent form, this theory postulates that:

1. Features in the history of any society and in the cultural environment in which it is located influence
2. the customary methods by which infants (and children) are cared for in that society, which have
3. enduring psychological and physiological effects on the members of that society, which are manifested in
4. the cultural projective-expressive systems of the society and the physiques of its members. (J. Whiting 1981: 155)

The Whiting model represented a new synthesis of anthropological and psychological theory. From anthropology came the functionalist proposition that different cultural domains were contingent on each other, rather than simply coexisting as accidents of history. From psychological theory came two central ideas that were widely accepted in the popular mind as well as among formal theorists. First was the concept of personality, defined as enduring dispositions to respond in certain ways under a variety of conditions. Second was the hypothesized primacy of early experience in establishing these dispositions. The theoretical relationships among culture, early experience, and personality were thus established, with the result that understanding the environments of infancy and early childhood took on great importance in psychological anthropology.

Research by the Whitings and their colleagues took a critical and innovative approach to specific psychological theories of the time, then translated them to cultural-level variables for validation. Whiting and Child's (1953) cross-cultural study of childrearing practices and folk theories of illness is a case in point. Drawing from behaviorist theory, Whiting and Child proposed that the psychoanalytic concept of fixation should be differentiated into positive and negative types. They proposed that, at the cultural level, widely shared areas of anxiety derived from harsh socialization practices would be expressed in beliefs about illness oriented to the relevant experiences of early childhood. In contrast, customary therapeutic practices were proposed as cultural expressions of positive fixation, following the idea that behavior that had been rewarded in early childhood would assume the psychological power to reduce anxieties about illness. A central finding derived from their cross-cultural test of ethnographic reports on seventy-five societies was that strict socialization practices (specifically early socialization, for example early weaning) were associated with attributions of patient responsibility for illness; on the other hand, permissive rearing was not associated with any particular pattern of illness. Whiting and Child viewed this pattern of results as confirmation of their differentiation of positive and negative fixation, suggesting that negative fixation would be a powerful predictor of adult customary beliefs and practices whereas positive fixation would not.

A further exploration of psychological constructs at the cultural level was entailed in research by J. Whiting and colleagues on relationships between mother–child sleeping arrangements and male initiation rites. They postulated that boy children who slept in contact with their mothers past early infancy would develop a female identity. This could be resolved at the cultural level through male initiation ceremonies that would break the tie with the mother (Burton and Whiting 1961; Whiting, Kluckhohn, and Anthony 1958). Alternatively, female identification by boys, if carried into adulthood, might be expressed in the cultural practice of couvade (Burton and Whiting 1961) or male pregnancy symptoms (Munroe and Munroe 1971). These relationships were demonstrated through cross-cultural patterns of co-occurrence.

Although the cross-cultural evidence on environments of early childhood and the "expressive systems" of later life were consistent with contemporary theories of psychological development, they were less than convincing to some. As LeVine (1970: 596–597) has pointed out,

> Customs like child-rearing practices and the variety of cultural behavior patterns with which they have been hypothetically linked tend to be associated with many other customs, and these multiple associations lend themselves to a variety of interpretations, some of them sociological or ecological rather than psychological. In the welter of multiple connections ... it is all too easy to find support of simple causal hypotheses by limiting one's investigation to a few variables rather than looking at the larger structure of relations in which they are embedded.

Furthermore, comparable data on the variables of interest was often not available in the ethnographic literature. For these reasons among others, work by the Whitings and their colleagues came to involve more collection of actual field data. With this came an increasing focus on the *earlier* links in the theoretical model of antecedents and consequents – that is, the relationships between the culturally constructed environments of childhood and the actual behavior of children at specified ages.

The centerpiece of this cross-cultural fieldwork effort was the Six Culture Study, organized by the Whitings and their colleagues in the early

1950s. The products of this work were, literally, voluminous: they included monographs reporting the results of fieldwork in each of six cultures around the world (B. Whiting 1963), a field manual (Whiting, Child, and Lambert 1966), an analysis of maternal beliefs (Minturn and Lambert 1964), and a psychocultural analysis of children's behavior (Whiting and Whiting 1975). The Six Culture Study made available for the first time detailed, systematic, and comparable information on the environments of childhood and children's daily lives and behavior within these settings in cultures as diverse as the Gusii of Western Kenya, the Rajputs of India, and a suburban New England community. This methodological achievement was made possible by the adoption of a standard set of protocols to be used in all the field studies. At the core of this was a system for observing the social behavior of children. Based on the idea that personality could be studied through naturally occurring behavior (rather than psychological tests) and drawing from learning and social-learning theory, the Whitings' behavior observation method entailed detailed observation of short segments of children's behavior at specified times and places. These were recorded in terms of "interacts," and further analyzed in relation to twelve basic categories of behavior such as nurturance, responsibility, dominance, and sociability. Although the categories themselves were considered universals, the question of how to categorize any particular "interact" relied upon the insights of members of the culture who were the actual observers and who could be expected to understand the intentions of actions more accurately than outsiders could.

The most significant theoretical results of the Six Culture Study were the patterns of relationships found between aspects of children's socio-cultural environments and their social behavior. Through extensive analysis of the behavior observations, the proportional occurrence of the twelve basic categories of "interacts" for each child was calculated. Average frequencies for each culture based on these proportional scores were then derived and subjected to multidimensional scaling. Two dimensions of difference among the children of the six cultures emerged. Dimension A differentiated nurturance and responsibility from dependence and dominance, while Dimension B contrasted sociable-intimate behavior with authoritarian and aggressive behavior. Dimension A was found to be related to social and technological complexity, with children from the most complex cultures scoring high on dependent and dominant behavior, while children from simpler cultures scored high on nurturant and responsible behavior. Dimension B contrasted family structure, with sociable-intimate behavior more characteristic of the cultures with nuclear families, and authoritarian behavior found more in cultures where extended families were the norm. Thus, for example, the Gusii children in Kenya (a technologically simple society) had high proportions of nurturant and responsible behavior (such as taking care of younger siblings) by contrast with children in India, who were more apt to engage in dominant or dependent behavior (such as bossing around a younger child, or seeking help from the mother). Children from the American community (technologically complex and characterized by nuclear families), on the other hand, were also high on dominant and dependent behavior, but were more apt to engage in sociable-intimate behavior than were children from the extended-family households of both Kenya and India.

From the perspective of anthropological theory, an interesting aspect of the Whitings' work is how the concept of culture became transformed by the research methodology of the Six Culture Study. To state it simply, culture came in this work to function as one of several independent variables that predict behavior in any given instance. As the Whitings wrote the Introduction to *Children of Six Cultures*, "if you want to predict the behavior of a preadolescent child, which would it be most important to know: his or her sex, age, birth order, the culture into which he was born, or the situation he was in at the moment you made your prediction?" (Whiting and Whiting 1975: 11). This approach represented a useful response to the need to sort out huge amounts of behavioral data on boys and girls of varying ages in different kinds of social settings across a wide variety of cultures. It laid the foundation for more recent work directed by Beatrice Whiting on the role of culture as a "provider of settings" which themselves have important influences on behavior (B. Whiting 1980; Whiting and Edwards 1988). The negative side of this approach, however, was that it relegated "culture" to a residual category of background variables, and divested it of its function as an integrative construct. Further, at the analytical level it did not allow for differences in the meanings of such other variables as age, sex, and sibling order. For example, what is the meaning of being a five-year-old girl with no younger siblings? In a middle-class American community, this is a normative status, whereas in rural highland Kenyan communities, the girl is likely to be a "spoiled" last-born of many children, or a child whose younger sibling has died. These factors, of course, are significant not only for the child's behavior but also for the behavior of others toward the child.

The Six Culture Study spanned more than two decades from its inception in the early 1950s to the publication of the behavioral analyses in the 1970s. During that period of time, some of the theoretical constructs which had stimulated its original formulation gave way to new approaches. As discussed by Shweder (1979a, 1979b), the central idea of "personality" as a set of consistent ways of reacting to a wide variety of situations, and the primacy of early experience in setting such patterns of response, did not hold up very well in a variety of studies. Better predictions could be obtained from the situation surrounding a given behavior than from the actor involved; yet situations, too, had problems for cross-cultural comparison since it could be argued that the cultural meanings of apparently similar situations (insofar as they could be found) might actually be quite different in different cultural settings. Thus, the relationships among culture, behavior, personality, and projective systems that were at the core of the Whiting model were now rejected by many (along with the "culture and personality" school more generally), and the anthropological rationale for studying the environments and behavioral development of children across cultures was greatly diminished. While issues of continuity in human development were being debated in psychology, anthropologists turned away from early childhood experience as a key to understanding the rituals and customary practices of adult life in other cultures; and other paradigms came to dominate this central theme in anthropological theory.

Cross-cultural research on child development

From the days of Margaret Mead, when human development was seen as residing at the core of cultural anthropology, the study of childrearing and child development in other cultures moved by the 1970s to a peripheral position in psychological anthropology. This very change, however, may have been essential for the creation of a theoretically fruitful interface with developmental psychology. The legacy of the Whitings, carried on by several generations of students and the Whitings themselves, was a strongly empirical approach to the study of childrearing and child development across cultures. From a focus on questions of adult personality and their hypothesized cultural correlates, attention came to focus on understanding universals and cultural structuring of developmental processes themselves. The anthropologists who interested themselves in these questions might find relatively few listeners within their own discipline, but they found a ready audience among developmental psychologists who were becoming dissatisfied with the limitations of trying to understand human psychological functioning within the confines of the laboratory. Growing attention to the child in context on the part of psychologists contributed to a confluence of cross-cultural research on children's development from both anthropological and psychological traditions (Jahoda 1982; LeVine, Miller, and West 1988; Segall, Dasen, Berry, and Poortinga 1990; Stigler, Shweder, and Herdt

1990). During the past two decades, thus, studies of human development within psychological anthropology have benefited from a new kind of integration of anthropology and psychology.

Recent research on human development in cultural context has addressed the problem, first raised by Mead, of validating Western psychological theories on a broader base of human experience. This has been a challenging task, but a relatively straightforward one in principle. During the last two decades, major current psychological theories have been put to cross-cultural tests. For example, Kagan (1973) used research on the development of Mayan Indian children in Guatemala to reexamine assumptions about continuity in development. Dasen's (1975) cross-cultural research on Piaget's stages of development has shown that the purported "stage" of a child's thinking is ecologically dependent. Edwards' (1982) research on moral reasoning in other cultures has shown how the conceptualization of the moral development stages themselves is based on Western social structure. Weisner (1981) has investigated the cultural mediation of stress in families, and Harkness (1987) has discussed postpartum depression as a "culture-bound syndrome," drawing from research on women in rural Kenya.

Anthropologists' early contributions to developmental theory were mainly to provide ethnographic exceptions to disprove Western-based generalizations. More recent work by both anthropologists and psychologists, in contrast, has sought ways of formulating cross-culturally valid principles of human development through a "derived etic" process, wherein Western developmental theories are reexamined as cultural products from the perspective of behavior and ethnotheories of other cultures (e.g. Lutz 1985; Harkness, Edwards, and Super 1981). Another approach has been to seek universals in the *structure* of human development as expressed in the timing of transitions. For example, research on infants' responses to their mothers' departure has shown similar age-related patterns in a wide variety of cultural settings; this finding has been interpreted as confirming a hypothesis, advanced by Kagan (1976), that the infant's ability to detect and evaluate events is dependent on the biologically based growth of cognitive capacities. Super's (1991) research on cognitive changes around age six in American and rural African children has also shown similarities in the shape of development, although actual performance levels in particular tasks are related to experiential factors such as formal schooling and literacy at home. Discussion of this large and important body of research is beyond the scope of this chapter, but the very bulk of the literature attests to the success of the anthropological message for psychology (for a fuller discussion, see Harkness and Super 1987).

Anthropological concepts of culture and psychological concepts of the person

Recent interaction between psychological anthropology and developmental psychology has proceeded from shared concerns about how to construct a valid data base for making generalizations about human development, and how to understand the ways that culturally constructed settings influence behavior in developmental context. Anthropology and psychology have also participated jointly in theoretical shifts in concepts of culture and the person. We turn now to these as a prelude to our review of current work on human development in psychological anthropology and prospects for the future.

A central metaphor in conceptualizations of culture is the "external–internal" dimension of contrast. Culture has been seen as providing an environment for individual thinking and action on the one hand, as a set of internal rules guiding such activity on the other. The outer manifestations or "products" of culture are contrasted with the inner "cultural information pool" or beliefs and values which create them. Behavior, which can be directly observed, is contrasted with ideas, emotions, and systems of meaning that are more hidden from view (Kluckhohn 1962; Kracke and Herdt 1987; LeVine 1973; Romney, Weller, and Batchelder 1986).

A perception shared by many is that within the field of psychological anthropology there has been a shift over the past twenty years or so from "external" to "internal" conceptualizations of culture. As D'Andrade commented in a 1981 discussion of culture theory:

> When I was a graduate student, one imagined people *in* a culture: ten years later culture was all in their heads. The thing went from something out there and very large to something that got placed inside. Culture became a branch of cognitive psychology. We went from "let's try to look at behavior and describe it," to "let's look at ideas." Now, how you were going to look at ideas was a bit of a problem – and some people said, "Well, look at language." That notion, that you look at idea systems, was extremely general in the social sciences. On, I think, the same afternoon in 1957 you have papers by Chomsky and Miller and in anthropology, Ward Goodenough. All signal an end to the era of "Let's look at people's behavior and see what they do." Before 1957 the definition of culture was primarily a behavioral one – culture was patterns of behavior, actions, and customs. The same behavioral emphasis was there in linguistics and psychology. The idea that cognition is where it's at struck all three fields at the same time – whether you do experiments or whether you look for intuitions or whether you talk to informants. (Shweder 1984: 7)

After reviewing several statements about culture, both pre- and post-1957, I am inclined to think that the "internal" side of culture has always seemed more central to psychological anthropologists, and that our perception of change in this regard is exaggerated. For example, Clyde Kluckhohn, in an essay on "the concept of culture" that was first published in 1945, concluded that "the essential core of culture consists of traditional (i.e. historically derived) ideas, and especially their attached values" (Kluckhohn 1962: 73). Likewise, the Whitings, in a chapter written for a psychological audience in 1960, characterized culture as "the formulation of the shared symbolic determinants of behavior" (Whiting and Whiting 1960, in Shweder 1980: 83). What has changed over the past two or three decades, I believe, is not so much what we think culture is, as how we conceptualize the person, what kinds of topics seem to be proper subjects for research, and what kinds of methods are available for their study. Briefly, "scientific" research as first established in experimental psychology meant the measurement of observable responses to external stimuli. As formalized in learning theory, the human mind was seen from an external perspective, as a *tabula rasa* on which could be written various patterns of thinking and action. The central emphasis here was on the person as a responding being; and the study of behavior was its logical expression. With the rise of cognitive approaches, the perspective in psychology shifted from an external to an internal view: the developing person was now seen as though "from within," as an originator of thoughts and actions which would in turn influence the external environment. The Western discovery of Vygotsky's theories of development has added a new dimension in thinking about "internal" development in interaction with the external world (e.g. Rogoff 1990; Wertsch 1985). The expression of this view of the person has been accompanied by the elaboration of new research modalities that attempt to gain more direct access to inner mental representations and processes. To these we now turn.

Recent work: culture, cognition, and language in human development

The rise of cognitive approaches to culture in the late 1950s, as described by D'Andrade (quoted in Shweder 1984), coincided in historical time with the early years of the Whitings' behaviorally oriented Six Culture Study. The more general paradigmatic shift in conceptualizations of human development and the person, however, has favored the elaboration in recent years of research directed to culturally organized learning, often accessed through language. The result in psychological anthropology and related fields has been a reformulation of "enculturation" as "the acquisition of culture" (Schwartz 1981). As this phrase adapted from child language acquisition suggests, the process of culture transmission is now viewed more from the perspective of the learner, who is seen as an active agent in developing and testing culturally structured ways of thinking and feeling. Three areas of research growing from this perspective have been particularly important in psychological anthropology: child language socialization, the socialization of affect, and the development of cultural models related to the self.

The process of learning to communicate through language is a central feature of human development as it is of the acquisition of culture. Ochs and Schieffelin (1984: 277) have described the mutuality of these two processes:

> (1) The process of acquiring language is deeply affected by the process of becoming a competent member of society; and (2) The process of becoming a competent member of society is realized to a large extent through language, by acquiring knowledge of its functions, social distribution, and interpretations in and across socially defined situations, i.e., through exchanges of language in particular social situations.

The first part of this statement is relevant to the debate in developmental psycholinguistics about the role of environmental input in language acquisition and the nature of language-learning processes. Research on child language socialization and development in other cultures has contributed to reformulations of just what kinds of environmental input are important in children's language learning (Blount 1990; Harkness 1988; Snow, Perlman, and Nathan 1987). A more fundamental theoretical contribution of this work has been to point out the ways in which language development can be seen as divergent across cultures, not only in the obvious fact that children learn different linguistic codes but also in the ways that language comes to be integrated and expressed in communication with the self and others (Harkness, in press; Snow 1989).

While child language socialization research in other cultures has made a theoretical contribution to developmental psycholinguistics, it is the role of language in the acquisition of culture (the second part of Ochs and Schieffelin's formulation) that has been of more central interest to anthropologists. Research on child language socialization has illustrated how social organization is communicated to children, and how the learning of particular kinds of linguistic routines figures in learning the rules of the culture. Watson-Gegeo and Gegeo (1977), for example, have shown how Samoan infants and young children are taught the mores of social interaction along with the structure of the language through calling-out and repeating routines. Ochs (1988) has discussed cross-cultural variations in caretakers' clarification responses to partially understood child utterances in relation to larger cultural values: while white middle-class mothers in the United States seem to prefer to verbalize a guess about what the child said, Samoan mothers more frequently seek clarification by getting the child to repeat the utterance. Ochs sees the Samoan pattern as part of a larger strategy for enculturation that relies heavily on repeated observation of behaviors.

As cross-cultural research on child language socialization has matured, there has been increasing recognition of the many ties between language development and other aspects of development, such as the learning of emotions, that are also culturally structured through the same mechanisms. For example, Miller's research on the role of narratives in the language environments of young children in a South Baltimore community (Miller and Sperry 1987; Miller and Moore 1989) shows how children are taught to use the narrative genre at the same time that they learn about culturally approved forms of expressing anger and aggression. Schieffelin (1979) and Ochs (1988) have documented the salience of emotion states in language structure and usage in Pacific cultures. A contrasting cultural scenario is presented by Harkness and Super's (1985a) analysis of "cultural scripts" for Kipsigis (Kenyan) mothers' responses to crying episodes by their two-year-old children, wherein it appears that speech and behavior in this setting are oriented to de-emphasizing awareness of inner emotional states.

Anthropological research on the socialization of emotion addresses issues in the acquisition of cultural-meaning systems as well as communicative skills. Lutz's research on the socialization of emotions on Ifaluk atoll (1988) in Micronesia is an example. Through a variety of methods including interviews, triads tests, and participant observation, Lutz has derived a model for the cultural construction of emotions. She contrasts the Ifalukian perspective, wherein the meanings of emotions are derived from their associated situations, with the Western folk psychology of emotions as more abstracted entities. Her analysis of individual variation in Ifalukian children's associations with the term *nguch* (meaning bored, tired, or fed up) is particularly interesting in that it indicates how variations in personal experience are related to the development of emotional understanding.

Both language socialization research and research on the development of emotional-meaning systems relate to the more general topic of how cultural models of the self are learned. Anthropological research within the cognitive science paradigm provides a framework for addressing this question. As defined by Quinn and Holland (1987: 6), cultural models are shared understandings that "frame experience, supplying interpretations of that experience and inferences about it, and goals for action." Research on cultural models has used the analysis of discourse (whether naturally occurring or in the context of interviews with the investigator) to derive patterns of propositions, themes, and metaphors that constitute cultural meaning systems. One striking finding that emerges from this research is the "thematicity" of cultural models from different domains within a single culture. An example is the use of the culturally constructed idea of "independence" in American parents' theories of child behavior and development, as described by Harkness, Super, and Keefer (1992). The idea of "independence" is a pervasive cultural theme in American life; it is one of "a small number of very general-purpose cultural models developed for special purposes" (Quinn and Holland 1987: 11). Harkness, Super, and Keefer (1992) propose that American parents use this general cultural model to develop specific models of early childhood development that allow re-framing of ostensibly negative child behavior in a culturally valued mode.

There is a tension in research on cultural models that comes of a disjunction between theory and methods. On the theoretical side, it has been suggested that cultural models have motivational and affective dimensions (D'Andrade and Strauss 1992). Nevertheless, in its focus on the "inner" version of culture, research on cultural models has relied virtually exclusively on the analysis of discourse rather than behavior. The question of how thought relates to action is problematic, and even more so in the context of cultural analysis, but it is one that future research will need to address. Cross-cutting this issue is another: how do cultural models get elaborated in the course of human development? Quinn (1992) has discussed how cultural models of American marriage develop as a result of experience from premarital to married states, and she speculates about the origins of these models in early childhood experience. There has been little if any research to date, however, that actually documents the development of cultural models in childhood and how they change in relation to cognitive and affective development as well as social experience. One promising theoretical approach to thinking about cultural models in human development is proposed by Holland and Valsiner (1988). They compare the idea of cultural models with Vygotsky's idea of "mediating devices," and suggest that Vygotsky's perspective on the development of inner representations through social interaction could be useful for anthropological research on the development of culturally shared understandings.

Toward a synthesis of behavioral and cognitive approaches

Anthropological thinking and research on human development, as reviewed here, have undergone a shift in paradigms from the behaviorally oriented field research of the Whitings' school to more recent studies that have focused on cognitive models of culture, accessed primarily through language. I have proposed that this methodological shift has resulted from a change in how both culture and the person are conceptualized. Especially important in this regard is the new perspective, derived from cognitive approaches in several fields, that sees the developing human as actively acquiring and indeed constructing knowledge of how the world works and what it means to be a person in it.

In the process of this paradigmatic shift, we have gained some powerful new tools for studying culture, especially the analysis of language productions, but there has also been a loss in the abandonment of the systematic behavioral observations that characterized earlier work in our field. This seems especially obvious in relation to research that relies entirely on informant interviews, but it is also true of research in the sociolinguistic tradition that focuses systematically only on certain specified kinds of speech events. This issue is discussed at greater length in Miller and Hoogstra's chapter in this volume; the point to be made here is that how people talk about their cultures and within their cultures needs to be studied in the context of how experience is culturally structured in everyday life.

One research framework that incorporates both behavioral and cognitive perspectives is the idea of the "developmental niche" propounded by Super and Harkness (1986). The developmental niche is a theoretical framework for studying cultural regulation of the micro-environment of the child, and it attempts to describe this environment from the point of view of the child in order to understand processes of development and the acquisition of culture. The developmental niche has three major subsystems which operate together as a larger system and each of which operates conditionally with other features of the culture. These are: (1) the physical and social setting in which the child lives; (2) culturally regulated customs of child care and childrearing; and (3) the psychology of the caretakers. These three subsystems share the common function of mediating the individual's developmental experience within the larger culture. Regularities in the subsystems, as well as thematic continuities from one culturally defined developmental stage to the next, provide material from which the child abstracts the social, affective, and cognitive rules of the culture, much as the rules of grammar are abstracted from the regularities of the speech environment. This framework has proved useful for the analysis of many aspects of child development and family life in cultural context (Blount 1990; Harkness, in press; Harkness and Super 1985, in press; Super and Harkness 1986; Segall, Dasen, Berry, and Poortinga 1990).

Conclusions

In psychological anthropology, as suggested at the beginning of this chapter, we have a heritage of two reasons for studying human development: in order to derive a more valid theory of human development, and in order to enhance our concepts of culture. In the first area, we have seen progress from the early contributions of Mead and others who pointed out cultural exceptions to Western-based generalizations, to the systematic seeking of universals and cultural variations in human development, to the most recent formulations of the cultural structuring of human development. In this progression, it becomes apparent that questions of culture and development have increasingly converged. On the developmental side, the child as a unit of analysis is increasingly being re-conceptualized as the child-in-context. At the same time, studies in language and the socialization of affect have pointed to the inseparability of these processes from culture acquisition. In the second area, our progress has been marked by shifts in paradigms that accompanied new empirical evidence or larger historical trends in concepts of the person. Culture, as suggested above, has always been defined at least partly in terms of mental representations and their attached values; the problem has been how to conceptualize the relationship between these individual phenomena and the collectively shared environment. Questions about personality as a predictor of behavior, and about continuity in human development in general, weakened the theoretical basis of the Whiting model, and with it the rationale for studying individual development in order to understand cultural belief systems. Recently, the rise of cognitive approaches has contributed to the rebirth of thinking about culturally shared individual ideas. At the same time, research in language socialization as both a privately understood and publicly utilized symbol system has shown how the dichotomy between internal and external visions of culture may be a false one (for a fuller discussion of this idea, see Miller and Hoogstra's chapter in this book). The next logical step in this enterprise will be to investigate how cultural models develop over the course of biological growth and socially constructed experience, and how they function not only to organize but also to direct actions. In carrying out this research agenda, it should become clear that human development in cultural context, far from occupying a peripheral position at the interface of two disciplines, is a central concern for both.

REFERENCES

Blount, B. G. 1990. Parental Speech and Language Acquisition: An Anthropological Perspective. *Pre- and Perinatal Psychology* 4(4): 319–335

Boas, F. 1930. Some Problems of Methodology in the Social Sciences. In L. D. White, ed., *The New Social Science* (pp. 84–98). University of Chicago Press

1948. Race, Language and Culture. New York: Macmillan

Brady, I., ed. 1983. Speaking in the Name of the Real: Freeman and Mead on Samoa. *American Anthropologist* 85(4): 908–947 (special section)

Burton, R. and J. W. M. Whiting. 1961. The Absent Father and Cross-sex Identity. *Merrill-Palmer Quarterly* 7(1): 85–97

Campbell, D. T. and D. W. Fiske. 1959. Convergent and Discriminant Validation by the Multitrait-Multimethod Matrix. *Psychological Bulletin* 56: 81–105

Cole, M., J. Gay, J. A. Glick, and D. W. Sharp. 1971. *The Cultural Context of Learning and Thinking*. New York: Basic Books

D'Andrade, Roy G. and C. Strauss, eds. 1992. *Human Motives and Cultural Models*. Cambridge: Cambridge University Press

Dasen, P. R. 1975. Concrete Operational Development in Three Cultures. *Journal of Cross-cultural Psychology* 6(2): 156–172

Edwards, C. P. 1982. Moral Development in Comparative Cross-cultural perspective. In D. A. Wagner and H. Stevenson, eds., *Cultural Perspectives on Child Development* (pp. 248–279). San Francisco: Freeman

Harkness, S. 1987. The Cultural Mediation of Postpartum Depression. *Medical Anthropology Quarterly* 1(2): 194–209

1988. The Cultural Construction of Semantic Contingency in Mother–Child Speech. In B. Blount, guest ed., Current Topics in Child Language Acquisition. *Language Sciences* 10: 53–67

In press. A Cultural Model for the Acquisition of Language: Implications for the Innateness Debate. In C. Dent and P. Zukow, eds., The Idea of Innateness: Effects on Language and Communication Research. *Developmental Psychobiology* 23(7)

Harkness, S., C. P. Edwards, and C. M. Super. 1981. Social Roles and Moral Reasoning: A Case Study in a Rural African Community. *Developmental Psychology* 17(5): 595–603

Harkness, S. and C. M. Super. 1985a. Child-Environment Interactions in the Socialization of Affect. In M. Lewis and C. Saarni, eds., *The Socialization of Emotions* (pp. 21–36). New York: Plenum

1985b. The Cultural Context of Gender Segregation in Children's Peer Groups. *Child Development* 56: 219–224

1987. The Uses of Cross-cultural Research in Child Development (vol. IV, pp. 209–244). Greenwich, CT: JAI Press

In press. The "Developmental Niche": A Framework for Analyzing the Household Production of Health. *Social Science and Medicine*

Harkness, S., C. M. Super, and C. H. Keefer. 1992. Learning to be an American Parent: How Cultural Models Gain Directive Force. In R. G. D'Andrade and C. Strauss, eds., *Human Motives and Cultural Models*. Cambridge: Cambridge University Press

Harris, M. 1968. *The Rise of Anthropological Theory*. New York: Thomas Y. Crowell

Holland, D. and J. Valsiner. 1988. Cognition, Symbols, and Vygotsky's Developmental Psychology. *Ethos* 16(3): 247–272

Jahoda, G. 1982. *Psychology and Anthropology: A Psychological Perspective*. New York: Academic Press

Kagan, J. 1973. Cross-Cultural Perspectives on Early Development. *American Psychologist* 28(11): 947–961

1976. Emergent Themes in Human Development. *American Scientist* 64: 186–196

Kluckhohn, C. 1962. The Concept of Culture. In C. Kluckhohn, ed., *Culture and Behavior* (pp. 19–73). New York: Free Press (originally published in 1945)

Kracke, W. and G. Herdt. 1987. Introduction: Interpretation in Psychoanalytic Anthropology. In W. Kracke and G. Herdt, guest eds., Interpretation in Psychoanalytic Anthropology. *Ethos* 15(1): 3–7

Laboratory of Comparative Human Cognition (LCHC). 1983. Culture and Cognitive Development. In P. Mussen, ed., *Handbook of Child Psychology: History, Theory, and Methods* (vol. I, pp. 295–356)

LeVine, R. A. 1970. Cross-Cultural Study in Child Development. In P. H. Mussen, ed., *Carmichael's Manual of Child Development* (3rd edn., vol. II, pp. 559–614). New York; Wiley

1973. *Culture, Behavior, and Personality*. Chicago: Aldine

LeVine, R. A., P. M. Miller, and M. M. West, eds. 1988. *Parental Behavior in Diverse Societies*. New Directions for Child Development, No. 40. San Francisco: Jossey-Bass

Levy, R. 1984. Mead, Freeman, and Samoa: The Problem of Seeing Things as They are. *Ethos* 12(1): 85–92

Lutz, C. A. 1985. Ethnopsychology Compared to What? Explaining Behavior and Consciousness among the Ifaluk. In G. M. White and J. Kirkpatrick, eds., *Person, Self, and Experience: Exploring Pacific Ethnopsychologies* (pp. 35–89). Berkeley: University of California Press

Lutz, C. A. 1988. *Unnatural Emotions: Everyday Sentiments on a Micronesian Atoll and their Challenge to Western Theory*. Chicago: University of Chicago Press

Mead, M. 1968. *Coming of Age in Samoa: A Psychological Study of Primitive Youth for Western Civilization* (first published 1928). New York: Dell

1972. *Blackberry Winter: My Earlier Years*. New York: William Morrow and Company

Miller, P. J. and B. B. Moore. 1989. Narrative Conjunctions of Caregiver and Child: A Comparative Perspective on Socialization through Stories. *Ethos* 17(4): 428–449

Miller, P. J. and L. L. Sperry. 1987. The Socialization of Anger and Aggression. *Merrill-Palmer Quarterly* 33(1): 1–31

Minturn, L. and Lambert, W. W. 1964. *Mothers of Six Cultures: Antecedents of Child Rearing*. New York: Wiley

Munroe, R. L. and R. H. Munroe. 1971. Male Pregnancy Symptoms and Cross-sex Identity in Three Societies. *Journal of Social Psychology* 84(1): 11–25

Ochs, Elinor. 1986. From Feelings to Grammar: A Samoan Case Study. In B. B. Schieffelin and E. Ochs, eds., *Language Socialization Across Cultures* (pp. 51–272). Cambridge: Cambridge University Press

1988. *Culture and Language Development: Language Acquisition and Language Socialization in a Samoan Village*. Cambridge: Cambridge University Press

Ochs, E. and B. Schieffelin. 1984. Language Acquisition and Socialization: Three Developmental Stories and their Implications. In R. A. Shweder and R. A. LeVine, eds., *Culture Theory: Essays on Mind, Self, and Emotion* (pp. 276–322). Cambridge: Cambridge University Press

Quinn, N. 1992. The Directive Force of Self Understanding: Evidence from Wives' Inner Conflicts. In R. G. D'Andrade and C. Strauss, eds., *Human Motives and Cultural Models*. Cambridge: Cambridge University Press

Quinn, N. and D. Holland. 1987. Culture and Cognition. In D. Holland and N. Quinn, eds., *Cultural Models in Language and Thought* (pp. 3–42). Cambridge: Cambridge University Press

Rogoff, B. 1982. Integrating Context and Cognitive Development. In M. E. Lamb and A. L. Brown, eds., *Advances in Developmental Psychology* (vol. II, pp. 125–170). Hillsdale, NJ: Erlbaum

1990. *Apprenticeship in Thinking: Cognitive Development in Social Context*. New York: Oxford University Press

Romney, A. K., S. C. Weller, and W. H. Batchelder. 1986. Culture as Consensus: A Theory of Culture and Informant Accuracy. *American Anthropologist* 88(2): 313–338

Schieffelin, B. 1979. Getting it Together: An Ethnographic Approach to the Study of the Development of Communicative Competence. In E. Ochs and B. Schieffelin, eds., *Developmental Pragmatics* (pp. 73–108). New York: Academic Press

Schieffelin, B. B. 1986. Teasing and Shaming in Kaluli Children's Interactions. In B. B. Schieffelin and E. Ochs, eds. *Language Socialization Across Cultures* (pp. 165–181) Cambridge: Cambridge University Press

Schwartz, T. 1981. The Acquisition of Culture. *Ethos* 9(1): 4–17

Segall, M. H., P. R. Dasen, J. W. Berry, and Y. H. Poortinga. 1990. *Human Behavior in Global Perspective: An Introduction to Cross-cultural Psychology*. New York: Pergamon Press

Shweder, R. A. 1979a. Rethinking Culture and Personality Theory. Part I: A Critical Examination of Two Classical Postulates. *Ethos* 7(3): 255–278

1979b. Rethinking Culture and Personality Theory. Part II: A Critical Examination of Two More Classical Postulates. *Ethos* 7(4): 279–311

1980. Rethinking Culture and Personality Theory. Part III: From Genesis and Typology to Hermeneutics and Dynamics. *Ethos* 8(1): 60–94

1984. A Colloquy of Culture Theorists. In R. A. Shweder and R. A. LeVine, eds., *Culture Theory: Essays on Mind, Self, and Emotion* (pp. 1–26). Cambridge: Cambridge University Press

Snow, C. E. 1977. Mothers' Speech Research: From Input to Interaction. In C. Snow and R. A. Ferguson, eds., *Talking to Children: Language Input and Acquisition* (pp. 31–50). Cambridge: Cambridge University Press

Snow, C. 1989. Understanding Social Interaction and Language Acquisition: Sentences are not Enough. In M. Bornstein and J. Bruner, eds., *Interaction in Human Development* (pp. 83–103). Hillsdale, NJ: Erlbaum

Snow, C., R. Perlmann, and D. Nathan. 1987. Why Routines are Different: Toward a Multiple-factors Model of the Relation between Input and Language Acquisition. In K. Nelson and A. van Kleeck, eds., *Children's Language* (vol. VI, pp. 65–98). Hillsdale, NJ: Erlbaum

Stigler, J. W., R. A. Shweder, and G. Herdt. 1990. *Cultural Psychology: Essays on Comparative Human Development*. Cambridge: Cambridge University Press

Super, C. M. 1991 Development Transitions in Cognitive Functioning in Rural Kenya and Metropolitan America. In K. Gibson, A. Petersen, and J. Lancaster, eds., *Brain and Development: Biosocial Perspectives* (pp. 225–251). Hawthorne, NY: Aldine de Gruyter

Super, C. M. and S. Harkness. 1986. The Developmental Niche: A Conceptualization at the Interface of Child and Culture. *International Journal of Behavioral Development* 9: 545–569

Watson-Gegeo, K. and D. Gegeo. 1977. From Verbal Play to Talk Story: The Role of Routines in Speech Events among Hawaiian Children. In S. Ervin-Tripp and C. Mitchell-Kernan, eds., *Child Discourse* (pp. 67–90). New York: Academic Press

Weisner, T. S. 1981. Cities, Stress, and Children: A Review of Some Cross-cultural Questions. In R. H. Munroe, R. L. Munroe, and B. B. Whiting, eds., *Handbook of Cross-cultural Human Development* (pp. 783–808). New York: Garland

Wertsch, J. V. 1985. *Vygotsky and the Social Formation of Mind*. Cambridge, MA: Harvard University Press

Whiting, B. B., ed. 1963. *Six Cultures: Studies of Child Rearing*. New York: Wiley

1980. Culture and Social Behavior: A Model for the Development of Social Behavior. *Ethos* 8(2): 95–116

Whiting, B. B. and C. P. Edwards. 1988. *Children of Different Worlds: The Formation of Social Behavior*. Cambridge, MA: Harvard University Press

Whiting, B. B. and J. W. M. Whiting. 1975. *Children of Six Cultures: A Psychocultural Analysis*. Cambridge, MA: Harvard University Press

Whiting, J. W. M. 1981. Environmental Constraints on Infant Care Practices. In R. H. Munroe, R. L. Munroe, and B. B. Whiting, eds., *Handbook of Cross-cultural Human Development* (pp. 155–180). New York: Garland

Whiting, J. W. M. and I. L. Child. 1953. *Child Training and Personality*. New Haven, CT: Yale University Press

Whiting, J. W. M., I. L. Child, W. W. Lambert, et al. 1966. *Field Guide of a Study of Socialization*. New York: Wiley

Whiting, J. W. M., R. Kluckhohn, and A. A. Anthony. 1958. The Function of Male Initiation Ceremonies at Puberty. In E. E. Maccoby, T. M. Newcomb, and E. L. Hartley, eds., *Readings in Social Psychology* (pp. 359–370). New York: Holt

Part III

The body's person

7 Putting people in biology: toward a synthesis of biological and psychological anthropology

James S. Chisholm

Introduction

Until recently the rift between biological and psychological anthropology was about as great as it could be. In her chapter for this book (chapter 8), Carol Worthman argues elegantly that the essence of these differences has been the one between Cupid and Psyche – between the views of human behavior as determined and as emergent. Biological anthropology has worked largely from the position that human behavior is determined – for example, by DNA sequences, endocrine substances, neural nets, and other biological phenomena that are relatively easy to describe objectively, count, and measure. Psychological anthropology, on the other hand, has typically seen human behavior as emergent, its essentially ineffable nature contingent on the dialectics of mind, self, and society.

This rift between biological and psychological anthropology, however, has not always been so formidable. Freud and Piaget, for example, each began his life's work because he saw implications of Darwin's theory of evolution by natural selection for understanding human motivation and thought (for Freud see Sulloway 1982; Leak and Christopher 1982; MacDonald 1986; for Piaget see Goodwin 1982; Piaget 1971, 1978). But despite this promising early alliance, biological and psychological anthropology drifted apart. With the emergence of Lionel Tiger and Robin Fox's "zoological perspective" (Tiger and Fox 1966, 1971), and their argument that no matter how cultural we are, we were primates first, and mammals before that, the gulf widened. And when William Hamilton (1964), Robert Trivers (1972), and E. O. Wilson (1975) used population genetics and mathematical models to solve Darwin's "special problem" (the evolution of altruism) the rift between biological and psychological anthropology appeared unbridgeable.

But appearances are sometimes just that, and there may be ways to recapture some of the early excitement that Freud and Piaget seem to have felt. In her chapter, Carol Worthman identifies areas of concern common to biological and psychological anthropology, and recommends liberal doses of communication across disciplinary lines. She also invites psychological anthropologists to collaborate with their biological colleagues, saying that they have "information and research techniques that can complement those of psychological anthropologists" (this book, p. 171). I agree, of course, for whatever else we may be, we are surely biological phenomena. But I also believe that biological anthropologists must seek out their psychological colleagues, for psychological anthropology has information and research techniques that can help us develop more fully some of the exciting recent advances in evolutionary biology and ecology. For me, psychological anthropology is "an anthropology with people in it" (as Robert Paul put it in a 1984 [p. 99] editorial in *Ethos*). As a *biological* anthropologist I assert that we must recognize the biology in people. As an *anthropologist*, however, I also assert that we must keep sight of the individual, the person – something for which biological anthropology is not particularly acclaimed. Following Paul's lead, my goal in this chapter is thus to "put people in biology."

I will begin with a description of the "adaptationist–mechanist" debate in biology, for anthropology is not the only discipline with "adversarial lovers" (to borrow Carol Worthman's metaphor). If many anthropologists are concerned, as Barkow put it, with the "distance between genes and culture" (Barkow 1984), they might take heart from those biologists concerned with the "distance" between genes (the organism's endowment of genetic possibilities) and *any* phenotypic trait (the actualization of a genetic potential in a particular environment). Second, reiterating another of Carol Worthman's themes, I will outline new ideas about development from the emerging biological field of life-history theory which foreshadow a reconciliation between the adaptationist and mechanist perspectives in biology. I believe these insights can also help biological and psychological anthropologists identify common ground. Finally, I will suggest that there is one aspect of this new focus on development that is especially conducive to a dialogue between biological and psychological anthropology: this is the concept of "strategy" as used in life-history theory. I believe that psychological anthropology has "information and research techniques" that can help us better apply the biological concept of strategy to humans.

The adaptationist–mechanist debate

The adaptationist school is biology's "Cupid" and the mechanist school is its "Psyche." Despite their different approaches and emphases, the adaptationist and mechanist positions are in fact complementary, and there is no necessary, fundamental opposition between them. There is a growing sentiment, however, that the adaptationist program has lately been overemphasized, and that with regard especially to the study of human behavior (and despite any connotations of its name), a corrective mechanist emphasis is now required. I hasten to stress that, ultimately, biologists see no real competition for the adaptationist perspective. In what follows I magnify the differences between the adaptationist and mechanist perspectives in order to characterize them more clearly – and to underline the point that a new mechanist emphasis can contribute to more sophisticated adaptationist models. I also believe that by exaggerating the adaptationist–mechanist differences, I can better suggest the value of an evolutionary perspective to psychological anthropologists, many of whom will be more familiar with the overemphasized adaptationist perspective embodied in the work of uncritical sociobiologists (see also Kitcher 1985).

The adaptationist perspective has its roots in genetics, population genetics, and demography. Combining the concepts and methods of these fields with sophisticated statistics and mathematics, the adaptationist tradition gave rise in the 1930s to biology's New Synthesis, with its wonderfully elegant and powerfully predictive formal models of how gene pools change and what selection should favor. There is no question that by providing a predictive, quantitative basis for evolutionary theory, adaptationists have achieved spectacular success. This success has resulted largely from a primary focus on *populations* and the *products* of adaptation by natural selection – that is, on relative differences in quantities of genes appearing in succeeding generations as a function of selection. Fitness is defined in terms of reproductive success, which is in turn typically defined as an individual leaving more copies of its genes in succeeding generations than other individuals in its population carrying different genes (e.g., Daly and Wilson 1983). Adaptationists thus tend to argue that in the long run natural selection maximizes – or optimizes – number of offspring. This approach has been the dominant one in biology since the New Synthesis, and has, since Wilson's *Sociobiology* (1975), been the most rapidly growing force in biological anthropology as well (see also Smith 1987; Parker and Maynard Smith 1990).

However, as the biologist Steven Stearns put it, because of the adaptationists' very success in modeling changes in gene frequencies, "the organism disappeared from view, and with it the phenotype" (1982: 238). Consequently, adaptationists sometimes seem to conflate phenotypic traits themselves with the genes "for" such traits – because they approach the organism as if it were the sum of its individual traits (e.g., Oyama 1985).

The mechanist school, on the other hand, has its roots in anatomy, physiology, embryology, and the European tradition of "whole organism" natural history and classical ethology. Where adaptationists focus on the products of adaptation, mechanists focus on the *process* of adaptation – how the qualities of individuals' genes and environments interact throughout development. Mechanists agree that ultimately differential reproductive success is what drives evolution, but they emphasize more the trade-offs between phenotypic quantity and quality, arguing that natural selection cannot be expected to maximize number of offspring at the expense of adaptations for survival, growth and development, and other preparations for adult life.

Adaptationists and mechanists agree that ultimately genes underlie everything an organism is or can be. But mechanists are less apt to confuse phenotypic traits with the genetic basis "for" such traits because the mechanist tradition has always emphasized that the environment also underlies everything an organism is or can be, and that the phenotype is *emergent* – contingent on the dialectic between organism and environment from conception to death (e.g., Bateson 1976, 1982; Hinde 1987, 1990; Oyama 1985; Stearns 1982; Lewontin 1978, 1982). For example, rather than viewing the genotype as a "blueprint for" the phenotype, as adaptationists are wont to, Goodwin (1972), a mechanist, prefers the metaphor of genotype as "hypotheses about" the phenotype. Mechanists stress that since selection operates on phenotypes, not genotypes (everyone agrees on this), it is the success of the phenotype that determines which genes get copied into the next generation. They also stress that selection does not "care" about the *source* of an organism's phenotypic adaptations: the efficient cause of survival, adaptive growth and development, learning, and other preparations for the business of being an adult may often come from, and be maintained by the organism's environment, whether physical, social, or cultural (e.g., Changeux 1985; Chisholm 1983, 1988; Chisholm and Heath 1987; Oyama 1985; Plotkin 1982; Plotkin and Odling-Smee 1979, 1981; Slobodkin and Rapoport 1974; Stearns 1982). Where adaptationists are concerned with what genes selection is expected to favor, mechanists are concerned with how the phenotype works, how it interacts with its environment, and especially, how it develops (Gould 1977, 1982; Gould and Lewontin 1979; Stearns 1982).

A frequent example of the adaptationist–mechanist debate concerns the evolution of the human chin (Gould and Lewontin 1979). The chin (the projecting wad of bone at the tip of our lower jaw) is a phenotypic trait of recent appearance in human evolution, and one which has long puzzled physical anthropologists. A popular adaptationist explanation for its appearance suggests that its mass functions as a shock absorber, mitigating the stress and strain of chewing after the evolution of smaller jaws and teeth. The mechanist explanation suggests, on the other hand, that the chin is an epiphenomenon, an accidental by-product of selection for reduced growth (relative to ancestral species) of the human "snout." As humans became less prognathic, their chins became more prominent, but there was no selection for chins, *per se*. The adaptationist view suggests that if a trait (e.g., the chin) exists, then there must be a gene (or genes) "for" that trait, and it must be (or have been) adaptive. The mechanist view suggests that the chin may not be a trait that is exposed to selection at all, that there is no gene "for" the chin, and that the chin is a phenotypic trait which is emergent, developmentally contingent on the interaction between adjacent growth fields in the face.

The critical issue is the "missing phenotype." Unless one has some understanding of the phenotype – how the organism works, how it develops – one cannot advance a sophisticated adaptationist argument. This is the trouble with narrow adaptationist arguments about human behavior, which sometimes seem to imagine that some behavior itself is the adaptation while they ignore the phenotypic traits that produce the behavior – the human brain or mind. As Symons puts it, "Darwin's theory of natural selection sheds light on human affairs only to the extent that it sheds light on phenotypic design, and design is usually manifested at the psychological level" (1989: 143). Consider, for example, Barkow's (1984) critique of Mildred Dickemann's (1979) sociobiological interpretation of preferential female infanticide. With data from a number of societies, Dickemann notes that female infanticide is concentrated among the wealthiest groups within each. This, she suggests, is because the sons of wealthy parents can provide them with more grandchildren than can their daughters – because sons can father more children than daughters can bear (especially when sons' wealth gives them the option of polygynous marriage). Female infanticide is thus seen as an adaptation to maximize reproductive success, at least in the hypergamous societies studied. Dickemann's data and analyses are impeccable, and there is a persuasive (adaptationist) rationale for her conclusions (Trivers and Willard 1973), but as Barkow points out, "Dickemann seems to be assuming that whenever the wealth and power of parents reach a certain level, a powerful but unconscious preference for sons over daughters is triggered" (1984: 370). With no understanding of the psychocultural processes that motivate individual parents preferentially to kill their daughters, it is difficult to claim that selective female infanticide is an evolved trait. Despite the fact that infanticide may increase reproductive success, as Dickemann suggests, infanticidal behavior *itself* cannot have been the focus of selection, and its effects on reproductive success are indirect at best, or entirely epiphenomenal. This is because infanticide –

or any other behavior – is exposed to selection only insofar as the psychological mechanisms that *produce* it are exposed to selection (see also Symons 1987). Thus, correlations between behavior and reproductive success do not in themselves constitute evidence for adaptation. To paraphrase the evolutionary biologist George Williams (1966), "the central biological problem is not reproduction as such, but *design* for reproduction." And as Darwin himself argued, it was not forms of behavior that evolved, but *motives* (Gruber 1974).

The moral is that we cannot confuse a trait – like the chin, or infanticide – with genes "for" that trait. We must instead understand how the trait works and where it comes from. Selection acts not only on behavior, but also on the developmental biological and psychological mechanisms that produce behavior. This perspective is key to the research program of what is lately being called "evolutionary" or "Darwinian" psychology, which is developing within biological anthropology as a mechanist correction to the field's long-standing adaptationist bias in the study of behavior (e.g., Barkow 1984, 1989; Barkow, Cosmides, and Tooby 1992; Cosmides and Tooby 1987, 1989; Symons 1987, 1989; Tooby and Cosmides 1989; see also the special issue of *Ethology and Sociobiology* [11(4/5), 1990]).

Life-history theory

Life-history theory is a recently emerging field of biology that combines the study of reproduction, growth and development, genetics, and ecology in an evolutionary context (e.g., Boyce 1988; Horn and Rubenstein 1984; Stearns 1976, 1977, 1982; Wittenberger 1981). It is also the field of biology where adaptationist–mechanist differences are most blurred. Its adaptationist concern is with how selection shapes broad aspects of organisms' entire life cycles, and its simultaneous mechanist concerns are with the development of the phenotype and reciprocal constraints and influences between ontogeny (individual lifespan development) and phylogeny (evolutionary history). A basic premise of life-history theory is that organisms have been selected for the optimal allocation of finite resources (time, energy, safety, etc.) to the inherently conflicting evolutionary demands of bodily maintenance, growth and development, and reproduction (mating and parenting). Most life-history theory research investigates the socioecological causes and fitness consequences of trade-offs between the various components of fitness (for example, those between mating effort and parenting effort; between slow growth with late reproduction and rapid growth with early reproduction; and between rearing a few "high-quality" offspring and many "lower-quality" offspring).

Life-history theory has special relevance for fostering a dialogue between psychological and biological anthropology because one of its conclusions is that human evolution has been characterized by natural selection for a high degree of behavioral flexibility – the capacity to develop a wide range of behavioral phenotypes, whose very adaptability is *contingent* on social–cultural and physical environmental influences encountered during development. To appreciate why life-history theory expects a high degree of behavioral/phenotypic flexibility in humans, we must briefly examine the life-history concepts of "r-" and "K- selection" and "bet-hedging" ("r" and "K" are technical terms whose definitions are not material here; see Chisholm 1988 and references above for more details).

The evolution of development

A major contribution of life-history theory has been in making sense of the bewildering diversity in the ontogenies of living organisms. In environments which change frequently and unpredictably, for example, there are often catastrophic mortality rates in which large numbers die, not so much because individuals are unfit but because they are unlucky. These conditions are associated with r-selection. When selection is thus undirected it does not work to produce a more efficient phenotype, but instead to produce a reproductive strategy based on rapid and massive reproduction. A reproductive strategy is a complex, a "package," of co-adapted phenotypic traits (anatomical, physiological, psychological, etc.) designed by natural selection to solve particular, expectable environmental problems. Under unpredictable conditions, r-selection is thought to favor a "package" of traits that includes rapid development, many offspring, minimal parental care, short birth interval, small body size, short lifespan, and relatively simple social behavior (i.e., the "r-strategy"). This is because the evolutionary payoff under these conditions goes to individuals who reproduce most rapidly and/or in the greatest number, for they are disproportionately represented in future generations by virtue of their headstart in re-colonizing empty niches after a period of catastrophic mortality.

On the other hand, as an adaptation to the higher levels of intraspecific competition that is typical of populations at environmental carrying capacity in less changeable and more predictable environments ("K-selection"), the essence of what is called the "K-strategy" is to ensure reproduction at replacement levels (i.e., low or zero population growth). This is because there is no evolutionary payoff in having large numbers of offspring in rapid succession (for this would intensify already high levels of intraspecific competition and endanger the survival or optimum development of all offspring). The "K-complex" includes slow development, few offspring, intensive parental care, long birth interval, large body size, long lifespan, and complex social behavior.

Consistent K-selection is believed to have favored the genetic basis for extensive behavioral flexibility (i.e., learning, or the capacity to be adaptively affected by one's environment, especially during development) because crowded, competitive, and intensely social environments are apt to change unpredictably over time spans very much shorter than genetic change can occur. For any organism, all conspecifics that it encounters are as much a part of its environment as any inanimate object or force of nature. Unlike inanimate objects and forces of nature, however, conspecifics pattern their behavior toward each other on the basis of how others behave toward them. In K-selective environments the most pressing and pervasive selective force is not inanimate nature or the behavior of other organisms, but the behavior of *conspecifics*. In these environments a succession of novel and shifting selective forces is virtually guaranteed because each individual learns, and is surrounded by others who also learn, and who generate novel behavior patterns *contingent* on their interactions with everybody else. Such, of course, is a good characterization of the social environment of hominid evolution, at least since the end of the Pleistocene, when our ancestors spread over the globe and constructed their subsistence activities, work loads, sexual divisions of labor, systems of exchange, social organizations, marriage patterns, and belief systems to suit their own histories and local conditions.

However, while humans seem clearly to possess a "package" of K-selected traits, the concepts of r- and K-selection themselves are not without their critics. The leading criticism is that the r–K model deals inadequately with the demographic consequences of different patterns of adult and juvenile mortality. The alternative model, termed "bet-hedging theory" (e.g., Stearns 1976, 1977; Wittenberger 1981), focuses explicitly on these consequences, and suggests that *they* may be the selective forces behind the r- and K-trait "packages" rather than the "classic" r- and K-environments themselves. When adult mortality is high, for example, or juvenile mortality is predictably low, bet-hedging theory predicts the "r-" complex of early maturity, high reproductive effort, and low parental investment per offspring (Wittenberger 1981: 358).

Nonetheless, while the r–K and bet-hedging theories have different ideas about the ultimate evolutionary source of human behavioral plasticity (learning), we still have an initial grasp of some of the mechanisms whereby this package of phenotypic traits may have been achieved. Examples include selection for the genetic basis of developmental patterns which produce neoteny (e.g., Gould 1977, 1982), and Jean-Pierre Changeux's

(1985) "epigenesis by selective stabilization." Changeux argues that while the fundamental architecture of the human brain seems genetically determined, there is nonetheless an *inherent* (i.e., genetically determined) "phenotypic variability" in the process of synapse formation, which provides the raw material for "neural selection" to favor the preservation or stabilization of those neural connections that have functional significance in a particular environment (physical, social, cultural, etc.). Changeux also notes that there is a progressive *decrease* in the determing effect of the genotype on the neural phenotype from invertebrates to vertebrates, from lower vertebrates to higher, and from nonhuman primates to humans because of the *indeterminacy* inherent in neural development processes. C. H. Waddington (in some ways the spiritual father of life-history theory) characterized the relationship of the genotype to the phenotype as one of "adaptive indeterminacy" (1968: 364), and even Sewall Wright, one of the founders of biology's "New Synthesis," argued that "[phenotypic plasticity] is not only of the greatest significance as a factor in evolution damping the effects of selection . . . but is itself perhaps the *chief object* of selection" (quoted in Stearns 1982: 240; my italics).

There are, however, costs as well as benefits to the evolution of learning, and there are thus limits on the behavioral plasticity obtained through enhanced learning, memory, and other cognitive capacities. A variety of these costs has been suggested (Fagen 1982; Johnston 1982), but foremost among them is "developmental fallibility," or the increased possibility of *failure* to learn and *inappropriate* learning (Johnston 1982). In other words, the very flexibility of behavior that is the benefit of an increased capacity for learning implies the cost of an increased likelihood of learning gone wrong. On these grounds we thus expect selection to have favored the genetic basis for psychological mechanisms which buffer the developing child against inappropriate learning, or which channel him or her into the locally most appropriate learning situations. The evolution of the capacity for intensive parental care and extensive teaching by parents and others are two obvious examples of such mechanisms in humans, but current efforts in life-history theory and evolutionary psychology are focusing on the developmental biology and socioecology of neuroendocrine and psychological factors that make some behaviors "easy" to learn and others "hard" to learn – i.e., on the identification and analysis of "learning biases" or "predispositions to learn."

Learning bias and culture

In their important contribution to "dual-inheritance theory" (the co-evolution of genes and culture), Boyd and Richerson (1985) deal broadly and creatively with questions about learning bias. Their overall concern is with how, given the fact of the cultural transmission of behavior, evolution might progress, and with the social and ecological conditions under which certain patterns or structures of cultural transmission (i.e., specific learning biases) might be adaptive. They provide a series of formal models showing how behaviors transmitted via the cultural inheritance system could be neutral or even maladaptive in terms of ordinary genetic reproductive success, but still persist. They also model the evolution of learning biases that can, in principle, account for the evolutionary origin and persistence of culture itself and individual cultural traditions.

They provide theoretical rationales and empirical evidence (from anthropology and social and developmental psychology) for the existence of a number of human learning biases, but the core of their argument is the Piagetian axiom that children are naturally (genetically) biased toward dynamic and evaluatory participation in their own learning, and are thus active partners in their own socialization and enculturation. This is opposed to individual trial-and-error learning, which may often be dangerous and time consuming, and to passive imitation or unquestioning acceptance of teaching, which are "unbiased" learning rules, suitable for traits like, say, grammar and syntax, which are both adaptively crucial and largely invariant in most children's learning environments. When adaptively crucial aspects of children's learning environments are sufficiently variable, however, passive imitation and unquestioning acceptance are less likely to be adaptive in terms of either natural selection or cultural integration. Boyd and Richerson's major contribution is in showing how natural selection could favor the evolution of more complex learning biases that would increase the probability that children would adopt the locally optimum trait even under conditions of variability and flux in their learning environments. These more complex learning biases involve the evaluation of alternative behavioral traits and models and the adoption of some of these traits disproportionately according to certain "rules of thumb" for evaluation (e.g., whether models for a trait are common or rare; whether models for a trait vary according to some criterion [like wealth, prestige, etc.]; whether the trait itself "works," i.e., whether it achieves some material or nonmaterial value). For me, Boyd and Richerson's work has two important implications; first, state-of-the-art research at the juncture of psychological and biological anthropology will now focus on identification and description of these "learning biases," and particularly on the mental images and processes that people use to evaluate alternatives and actually to *produce* the behavioral traits they have seen modeled (or to invent new ones). Second, such a focus itself demands attention to "local knowledge," for traits to be modeled (or not) only exist in, and have value or meaning by virtue of, a local context. Shore (1988) might have been speaking for this sort of approach when he said "each of us lives out our species nature only in a specific local manifestation, and ... our cultural and historical peculiarity is an essential part of that nature" (p. 170).

Alternative reproductive strategies

The behavioral–developmental plasticity of K-selected animals produces a high degree of intraspecific variation in behavior, and consequently more complex social behavior. This is because selection favors animals who *can be* adaptively affected by their developmental environment. There are thus more *ways* in which individuals can differ from each other. Because of its theoretical rationale for expecting the evolution of behavioral flexibility, one of life-history theory's major concerns is with understanding all this variance. Instead of focusing on "normal," "average," or "species-typical" behavior, life-history theory emphasizes the analysis of patterns of individual *differences* in behavior according to socioecological factors – especially those encountered during development. The most exciting result of this approach is the realization that different developmental environments may entail adaptive "alternative developmental strategies." What develops may be any aspect of the phenotype, but there is special interest in the development of alternative mating and parental investment strategies, because of their very direct and immediate impact on the evolutionary goal of reproduction. Developmental fallibility in the arenas of mating and parenting is likely to have been pervasively selected against, and it is in these arenas that we would most expect to find examples of human learning biases that buffer and channel against such fallibility.

Life-history theory predicts that the development of alternative reproductive and parental investment strategies will be contingent on those aspects of an organism's developmental niche that are reliable predictors of adult conditions intimately affecting fitness which nonetheless fluctuate unpredictably over a predictable range of values – that is, when the *timing* of change is largely unpredictable but the *value* or *direction* of the change is predictable (e.g., Fagen 1982; Horn and Rubinstein 1984). We expect, in other words, that individuals will have been selected to be affected by those early experiences which happened to provide an "early warning" of social and economic conditions they would encounter as adults. For example, Pat Draper and Henry Harpending (1982, 1987, 1988) and Jane and Chet Lancaster (Lancaster and Lancaster 1983, 1987), among others, have suggested that for most of human evolution the success of adult reproductive and parental investment strategies was crucially dependent on such variable environmental features as population density; the quality and distribution of resources; the nature and frequency of environmental hazards; and the sex ratio and availability of appropriate mates. While the timing of change in these aspects of socioecology usually could not be forecast over very long time periods, the range of values assumed by each component, or at least their direction of change, was probably more predictable. One may not have known *when* a change would occur but still have some confidence about what it would entail when it did – by reference to current conditions and the recent past, to the beliefs, attitudes, and behavior of older people who know better the more distant past, or even to myths and legends. Under these circumstances we expect selection to favor developmental sensitivity to harbingers of change, and children are hypothesized to be most developmentally sensitive to, or affected by, those aspects of the developmental niche that were the most consistent bellwethers for the conditions they would face when they began to lay their reproductive potential on the line.

The absent-father syndrome

Draper and Harpending (1982, 1987, 1988) suggest in particular that because sex itself is the universal and most immediate component of reproductive success, children might be expected to be especially sensitive to the mating and parenting behaviors of their parents and other adults with whom they interact frequently – for these adults will typically already have committed themselves to a mating and parenting strategy under physical and social environmental conditions likely to be similar to those the children will face in little more than a decade. From this premise they provide an illuminating life-history-theory reinterpretation of the "absent-father syndrome." They propose the existence of an evolved sensitivity to the presence or absence of an investing male because in the environment of human evolutionary adaptedness (Bowlby 1969) father absence or presence (or degree of father involvement) was a reliable early predictor of socioecological conditions in which the reproductive success of each sex is likely to have depended on a degree of separation between the sexes. In non-Western societies, for example, fathers tend to be absent (or less involved with children) under the conditions associated with polygyny, with "aloof" rather than "intimate" relations between husbands and wives, and with high levels of intergroup antagonism or warfare (e.g., Alcorta 1982; Divale and Harris 1976; West and Konner 1976; Whiting and Whiting 1975). Under these conditions (i.e., an "r-selective" environment, and/or one with high levels of adult mortality), high reproductive output and relatively low parental investment are likely to do better – for both sexes – than high parental investment in a small number of offspring.

In industrial societies, however, fathers are typically absent for different reasons: poverty and racial prejudice, and associated high levels of incarceration and mortality among young adult males; high rates of divorce; imbalanced sex ratios; and misguided social welfare programs (e.g., Burton 1990; Geronimus 1987; Guttentag and Secord 1983; Stack 1974). A particular strength of Draper and Harpending's work is the evidence they amass that despite the reasons for father absence or low involvement, its developmental effects are strikingly similar in both Western societies, where it is non-normative and often seen as "social pathology," and non-Western societies, where it is entirely normal. In both settings father-absent boys tend to reject authority, tend to exaggerate their masculinity and engage frequently in aggressive and other dangerous activities, tend to denigrate females and femininity, and to evidence an exploitative attitude toward sexual relations with women. In Western settings father-absent girls tend to show a precocious interest in sex, tend to denigrate males and masculinity, and tend to exhibit little willingness to maintain a long-term sexual–emotional bond with one man. In non-Western settings, however, these effects on girls are often difficult to discern, possibly because of the biases of male ethnographers and the practical and ethical difficulties for either sex in studying sexual behavior in most small-scale societies. Another factor, however, is that in many such societies young girls are married before or shortly after menarche (Whiting, Burbank, and Ratner 1986), and their sexuality may thus be controlled by more people – by husbands, co-wives, and in-laws, as well as parents – for more of their lives. But it is also typically true in non-Western father-absent societies that there is considerable antagonism between the sexes (see references in Draper and Harpending 1982).

The cross-cultural consistency in the developmental effects of father absence would seem difficult to explain in terms of standard learning theories, not just because of the immense variability in cultural constructions of fatherhood and the family, but especially because the same effects seem to occur where fathers are "normally" and "non-normally" absent. Life-history theory, on the other hand, provides a rationale for expecting father presence/absence to be a salient component of the developmental niche: children are sensitive to father presence/absence (or involvement) because it entrains the *learning* and *practice* of cognitive, perceptual, and socioemotional traits that tend to be adaptive (in the sense of both biological adaptation and sociocultural integration) in the kinds of socioeconomic environments where, during human evolution, fathers have been typically absent or present.

Part of the motivation to learn and practice particular behaviors and interactive styles contingent on father presence/absence is likely to derive from the effects of varying degrees of father involvement on physiological and neuroendocrine development. That is, focusing as it does on the phenotype, and recognizing that selection does not act on behavior but on the "organs" of behavior, life-history theory expects the existence of a "package" or "complex" of morphological, physiological, and endocrine traits that underlie or are associated with the psychological processes that actually produce the behaviors we see. It is thus interesting to note that father-absent girls (at least in Western societies) are reported to reach menarche significantly earlier than father-present girls (Jones, Leeton, McLeod, and Wood 1972; Surbey 1990). While this finding requires replication in larger samples with better controls, it is consistent with Draper and Harpending's model and life-history theory predictions in that the proposed adaptive function of the father-absent reproductive strategy is to increase fertility early in a woman's reproductive career – and it is known from a number of studies that early-maturing girls (again in Western societies) engage in sexual intercourse earlier than later-maturing girls (e.g., Bernard 1975; Cvetkovich, Grote, Lieberman, and Miller 1978; Udry and Cliquet 1982), which would tend to accomplish this. It is also beginning to look as though early and frequent sexual intercourse may have a cumulatively enhancing effect on women's reproductive function (Cutler and Garcia 1980; Cutler, Preti, Huggins, Erickson and Garcia 1985). Further, although there are again sampling and measurement problems, there is some evidence that anorgasmic women are more likely than others to report strained relations with their fathers, or having grown up without a father (Fisher 1973; Offit 1981; Uddenberg 1974). The obvious speculation in this context is that anorgasmia as a developmental consequence of father-absence might constitute part of a "learning bias" – a psychobiological mechanism "predisposing" some women to seek new partners who can help them achieve orgasm (see also Rancour-Laferriere 1985). Such a mechanism might simultaneously "predispose" some women to denigrate males and masculinity. Whereas standard learning theories would seem to have difficulty accounting for this apparent covariance of behavioral and physiological–maturational traits among father-absent girls, it makes sense in terms of a co-evolved "package" of phenotypic design features in the service of alternative reproductive strategies.

Although intriguing, it is clear that additional research is required before Draper and Harpending's "absent-father" model can be considered validated. I have nonetheless described it at some length because it is the best current example of the application of life-history theory to an important domain of human psychology, because it organizes so many otherwise disparate findings, and because the "absent-father syndrome" is a venerated topic in psychological anthropology. Other theoretically sophisticated (and not mutually exclusive) treatments of the contingent development of alternative reproductive strategies exist, but are less fully developed. Lancaster and Lancaster (1983, 1987), for example, suggest that the developing child's perception of resource predictability is the primary source of differences in reproductive strategies, instead of father presence/absence. Life-history theory does emphasize individual differences in the distribution of resources in the development of alternative reproductive strategies (e.g., Stearns 1976), but to the extent that father presence/absence is (or was) correlated with the flow of resources a child might experience, the absent-father and resource-flow models could still be congruent. Another example is the recent work of Belsky, Steinberg, and Draper (1991), who argue that what makes a difference in the development of alternative reproductive strategies is not likely to be father absence *per se*, or poverty *per se*, but any early, consistent psychological distress that contributes to insecure attachment and/or a basically mistrustful view of social relations and the world. I think this approach is promising because it highlights the psychological effects of differences in early experience, and thus opens the *child's* point of view to consideration from an evolutionary perspective. Such a focus on the environmental (social and physical) perceptions of *children* (rather than those of evolutionary ecologists) will clearly be an important component of future research on the development of alternative strategies.

A fundamental tenet of life-history theory is that selection does not favor good genes, but a *reliable association* between good genes and a good environment (Lewontin 1978; Oyama 1985; Wachs 1983; West, King, and Arberg 1988). The absent-father and resource-flow models of the development of alternative male and female reproductive strategies contingent on early socioecology are consistent with this notion because they suggest that human perceptual and affective mechanisms may have evolved to "channel" children's opportunities and motivations for learning, dependent on their early environment. Thus, people, like other organisms, *do* make their own environments (e.g., Scarr and McCartney 1983), but along the way some of their choices about interactions and social environments may be constrained by the reliable developmental effect of particular socioecological factors on inherently plastic cognitive, perceptual, and socioemotional processes. This is the life-history conception of strategy.

Life-history theory argues that there is never any theoretical or logical requirement that any organism ever be conscious of following some strategy – indeed, maturational and physiological processes (like age at menarche, for example) are often considered as part of a strategy. A strategy is said to exist when it is observed that certain behaviors (and/or maturational or physiological processes) which enhance or maintain fitness (however that may be defined) are contingent on evolutionarily significant aspects of the environment. It is then said that the organism is behaving "*as if*" it were following some particular alternative strategy – which might be thought of as a series of hierarchically arranged, conditional, "if–then" propositions. I believe that psychological anthropology can help biological anthropology understand better what human strategies might look like – perhaps especially in grasping the mechanisms and processes underlying that crucial "as if" qualification (see also Callan 1984). If people sometimes – or often – act "as if" they were following a series of "if–then" propositions, what are these propositions, and how do people learn them, and "follow" them?

Human strategies

The central lesson from life-history is that we need to study the developmental processes underlying the emergence of phenotypic traits (very especially those, like preferential female infanticide, that occasionally seem to have important adaptive consequences). If we are interested in humans, and if the phenotypic traits we are interested in are the broad classes of behavior involved in alternative strategies for mating and marriage, parenting, resource accrual, or anything else, then necessarily we are interested in the cognitive, perceptual, affective, linguistic, moral, and other developmental processes involved in the emergence and maintenance of locally available behavioral options. For example, if individual differences in parental investment have had consistent effects on fitness, for a sufficiently long time, then we might expect individual differences in patterns of cognitive, perceptual, and social–emotional development to co-vary with alternative investment strategies and to be developmentally contingent on the same socioecological factors as the observed behaviors that we used to define the alternative strategies in the first place.

In fact, a number of psychological anthropologists are advocating similar kinds of thinking and are already providing the kinds of data useful to human life-history research. One promising approach is that of Charles Super and Sara Harkness (1986), whose concept of the "developmental niche" suggests how culturally constructed theories about the nature of children are contingent on parents' perceptions of the larger social–cultural and physical environment, and how these ethnotheories in turn affect parents' perceptions of children's cognitive, perceptual, and moral capacities, and thus also parental treatment of children. Victoria Burbank (1988; Burbank and Chisholm, in press), for example, has shown how an externally imposed change in marriage options has entrained differences in ethnotheories of appropriate mate choice between teenage Australian Aboriginal girls and their parents, one consequence of which is increased parent–offspring conflict and a marked increase in single parenthood and "incorrect" marriages. And in another Australian Aboriginal group, Annette Hamilton (1982) has shown how children of such "incorrect" marriages may be neglected because of ambiguous cultural expectations about the responsibilities of certain classes of kin toward the child. And as Carol Worthman also noted in her chapter, Robert LeVine (1979, 1988) and Nancy Scheper-Hughes (1985) suggest how parents' perceptions of their children's "survivability" may affect parental investment, and how such perceptions may be contingent on biological properties of the child, local infant-mortality rates, and estimates of future resources the parents may be able to marshall for the child. On the basis of their cross-cultural work, LeVine and Scheper-Hughes argue that "mother-love" is not genetically determined, that mothers are not obligated by their X chromosomes to become "bonded" to their children in the way that many attachment theorists (on the basis of their laboratory research on predominantly white, middle-class mothers in Europe and America) seem to have assumed (for an overview of these issues see Lamb, Thompson, Gardner, Charnov, and Estes 1984).

The view that "mother-love" is not obligate – but situationally contingent on the nature of the mother and child and maternal perceptions of present and future social–emotional and material support for herself and her baby – is the accepted view in life-history theory. With its rationale for expecting a high degree of behavioral flexibility in humans and its commitment to understanding behavioral variability in terms of phenotypic design and socioecological context, life-history theory is suspicious of claims of invariant human nature, and recognizes that women, like other females, are not "designed" for unthinking maternal love and solicitude regardless of conditions, but for the "wise" management of their reproductive and parental capacities contingent on their particular histories and local conditions – as the research of LeVine and Scheper-Hughes shows. Scheper-Hughes, for example, argues that where infant mortality rates are high, mothers will "hedge their bets" and "protect themselves from strong, emotional attachment to their infants through a form of nurturance that is, from the start, somewhat 'impersonal'" (1985: 311). Life-history theory would predict this (see, for example, Stearns' [1976] discussion of reproductive "bet-hedging"). There is nothing in life-history theory that entails the notion that parental love and care are inherited or genetically determined. Instead, they are seen as situationally determined. Life-history theory does suggest that we are "designed" to be sensitive to – to perceive and respond contingently to – certain aspects of our social/cultural and physical environments that have had the most consistent impact on fitness during human evolution. (For viewpoints on the "wise" allocation of parental love and other resources see Burgess and Draper 1989; Burton 1990; Chisholm and Heath 1987; Daly and Wilson 1980; Gelles and Lancaster 1987 [especially the chapters by Daly and Wilson and Wilson and Daly]; Geronimus 1987; Hausfater and Hrdy, 1984.) One goal of the life-history approach is to investigate the role of phenotypic design (e.g., alternative developmental strategies and learning biases) in the perception of these contingencies.

Conclusion

This sort of research by psychological anthropologists provides empirical evidence of how perceptions of the social–cultural and physical environments condition individual decisions about mating and parenting; life-history theory suggests why this should be the case. What we need now is a *natural history* of what Ward Goodenough called "standards for perceiving, believing, evaluating, communicating, and acting" (1970: 99) – and biological anthropology must take seriously the notion that these standards are part of the human phenotype. This will require biological anthropologists to enlist the aid of their psychological colleagues, for a natural history of human beliefs, values, and expectations demands a sophisticated understanding of diverse cultural distinctions as a basis for generating useful typologies. When the variance in these typologies "maps onto" the variance in individuals' developmental experience with such factors as local population density and frequency of social interactions, resource availability, environmental hazards and morbidity/mortality rates, the sex ratio and availability of mates, then biological anthropology will be able to describe human strategies in terms not only of behavior and biology, but also in terms of "psychocultural phenotypes." Life-history research in humans will do well to consider how different peoples construct the meanings that *they* associate with the behaviors and socioecological factors of interest to the scientist, because too narrow a focus on behavior may blind us to differences in the standards people use for perceiving and evaluating their socioecology, for holding beliefs about it, for communicating about it, and ultimately for acting. Without knowledge of these standards we are without an important dimension of the human phenotype, and unsure as to why the behavior we observe agrees (or not) with predictions from evolutionary ecology, whether adaptationist or mechanist. Life-history theory emphasizes the socioecological causes of alternative strategies, but anthropologists applying the principles of life-history theory must consider how local cultures structure individuals' perceptions of resources, and standards for evaluating resources and behavioral alternatives (for analogous arguments see Draper 1989; LeVine and White 1987).

This is especially important for life-history approaches in anthropology because a critical category of resources for humans seem to be *emotional* resources. By "emotional resource" I mean the value – the emotional and/or moral satisfaction – that accrues to social interactions and bonds that are perceived as continuing and somehow "worthwhile." The optimality arguments of mainstream evolutionary ecology usually focus on "resources" and "value" that have a *material* nature. One reason for this is that there will often be (or have been) an evolutionarily adaptive connection between the tendency to experience certain perceptions or feelings in certain situations and to enjoy certain material rewards as a result. Another reason, however, is that material items like number of offspring and kilocalories per hour are easier to define and measure than aspects of the human psyche like satisfaction, fear, or pride that have a nonmaterial value.

The metaphorical ("as if") application of the concept of strategy to humans – or any species – is not wrong. It's just that with people we have the means to do so much better. We are animals, but for very good evolutionary reasons we are not *just* another animal. For a mature biological anthropology, and one that can capitalize on the excitement that life-history theory is bringing to biology, we need now to put people in biology. This will include the adoption of methods used by psychological anthropologists for describing variation in the human psyche, for that is what stands at the intersection of human biology and the local environment.

NOTE

My thinking about the relationships between biological and psychological anthropology owes much to Victoria K. Burbank's special insight and suspicion of received wisdom. I have been helped also by the comments of Monique Borgerhoff Mulder, Pat Draper, Jeff Long, Cathy Lutz, and Geoff White (who are nonetheless unlikely to agree with everything I have said). The preparation of this chapter was supported in part by the Agricultural Experiment Station, University of California, Davis.

REFERENCES

Alcorta, C. S. 1982. Paternal Behavior and Group Competition. *Behavior Science Research* 17: 3–23

Barkow, J. 1984. The Distance between Genes and Culture. *Journal of Anthropological Research* 40: 367–385

1989. *Darwin, Sex, and Status: Biological Approaches to Mind and Culture*. Toronto: University of Toronto Press

Barkow, J., L. Cosmides, and J. Tooby, eds. 1992. *The Adapted Mind: Evolutionary Psychology and the Generation of Culture*. New York: Oxford University Press

Bateson, P. P. G. 1976. Rules and Reciprocity in Behavioral Development. In P. P. G. Bateson and R. A. Hinde, eds., *Growing Points in Ethology*. Cambridge: Cambridge University Press

1982. Behavioural Development and Evolutionary Processes. In King's College Sociobiology Study Group, Cambridge, *Current Problems in Sociobiology*. Cambridge: Cambridge University Press.

Belsky, J., L. Steinberg, L. and P. Draper. 1991. Childhood Experience, Interpersonal Development, and Reproductive Strategy: An Evolutionary Theory of Socialization. *Child Development* 62: 647–670

Bernard, J. 1975. Adolescence and Socialization for Motherhood. In S. E. Dragastin and G. H. Elder, eds., *Adolescence in the Life Cycle*. New York: John Wiley

Betzig, L., M. Borgerhoff Mulder, and P. Turke, eds. 1988. *Human Reproductive Behavior: A Darwinian Perspective*. Cambridge: Cambridge University Press

Bowlby, J. 1969. *Attachment*. New York: Basic Books

Boyce, M. S., ed. 1988. *Evolution of Life Histories of Mammals*. New Haven: Yale University Press

Boyd, R. and P. J. Richerson. 1985. *Culture and the Evolutionary Process*. Chicago: University of Chicago Press

Burbank, V. K. 1988. *Aboriginal Adolescence: Maidenhood in an Australian Community*. New Brunswick, NJ: Rutgers University Press

Burbank, V. K. and J. S. Chisholm. In press. Adolescent Pregnancy and Parenthood in an Australian Aboriginal Community. In G. Herdt and M. Busse, eds. *Adolescence in the Pacific*. Cambridge: Cambridge University Press

Burgess, R. L. and P. Draper. 1989. The Explanation of Family Violence: The Role of Biological, Behavioral, and Cultural Selection. In L. Ohlin and M. Tonry, eds., *Crime and Justice: An Annual Review of Research* vol. XI. Chicago: University of Chicago Press

Burton, L. M. 1990. Teenage Childbearing as an Alternative Life-course Strategy in Multigenerational Black Families. *Human Nature* 1(2): 123–143

Callan, H. 1984. The Imagery of Choice in Sociobiology. *Man* (N.S.) 19: 404–420

Caro, T. M. and P. P. G. Bateson 1986. Organization and Ontogeny of Alternative Tactics. *Animal Behavior* 34: 1,483–1,499

Changeux, J.-P. 1985. *Neuronal Man*. Translated by L. Carey. New York: Pantheon

Chisholm, J. S. 1983. *Navajo Infancy: An Ethological Study of Child Development*. New York: Aldine

1988. Toward a Developmental Evolutionary Ecology of Humans. In K. MacDonald, ed., *Sociobiological Perspectives on Human Development*. New York: Springer-Verlag

Chisholm, J. S. and G. D. Heath 1987. Evolution and Pregnancy: A Biosocial View of Prenatal Influences. In C. M. Super, ed. *The Role of Culture in Developmental Disorder*. New York: Academic Press

Cosmides, L. and J. Tooby. 1987. From Evolution to Behavior: Evolutionary Psychology as the Missing Link. In J. Dupre, ed., *The Latest on the Best: Essays on Evolution and Optimality*. Cambridge, MA: MIT Press

1989. Evolutionary Psychology and the Generation of Culture, Part II. *Ethology and Sociobiology* 10: 51–97

Cutler, W. B. and C. R. Garcia 1980. The Psychoneuroendocrinology of the Ovulatory Cycles of Women. *Psychoneuroendocrinology* 5:89–111

Cutler, W. B., G. Preti, G. R. Huggins, B. Erickson, and C. R. Garcia. 1985. Sexual Behavior Frequency and Biphasic Ovulatory Type Menstrual Cycles. *Physiology and Behavior* 34: 805–810

Cvetkovich, G., B. Grote, E. J. Lieberman, and W. Miller. 1978. Sex Role Development and Teenage Fertility-Related Behavior. *Adolescence* 8(50): 231–236

Daly, M. and M. Wilson 1980. Discriminative Parental Solicitude: A Biological Perspective. *Journal of Marriage and the Family* 42: 277–288

1983. *Sex, Evolution and Behavior* (2nd edn.) Boston: Willard Grant Press

Dickemann, M. 1979. Female Infanticide, Reproductive Strategies, and Social Stratification: A Preliminary Model. In N. A. Chagnon and W. Irons, eds., *Evolutionary Biology and Human Social Behavior*. North Scituate, MA: Duxbury Press

Divale, W. T. and M. Harris. 1976. Population, Warfare, and the Male Supremacist Complex. *American Anthropologist* 78: 529–537

Draper, P. 1989. African Marriage Systems: Perspectives from Evolutionary Ecology. *Ethology and Sociobiology* 10: 145–169

Draper, P. and H. Harpending. 1982. Father Absence and Reproductive Strategy: An Evolutionary Perspective. *Journal of Anthropological Research* 38: 225–273

1987. Parent investment and the child's learning environment. In J. B. Lancaster, A. S. Rossi, J. Altmann, and L. R. Sherrod, eds., *Parenting Across the Life Span: Biosocial Dimensions*. New York: Aldine de Gruyter

1988. A Sociobiological Perspective on the Development of Human Reproductive Strategies. In K. MacDonald, ed., *Sociobiological Perspectives on Human Development*. New York: Springer-Verlag

Fagen, R. 1982 . Evolutionary Issues in the Development of Behavioral Flexibility. In P. P. G. Bateson and R. A. Hinde, eds., *Perspectives in Ethology*, vol. V. New York: Plenum

Fisher, S. 1973. *The Female Orgasm: Psychology, Physiology, Fantasy*. New York: Basic Books

Gelles, R. J. and J. B. Lancaster, eds. 1987. *Child Abuse and Neglect: Biosocial Dimensions*. New York: Aldine de Gruyter

Geronimus, A. T. 1987. On Teenage Childbearing and Neonatal Mortality in the United States. *Population and Development Review* 13(2): 245–279

Goodenough, W. 1970. *Description and Comparison in Cultural Anthropology*. Chicago: Aldine

Goodwin, B. C. 1972. Biology and Meaning. In C. H. Waddington, ed., *Towards a Theoretical Biology* vol. III. Chicago: Aldine

1982. Genetic Epistemology and Constructionist Biology. *Revue Internationale de Philosophie* 142–143: 527–548

Gould, S. J. 1977. *Ontogeny and Phylogeny*. Cambridge, MA: Harvard University Press

1982. Change in Developmental Timing as a Mechanism of Macroevolution. In J. T. Bonner, ed., *Evolution and Development*. Dahlem Konferenzen. New York: Springer-Verlag

Gould, S. J. and R. C. Lewontin 1979. The Spandrels of San Marco and the Panglossian Paradigm: A Critique of the Adaptationist Programme. *Proceedings of the Royal Society of London B* 205: 581–598

Gruber, H. E. 1974. *Darwin on Man*. New York: Dutton

Guttentag, M. and P. F. Secord. 1983. *Too Many Women? The Sex Ratio Question*. Beverly Hills: Sage Publications

Hamilton, A. 1982. Child Health and Child Care in a Desert Community, 1970–1971. In J. Reid, ed., *Body, Land, and Spirit: Health and Healing in Aboriginal Society*. St. Lucia, Queensland: University of Queensland Press

Hamilton, W. D. 1964. The Genetical Evolution of Social Behavior, I and II. *Journal of Theoretical Biology* 12: 12–45

Hausfater, G. and Hrdy, S. B., eds., 1984. *Infanticide: Comparative and Evolutionary Perspectives*. New York: Aldine de Gruyter

Hinde, R. A. 1987. *Individuals, Relationships, and Culture: Links Between Ethology and the Social Sciences*. Cambridge: Cambridge University Press

1990. The Causes of Development from the Perspective of an Integrated Developmental Science. In G. Butterworth and P. Bryant, eds., *Causes of Development: Interdisciplinary Perspectives*. London: Harvester Press

Horn, H. S. and D. J. Rubenstein. 1984. Behavioural Adaptations and Life History. In J. R. Krebs and N. B. Davies, eds., *Behavioural Ecology: An Evolutionary Approach* (2nd edn.) Oxford: Oxford University Press

Johnston, T. D. 1982. Selective Costs and Benefits in the Evolution of Learning. In J. S. Rosenblatt, R. A. Hinde, C. Beer, and M-C. Busnel, eds. *Advances in the Study of Behavior* (vol. XII). New York: Academic Press

Jones, B., J. Leeton, J. McLeod, and C. Wood 1972. Factors Influencing the Age of Menarche in a Lower Socioeconomic Group in Melbourne. *Medical Journal of Australia* 2: 533–535

Kitcher, P. 1985. *Vaulting Ambition*. Cambridge, MA: MIT Press

Lamb, M. E., R. A. Thompson, W. P. Gardner, E. L. Charnov, E. L., and D. Estes. 1984. Security of Infantile Attachment as Assessed in the "Strange Situation": Its Study and Biological Interpretation. *Behavioral and Brain Sciences* 7: 127–171

Lancaster, J. B. and C. S. Lancaster. 1983. Parental Investment: The Hominid Adaptation. In D. J. Ortner, ed. *How Humans Adapt: A Biocultural Odyssey*. Washington, DC: Smithsonian Institution Press

1986. The Watershed: Changes in Parental Investment and Family-Formation Strategies in the Course of Human Evolution. In J. B. Lancaster, A. S. Rossi,

J. Altmann, and L. R. Sherrod, eds., *Parenting Across the Life Span: Biosocial Dimensions*. New York: Aldine de Gruyter

Leak, G. and S. B. Christopher. 1982. Freudian Psychoanalysis and Sociobiology: A Synthesis. *American Psychologist* 37(3): 313–322

LeVine, R. A. 1979. Child Rearing as Cultural Adaptation. In P. H. Leiderman, S. Tulkin, and A. Rosenfeld, eds., *Culture and Infancy*. New York: Academic Press

1988. Human Parental Care: Universal Goals, Cultural Strategies, Individual Behavior. In R. A. LeVine, P. M. Miller, and M. M. West, eds., *Parental Behavior in Diverse Societies*. New Directions for Child Development 40. San Francisco: Jossey-Bass

LeVine, R. A. and M. White., 1987. Parenthood in Social Transformation. In J. Lancaster, J. Altmann, A. Rossi, and L. Sherrod, eds., *Parenting Across the Lifespan: Biosocial Dimensions*. New York: Aldine de Gruyter

Lewontin, R. C. 1978. Adaptation. *Scientific American* 239: 212–233

1982. Organism and Environment. In H. C. Plotkin, ed., *Learning, Development, and Culture*. London: John Wiley

MacDonald, K. 1986. *Civilization and its Discontents* Revisited: Freud as an Evolutionary Biologist. *Journal of Social and Biological Structures* 9: 213–220

Offit, A. 1981. *Night Thoughts: Reflections of a Sex Therapist*. New York: Congdon and Lattes

Oyama, S. 1985. *The Ontogeny of Information: Developmental Systems and Evolution*. Cambridge: Cambridge University Press

Parker, G. and J. Maynard Smith. 1990. Optimality Theory in Evolutionary Biology. *Nature* 348: 27–33

Paul, R. 1984. Editorial. *Ethos* 12(2): 99–104

Piaget, J. 1971. *Biology and Knowledge*. Chicago: University of Chicago Press

1978. *Behavior and Evolution*. New York: Pantheon

Plotkin, H. C., ed. 1982. *Learning, Development, and Culture*. London: John Wiley

Plotkin, H. C. and F. J. Odling-Smee. 1979. Learning, Change, and Evolution. *Advances in the Study of Behavior* 10: 1–41

1981. A Multiple-Level Model of Evolution and its Implications for Sociobiology. *The Behavioral and Brain Sciences* 4: 225–268

Rancour-Laferriere, D. 1985. *Signs of the Flesh: An Essay on the Evolution of Hominid Sexuality*. New York: Mouton de Gruyter

Scarr, S. and K. McCartney. 1983. How People Make Their Own Environments: A Theory of Genotype → Environment Effects. *Child Development* 54: 424–435

Scheper-Hughes, N. 1985. Culture, Scarcity, and Maternal Thinking: Maternal Detachment and Infant Survival in a Brazilian Shantytown. *Ethos* 13: 291–317

Shore, B. 1988. Interpretation under Fire. *Anthropological Quarterly* 61(4): 161–176

Slobodkin, L. B. and A. Rapoport. 1974. An Optimal Strategy of Evolution. *Quarterly Review of Biology* 49: 181–200

Smith, E. A. 1987. Optimization Theory in Anthropology: Applications and Critiques. In J. Dupre, ed., *The Latest on the Best: Essays on Evolution and Optimality*. Cambridge, MA: MIT Press

Stack, C. B. 1974. *All Our Kin: Strategies for Survival in a Black Community*. New York: Harper & Row

Stearns, S. C. 1976. Life History Tactics: A Review of the Ideas. *Quarterly Review of Biology* 51(1): 3–47

1977. The Evolution of Life History Traits: A Critique of the Theories and A Review of the Data. *Annual Review of Ecology and Systematics* 8: 145–171

1982. The Role of Development in the Evolution of Life Histories. In J. T. Bonner, ed. *Evolution and Development*. Dahlem Konferenzen. New York: Springer-Verlag

Sulloway, F. 1982. Freud and Biology: The Hidden Legacy. In W. R. Woodward and M. G. Ash, eds., *The Problematic Science: Psychology in Nineteenth-century Thought*. New York: Praeger

Super, C. and S. Harkness. 1986. The Developmental Niche: A Conceptualization at the Interface of Child and Culture. *International Journal of Behavioral Development* 9: 545–569

Surbey, M. 1990. Family Composition, Stress, and Human Menarche. In F. Bercovitch and T. Zeigler, eds., *The Socioendocrinology of Primate Reproduction*. New York: Allan Liss

Symons, D. 1987. If we're All Darwinians, What's the Fuss About? In C. B. Crawford, M. F. Smith, and D. L. Krebs, eds., *Sociobiology and Psychology*. Hillsdale, NJ: Lawrence Erlbaum

1989. A Critique of Darwinian Anthropology. *Ethology and Sociobiology* 10: 131–144

Tiger, L. and R. Fox. 1966. The Zoological Perspective in the Social Sciences. *Man* 1(1): 75–81

1971. *The Imperial Animal*. New York: Holt, Rinehart, and Winston

Tooby, J. and L. Cosmides. 1989. Evolutionary Psychology and the Generation of Culture, Part I. *Ethology and Sociobiology* 10: 29–49

Trivers, R. L. 1972. Parental Investment and Sexual Selection. In B. Campbell, ed., *Sexual Selection and the Descent of Man*. Chicago: Aldine

Trivers, R. L. and D. E. Willard 1973. Natural Selection of Parental Ability to Vary the Sex Ratio of Offspring. *Science* 179: 90–92

Uddenberg, N. 1974. Psychological Aspects of Sexual Inadequacy in Women. *Journal of Psychosomatic Research* 18: 33–47

Udry, J. R. and R. L. Cliquet. 1982. A Cross-Cultural Examination of the Relationship Between Ages at Menarche, Marriage, and First Birth. *Demography* 19(1): 53–63

Wachs, T. 1983. The Use and Abuse of Environment in Behavior-Genetic Research. *Child Development* 54: 396–407

Waddington, C. H. 1968. The Theory of Evolution Today. In A. Koestler and R. Smythies, eds., *Beyond Reductionism*. New York: Macmillan

West, M. J., A. P. King, and A. A. Arberg. 1988. The Inheritance of Niches: The Role of Ecological Legacies in Ontogeny. In E. Blass, ed., *Developmental Psychobiology and Behavioral Ecology*. New York: Plenum

West, M. M. and M. J. Konner. 1976. The Role of the Father: An Anthropological Perspective. In M. Lamb, ed. *The Role of the Father in Child Development*. New York: John Wiley

Whiting, J. W. M. and B. Whiting. 1975. Aloofness and Intimacy of Husbands and Wives: A Cross-Cultural Study. *Ethos* 3: 183–207

Whiting, J. W. M., V. Burbank, and M. Ratner. 1986. The Duration of Maidenhood Across Cultures. In J. B. Lancaster and B. A. Hamburg, eds., *School-Age Pregnancy and Parenthood: Biosocial Dimensions*. New York: Aldine de Gruyter

Williams, G. C. 1966. *Adaptation and Natural Selection*. Princeton: Princeton University Press

Wilson, E. O. 1975. *Sociobiology: The New Synthesis*. Cambridge, MA: Harvard University Press

Wittenberger, J. F. 1981. *Animal Social Behavior*. Boston: Duxbury Press

8 Cupid and Psyche: investigative syncretism in biological and psychosocial anthropology

Carol M. Worthman

Tension between body and mind has been integral to Western views of human existence. This ancient theme finds expression in a pair of adversarial lovers, the god Cupid and the mortal Psyche, whose remarkable durability in Western imagination attests to the persistence of the tension they represent. Cupid's arrows incite passions in their victims, implying a humoral causality in experience similar to the attribution: "hormones made him do it." Psyche, on the other hand, embodies the human capacity to create a self-determined, evolved persona. Representing the divide between views of human behavior as determined or emergent, Cupid and Psyche have long been consigned to alienation in Western conceptions (Popper and Eccles 1983: 148–210).

Several conceptual trends in this and the previous century have, however, recognized synergy between biology and culture in human experience. Although Cartesian views had reinforced the distinction of mind from body (LeDoux 1986), the nineteenth century brought renewed efforts to unite these elements because the mind was considered the fulcrum of biosocial coevolution. Thinkers from Darwin to Freud (1895) subscribed to this notion, which, along with linear cultural evolution and "primitive mind," was subsequently rejected by social anthropologists in favor of superorganismic views of self and culture (reviewed in Hallowell 1960; Kroeber 1917). Again, research directions diverged to social and biological paradigms for explaining human diversity. These paths collided spectacularly when sociobiological theory precipitated awareness that both paradigms claim overlapping explanatory domains: motivation, social behavior, and the constitution of self.

This chapter will consider why Cupid and Psyche should be reunited in the study of human experience. It surveys strides in anthropology, psychology, and physiology that make their reintegration necessary and possible. The fact is, that Cupid and Psyche, while divorced conceptually, continue to "carry on" under our noses: their relationship represents a central dimension in human experience that has often remained hidden not only from social scientists but also from subjective perception. The "work of culture" relies significantly on "body work": data reviewed in this chapter demonstrate that cultural influences on cognition and behavior are grounded in a "hidden dimension" of their interaction with biological structure and function. One dynamic behind this dimension is that ontogeny is a central feature of individual human adaptation, so that structure and function are "designed" to interact with the (largely social) environment to determine perception and behavior. Complementarily, culture is often "designed" to play upon biological features. My task in this chapter is to explore briefly the implications of biology for psychological anthropology, to attempt an integration of current knowledge, and to share a vision of the routes to important questions that a biopsychological anthropology of human experience might open.

Overview

Psychological anthropologists remain in at least two "minds" about foundations for human experience. Of late, we have seen rejection of a search for psychological universals and reclamation of the realm of the subjective as an independent, locally constructed domain (Harré 1986; Lutz 1985; Shweder 1984). Further, the central role of culture has been asserted by some to determine not only patterns of feeling and thought, but also the primary affects of a likewise socially constructed self (Geertz 1980; Rosaldo 1984). These concepts, by reaffirming the multilevel and plastic properties of subjectivity and self, have focused anthropological attention on processes of social construction. Recently, in developing the concept of cultural psychology, Shweder (1990) stresses the dialectic between intentional worlds (cultures) and intentional persons (psyches), in which intentionality is action guided by mental constructs. To elaborate this dialectic relationship, Shweder draws on frameworks for analyzing genotype–environment interactions (Scarr and McCartney 1983) as a model for mutually constituting dimensions. Because he sets cultural psychology at the person–environment level, Schweder bypasses the genotype–environment (or phenotypic) level. This chapter argues that the latter level is crucial: it aims to show that the person is actively constituted as a phenotype that is, in turn, constituted by the intentional person and the environment (intentional or not). Since phenotype results from a process, this perspective is developmental or historical.

In this chapter, I argue for cultural *bio*psychology on the basis that full understanding of processes of social construction and the work of culture will depend on integrating brain and body as substantive substrates of experience. This is one route by which anthropology, while viewing societies and individuals as historical products, may yet escape becoming historical analysis by renewing its attention to the proximal, contingent processes that shape social phenomena, as acted and experienced by individuals. Further, it will be argued that quantitative and "encorporated" thinking of this kind is necessary to achieve a truly critical, reflexive anthropology. In the first section, on mind and matter, I discuss current understanding of neural development and function to illustrate how biology displays emergent properties which possess a spectrum of relationships (from independent to dialectic) to emergent properties of culture. Then, human development, emotion, and illness are analyzed in turn to demonstrate how the person–body–culture dynamic operates. Human development, which perhaps most vividly and accessibly exhibits these co-emergent processes, is discussed first. The next section deals with emotion, emphasizing its conditioned, physiologic dimensions. Finally, it is urged that viewing person, body, and culture as mutually constituting domains can address dysfunction as well as function, and is needed to explain illness more fully.

Mind and matter

The role of the body in the mind has been considered as a significant source of primary metaphors in thought (Douglas 1970; Lakoff and Johnson 1980; Johnson 1987), a concept that has richly illuminated the body's role as a referential locus for everyday experience. Complementary to this perspective we may further ask: what about the mind in the body? Recently, neuroscientists have contributed models of mind and self that include structural–functional properties of brain. Examples include Winson's (1986) reformulation of the bases of the unconscious and Sacks' (1987) analyses of neurologically deficient states for the foundations of self and self-aware experience. Changeux (1985) has presented a closely reasoned, well-supported argument for the developmental–neurologic bases of human imagination, while Edelman has proposed that selection processes underlie neural organization and perception (Edelman 1978, 1987).

Two aspects of the extraordinary picture of the neurobiology of mind which has emerged have significant implications for psychological anthropology: first, much fine structure and function of the brain arises with experience, which apparently shapes them through an ontogenetic selection process of stimulus reinforcement and pruning. Receiving and processing information thus actively configure neural circuits and the larger functional complexes of association and memory (Changeux 1985; Edelman 1987). Second, the workings of the nervous system preclude a concept of "authentic," pre-interpretive sensory reality that is independent of culturally or historically shaped interpretive schemata. Considered together, these two insights suggest that the biological construction of reality is both in part independent of and partly interactive with the social construction of reality for the individual. The first point will be expanded in the subsequent section on development; the lack of a raw authentic sensory reality is discussed below.

Biology of the brain is the dynamic substrate of human experience. Current theory and data about cerebral function strongly affirm the absence of uninterpreted, "pure" experience. Rather, all subjective awareness is the result of interpretive processes on at least three prior levels. First, neural circuits are themselves integrating, with patterns of function and association that are unique historical products. Thus, the pattern of inputs to the brain denoting a stimulus reflects the organization of sensory input as well as the stimulus itself. Second, sensory modalities such as sight and hearing are represented in multiple areas of the brain, each of which generates a slightly different picture of any input. The number of areas to which visual information is projected in the human brain is not known, but the rhesus macaque has eight in the association regions near the primary visual cortex, compared to two in the hedgehog. Likewise, the ear connects to six cortical areas in the rhesus, as opposed to three in the tree shrew or two in the squirrel. This proliferation of sensory representations in the primate brain may greatly enhance the number and complexity of contextual features that are attended to. Each representation delineates a specific attribute (such as movement or surface orientation in visual images) that complements and "competes" with representations from other areas (Baron 1987: 134–213; Changeux 1985: 117–119).

The "Rashomon effect" (Heider 1988) therefore has a biological basis: the question "Why do you see things as you do?" comprises a neurological as well as a psychosocial dimension, for any perception is composed of multiple representational variants and is thus heterologous. Furthermore, a third level of preconscious sensory interpretation is created through extensive processing (integration and editing) by the brain of incoming sensory stimuli that precedes their reaching conscious awareness. Libet and colleagues (Libet, Wright, Feinstein, and Pearl 1979) have demonstrated that the organization of cerebral operation creates a half-second gap of preconscious central sensory processing before we become subjectively aware of a sensory input: while incoming sensory information takes just 15–25 msec to reach the brain, we become conscious of it only one half-second later. Rapid, even complex and purposive, behavioral responses that arise in the interim do so un- or preconsciously (Libet 1978). The timing gap is concealed from our conscious selves by temporal referral of subjective awareness of a stimulus backward to the time of its initial arrival in the brain.

Thus, subjective perception ("consciousness") is in many essential ways a preedited, preconscious construct. Recognition that the brain operates through multiple parallel processing, of which subjective consciousness represents only a small segment, has reinforced the notion of a "plurality of consciousness" (Oakley and Eames 1985). The presence of multiple streams of central information processing, outside of subjective awareness, has been shown in split-brain patients, hypnosis, and anaesthesia to contribute to affect, memory, and motivation. The extent of subliminal processing has even led some psychologists to question the centrality of subjective awareness in behavior responses (Dixon 1981; Pöppel 1988: 134–147). Such data furthermore suggest how many aspects of social life may relate to streams of consciousness outside of subjective awareness; they support propositions by symbolic and structural anthropologists that the power of certain experiences (symbol, ritual, or myth) arises partly from appeal to pre- or peri-conscious awareness. Moreover, they strongly validate psychological anthropology's attention to the unconscious as an important stage for socially mediated experience that also grounds human action.

The currency of perception, then, is not "pure" sensory input, but multiple overlapping representations that are selected in a neural system the properties of which are a product of ongoing and prior activity. Cerebral function is thus predicated on emergent properties. This insight points to a larger reason why biology significantly contributes to the varieties of human experience.

The preeminent role ascribed to culture in development and dynamics of self has devolved in part from the assertion that biology plays an insufficiently large part in human experience to contribute significantly to its elucidation. That this role is open to question comes mainly from the widespread assumption, among biologists and social scientists alike, that culture and self are emergent, while biology is determined. In this view, emergent features possess transcendent properties that cannot be explained as the sum of constituent parts, while determined ones can. The emergent qualities of society and self are adduced to explain the enormous variation we observe in both, while biology should provide the material basis of species universality and the broad physical boundaries of potential. According to this outlook, explanations for the majority of meaningful human variation (i.e., the range of human experience) derive from properties of culture and mind.

Over a century of progress in life sciences has blurred the emergent–determined dichotomy by abundantly demonstrating that biology, too, is emergent in life histories. Genetics provides the programmatic basis of individual variability. But ontogeny (development of the individual) evidences adaptive physical indeterminacy and sensitivity to experience that bring an emergent dimension to phenotypic variability. Thus, corporeal selves are also contingent: culturally mediated experiences can place an indelible stamp on function and physique. The converse is also true: biology and culture are dialectically related in human experience.[1]

Development

Conclusions of the previous section will here be applied to central questions in psychological anthropology, namely, the shaping of the emerging self and the bases of adult experience. Psychological anthropology has for some time concerned itself with child development, especially with the influences of childrearing practices on psychosocial and physical development (see Harkness, this book). Numerous investigators (e.g., John Whiting [Gunders and Whiting 1968; Landauer and Whiting 1980], Charles Super [1976], James Chisolm [1983], and Melvin Konner [1977]) have examined this interaction in infants and young children in specific cultural settings. Such studies have demonstrated direct effects of culturally prescribed parental behaviors on the physical as well as behavioral and cognitive development of children. To a large degree, however, the study of culture and personality has been founded on a perspective of culturally constructed ontogeny. In this section, I will discuss why attention to biologic processes can considerably augment our understanding of socialization and individuation.

Both the contingent and determined qualities of physical form and function are nowhere more apparent than in human development. At conception, the organism is endowed with genetic potentials that are already interacting with their milieu. Subsequent development normally describes a guided trajectory to produce a viable adult. However, it is neither efficient nor practicable that all aspects of development be programmed; instead, boundaries are set and patterns established that enable details of structure and operation to emerge. Developmental processes demonstrate sensitivity to context; some functions even depend on stimuli from the environment to shape their normal differentiation. Indeed, certain functional domains may be more likely to display developmental contingency and plasticity than others: information processing is such a domain. Early development of the peripheral and central nervous systems is characterized by overproduction of neurons, dendrites, and synapses. Pruning of excess through differential neuronal and synaptic death responds to patterns of stimulus and use that selectively stabilize pathways (Edelman 1987). Not only fine structure of the nervous system, but also aspects of its organization are designed to be contingent on patterns of stimulation for guiding development. The brain provides numerous examples of this phenomenon, one of the best-studied though less subtle of which is the dependence of structural organization of the visual cortex on receiving stimuli during a critical developmental period (LeVay, Wiesel, and Hubel 1981). Pathology provides a vivid example: an infant with congenital cataracts will experience irreversible impairment of depth perception if the condition is rectified late.

Susceptibility of structures and functions of the developing body to environmental inputs creates windows of maturational process called critical, or sensitive, periods (Cowan 1979; Gottlieb 1973). Insofar as culture determines the experiences to which the developing individual is exposed, it also may influence development in sensitive periods. Language acquisition is a well-studied instance (Changeux 1985: 241–246). Early language exposure influences ability to discriminate phonemes (i.e., frequency patterns): individuals not exposed to phonetic contrasts in childhood do not distinguish them as categories in adulthood (Winson 1986: 163–168). On the broadest level, the child depends on learning opportunities during the language-acquisition phase in order to attain speech competence. Children deprived of these opportunities experience considerable difficulty in learning to speak and understand language later. The difficulty is most severe among socially deprived feral children, for as Ochs and Schieffelin (1984) have pointed out, socialization processes are intimately bound to the social context of language acquisition.

In short, the person, or phenotype, is the outcome of interactive cultural-contextual and biological processes. Behavior and cognition, as well as physical attributes, all emerge through this dialectic. Therefore, we need to study all three domains if we are to understand how persons – experiences and behaviors – are constituted.

Given that many biological parameters, such as brain structure, are not directly accessible, how might anthropologists probe the interplay of biology and culture in ontogeny? Knowledge of the physical status of developing individuals can provide a basis for comparison within and between groups, thus partly resolving a central tension in anthropology. The discipline exhibits tension between particularist and generalist analysis, for particularist analysis reveals local process and variation, while summary characterization allows comparative analysis. In the above example on language acquisition, generalizations about parenting in one society must be made to compare it with another, while details about parental behaviors within the society are requisite for dynamic analysis. Selective inclusion of biological variables would help to delineate the bases of variability on both levels, by providing index variables for comparison across individuals and societies. For example, the largely universal physiology of growth and function provides indices with cross-population validity. Thus, if a young person is identified as being in the speech-acquisition phase or in a pubertal stage 2, he/she can be characterized for comparison of experience within and between cultures.

The corporeal dimension (especially, infant and child wellbeing) has lately been included in studies of parental behaviors. Factors that influence parenting styles and strategies, particularly of mothers, have been studied by Robert LeVine (1979) and Nancy Scheper-Hughes (1985). Scheper-Hughes' Brazilian study demonstrated that maternal behavior is not passively shaped by culture and biology, but also rationally self determined by maternal perception of her material circumstances and of the viability of the child. Jenkins and Heywood (1985) reported that caregiving by Amele (lowland Papua New Guinea) mothers is guided by their judgment of their infant's status within a six-stage emic model of infant development.

On a more proximal level, the physical status of an individual is relevant to the concerns of psychological anthropology in at least three important ways: first, it influences the social treatment of the individual; second, it is an autonomous source of subjective experience; third, it mediates specific effects exerted by experience. These points will be discussed in turn.

Perceptible physical status exerts pervasive effects on social treatment of individuals across the life cycle. Every society has schedules of experiences that are linked to physical condition. The emic model guiding infant treatment by Amele mothers, mentioned above, is an example. Physical maturational statuses that societies have been reported to target for cultural management include suckling, weaning, teething, walking, talking, pubertal onset, menarche, and height gain or size. Socially regulated domains often linked to physical ontogeny include diet (composition, timing, and quantity), rites of passage and rituals, work, sexuality, and residence. Thus, social assignment of activities, roles, and statuses frequently attends to the physical state of the asignee, and changes in physical state commonly trigger changes in social treatment and role assignment. Physical statuses that are monitored are many, ranging from gender and size to wellness and reproductive state.

Too often, social scientists have viewed physical states as static categories, rather than as physiologically dynamic potentials. Societies, however, have *not* missed this point. Society not only pays attention to the physical condition of its members, but may also time experiences to coincide with biologically mediated sensitivities or capacities in the individual that modulate the effect of cultural interventions. Study of Kikuyu adolescents in Kenya (Worthman 1987) found that socializing events (circumcision, clitoridectomy, removal to a boys' house) were temporally linked to physical development (breast stage, height attainment, seminal emission). These linkages were not all explicit at the prescriptive or conscious level. Such practices not only target psychosocial status but also select individuals in a specific range of developmental states. In this case, society uses the sign of pubertal development as an entrainer, or timer, of cultural interventions in experience. That some experiences are offered solely to individuals in specific physical states may mean not only that that state (e.g., reproductive maturity, illness) is a social problem to be managed or interpreted, but also that a biological vulnerability or potential is being culturally shaped or exploited.

Further, physical processes themselves generate experience. Shifts in developmental stage illustrate this vividly: the fear of strangers experienced by an infant achieving sufficient brain maturation to perceive pattern incongruences, the novel realizations ushered in when a child attains a new cognitive plane, or the new sensations engendered by physical changes and endocrine states of puberty exemplify bodily contributions to experience. These are plastic to social construction.

Finally, physical states may mediate effects exerted by experience; social construction of experience may be designed to enhance these effects. Society commonly employs two means to enhance physiologic homogeneity of social actors. The first, selection on the basis of physical status, was discussed above; the second, entrainment, is invoked when specific experiences involve complex behavioral schedules that have a common large effect on the physiology of participants (e.g., spirit quests, Gregorian chants, !Kung healing dances). Rites of passage regularly employ both devices, combining participant selection with subjection to a behavioral regimen (diet, activity, social stress) that assures a convergence of physiological states (Lex 1979). Direct social control over physiological condition is thereby effected. Studies of puberty rites have often overlooked the point that optimal *physical* development (culturally defined) is frequently an overt social goal. Male initiation in several New Guinea societies (Herdt 1982) exemplifies orchestration of massive, sustained social regulation of physical experience in conjunction with ritual and formal socialization.

At this point, we could all cite innumerable instances of relative cultural indifference to physical state in determining experience. For instance, for every society that ties circumcision to a maturational marker such as menarcheal status, we encounter others that link it to arbitrary social statuses or cycles (e.g., parental status, age-set formation) or some vague range of sizes and ages. Rather than being refuted by this enormous cultural variability, the relevance of biology to comparative psychological anthropology arises most obviously from this fact. Indeed, explanations for variability in the evolution of self and adult experience must rest in part on examination of cultural variability in this respect. To extend the example of circumcision: the operation's cognitive impact and behavioral outcome can be expected to differ in a culture that ties this event closely to physical status (motor skills, size) from one where it occurs anywhere between ages eleven and twenty-one.

Why anticipate that timing of experiences relative to physical developmental status will have important effects on cognition, affect, and behavior? Critical or sensitive periods, discussed previously, open windows of differential sensitivity or developmental vulnerability to environmental inputs. Maturational shifts are frequently accompanied by periods of accelerated learning. Endocrine changes that drive or coincide with these shifts influence motivational and affective states that are quickly reinforced by learning (Worthman 1990). Ontogeny, then, is punctuated by periods of "prepared learning" during which exposure to certain experiences may have long-term organizational impact; exposure to the same experiences at other times may have little effect.

Hence, not only the existence and content but also the manner of timing rites of passage and other culturally determined experiences may shape the emergent self. In addition, the degree of fit between cultural interventions and physical maturational status may vary widely among individuals and contribute to interindividual differences in quality and impact of experience. On the population level, these effects of relative timing may even contribute to degree of population variation with respect to personal developmental history and organization of self.

The concept of relative timing provides a basis for generating testable hypotheses. Relevant field data could readily be collected by addressing the following questions. (1) On what basis is an individual included in or excluded from an experience? For instance, for what reasons is a boy circumcised or moved out of the house at one time rather than another? For any ritual life history event, the ethnographer should ask: why this person? Why now? These questions should be answered on a case-by-case basis to obtain a profile of operative criteria for access to experience. Data on perception and decision-making processes in the cultural construction of experience will also be collected in this way. (2) What are the explicit or implicit biological concomitants of these criteria? (3) What is the interindividual variation in timing of and exposure to experiences? What implications does this variability have for quality and outcomes in life history?

In his introduction to a volume of *Ethos* on "Self and Emotion," Robert Levy identifies the need to "show how in various places passions and selves *are* locally shaped" and "that cultural experience affects not only the field of actions, but the very structure of the actor, that it, in Rosaldo's words, 'constitutes individuals as subjects'" (Levy 1983: 129). The views presented here are entirely congruent with this purpose, except that biology is included as a part of the shaping process, operating dialectically with culture and physical context. Persons are indeed "locally shaped," and culture is a major factor in that process. The self, however, is also grounded in biological experience. Hence, I would strongly concur that the "very structure of the actor" is an outcome of this local process, but that process is a dialectical one involving biological, sociocultural, and material conditions. In that event, culture constitutes subjective individuality no more than biology does. To contribute significantly to a process is not wholly to constitute it.

To summarize the argument thus far: physiologic and cognitive function are, with affect, co-emergent in ontogeny under the mutually constituting influence of culture, with the theater of experience located within *and* outside the person. Physical development represents a series of emerging states that form altered bases of experience, in terms of cognitive-behavioral capacity and biologically based awarenesses. This biologically regulated process exhibits exquisite sensitivity, as it logically should, to many aspects of experience. However, the bases on which individuals are exposed to culturally determined experiences vary significantly between and even within populations. Timing and degree of social accommodation of or indifference to physical states can be a determining factor in the quality and impact of experience – whether it will provoke passing or enduring attitudes.

This developmental model can be hypothetically illustrated by tracing a linkage of menses to puberty rituals and timing of marriage. At her first menses (Time 1), the girl reports her condition to others, or they recognize it. This cue triggers her exposure to rituals of isolation, purification, and adult-role instruction. After first menses and its attendant experiences (Time 2), she is a different person, both as she is perceived and treated by others, and as she experiences and perceives herself. The combination of altered diet, movement restrictions, and boredom experienced in isolation at the time of first menses interacted with her newly adult endocrine state to link into explicit teaching about adult female roles (sexuality, childbearing, and the social control exerted over her new reproductive power) to imprint culturally intended and unintended effects on the organization of feeling and behavior. At Time 2, she may not consciously feel different, but cultural and personal expectations lead her to try to act and feel differently, creating a novel form of self-alienation that may or may not find resolution in culturally prescribed adult gender roles. Furthermore, if her marriageability is enhanced by her being early maturing (that is, she was relatively young at Time 1) (e.g., Kipsigis; Borgerhoff-Mulder 1988), then the initial cue will entrain early marriage to a higher-status spouse, with a larger number of children subsequently born. This chain of experiences will alter her physical state, behavior, and feeling over the rest of her lifetime.

To some degree, the perspective outlined here attempts to operationalize cross-cultural studies by psychological anthropologists who have examined childrearing practices to explain cultural differences in patterns of adult behavior such as warfare, gender roles, and sexual behavior (e.g., the work of John and Beatrice Whiting, Herbert Barry, Carolyn and Melvin Ember, and Alice Schlegel). This approach has uncovered patterns of association; the strategy suggested here may identify proximal processes that create these patterns.

Emotion: passion and sentiment

Earlier sections of this discussion have touched on emotion, for the cultural role in shaping or defining affect is generally conceived as operating ontogenetically. In Western tradition, emotions have often been contrastingly segregated into the innate, pre-rational or irrational and biologically driven (passion), and the acquired, rational or culturally constructed (sentiment) (Gordon 1981; Frank 1988). Both, however, are tightly interwoven threads of subjectivity, for physical and functional properties of mind are fundamentally indissociable. General consensus among anthropologists on this point in principle, is, however, effectively overshadowed by differences over the degree to which biology contributes to diversity in personal experience and, therefore, the extent to which it should be considered in explaining that diversity.

The dynamic role physical processes play in creating and shaping emotion is well documented. Our brains are awash with biochemicals, some of which function as regulators of activity in many neurons. Disturbances of biochemical regulation (via excess, neuronal insensitivity, etc.) have been repeatedly linked to affective-behavioral disorders such as depression or manic-depression (Whybrow, Akiskal, and McKinney 1984: 119–150). The complex biochemical milieu of the brain also shapes affect on much more subtle levels. Products generated by patterns of activity, diet, stress, and reproductive function modulate brain activity

(Wurtman 1979; Rubin, Reinisch, and Haskett 1981; Winson 1986: 192–202). Such modulations influence physiological *and* behavioral regulation, often via feelings that alter thresholds of behavior. Among extensive supporting data are recent demonstrations that steroid metabolites – products of many normal endocrine functions – affect nerve excitability in the brain (Majewska, Harrison, Schwartz, Barker, and Paul 1986; Gold, Loriaux, and Roy 1986). The well-recognized association of steroid hormone fluctuations with mood patterns may thus be explained.

Context and learning operate interdependently with physical process to shape experience and response. Research on the neural and endocrine substrates of mind, mood, and behavior has consistently demonstrated context-sensitive and learned components. (See, for example, Sacks 1987: 43–53; Koeske and Koeske 1975; Smith, Udry, and Morris 1985, but see also Udry, Billy, Morris, Groff, and Raj 1985). Emotions also have physiological correlates that form key elements of the affective experience of emotion (Ekman, Friesen, and Ellsworth 1983). To relate to the example noted above, an individual who is stressed – for whatever reason – will produce elevated cortisol levels that promote depression of the central nervous system.[2] Translation of that neurologically "depressed" state into affective experience and overt behaviors, as well as the reasons for the original perceived stress, are both subject to learning and culturally shaped interpretation.[3] Further, subsequent elevation of cortisol and its physiologic correlates[4] can provoke feelings of anxiety, because of previous experience of how stress "feels." Other well-studied examples include the biopsychosocial dynamics of asthma, and interaction of gonadal hormones with mood and behavior in men, as well as over the menstrual cycle in women (Vincent 1990). Biopsychosocial relationships have been demonstrated to have strong learned and cultural along with common intrinsic components. Therefore, physical and learned, or culturally constructed, dimensions are indissociable *interactive* elements in emotion.

Conversely, anthropologists might consider how culturally shaped patterns of consumption and activity influence motivation and affective tone of individuals. Analyses of patterns of oral consumption – of sugar and tea (Mintz 1985), or alcohol and tobacco (Knauft 1987) – have revealed their role in effecting an interface between individual and group. Treatment of specific consumption patterns as forms of substance use, however, sets them in a special category, offset from ordinary consumption. Consumption habits can also be seen to lie on a continuum of influence by things taken into the body on the affective state of the individual: certain drugs may exert enormous influence on perception, but, for instance, even the protein composition of a meal has been shown to influence neurotrans mitter levels in the brain (Wurtman 1979). More simply, lack of food – hunger – also powerfully organizes behavior and influences perception (Frank 1988: 51–53; Scheper-Hughes 1988). Culture, of course, characteristically shapes diet, including composition, adequacy, and timing of meals (Cassidy 1982; Ritenbaugh 1982a). To focus on specific substances with respect to how they serve both proximate (mood or physiologic toners) and remote (geopolitical, economic) structural processes is to stop short of a larger insight that sociodynamically patterned diet and activity exert this effect daily, from development through maturity. The work on specific behavioral effects of dietary deficiencies (implicating seasonal vitamin-D deficiency in *pibloktok* among Inuit [Foulks and Katz 1972; Katz and Foulks 1970], calcium deficiency in possession behavior among women [Kehoe and Giletti 1981]) illustrates the interplay among culturally patterned behavior (diet) and individual behavioral outcomes which are, in turn, expressed within culturally prescribed scripts (Locke and Kelley 1986).

The classic distinction between passion and sentiment has also been questioned by psychological anthropologists, but on a very different basis: it has been argued that biologically based passions lack an antecedent or independent role in subjective experience because they are entirely apprehended and interpreted within culturally constructed frameworks (Geertz 1980; Scheper-Hughes and Lock 1987). Culture is concluded to be the basis on which emotion is to be understood, because "without culture we would simply not know how to feel" (Scheper-Hughes and Lock 1987: 28) because "ideation, subtle or otherwise, is a cultural artifact" (Geertz 1983: 152). These statements are succinct summaries of the rich contemporary work on emotional experience, and are supported in principle by abundant evidence. However, the overall reasoning is circular and syllogistic when the implicit conclusion drawn is that culture defines knowledge and feeling, relegating material/physical conditions to passive text, not active force in human experience.

This latter objection does not, as has been suggested, mistake interpretation for "commitment to idealism, to a subjectivist conception of social reality, or to a denial of the force of ambition, might, accident, cleverness, and material interest in determining the life chances of men" (Geertz 1980: 135); rather, it notes the current appearance of generalized schema and rhetoric about human experience that nevertheless leave very little room for them. The indissociability of biological and cultural contributions to affective experience cannot be a reason for concluding that biological factors scarcely contribute to the extraordinary varieties of human experience. As outlined above, bodily experiences provide both the dynamic and the substrate for culturally constructed emotion; indeed, they may independently evaluate them. For instance, the culturally constructed emotions of love or revulsion may be powerfully validated (or discredited) in individual experience by their expected physiological concomitants (or lack thereof).[5] In her recent book on emotion, Lutz (1988: 210) identifies a middle ground based on a strategy "to critique essentialism in the understanding of emotion and to explore the relatively neglected ways in which social and cultural forces help to give emotions their observed character."

Thus, I agree with some on the synergistic relationship of biology and culture in emotion, but differ from most in my conclusion that the two must also be studied in tandem in order to understand the bases of affective experience. The query of some psychological anthropologists, "whether any expression of human emotion and feeling . . . is ever free of cultural shaping and cultural meaning" (Scheper-Hughes and Lock 1987: 28), can be counterbalanced with the question whether it is ever free of biological shaping and physiological concomitants: evidence suggests that the answer is "no" to both.

Linkage of affective states to behavior requires a concept of how these connections are made. Recent discussions of motivation (D'Andrade 1990) and intentionality (Shweder 1990) draw heavily on the notion of schemata, which are learned, culturally constituted conceptual templates that humans use to interpret, predict, and organize experience and behavior. These concepts can be amplified to include a biological dimension. A starting point is Shweder's (1987: 43) observation that:

> Instead of being arbitrary, there seems to be a moderate degree of motivation to the way body parts and words for body parts get used to give expression to states of mind . . . that certain aspects of physiological, motoric and interpersonal functioning – grasping, buckling at the knees, body hair standing on edge – provide a minimal universal ground for a folk psychology of body meanings.

In addition to providing a common base for metaphor (Johnson 1987) and certain emotional expressions, physical experiences activate and drive powerful internal schemata for organizing affect and motivation. Smells, for instance, can be potent evokers of memory and association. Sambia men plug their noses during intercourse to prevent inhalation of vaginal odor (Herdt 1990): in a Highland New Guinea society with highly socialized gender antagonism, the smell may actuate the very antagonism schema that must be overcome to have intimate contact with a woman.

Figure 1 puts the argument concerning the role of biology in affect into graphic form. In this view, learning of schemata for interpretation and organization of experience occurs not just through internalization, but also by forging linkages between physiologic states and interpretive–

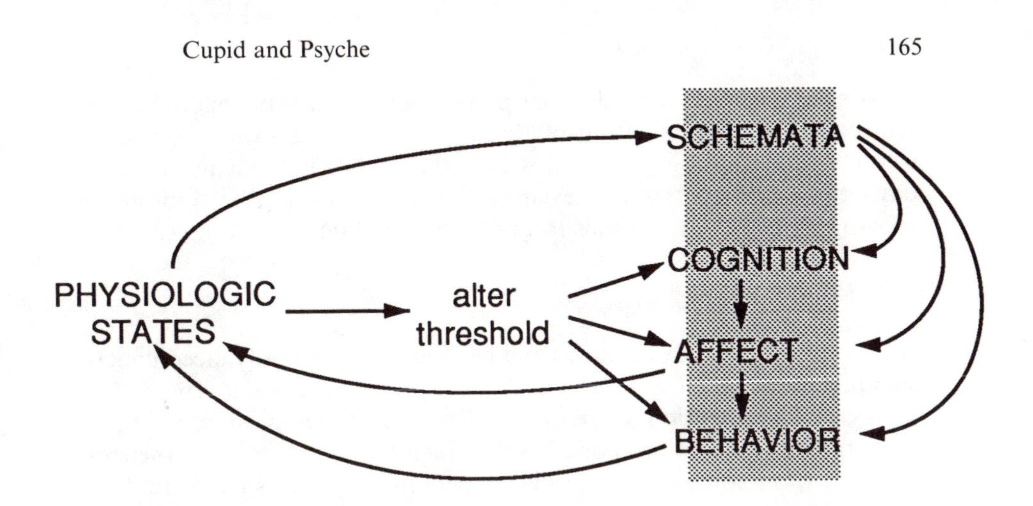

Figure 1

organizational schemata. Thus, physiologic states have both direct and indirect (via schemata) effects on affect and behavior. Physiologic states alter the threshold to certain cognitive states, affective states, and behaviors. Further, physical states can trigger or evoke schemata that, in turn, entrain their cognitive, affective, and behavioral components in the individual. Note that this synchronic model has a diachronic or developmental–historic background, in which structural and functional plasticity have interacted with context, previous affects, and behaviors, to shape ongoing function (phenotype). Learning forms an important link among all components. This is an internal model, and has omitted the important effects of external social milieu and environmental conditions.

To take testosterone levels in adult men as an example: testosterone is known not to cause men to act aggressively or engage in intercourse, but to alter the threshold to engage in these and other high-intensity, high-energy activities involving large muscle effort. Further, the hormone enhances feelings of wellbeing and changes cognitive performance (reduces fatigue in repetitive tasks). Testosterone is, moreover, context sensitive, dropping sharply in response to stress or malnutrition. Activity also affects androgen levels: moderate-to-vigorous sustained exercise elevates testosterone, while work to exhaustion depresses it (Worthman and Konner 1987). Some data suggest that, during puberty, facilitated learning occurs in linking testosterone levels to schemata concerning sexuality, aggressiveness, and gender identity. Thus, in men, testosterone both influences cognition, affect, and behavior, and triggers schemata for certain gendered roles. Through these various routes, feelings of lust, anger, stress, or exhaustion would be partly constituted and evoked by endocrine dynamics, a hidden but potent element in experience. I think that comparative elucidation of the interplay among social, cognitive-affective, and physiological processes in the lives of individuals in everyday settings represents a most exciting and challenging potential for novel anthropological contributions to understanding human experience.

Illness and healing

Anthropological study of illness and healing has greatly advanced understanding of the social construction of these processes, but it is remarkable for a general inattention to physiology. The lack of biological information is surprising because corporeal wellbeing (if not of patients, then of someone or of some institution) is almost universally at stake here. One reads works on healing practices and medical belief systems without learning anything about the patient (his/her physical properties, or feeling and experience) (Katz 1985), and one burns to know *anything* concrete about the physical–physiological statuses of participants – patients, healers, and attendants alike (Kleinman and Good 1985; Kleinman, Kunstadter, Alexander, and Gate 1978). This disregard may be largely explained by a perceived necessity to establish the importance of social or symbolic analysis for reinterpreting medical practices, wellness, and illness, against the prevailing biomedical materialist paradigm.

At this juncture, greater attention to the physical dimension of illness and healing would significantly deepen our knowledge of these phenomena. A dialectical relationship between cultural and material reality definitely pertains, but *how* that relationship works is largely unknown: biological process participates as a defining dynamic, but not as an independent variable. Hahn and Kleinman (1983a) suggest as much and advocate a perspective of "material–ideal interactionism" or "aspectualism" (i.e., one that views the relationship of the material and the ideal/subjective as dialectic, being mutually defining and transforming facets of social reality). They urge that:

> Anthropologists must explore the material constraints on the social construction and production of "reality," and the reciprocal shaping of nature by its social production and construction . . . [We] contend that the material–ideal interactionist framework will emerge as the one most valid in the anthropological account of human and social affairs. We support the *aspect* version of this framework, in which society, mind, and body are not, in Cartesian fashion, separate sorts of entities which interact, but rather aspects common to human events. (p. 322)

Further, they urge the suitability of biomedicine as a testing-ground for this outlook, using interdisciplinary research that combines cultural–ethnographic analysis with clinical and epidemiologic methods.

For example, 30 to 60 per cent of cures effected by modern Western medicine are ascribed to the widely recognized but empirically obscure "placebo effect" (Brody 1983; Hahn and Kleinman 1983a; Moerman, 1983). This effect will doubtless yield only to biopsychocultural study, for all three domains inhere to the processes of wellness and illness. As was argued in the section on emotion, affects and perceptions influence physical status. For instance, the suppressive influence of the hormones of stress on immune competence has been well described (Marx 1985), and social–physiological effects on endogenous production of opiates are also known, though they are still only poorly understood. Conversely, the body itself provides cues to its status that constitute one basis of subjectivity (LeDoux 1986: 309–327). In addition, physical states and individual differences may open windows of differential physiological vulnerability on which culture acts to shape immediate affects and even permanent cognitive style.

Thus, the individual's relationship to and apperception of physical states is defined by the states themselves and by contextually mediated experiences, with learning and memory as intermediaries. An excellent example is *latah*. Partial explanations of this phenomenon have been offered that address its multiple dimensions (emic symbolic, sociodynamic, neurophysiologic, psychodynamic, ethologic, sociologic, cognitive), on a local as well as cross-cultural basis (e.g., Kenny, Ohnuki-Tierney, and Simons in Simons and Hughes 1985). We need to seek means by which competing understandings of a given social phenomenon may be weighed and placed within an integrated framework. Empirically informed derivation of such a framework should be a central goal for anthropology. Thus, *latah* should be understood not simply through its disparate aspects, but also as an instance of how those aspects interact. For this reason, Simons' (in Simons and Hughes 1985) analysis seems the most complete to date because it integrates several dimensions to explain why and how given individuals become *latah*.

Simon starts from the premise that "various forms of the *latah* reaction are culture-specific exploitations of a neurophysiologically determined behavioral potential" (Simons and Hughes 1985: 44). The startle response is a shared human fixed-action pattern that is provoked by sudden stimuli. Liability to startle is both a trait (inherently lower threshold for reaction) and a state (hyperaroused or distracted states lower the startle threshold). Some societies recognize, anticipate, and amplify individual differences in responsiveness, or predisposition to startle: these societies, scattered around the world, label and contain roles for "startlers," and actively induct vulnerable individuals into those roles. While patterns of the startle reflex are universal, the ways in which these are elaborated behaviorally, enacted interpersonally, and invested with meaning are local, or culture specific. Malay *latahs* are distinct from Maine jumpers and Ainu *imu bakko*, though all arise from elaborations of the startle response. Fundamental to the existence of phenomena such as *latah* is the existence of the startle reaction, of individual differences in degree of arousability, and of a physiological capacity to reinforce the reaction through attention capture and repeated or self stimulus. Fundamental to the absence of the phenomenon in a population is the failure culturally to "exploit" a physiologic potential. The lack of *latah*-like roles and behaviors in such societies – even though they contain individuals who startle easily – points to the importance of cultural process in the elicitation of the pattern in an individual.

This last point about *latah* – the harnessing of biological processes or potentials to cultural ends, with synergy of biology and culture in constructing individual experience – illustrates the central theme of this chapter. Applied to medical anthropology, this insight suggests that the social construction of symptom formation would be further elucidated by answers to simple physiological questions, e.g., did the patient – or caregiver, or other participants – have a fever? Did he/she suffer iron deficiency? A similar research strategy to that suggested earlier for studies of development could be employed. That is, physical measures could be used to characterize biologic state for correlation with cultural treatment of persons in that state. Ritenbaugh (1982b) has applied this strategy in her analysis of obesity as a cultural construct in the United States, by examining the criteria for obesity against the actual distribution of weight and morbidity. Further, knowledge of individual weight and body shape augments interpretation of individual self image as well as perception and treatment by others. A genuinely critical medical anthropology should be eager to employ quantitative analysis because measurable differences in resource distribution and wellbeing are key outcome measures of dominance and inequity. This strategy is used by physical anthropologists. For example, Bielicki (1986) has used Polish data on adolescent development to demonstrate marked developmental differences by parental occupation, thus critiquing state rhetoric of social equity; conversely, similar data for Sweden and Norway showing no such association (Brundtland, Liestøl, and Walloe 1980; Lindgren 1976) have validated those societies' claims of equitable resource distribution. Medical anthropology could build on its existing record of integration of epidemiologic and biologic measures with interpretive analysis of sociodynamics to illuminate critically the social construction (in both senses: creation and interpretation) of illness and wellness (reviewed in Inhorn and Brown 1990).

Relevant clues to what, physically, is "going on" in the contexts of illness and healing provide insights into what, inter- and intra-subjectively, is going on as well. The intellectual distances across anthropology are reflected in the fact that medical anthropologists regularly collaborate with clinical or biomedical researchers, but seldom with biological anthropologists or human biologists. That predilection is understandable, both because medical anthropology targets the hegemony of biomedicine, and because biomedical research is relatively well funded. But there are limitations to this approach. Existing biomedical techniques often are not readily applicable to field research settings among "normal" or remote populations. Moreover, these techniques are tuned to address questions framed under biomedical paradigms, and may need to be modified to address different kinds of problems. By contrast, bioanthropological research already focuses on individual differences, historic (mainly ontogenetic) processes, and local dynamics – issues that concern many social anthropologists, though framed differently. Indeed, biological anthropologists have frequently pioneered adaptation of existing biomedical techniques for anthropological purposes, as in the study of human development or reproduction (Lasker and Mascie-Taylor 1989).

In sum, appropriate collection of physical data in medical anthropology would lead not to abrogation of social by physical process, but to appreciation of the power of each for the other and clarification of their respective operational domains. Only in this way will important questions about human suffering/dysfunction and its alleviation be answered.

In favor of collaborative multidisciplinary research

The purpose of this chapter is to urge the relevance of biological parameters to the aims of psychological anthropology and to show that the state of knowledge makes a unified approach feasible. I am not suggesting that this approach should replace existing paradigms, but that it should augment them. Nor am I assuming that all, or even many, psychological anthropologists will wish to take up biocultural inquiry. Rather, I am arguing for a place for such research. We can now transcend prior assumptions and assertions about the relative contributions of culture and biology to human mind and experience to *test* their respective roles. Most data suggest that they will operate in a dialectic manner in ontogeny and function. This makes our task considerably more exciting but also more difficult, for we are dealing with a "five-dimensional problem," that is, a phenomenon that occurs in the standard three dimensions through time and across levels of organization (in the sense of Berger and Luckmann 1966, and Bateson 1972).

Although contemporary anthropologists have leveled appropriate critiques at the oppositions of mind–body, nature–culture as culture-bound constructs, their critical reflexivity has rarely extended to attempts to bridge these constructs in the conduct of anthropological research. Shore (1988) has proposed a stratigraphic model. He points out that the holistic emphasis in anthropology fuels critical discourse that disparages partial explanations for their incompleteness, and leads to exclusive and overgeneralized rather than accumulative and localized explanations. He suggests anthropologists grant one another the freedom to pursue rigorous partial accounts, and practice modesty in their explanatory claims. This constructive suggestion is salutary for salving the discipline's internecine rubs; but plurality in explanatory modes must be conceived within an integrated framework, such as that advanced by Shore and Hahn and Kleinman (1983a). It should therefore not be assumed that a *laissez-faire* attitude heralds an extinction of anthropology's commitment to holism, a relinquishing of our original quest for a full account of human experience.

This point is worth emphasizing because what would be ceded would probably be the integration of cultural and physical dimensions. Part of anthropology's task has been epistemological, an intellectual undertaking toward conceptual means of incorporating "the mental and the material" in discourse and inquiry. Studying the relationship of these dimensions is an important enterprise that addresses a major lacuna in Western thought. A retreat from that epistemological program would be a loss, analogous to biology's retreat to the molecular level. Indeed, at present this is a unique, though most difficult element of the anthropological enterprise, for no other discipline retains that concept at the center of its mandate: no others place the relationship of cultural and material dimensions among their central empirical questions.

While each of us varies in our inclination and ability to face this particular epistemological challenge, its maintenance in anthropology's program acts as a goad to prompt repeated attempts at synthesis, a reintegration of the various domains in which we work. These attempts provoke us to remain conversant with various modes of inquiry and discourse within the discipline, create a common basis for intellectual dialogue, and constitute an uncommon wellspring of reflexive but constructive criticality. Ignorance, and preferences in styles of observation, thought, and discourse are excellent reasons to avoid one set of intellectual questions and choose another, but they do not justify denigration or dismissal of the path not taken. Examination of the roles of culture and biology in human experience has, regrettably, become concatenated for some with symbolic polarities (purity : pollution, natural : unnatural, traditional : Western, emergent : determined), compounded by intellectual xenophobia. The strife may be constructive, however, insofar as it continually piques us to surmount our own cultural baggage in order to survey conceptions of humanity and evaluate the anthropological enterprise.

Analogous to the need to allow a more inclusive, rather than exclusive, explanatory approach, is the need for cooperative, collaborative research. Obviously, no single individual commands sufficiently broad expertise to realize a multidimensional study single-handedly. For collaborative studies, an implicit model for the conduct of anthropological research will need to be expanded from the single-investigator and, especially, single-analyst approach. Such an expanded model is furthermore at odds with the structure for attaining recognition in the discipline, which has been characterized by individualism and the semi-alienation of frontierism; acceptance of multiplex responsibility for multiplex discoveries will need to be granted. In addition, we will need to evaluate one another's contributions based as much on the gradual accumulation of knowledge, as on insightful extrapolation or conceptual exclusion. Intellectual palimpsest, a discounting of information that accompanies rejection of conceptual frameworks, may thereby be avoided.

This chapter aims to encourage psychological anthropologists to consider collaboration with their colleagues in biological anthropology, who may often be found to be receptive (or at least educable) to more broadly framed questions about human experience. Better, these colleagues have information and research techniques that can complement those of psychological anthropologists. The education process would be mutual. Biological anthropologists focus on sources of physical variation on the individual and population level, with attention to the cultural sources of that variation. But they should attend more to the interaction of biological with psychosocial dynamics. Much could be learned from greater descriptive specificity or simple measures on the physical status of individuals, including measures of developmental, reproductive, or nutritional state. There is a wealth of minimally invasive physical measures that could be incorporated into field studies and made to complement, not drive out or supplant, other methods of inquiry.

Conclusion

This chapter has treated mind–body not as a problem but as a phenomenon to be studied. It has shown that experience, behavior, and the "self" are all grounded in two emergent aspects, cultural and physical, which are furthermore co-emergent in individuals. For this reason, fuller understanding of the one aspect cannot be achieved without consideration of the other, and is predicated on a multidisciplinary research paradigm. The material surveyed here has demonstrated how biological processes, although "hidden" from subjective consciousness and casual inspection, represent a significant theater of operation for social processes on the individual level. Therefore, a truly critical anthropology should view attention to the physical domain as central to deconstructive analysis that uncovers these processes. I suggest that psychological anthropology employ investigative syncretism, an openness to incorporating study of physical process. Likewise, anthropologists who have concentrated on biological aspects of human variation should recognize the need for contextual and affective analysis.

The problem with actualizing the syncretic approach is that empirical and conceptual frameworks are needed, for we are not used to thinking about questions in biocultural terms. Methods, too, are lacking: psychological anthropology has not historically focused on the individual (see Chisholm, this book), so there is a dearth of individual outcome measures that could be linked to biological data on individuals. Some investigators have made a start in this direction, though largely in conceptual rather than empirical work. Many have continued to draw on substantive substrates for insights into self and affect (Levy 1984; D'Andrade 1981, 1984). Some psychological anthropologists, as well as philosophers of mind and experience (Dennett 1978; Eccles 1982; reviewed in Churchland 1984), have lately moved to incorporate physical–psychological dimensions in their schemata. For instance, a 1982 issue of *Ethos* was devoted to endorphins and altered states of consciousness. Another instance is the application of a biogenetic structuralist model to analysis of ritual by Lex (1979) and D'Aquili and Laughlin (1979). Locke and Kelly (1986) have presented a multidimensional model for comparative analysis of altered states of consciousness. They, as well as others (Bourguignon, Bellisari, and McCabe 1983), have emphasized the "extreme complexity" of these states. Nevertheless, increasingly, anthropologists are attempting multidimensional analyses. With subdisciplinary dialogue and collaboration when appropriate, anthropology will move further toward fulfilling its promise fully to represent the human experience.

This congenial prospect returns us to the fates of Cupid and Psyche. Here, the divine male (Cupid), curiously, represents humoral and deterministic bases of human experience, whereas the mortal female (Psyche) embodies the transformation of nature. One might say that they symbolize the inherently multidimensional aspect of human existence, an intrinsic dialectic between biology and culture that has been emphasized throughout this chapter. We may expect that their reunion in Western thought would, like any good marriage, result not in simple fusion but in a bond of creative tension.

NOTES

I thank Bradd Shore, Robert Paul, Edward Schieffelin, Melvin Konner, and Bruce Knauft, generous colleagues who read versions of this paper, and have shared ideas and sources in our discussions on these topics. This work was supported in part by a Faculty Scholar award from the William T. Grant Foundation.

1 A rather different, but conceptually analogous, outlook is Lakoff's (1987: xiv–xv) experientialist (one could also call it ecological) view of thought as shaped by both the body and the situations in which it arises.

2 While there are many psychological correlates of stress (e.g., up-regulation of the cardiovascular system, suppression of immune and gastrointestinal function), the observation that cortisol alters blood–brain barrier permeability (Long and Holaday 1985) suggests a further route by which the physiology of stress may redound to further alteration of cognitive–affective states.

3 For a good example of the learned, biological, and cultural components of emotion, see the study of socialization for substance use and regulation of emotional expression in managing male social relations among Gebusi (Knauft 1987).

4 Adrenocorticotropic hormone (ACTH) release by the pituitary is activated from the CNS by stress and induces release of cortisol by the adrenal gland. ACTH receptors are found in the brain, and ACTH has been shown to exert a central effect on affect. Disagreement exists over whether cortisol has a similar direct influence.

5 Lutz (1988: 100–101) provides an excellent example in the postpartum women on Ifaluk: there, maternal anger or distress is taken as a sign of maternal isolation and oppression by her domestic and nurturant duties, a state due to lack of assistance or support by others. Postpartum depression is interpreted not as a failure of maternal adjustment or love for the infant, but as justified perturbation reflecting a social failure in responsibility by others. While postpartum depression occurs in both Ifaluk and American societies, the attributed causes (internal) and behavioral-affective outcomes (depression) are markedly different in American women, and lead to a questioning of *maternal* adjustment.

REFERENCES

Baron, R. J. 1987. *The Cerebral Computer: An Introduction to the Computational Structure of the Human Brain*. Hillsdale, NJ: Lawrence Erlbaum

Bateson, G. 1972. *Steps to an Ecology of Mind*. New York: Ballantine

Berger, P. and T. Luckmann. 1966. *The Social Construction of Reality*. New York: Doubleday

Bielicki, T. 1986. Physical Growth as a Measure of the Economic Well-Being of Populations: The Twentieth Century. In F. Falkner and J. M. Tanner, eds., *Human Growth* (2nd edn, vol. III, pp. 283–305). New York: Plenum

Borgerhoff-Mulder, M. 1988. Kipsigis Bridewealth Payments. In L. Betzig, M. Borgerhoff-Mulder, and P. Turke, eds. *Human Reproductive Behaviour*. Cambridge: Cambridge University Press

Bourguignon, E., A. Bellisari, and S. McCabe. 1983. Women, Possession Trance Cults, and the Extended Nutrient-Deficiency Hypothesis. *American Anthropologist* 85, 413–416

Brody, H. 1983. Does Disease have a Natural History? *Medical Anthropology Quarterly* 14: 19–22

Brundtland, G. H., K. Liestøl, and L. Walløe. 1980. Height, Weight, and Menarcheal Age of Oslo Schoolchildren During the Last 60 Years. *Annals of Human Biology* 7: 307–322

Cassidy, C. M. 1982. Protein Energy Malnutrition as a Culture-Bound Syndrome. *Culture, Medicine and Psychiatry* 6: 325–345

Changeux, J-P. 1985. *Neuronal Man* Translated by L. Garey. New York: Pantheon

Chisholm, J. S. 1983. *Navajo Infancy: An Ethological Study of Child Development*. New York: Aldine

Churchland, P. M. 1984. *Matter and Consciousness*. Cambridge, MA: MIT Press

Cowan, W. M. 1979. In F. O. Schmitt and F. G. Worden, eds., *The Neurosciences Fourth Study Program* (pp. 59–79). Cambridge, MA: MIT Press

D'Andrade, R. G. 1981. The Cultural Part of Cognition. *Cognitive Science* 5, 179–195

1984. Cultural Meaning Systems. In R. A. Shweder and R. A. LeVine, eds., *Culture Theory: Essays on Mind, Self and Emotion* (pp. 88–119). Cambridge: Cambridge University Press

1990. Some Propositions about the Relations Between Culture and Human Cognition. In J. W. Stigler, R. A. Shweder, and G. Herdt, eds., *Cultural Psychology* (pp. 65–129). Cambridge: Cambridge University Press

D'Aquili, E. G. and C. D. Laughlin. 1979. The Neurobiology of Myth and Ritual. In E. G. d'Aquili, C. D. Laughlin, and J. McManus, eds., *The Spectrum of Ritual* (pp. 152–182). New York: Columbia University Press

Dennett, D. C. 1978. *Brainstorms: Philosophical Essays on Mind and Psychology*. Cambridge, MA: MIT

Dixon, N. F. 1981. *Preconscious Processing*. New York: John Wiley

Douglas, M. 1970. *Natural Symbols*. New York: Vintage

Eccles, J., ed. 1982. *Mind and Brain*. Washington: Paragon House

Edelman, G. M. 1978. Group Selection and Phasic Reentrant Signaling: A Theory of Higher Brain Function. In G. M. Edelman and V. B. Mountcastle, eds., *The Mindful Brain* (pp. 51–100). Cambridge, MA: MIT Press

1987. *Neural Darwinism: Theory of Neuronal Group Selection*. New York: Basic Books

Ekman, P., W. V. Friesen, and P. Ellsworth. 1983. Autonomic Nervous System Activity Distinguishes Among Emotions. *Science* 221: 1,208–1,210

Ellenberger, H. F. 1970. *The Discovery of the Unconscious*. New York: Basic Books

Foulks, E. F. and S. H. Katz. 1972. Biobehavioral Adaptation in the Arctic. In E. S. Watts, F. E. Johnston, and G. W. Lasker, eds., *Biosocial Interrelations in Population Adaptation* (pp. 1–11). New Orleans: Tulane University Press

Frank, R. H. 1988. *Passions Within Reason*. New York: W. W. Norton

Freud, S. 1895. Project for a Scientific Psychology. In J. Strachey, ed., *The Standard Edition of the Complete Psychological Works of Sigmund Freud* (vol. I, pp. 283–387). London: Hogarth Press, 1953

Geertz, C. 1980. *Negara: The Theater-State in Nineteenth Century Bali*. Princeton: Princeton University Press

1983. *Local Knowledge: Further Essays in Interpretive Anthropology*. New York: Basic Books

Gold, P. W., D. L. Loriaux, and A. Roy. 1986. Responses to Corticotropin-Releasing Hormone in the Hypercortisolism of Depression and Cushing's Disease. *New England Journal of Medicine* 314: 1,329–1,335

Gordon, S. I. 1981. The Sociology of Sentiments and Emotion. In S. L. Rosenberg and R. H. Turner, eds., *Social Psychology: Sociological Perspectives* (pp. 562–592). New York: Basic Books

Gottlieb, G. 1973. In G. Gottlieb, ed., *Studies on the Development of Behavior and Nervous System* (vol. I, pp. 3–45). New York: Academic Press

Gunders, S. and J. W. M. Whiting. 1968. Mother–Infant Separation and Physical Growth. *Ethnology* 2: 196–206

Hahn, R. A. and A. Kleinman. 1983a. Biomedical Practice and Anthropological Theory: Frameworks and Directions. *Annual Review of Anthropology* 12: 305–333

1983b. Belief as Pathogen, Belief as Medicine: "Voodoo Death" and the "Placebo Phenomenon" in Anthropological Perspective. *Medical Anthropology Quarterly* 14(3): 16–19

Hallowell, A. I. 1960. Self, Society, and Culture in Phylogenetic Perspective. In S. Tax, ed., *Evolution after Darwin* (pp. 309–371). Chicago: University of Chicago Press

Harré, R., ed., 1986. *The Social Construction of Emotions*. Oxford: Blackwell

Heider, K. G. 1988. The Rashomon Effect: When Ethnographers Disagree. *American Anthropologist* 90: 73–81

Herdt, G. H., ed., 1982. *Rituals of Manhood: Male Initiation in Papua New Guinea*. Berkeley: University of California Press

1990. Sambia Nosebleeding Rites and Male Proximity to Women. In J. W. Stigler, R. A. Shweder, and G. Herdt, eds., *Cultural Psychology* (pp. 366–400). Cambridge: Cambridge University Press

Inhorn, M. C. and P. Brown 1990. The Anthropology of Infectious Disease. *Annual Review of Anthropology* 19: 89–117

Jenkins, C. L. and P. F. Heywood. 1985. Ethnopediatrics and Fertility Among the Amele of Lowland Papua New Guinea. In V. Hull and M. Simpson, eds., *Breastfeeding, Child Health, and Child Spacing: Cross-Cultural Perspectives* (pp. 11–34). London: Croom Helm

Johnson, M. 1987. *The Body in the Mind*. Chicago: University of Chicago Press

Katz, R. 1985. *Boiling energy*. Cambridge: Harvard University Press

Katz, S. H. and E. F. Foulks. 1970. Mineral Metabolism and Behavior: Abnormalities of Calcium Homeostasis. *American Journal of Physical Anthropology* 32: 299–304

Kehoe, A. B. and D. H. Giletti. 1981. Women's Preponderance in Possession Cults: the Calcium-Deficiency Hypothesis Extended. *American Anthropologist* 83: 549–561

Kleinman, A. and B. Good, eds., 1985. *Culture and Depression: Studies in the Anthropology and Cross-Cultural Psychiatry of Affect and Disorder*. Berkeley: University of California Press

Kleinman, A., P. Kunstadter, E. R. Alexander, and J. L. Gate. 1978. *Culture and Healing in Asian Societies*. Cambridge, MA: Schenkman Publishing

Knauft, B. 1987. Managing Sex and Anger: Tobacco and Kava Use Among the Gebusi of Papua New Guinea. In L. Lindstrom, ed., *Drugs in Western Pacific Societies: Relations of Substance* (pp. 73–98). Lanham, MD: University Press of America

Koeske, R. K. and Koeske, G. F. 1975. An Attributional Approach to Moods and the Menstrual Cycle. *Journal of Personality and Social Psychology* 31: 473–478

Konner, M. J. 1977. Infancy Among the Kalahari Desert San. In P. H. Leiderman, S. Tulkin, and A. Rosenfeld eds., *Culture and Infancy* (pp. 287–328). New York: Academic Press

Kroeber, A. 1917. The Superorganic. *American Anthropologist* 19: 163–213

Lakoff, G. 1987. *Women, Fire and Dangerous Things*. Chicago: University of Chicago Press

Lakoff, G. and M. Johnson. 1980. *Metaphors We Live By*. Chicago: University of Chicago Press

Landauer, T. K. and J. W. M. Whiting. 1980. Correlates and Consequences of Stress in Infancy. In R. Munroe, R. Munroe and B. B. Whiting, eds., *Handbook of Cross-Cultural Research in Human Development* (pp. 355–75). New York: Garland

Lasker, G. W. and Mascie-Taylor, eds. 1989. *Applications of Biological Anthropology to Human Affairs*. Cambridge: Cambridge University Press

LeDoux, J. E. 1986. The Neurobiology of Emotion. In J. E. LeDoux and W. Hirst, eds., *Mind and Brain: Dialogues in Cognitive Neuroscience* (pp. 300–360). Cambridge: Cambridge University Press

LeVay, S., T. N. Wiesel and D. Hubel. 1981. The Postnatal Development and Plasticity of Ocular-Dominance Columns in the Monkey. In F. O. Schmitt, F. G. Worden, G. Adelman, and S. G. Dennis, eds., *The Organization of the Cerebral Cortex* (pp. 29–45). Cambridge, MA: MIT

LeVine, R. A. 1979. Child Rearing as Cultural Adaptation. In P. H. Leiderman, S. Tulkin, and A. Rosenfeld, eds., *Culture and Infancy* (pp. 15–27). New York: Academic Press

Levy, R. I. 1983. Introduction: Self and Emotion. *Ethos* 11: 128–134

1984. Emotion, Knowing, and Culture. In R. A. Shweder and R. A. LeVine, eds., *Culture Theory: Essays on Mind, Self and Emotion* (pp. 214–237). Cambridge: Cambridge University Press

Lex, B. 1979. The Neurobiology of Ritual Trance. In E. G. d'Aquili, C. D. Laughlin, and J. McMannus, eds., *The Spectrum of Ritual* (pp. 117–151). New York: Columbia University Press

Libet, B. 1978. Neuronal vs. Subjective Timing for a Conscious Sensory Experience. In P. A. Buser and A. Rougeul-Buser, eds., *Cerebral Correlates of Conscious Experience* (pp. 69–82). Amsterdam: North-Holland

Libet, B., E. W. Wright, B. Feinstein, and D. K. Pearl. 1979. Subjective Referral of the Timing for a Conscious Sensory Experience. *Brain* 102: 193–224

Lindgren, G. 1976. Height, Weight and Menarche in Swedish Urban School Children in Relation to Socioeconomic and Regional Factors. *Annals of Human Biology* 3: 501–528

Locke, R. G. and E. F. Kelly. 1986. A Preliminary Model for the Cross-Cultural Analysis of Altered States of Consciousness. *Ethos* 14: 3–55

Long, J. B. and J. W. Holaday. 1985. Blood-Brain Barrier: Endogenous Modulation by Adrenal-Cortical Function. *Science* 227: 1,580–1,583

Lutz, C. 1985. Ethnopsychology Compared to What? Explaining Behavior and Consciousness Among the Ifaluk. In G. M. White and J. Kirkpatrick, eds., *Person, Self, and Experience: Exploring Pacific Ethnopsychologies* (pp. 35–79). Berkeley: University of California Press

Lutz, C. 1988. *Unnatural Emotions: Everyday Sentiments on a Micronesian Atoll and their Challenge to Western Theory*. Chicago: University of Chicago Press

Majewska, M. D., N. L. Harrison, R. D. Schwartz, J. L. Barker, and S. M. Paul. 1986. Steroid Hormone Metabolites are Barbiturate-Like Modulators of the GAVA Receptor. *Science* 232: 1,004–1,007

Marx, J. L. 1985. The Immune System "Belongs in the body." *Science* 227: 1,190–1,192

Mintz, S. W. 1985. *Sweetness and Power*. New York: Penguin Books

Moerman, D. E. 1983. General Medical Effectiveness and Human Biology: Placebo Effects in the Treatment of Ulcer Disease. *Medical Anthropology Quarterly* 14(3): 13–16

Oakley, D. A., and L. C. Eames. 1985. The Plurality of Consciousness. In D. A. Oakley, ed. *Brain and Mind* (pp. 217–258). New York: Methuen

Ochs, E., and B. B. Schieffelin. 1984. Language Acquisition and Socialization: Three Developmental Stories and Their Implications. In R. A. Shweder and R. A. LeVine, eds., *Culture Theory: Essays on Mind, Self and Emotion*. (pp. 276–320). Cambridge: Cambridge University Press

Pöppel, E. 1988. *Mindworks: Time and Conscious Experience*. Translated by T. Artin. Boston: Harcourt Brace Jovanovich

Popper, K. R. and J. C. Eccles. 1983. *The Self and its Brain*. London: Routledge & Kegan Paul

Ritenbaugh, C. 1982a. New Approaches to Old Problems: Interactions of Culture and Nutrition. In N. Chrisman and T. W. Maretzki, eds., *Clinically Applied Anthropology* (pp. 141–178). Boston: D. Reidel

1982b. Obesity as a Culture-Bound Syndrome. *Culture, Medicine and Psychiatry* 6: 346–361

Rosaldo, M. 1984. Toward an Anthropology of Self and Feeling. In R. A. Shweder and R. A. LeVine, eds., *Culture Theory: Essays on Mind, Self and Emotion*. (pp. 137–157). Cambridge: Cambridge University Press

Rubin, R. T., J. M. Reinisch, and R. F. Haskett. 1981. Postnatal Gonadal Steroid Effects on Human Behavior. *Science* 211: 1,318–1,324

Sacks, O. 1987. *The Man Who Mistook His Wife for a Hat*. Cambridge, MA: HarperPerennial

Scarr, S. and K. McCartney. 1983. How People Make Their Own Environments: A Theory of Genotype → Environment Effects. *Child Development* 54: 424–435

Scheper-Hughes, N. 1985. Culture, Scarcity, and Maternal Thinking: Maternal Detachment and Infant Survival in a Brazilian Shantytown. *Ethos* 13: 291–317

1988. The Madness of Hunger: Sickness, Delirium, and Human Needs. *Culture, Medicine and Psychiatry* 12: 429–458

Scheper-Hughes, N. and M. Lock. 1987. The Mindful Body: A Prolegomenon to Future Work in Medical Anthropology. *Medical Anthropology Quarterly* 1: 6–41

Shore, B. 1988. Interpretation Under Fire. *Anthropological Quarterly* 61: 161–176

Shweder, R. A. 1984. Anthropology's Romantic Rebellion Against the Enlightenment, or There's More to Thinking than Reason and Evidence. In R. A. Shweder and R. A. LeVine, eds., *Culture Theory: Essays on Mind, Self and Emotion* (pp. 27–66). Cambridge: Cambridge University Press

1987. How to Look at Medusa Without Turning to Stone. *Contributions to Indian Sociology* 21: 37–55

1990. Cultural Psychology – What is It? In J. W. Stigler, R. A. Shweder, and G. Herdt, eds., *Cultural Psychology* (pp. 1–43). Cambridge: Cambridge University Press

Simons, R. C. and C. C. Hughes, eds., 1985. *The Culture-Bound Syndromes.* Dordrecht: D. Reidl Publishing

Smith, E. A., J. R. Udry, and N. M. Morris. 1985. Pubertal Development and Friends: A Biosocial Explanation of Adolescent Sexual Behavior. *Journal of Health and Social Behavior* 26: 182–192

Super, C. M. 1976. Environmenal Effects on Motor Development: The Case of African Precocity. *Developmental Medicine and Child Neurology* 18: 561–567

Udry, R. J., J. O. G. Billy, N. M. Morris, T. R. Groff, M. H. Raj. 1985. Serum Androgenic Hormones Motivate Sexual Behavior in Adolescent Boys. *Fertility and Sterility* 43: 90–94

Vincent, J-D. 1990. *The Biology of Emotions.* Oxford: Blackwell

Whybrow, P. C., H. S. Akiskal, and W. T. McKinney. 1984. *Mood Disorder: Toward a New Psychobiology.* New York: Plenum

Winson, J. 1986. *Brain and Psyche.* New York: Vintage Books

Worthman, C. M. 1987. Interactions of Physical Maturation and Cultural Practice in Ontogeny: Kikuyu Adolescents. *Cultural Anthropology* 2: 29–39

1990. Socioendocrinology: Key to a Fundamental Synergy. In F. Berkovitch and T. Ziegler, eds., *Socioendocrinology of Primate Reproduction* (pp. 187–212). New York: Wiley-Liss

Worthman, C. M. and M. Konner. 1987. Hunting Alters Testosterone Daily Rhythm in !Kung San Hunter-Gatherer Men. *Psychoneuroendocrinology* 12: 449–458

Wurtman, R. J. 1979. Precursor Control of Transmitter Synthesis. In A. Barbeau, J. H. Growdon, and R. J. Wurtman, eds., *Nutrition and the Brain.* Vol V: *Choline and Lecithin in Brain Disorders* (pp. 1–12). New York: Raven Press

Part IV

Psychiatry and its contexts

9 Culture and psychopathology: directions for psychiatric anthropology

Byron J. Good

During the past twenty years, psychiatry in Europe and North America has undergone the most extraordinary paradigm shift of this century. Journal publications, research dollars, and treatment orientations all reflect a shift in dominance from psychoanalytic discourse to biological, from a focus on psychological processes to classification of symptoms, from a primary interest in affect and its economy to cognition, and from investments in community psychiatry to biological research and pharmacological treatment. This change poses a serious challenge for the anthropologist interested in the role of culture in psychopathology, raising questions about what directions anthropological research should take in the coming decade. It also raises the specter of declining interest in the social and cultural dimensions of mental illness in the psychiatric profession and public policy. One might have anticipated that these changes in psychiatry would have provoked, among anthropologists, both a sharp critique of the reification of medicalized disease categories and a sense of despair, as funding agencies such as the US National Institutes of Mental Health (NIMH) increasingly reorient their mission and review committees to focus on the molecular biology and genetics of disease entities. What is most striking in reviewing the anthropological literature, however, is that there has been almost *no* anthropological response. With rare exceptions, our journals provide little evidence that anthropologists are even aware that the world of psychiatry has changed in the past two decades. Many in our field *are* aware, of course. However, cognizance of changes in psychiatry has yet to produce a new agenda of theorizing and research for anthropologists interested in the cross-cultural study of psychopathology.

It is my belief that current events in psychiatry offer not only obstacles but important new opportunities for psychiatric anthropology and cross-cultural psychiatry. I make this argument with some trepidation. It is far more fashionable in anthropology to criticize or even ridicule psychiatry's construction of diagnostic categories than to suggest a research agenda formulated in terms of them. Indeed, were this review designed for a psychiatric readership, the heart of the chapter would be a challenge to the validity of such categories, formulated in cultural terms. However, it is disturbing that anthropology has had so little engagement with psychiatry at a time in which such extraordinary change has been coupled with such great advances in neurobiology. Psychological anthropologists have given close attention to developments in cognitive psychology and human development, and have contributed to those fields. They have, however, paid far less attention to contemporary currents in abnormal psychology and psychiatry.

More than fifty years ago, Edward Sapir, having worked with Harry Stack Sullivan at Chicago, outlined a research agenda that began with cross-ethnic and cross-cultural studies of normal personality, then moved on to studies of psychopathology, schizophrenic illness in particular, among these groups. He concluded: "one of the crying needs in the whole field of human behavior [is] to discover what maladjustment means in the remoter cultures" (quoted in Darnell 1986: 166). Over the decades, that challenge has been taken up by anthropologists collaborating with American or non-American psychiatrists; one thinks of Caudill at the National Institute of Mental Health and in Japan, of Bateson in Palo Alto, Wallace in Philadelphia, or anthropologists currently working at the Neuropsychiatric Institute at University of California, Los Angeles (UCLA) and in Montreal. However, anthropology has not yet forged a substantial response to changes in psychiatry over the past two decades. It is time to sound Sapir's call once again.

In the following pages, I outline several directions our research may take us in the coming decade. Before turning to discuss these, however, let me say a few more words about the reconceptualization of psychopathology within contemporary psychiatry.

The "Neo-Kraepelinians" and the conceptualization of psychopathology

The so-called "Neo-Kraepelinian Movement" developed in the 1960s in a climate of anti-classification sentiments and sharp criticism of the diagnostic process. In a recent book on psychiatric classification, Blashfield (1984) identifies several foci of criticism of psychiatric classification that had emerged by this time. First, a set of studies, beginning in 1949 and culminating in the late 1960s, provided evidence that interclinician reliability in making diagnostic judgments was extremely low. From an early study by Ash (1949), which showed that three research psychiatrists agreed on diagnoses of only 20 percent of fifty-two patients, through a major study by Cooper and his colleagues in the late 1960s, showing that

American psychiatrists are much more likely to diagnose patients as schizophrenic and British psychiatrists to diagnose them as suffering an affective disorder (Cooper, Kendall, and Gurland 1972), increasing evidence was provided of the lack of reliability of psychiatric classification. Second, research suggested that much of the disparity in diagnosis resulted from inadequacies of the nosological system rather than simply differences among clinicians. For example, Ward and Beck (1962) found that disagreement in diagnosis resulted in 5 percent of the cases from changes in the patients, 32 percent from differences among diagnosticians, and 62 percent from inadequacies of the nosology. In addition to these studies demonstrating poor reliability of psychiatric diagnosis, the 1960s produced political criticisms of the diagnostic enterprise. Critics claimed that the medical model of psychiatric classification was an expression of the dominance of the medical profession and provided reductionistic rather than humanistic accounts, and labeling theorists developed the argument that diagnostic categories produce what they claim to represent and reflect.

These criticisms of psychiatric diagnosis, Blashfield argues, stimulated efforts to reconstitute psychiatric nosology. A group of prominent research psychiatrists argued that the essential problems were not with those making the diagnoses – the practicing clinicians – but with the current nosological system itself, a system which they argued could not be applied reliably. In particular, they were convinced that a classification system based on etiology, on the psychological factors that produce disorders of character and neurotic symptoms (as held by psychoanalytic theory), might serve well for psychotherapy but could never produce reliable diagnoses. Thus, they focused their criticisms on the current diagnostic manual (*DSM* II, the second edition of the American Psychiatric Association's *Diagnostic and Statistical Manual*), and set out to develop an alternative, research-based system of psychiatric diagnosis formulated in terms of description rather than etiology.

In 1978, Klerman made explicit the propositions associated with the "Neo-Kraepelinians." In general, their position represented a reawakening of the interests in description and classification of Emil Kraepelin, the nineteenth-century German psychiatrist. They conceived psychopathology according to a medical model, and represented mental illnesses as discrete disorders. They held that clear, reliable criteria should be developed to differentiate disorders, and that these criteria should be valued and taught in psychiatric residency programs. And they argued strongly that quantitative techniques should be used to improve reliability and to investigate the validity of diagnostic criteria.

Most prominent among the Neo-Kraepelinians were Samuel Guze and

Eli Robins of Washington University in St. Louis, George Winokur, who moved from Washington University to the University of Iowa, and Don Klein and Robert Spitzer at the New York State Psychiatric Institute, as Blashfield confirmed through a citation analysis. These five researchers were most closely associated with the development of the new approach to psychiatric diagnosis. The Washington University group developed the Feighner Criteria, and Spitzer was chair of the committee that developed the revision of the American Psychiatric Association's *Diagnostic and Statistical Manual of Mental Disorders* (3rd edition) or *DSM* III (APA 1980). The most important epidemiological instruments designed to provide reliable research diagnoses are also associated with these groups, with the Diagnostic Interview Schedule (DIS) being developed at Washington University and the Schedule of Affective Disorders and Schizophrenia (SADS) in New York. Spitzer stressed that special attention should be given to the reliability of diagnosis. "Reliability doesn't guarantee validity," he argued, "but a lack of reliability ensures a classification system will not be valid" (Spitzer and Fleiss 1974: 341). This position provided the framework for a wide range of investigations that began in the late 1960s and continues to the present.

Insiders' histories, such as that provided by Blashfield, offer very little real sociology of knowledge of the transformation of psychiatric diagnostic practices over the past two decades, omitting social and political-economy factors entirely. Several of these were clearly important. By the late 1960s, pharmaceutical agents with specific effects on psychosis, depression, mania, and anxiety had been developed. Clinical trials of these drugs depended on reliable diagnostic criteria, as did genetic and psychophysiological research. The pharmaceutical industry was thus heavily invested in the development of the new research diagnostic criteria. These diagnostic and pharmacological developments were linked to the dramatic changes in neurobiology, where studies of neurotransmission provided the prospects of understanding the physiological mechanisms of pharmaceutical agents and ultimately of psychopathology. In addition to these changes in the basic sciences and medical treatments of mental illness, the paradigm shift in psychiatry was associated with reorganization of mental health services. The deinstitutionalization movement, driven in large measure by social and political criticisms of psychiatric incarceration and its effects, ironically served to foster the consignment of the ill to private "institutions" and the streets, and to limit treatment of the psychiatrically ill to outpatient medication clinics. Medicalized diagnoses served such outpatient treatment. The sharp rise in third-party reimbursement of psychiatric services – during the 1970s – also provided a spur to the integration of psychiatric diagnostic practices with those of other medical subspecialties. Reimbursement practices, including reimbursement by "diagnostically related groups" (DRG's) in recent years, continue to play a critical role in promoting attention to diagnosis among clinicians. Ironically, the anti-psychiatry movement in its contemporary forms has often brought its sharpest criticisms to bear on social and psychological theories and research, especially on studies of personal and familial etiologies, thus providing support for a narrow biological definition of psychopathology that removes all responsibility for madness from individuals and their families. The reorganization of the NIMH around disease categories – the schizophrenia branch, sections devoted to anxiety disorders and affective disorders in the clinical branch – both reflects and has continued to support the reorientation of psychiatric research to the new disease paradigm. When a critical sociology of the recent reorientation of psychiatric knowledge is ultimately written, social and political forces such as these will take their place alongside developments in biological psychiatry and psychopharmacology as crucial in the formation of contemporary understandings of mental illness and therapy. And while critics of the disciplinary gaze instantiated in the asylum often succeeded in the release of its inmates, research has taken a largely biological path and investment in humane care continues to decline (Eisenberg 1986).

What has emerged from these diverse social forces and scientific advances in neurobiology has been a sharp reconceptualization of psychopathology. The new paradigm has several characteristics. First, attention is focused on *categories* of disorder, rather than on level of distress, and psychiatric diseases are held to be *discrete* and *heterogenous*, that is, non-overlapping and distinguishable (Weissman and Klerman 1978). Second, criteria of categories are held to be *symptoms* (that is, positive markers that can be reliably elicited), rather than etiology. Third, the central research program in psychiatry is held to be the identification of the distinctive pathophysiology, course, and effective treatment forms characteristic of each diagnostic group. Fourth, efforts are made to extend this conceptualization from the major mental illnesses – schizophrenia, depression, manic-depressive illness – to all psychiatric phenomena (somatization, generalized anxiety, agoraphobia, drug abuse, personality disorders). And finally, additional research is aimed at the conceptualization and identification of the distinguishing features of diagnostic categories in neurophysiological, cognitive, psychodynamic, and social terms – as well as the development of integrative theories.

This reconceptualization of psychopathology has had strong influences not only on clinical practice – as well as billing procedures – but on social psychiatry and social epidemiology as well. Whereas the previous paradigm had led to epidemiological research focusing on correlations between social variables and *level* of psychological distress (levels of symptoms or disability), the new paradigm has led to an increased interest in identification of characteristics that make individuals vulnerable to *particular* diseases, to triggering events likely to lead to the onset of a disorder, and to factors that promote chronicity or recovery from a particular disease. Taken together with advances in neurobiology, these changes represent a dramatic shift in the organization of psychiatric concepts and research, a change with implications of a similar magnitude for social and cross-cultural research as for clinical and biological studies.

These changes should serve as a stark challenge to anthropology and our studies of psychopathology. The new psychiatry's conceptualization of human suffering stands in sharp contrast to an anthropological vision, and criticism of claims of universality of psychiatric diagnoses is almost second nature to anthropologists. Diagnostic categories reify Western ethnopsychological concepts, decontextualize symptoms, fail to attend to cultural forms and personal meanings, and fall prey to the category fallacy. It is easy for us to marshall such arguments, and in the company of psychiatrists we often do so. (For a cogent summary of such criticisms and the challenge they present to psychiatry, see Kleinman 1988.)

Several issues, however, should give us pause. First, the old psychoanalytically based classification of psychopathology as represented by *DSM* II *was* extraordinarily unreliable, even when applied within American culture, and provided an extremely poor basis for cross-cultural comparison. Its use by psychiatrists in the Third World often resulted in discussions of the cultural patterning of psychopathology in very ethnocentric and evolutionary terms. In societies where fears of witchcraft and rich somatic idioms are characteristic of psychopathology, weak egos and primitive defenses were said to abound, and those who suffer were held to be inappropriate candidates for psychological treatment. Surely a more descriptive, less etiological language of psychiatry offers significant advantages for both treatment and research.

Second, research over the past two decades has offered increasingly strong evidence that several psychiatric conditions – schizophrenia, manic-depressive disorder, major depression, and some forms of anxiety – are distinctive in their phenomenology, social origins, prognosis, and psychobiology. It seems increasingly naive to argue for pure cultural relativism in the study of psychopathology. It is troubling to find that many anthropologists, who would be quick to deny their adherence to the mind–body dichotomy, still demand radically different forms of analysis of conditions such as diabetes, on the one hand, and schizophrenia or depression, on the other. Although disordered physiology plays a more powerful role in constraining and organizing some forms of illness and suffering than others, it is clear that physiological processes, character, psychological coping patterns of individuals, and a society's cultural meanings and social responses are deeply involved in shaping *all* forms of illness. The world of suffering is simply not divided between diseases of the body, disguised with a veneer of cultural beliefs, and diseases of the mind, constituted by a society's culture-bound definition of abnormality and deviance. Anthropological efforts to reduce psychopathology to cultural psychology are as mistaken as psychiatry's reduction of suffering to disordered physiology.

Thus, I would argue that while recent developments in psychiatry do indeed direct attention away from the social and cultural dimensions of psychopathology, and should therefore be addressed critically, they also offer important new opportunities for theorizing and research among psychiatric and psychological anthropologists. In the remainder of this chapter, I will outline three general domains to which I believe we should direct our attention in the 1990s. First, we should develop, through ethnographic and historical research, a sociological and cultural critique of psychiatric knowledge and practice. Second, we should submit the new diagnostic categories and their criteria to systematic cross-cultural investigation. Third, we should develop autonomous theorizing and research in psychiatric anthropology, which includes a critical examination of the heterogeneity hypothesis. Let me address each of these in turn, using examples from research I have done with my colleagues on anxiety disorders.

The critical sociology of psychiatry knowledge and practice

The rapid changes in psychiatry offer an unusual opportunity for cultural–historical and direct ethnographic research on the social construction of psychiatric knowledge. Let me illustrate with an example from the construction of anxiety disorders, rather than depression or schizophrenia.

In the fall of 1983, I attended a conference on Anxiety and Anxiety Disorders, organized by the Anxiety Section of the Clinical Division of the NIMH, in order to provide a cross-cultural review of the literature on anxiety disorders (see Tuma and Maser 1985, for the conference papers and proceedings). There was a tremendous sense of excitement and energy at the conference. The leaders of the conference compared it to the National Institutes of Health conference on depression, held ten years earlier, which provided the framework for studies of depression in the 1970s. There was a feeling of enormous progress in the past two or three years in the study of anxiety. Neurotransmitters associated with anxiety and the efficacy of anxiolytic medications had been isolated. A consensus was emerging about discrete subcategories of anxiety disorders. The findings from the NIMH-sponsored ECA studies (the "Epidemiological Catchment Area" studies – community studies of prevalence of psychopathology, using the Diagnostic Interview Schedule) were just coming out of the computers, indicating distinctive genetic and psychosocial characteristics of the subtypes of anxiety disorders. And new understandings of anxiety were emerging, integrating traditional psychological studies and animal models, current clinical research, epidemiological findings, psychoneuroimmunological models developed by the endocrinologists, and basic cell-biology research on neurotransmitters. Organized predominantly by the Neo-Kraepelinians, the conference exuded a sense of excitement that at last the mighty stronghold of psychoanalysis, anxiety, was successfully being attacked by the weapons of science. There was but a single psychoanalytic paper at the conference, and talk in the corridors was of the psychoanalytic dinosaurs, just ready to disappear from the face of the earth.

In this conference, panic disorder was the central exhibit. As Robert Spitzer concluded at the end of the conference, "I would predict that the major growth industry in this field in the next decade will be panic!" Why panic disorder? In the late 1970s and early 1980s, increasing research attention was focused on anxiety attacks or panic attacks. A clear model was formulated of spontaneous, biologically triggered attacks as a discrete psychiatric disorder, and one with special importance since it often led through generalized learning to other forms of anxiety disorders. There were several contributions to the construction of panic disorder (see Klerman 1985). First, the discovery that some classes of pharmaceuticals have specific effects on panic disorder, distinct from those which affect generalized anxiety, was a powerful argument for the heterogeneity hypothesis. Particularly interesting was the fact that benzodiazapines, used for the treatment of generalized anxiety, were not effective in the treatment of recurrent panic attacks, while the monoamine oxidase (MAO) inhibitors, usually considered antidepressants, were effective in halting such attacks (Klein 1980). In addition to this pharmacological evidence, physiological evidence of the discreteness of panic disorder was emerging from research suggesting that sodium lactate would precipitate anxiety attacks among persons meeting criteria for panic disorder but not among other persons. Third, in addition to clear diagnostic criteria, a central phenomenological criterion of panic disorder was emerging: that the attacks are "unprovoked" or experienced as coming "out of the blue." Fourth, a series of papers had recently argued that agoraphobia, a severe and little-understood psychiatric condition, could be explained as a generalization of anxiety associated with those locations in which one first suffered a panic attack to other places, and a gradual development of an irrational fear that leaving one's house, particularly without the support of another person, might provoke an anxiety attack (Klein 1980). Finally, panic disorder provided a biological explanation which challenged a core claim of psychoanalysis – that acute anxiety is provoked by the surfacing of unconscious conflicts associated with some seemingly unrelated stimulus. Thus, several important symbolic dimensions were central to the reconstruction of anxiety attacks into panic disorder: the disorder was conceived as *discrete*, as *unprovoked*, as having symptoms that directly map onto the *physiological substrate*, and as producing *secondary elaborations* that make sense of other distinctive anxiety disorders.

The social construction of psychiatric categories such as this is amenable to critical historical, sociological, and anthropological analysis. First, if we take as our focus the diagnostic categories, it is obvious that not only has psychiatric ideology in general changed – several times, in fact – over the past 100 years, but that particular disorders have distinctive cultural histories. Some parts of that history have been written for depression (e.g., Jackson 1986), schizophrenia (e.g., Foucault 1966), and neurasthenia in Asia (e.g., Kleinman 1986; Lin 1989), as also for non-psychiatric disease categories such as venereal diseases (Brandt 1985). Anxiety, as depression, schizophrenia, and hysteria, has a distinctive cultural history in Western society, associated with neurasthenic women, traumatized soldiers, and the pressures of modernity and industrialization. In this it sharply diverges from the cultural history of schizophrenia, associated with asylums, chronic disability, the fractured self, and the ship of fools.[1] Anxiety also has a long history as a site for debates between advocates for psychoanalytic and psychophysiological explanations of distress. Meanings implicit in theorizing about anxiety disorders, as well as explicit theoretical debates about the nature and causes of anxiety disorders, are grounded in this cultural history.

The reconceptualization of anxiety bears within it not only dimensions of its cultural history, but important characteristics of the research actively underway today on anxiety disorders. Anthropologists have an unusual opportunity at this juncture to conduct ethnographic research on the construction and reconstruction of psychiatric diseases in precisely such settings. New diseases are being "identified" – that is, both recognized and constructed – in anxiety-disorder clinics, in sleep-disorder laboratories, in treatment centers for Post-Traumatic Stress Disorder (PTSD) (especially for American veterans of the Vietnam War),[2] and in specialized depression research centers. These are potential sites for important ethnographic research.

In ethnographic research on the contemporary construction of anxiety disorders, one rather unexpected finding is likely to emerge. Although the development of diagnostic criteria is central to the Neo-Kraepelinian psychiatry and has been a central focus of research, a review of both the clinical and popular literature on panic disorder suggests that the disorder is constructed far more through the development of *prototypical case accounts* or prototypical illness narratives than through the establishment of criteria.[3] David Sheehan, one of the leading proponents of the category panic disorder, begins his popular book entitled *The Anxiety Disease* (Sheehan 1983) with a "typical case" of a young, healthy woman who suddenly develops panic attacks, and her fiancé who cannot understand her condition and as a consequence subtly victimizes her for her condition. The book is organized around "the story of Adam and Maria," a story designed to "encapsulate the plight of a group of the population who are misunderstood by the world of normal people ... their descent into terror, their peculiar experiences. It is also about the beginning of the liberation of these people. And their journey to freedom" (Sheehan 1983: 8). In the story, Maria suffers her first mild spell at age twenty-three having finished college and now happily working in a new job – while with friends. "One evening she was out eating with friends, when suddenly she felt light-headed, dizzy" (p. 19). The spell occurs while she is under no stress ("She had been discussing their next vacation together with her friends ... What could be more pleasant?" [p. 20]). The spells continue occasionally for three months, when she suddenly experiences her first devastating attack of panic. Again, it happens without provocation: "She was out shopping in a mall when it overcame her. There was nothing special about the evening. Nothing unpleasant had happened to her that day" (p. 37). Terrified, she seeks medical advice, only to be told by her physician that there are no objective findings. The following stages of her illness are recounted – continued panic attacks, with a growing hypochondriasis and embarrassing encounters with the medical profession; the development of phobias, leading eventually to agoraphobia and depression; a split with her boyfriend, who cannot understand her problem. After Maria has made various unsuccessful attempts to find medical and psychiatric treatment, her boyfriend discovers a story about panic disorder in a science magazine, reads into the matter in the library, and informs Maria of his findings. Together, they seek out and finally attend an anxiety-disorder clinic, where her condition is correctly diagnosed, the correct drug (imipramine) is prescribed, and she is helped through her continued anxiety by a dedicated and supportive physician ("He had no fear of this fear disease. Indeed, she could see that he took pleasure in the struggle" [p. 187]). In the end, we see her moving toward the future, with growing self-assurance and independence, with only occasional bouts of anxiety recurring.

This scenario calls to mind D'Andrade's discussion elsewhere in this volume of the role of "schemas" or "prototypes" in cognition and the cultural organization of knowledge. Although the current diagnostic manual is organized in criterial terms, it seems likely that the construction of prototypical illness narratives, paradigmatic cases which come to serve clinicians (and thus the public) as prototypes for a form of disorder, may be far more powerful rhetorically than are diagnostic criteria, and may indeed be far more central to the diagnostic process as well. And what is the prototype, the core image, that is constructed of panic disorder in the literature? It is of an idealized, healthy individual, residing in a secure setting in which a sense of vulnerability is unreasonable and in which it is fairly easy to determine which fears one suffers that others in the same setting do not share. This person suffers a single, discrete disorder, a series of unprovoked attacks of fear or anxiety, a rush of biological symptoms, interpreted as a cue of danger, that come to play a fundamental role in structuring the individual's life experience. This person's problems are amenable neither to psychotherapy nor to traditional antianxiety medications. When correctly diagnosed, however, the condition can be successfully treated with medication and supportive therapy.

The analysis here is not meant to suggest that psychiatrists do not treat patients who quite closely resemble the prototype. Many do. My argument is rather that anthropologists have a special opportunity to investigate the construction of illness categories in psychiatry today by focusing on specialized research clinics, and that careful attention should be given to the development and popularization of prototypical narratives. These narratives have an important ideological component – panic-disorder patients are often characterized as middle class, anglo, and essentially healthy, individuals whose illness could only be understood as an endogenous, biological eruption. And the account authorizes a particular vision of this condition as fundamentally biological and its treatment as a form of medical practice, with diagnosis and prescription as its central activities. We might examine the extent to which such prototypes produce "systematic distortions" – of the type described by Shweder and D'Andrade (1980) – in the perception by clinicians and researchers of aspects of the patients' stories, a process that might be compared with the perceptual distortions of clinicians operating within other frameworks. And we might certainly examine how the focus on particular conditions as paradigmatic reproduces a model that maximizes the expertise and efficacy of particular researchers and clinicians and minimizes attention to features of conditions best kept outside the province of their attention.[4]

Historical and ethnographic research on the construction of psychiatric knowledge about particular illness conditions can be quite usefully complemented by direct anthropological studies of persons suffering the conditions identified by researchers and clinicians. A further example from my research on panic disorder will illustrate. Along with a postdoctoral fellow and graduate student, I carried out a preliminary study that raises questions about the social and cultural shaping of this diagnostic entity.[5] We developed a brief screening instrument, based on the *DSM* III criteria for panic disorder, and administered it to 100 patients in a poor, inner-city primary-care clinic. Forty of the 100 patients screened positive for having at some time in their lives suffered attacks with symptoms of those of panic disorder. About half of these cases indicated a history of heart disease, diabetes, or epilepsy, and others of alcoholism and other psychiatric disorders. For us, the so-called "discreteness" of the disorder was called into sharp question. It was often quite difficult, even in intensive interviews, to determine whether alcohol had been used to self-medicate for anxiety attacks, or whether the reported attacks were secondary to alcohol abuse. It was similarly difficult to distinguish the anxiety attacks from other psychiatric disorders, and in some cases the overlap with medical conditions causing episodes of anxiety and altered states of consciousness produced an extremely complex picture.

The issue of the "spontaneity" of the attacks raised equally difficult problems. A 56-year-old woman told an interviewer of being raped as a child and of never having told anyone, including a physician. A woman in her late thirties described her life history as including the death of one of her infants, brain-damage to another of her children with whom she now lived, and abandonment by her husband, as well as medical diagnoses of diabetes, high blood pressure, and "possible epilepsy." Another woman in her forties described a history of severe panic attacks, which began when she was a juror in a murder trial and which, in psychotherapy, she came to associate with her mother's having become psychotic and being institutionalized while the interviewee was a teenager. All of these persons met criteria for panic disorder. All three met *DSM* III criteria for suffering "unprovoked" attacks. In the face of such case data, it seems unlikely that a neat distinction between endogenous, unprovoked (i.e. biological) attacks and exogenous, provoked (i.e. psychological) attacks can be maintained (see Aronson 1987, for a similar view).

The Diagnostic Interview Schedule asks as the primary screening question: "Have you ever had a spell or attack when all of a sudden you felt frightened, anxious, or very uneasy in situations when most people would not be afraid?" This question did not make it easy to determine whether the anxiety attacks were unprovoked. In some other cases – of persons we interviewed who lived in quite dangerous halfway houses or on the street – the very question of having spells of feeling frightened when others would not be afraid was essentially meaningless. It thus became increasingly clear to us that the image of the person suffering panic disorder in the prototypical case accounts is *in part* an ideological construct, that is, it represents as prototypical not only a set of symptoms but a view of the person, social context, and life story that reproduces conventional knowledge about social relations in American society (see Young 1980).

One response of anthropology to the new developments in psychiatry should thus be a critical sociology of psychiatric knowledge, supported by research focused clearly on the contemporary reconstruction of psychiatric disease categories.

Cross-cultural research on diagnostic categories and their criteria

The second general domain of research that I have suggested as a response to the contemporary claims of psychiatry is the following: we have an opportunity to submit the new diagnostic categories and their criteria to systematic cross-cultural research, both through combined clinical and ethnographic research and through collaborating in epidemiological studies. Such research has a special urgency. *DSM* III has been officially translated into ten languages and is used by psychiatrists worldwide to make treatment decisions. As advances are made in psychoactive drugs, medication decisions, both in the US and worldwide, have increasingly serious consequences (see Good and Good 1986). Inappropriate use of neuroleptics, based on misdiagnosis of schizophrenia, often masks brief psychoses and produces chronicity rather than benefit. Failure to make appropriate use of antidepressant medications or lithium because of misdiagnosis can also needlessly prolong suffering and increase the risk of suicide. Thus research that examines the cultural patterning of major psychiatric disorders has potentially important consequences.

Cross-cultural research provides an opportunity to assess the claims of universality of the contemporary Neo-Kraepelinians and to develop a specific and detailed cultural response. The diagnostic approach represented by *DSM* III, as well as the current International Classification of Diseases (ICD 10), and various epidemiological instruments designed to provide diagnoses, provide very explicit symptomatic criteria for psychiatric conditions, conceived as disease entities. These may serve the anthropologist as hypotheses for investigating the cultural patterning of psychopathology, and provide the basis for collaboration both with clinicians and epidemiologists. I make no attempt here to review this important research domain,[6] but will rather illustrate briefly from what we currently know about anxiety disorders.

Although current theories of anxiety disorders have not been systematically investigated cross-culturally, what evidence we have suggests that neither diagnostic criteria nor subcategories of anxiety disorders found among Americans and Europeans are likely to be universal (see Good and Kleinman 1985, for a review). There may be higher levels of similarity, however, than many anthropologists would anticipate. Cultural differences might be summarized in four ways. First, nearly all anthropological research in this area demonstrates that an extremely rich and diverse somatic language is associated with anxiety, and that somatic idioms are culturally distinctive (see Kleinman 1988, and Good and Kleinman 1985, for a summary). Development of criteria for anxiety disorders that reflect semantic domains as well as psychophysiological disturbances, the definition of somatization disorders, and a basic understanding of the relation between "psychologization" and "somatization" of distress all hinge on interpretations of research in this area. Second, the ubiquitous language of nerves provides an interesting complex of issues for research. Studies of neurasthenia in Asian societies (e.g., Reynolds 1976; Kleinman 1986; Lin 1989) suggest that persons self-labeled as neurasthenic and traditionally so diagnosed meet criteria both for anxiety and depressive disorders, calling into question the validity of the distinction as represented in *DSM* III for some persons in Chinese and Japanese cultures. The nature of neurasthenia has been the focus of psychiatric theorizing, distinctive psychotherapies, and extensive empirical research in Asian societies (for a collection of essays on neurasthenia by Asian psychiatrists and social scientists, see Lin 1989). Distinctive schools of thought, such as those associated with various Chinese universities or Morita psychotherapy in Japan, have nosological systems which categorize subtypes of neurasthenia in a fashion suggesting both important similarities and differences to American categories of anxiety disorders (e.g., Russell 1989). And the increasing influence of Western psychiatry has led to sharp professional debates about the appropriateness of *DSM* III or ICD 10 for the Asian context. But illnesses of nerves are not confined to Asia. For example, a history of anthropological and psychiatric work on *nervios* among various Latin cultures indicates that rich local idioms are associated with what anglo psychiatrists conceptualize as anxiety disorders, and may help to explain the traditional finding of extremely high levels of psychopathology among Latinos, especially Puerto Ricans (see Guarnaccia, Good, and Kleinman 1990, for a discussion; cf. Scheper-Hughes in this book). The relationship between pathology, the articulation of personal suffering and human misery in the idiom of nerves, and the use of the nerves idiom as a "form of resistance" (e.g. Lock 1990) is also raised in a complex way by this research.

Third, hypotheses about the specificity of panic disorder, its onset outside the context of psychosocial stressors, and its relationship to agoraphobia deserve careful attention cross-culturally. For example, Puerto Ricans have long been observed to suffer *ataques de nervios*, attacks which include physical distress and anxiety and may include loss of consciousness. These attacks may occur under stress (such as during grief) or without immediate psychosocial provocation. One might well hypothesize that panic attacks as described in current psychiatric literature would be interpreted and experienced by Puerto Ricans as belonging to a larger domain of *ataques*, and that the culture-specific domain would provide more valid data in both clinical and epidemiological research than the narrower category "panic disorder." Support for this view is provided by the work by Guarnaccia and his colleagues in Puerto Rico. For example, Guarnaccia has demonstrated the importance of *ataques* as a phenomenological construct (Guarnaccia *et al.* 1989), and he and his colleagues have shown that it is possible to reinterpret data gathered using the Diagnostic Interview Schedule in a community study and to develop an *ataques de nervios* scale which solves a number of problems in the data analysis (Guarnaccia, Rubio-Stipec, and Canino 1989).

Finally, we might note that culturally distinctive etiological concepts – witchcraft, "stress," fright or startle, spirit attack – organize illness experience, categories, and symptoms, and that even when illness is clearly recognizable as an anxiety or depressive disorder its phenomenology and symptoms are culturally distinctive as well. For example, research in Africa suggests that anxiety disorders are associated both with highly elaborate somatic complaints (Ebigbo 1982) and with dreams of witchcraft and fears of infertility (A. Leighton, Lambo, Hughes, D. Leighton, Murphy, and Mecklin 1963). Diagnostic criteria developed from middle-class American patients and simply translated for use in non-Western cultures are thus certain to miss many pathognomic symptoms.

Anthropologists have focused attention on culture-bound disorders almost entirely to the exclusion of studies of brief psychoses, schizophrenic disorders, manic-depressive illness, depression, and anxiety disorders. The current classificatory system suggests quite specific hypotheses which may both provide a useful basis for cross-cultural comparison and stimulate a serious anthropological critique of contemporary psychiatry. In particular, the anthropological literature is unambiguous on one significant aspect of current psychiatric diagnosis.

Culture plays a profound role in the experience and expression of symptoms – in the process of symptom-formation. We would therefore expect that diagnostic criteria defined as *symptoms* will vary cross-culturally.

An agenda for anthropological studies of psychopathology

These suggestions then provide an entrée to the question of how we might expect to develop a program of anthropological studies of psychopathology which is not a reflex of a medicalized psychiatry but which explores issues provoked by an encounter with contemporary psychiatry. What do anthropologists have to offer? How should we study madness in the coming decade? I want to make several suggestions.

First, following my comments earlier in the chapter, I suggest we focus attention on specific disorders rather than on general distress, and on the major categories of psychopathology as well as on native categories of illness. Although there are noteworthy examples of such work in the past, it is remarkable how little current anthropological work begins with a simple level of psychiatric sophistication, establishes criteria for cases to be studied, and explores the influence of culture on specific types of psychopathology. Kleinman's work on depression and neurasthenia (1986) stands as the most important recent work growing out of this model; some current work on schizophrenia (e.g., Jenkins 1988; Corin 1990) follows this approach; and the *Culture and Depression* collection (Kleinman and Good 1985) was intended to stimulate and contribute to such a direction for research.

Second, I believe we should study psychopathology as "phenomenological reality." The Neo-Kraepelinians claim that their work is descriptive, and that descriptions of the phenomenology of particular disorders, rather than etiological theorizing, are central to their enterprise. However, "phenomenology" in the descriptive-psychiatry tradition seldom denotes more than frequency of symptoms and typical prognosis, bearing little relationship to the accounts of experience found in the phenomenological traditions of psychiatry and the social sciences. Here anthropology has the potential to make a major contribution. Rich phenomenological accounts based on cross-cultural research, work which focuses on *lived experience*, on the disturbances of experience of time, space, person, affect, thought, and embodiment, associated with psychopathology in various societies, would serve as a data base for renewed discussion of the role of culture in shaping psychopathology. Accounts which draw on methods of research and analysis such as those of Hallowell, continental phenomenologists, and contemporary medical anthropology have the potential to revivify and reconstitute the notion of the phenomenology of depression or schizophrenia (for recent examples, see Corin 1990, and Strauss and Estroff 1989). Such research can provide a solid critique of so-called "phenomenologies" of contemporary psychiatry, showing the extent to which such descriptions are organized around symptom criteria known or presumed to reflect biological categories, rather than around categories of experience.

Sapir wrote in 1932: "The morbidity . . . that the psychiatrist has to deal with seems for the most part, to be not a morbidity of organic segments or even of organic functions but of experience itself" (Sapir 1966: 144–145). Were he writing today he might well make less of a dichotomy between disorders of organic function and experience. He would surely, however, be disappointed by the failure of anthropologists to provide cross-cultural studies – both descriptive and analytic – of disorders of experience. Especially important may be studies that provide descriptions of experiences longitudinally, beginning with those at the onset of illness. The classic work of Chapman (1966) on schizophrenia suggests there is fairly rapid socialization of experience, that communicating and accounting for experience takes on culturally stereotyped form quite soon after initial awareness of hallucinations or other extraordinary experiences. Phenomenological accounts of this process in non-Western settings would provide a major contribution to our understanding of the enculturation of disordered experience.

In order for such work to progress, however, we will need to develop a far more clear and explicit framework for such phenomenological research and descriptions. Rich case accounts will be useful but not adequate. Such research should be designed to provide solid evidence *both* for cross-cultural similarities and differences in particular forms of psychopathology, and also for within-culture differences between types of disorder.

Third, I suggest we study madness as "interpreted disorder." Many of the experiences of madness, especially the early experiences, have an iconic quality. They are irruptions of the mysterious; they are experienced as an "it," *das id*, the other in the midst of the self. They seem to display unsocialized nature in unwelcome form. Godfrey Lienhardt's (1961) classic description of the possessing divinities of the Dinka describes how the healer calls forth the possible origins of suffering until the spirit names itself, that is, until the iconic becomes more fully symbolized. And as the spirit takes form, it emerges into a world of *symbolic complexes*, of domains of symbolized experience – not of isolated symptoms, but into a world in which a symptom, that is, a symbolized experience, *already belongs* to a cultural domain, a domain of intersubjective meanings, a network that entails a complex of symbolized meanings. What is remarkable about *DSM*-III-style symptom criteria is the total failure to recognize the *semantic* domains associated with particular illnesses, the naive assumption that biology continues to show itself iconically, the naive unawareness that nature irrupting in the self is quickly socialized, and that symptoms themselves are socialized articulations. Despite such socialization, however, illness maintains its power to reveal the form of the Other, and consequently has ontological significance. It can't be wished away. It maintains a sense of mystery, even as it is increasingly socialized and reintegrated into the economy of the self. It thus provokes ongoing efforts at understanding, processes of "labeling" and ritual management, efforts to "emplot" the disorder in a narrative form that makes sense of it and provides the grounds for efficacy and control (Good 1990). The interpretive processes through which this socialization occurs are ultimately *only* amenable to ethnographic and clinical analysis.

Fourth, we should study madness as "disordered interpretation." Disordered interpretations – changes in the way the self, social relations, the social environment are perceived and understood – are part of all serious illness, especially chronic or life-threatening illnesses. However, it lies at the heart of psychopathology (see Good and Good 1985). It is essentially what we *mean* by *psycho*pathology. Anxiety disorders *are* pathological interpretations of some aspect of the world as threatening, provoking irrational fears and unusual responses, for example. Cross-cultural research on disorders of the interpretive processes associated with psychopathology should provoke a serious engagement with the cognitive tradition of psychotherapy and psychological theorizing. Aaron Beck and his colleagues have provided accounts of depression (Beck 1976), and more recently of anxiety disorders (Beck and Emery 1985), as the product of disordered cognitive processes, a set of "errors" in logic and reasoning which shape perception and interpretation and produce syndromes of disordered experience. Their work suggests testable hypotheses. Is the logic they describe a universal logic, as they seem to believe, or a cultural and culture-specific logic, as anthropologists would expect? Do universal disorders of cognition and perception produce culture-specific illness forms? Or are disorders of cognition and perception themselves culturally variable?

Fifth, we should study madness as "situated discourses." Sociologists of science have noted recently that dramatically diverse pictures of scientists and their work can be assembled precisely because of the failure to identify the types of discourse being used as the basis for the portrait (Gilbert and Mulkay 1984). Similarly, extremely diverse pictures of madness in a given culture can be drawn, often because of failure to link discourse to delimited and contextualized narratives. Complaints by the sufferers, illness narratives by family members, medical texts, formal exegesis by healers, ritual or clinical discourse by healers, formal clinical talk by professional practitioners, informal talk by the same, written case notes by professionals – all produce distinctive perspectives on the cultural domain of madness. An analysis of types of discourse and their organization as cultural genres should accompany our analyses of what these sources tell us about psychopathology.

Sixth, we should study madness as emerging from and reshaping life histories. I note what may be obvious to psychological anthropologists for several reasons. Attention to "discourse" in postmodernist writing (including, for example, Foucault's writings on madness) has often explicitly denied analytic status to the "subject," resulting in a failure to attach texts to authors, narratives to narrators, and discourse to the experiences of the interlocutors. Patients speak out, however, resisting the caricature of their experience by clinicians, healers, or family members, or the appropriation of their suffering as "discourse," reasserting the mystery of their experience. Doctors, nurses, and healers not only justify their work, but express their hopes, their longing to overcome helplessness in the face of the intractability of chronic illness and the suffering of those they treat. Subordination of the individual lives of sufferers and healers to "discursive processes" often obscures the character of suffering *and* of healing. A return to intensive studies of life history and personal experience in cross-cultural investigations of psychopathology is thus overdue.

Seventh, we should direct explicit attention to the effects of culture on the *course and outcome* of psychopathology. One of the most dramatic findings of cross-cultural research of the past several decades comes from the results of the World Health Organization's International Pilot Study of Schizophrenia (IPSS) (WHO, 1979) and the more recent Determinants of Outcome Study.[7] Researchers identified persons suffering recent onset of psychosis and meeting criteria for schizophrenia in societies in both the developed and the developing world, then followed their course in ensuing years. In the original IPSS, a three-year follow-up found that sufferers in countries in the developing world did much better than those in the developed countries. For example, whereas only 11 percent of the cases in Denmark were recovered after three years, in Nigeria and India respectively 49 percent and 51 percent of individuals had recovered. These findings were debated, and the Determinants of Outcome Study was undertaken to explore in more detail the potential contributions to the course of schizophrenic illness.

Findings of this study are consistent with the earlier research (Sartorius, Jablensky, Korten, Ernberg, Anker, Cooper, and Day 1986). While further work is needed to reproduce and explain these apparent findings, we now have the basis for believing that culture has a profound effect on the course of illness, even on such an illness as schizophrenia, long defined (by Kraepelin and his followers) by its seemingly inevitable course of chronic deterioration. Many chronic illnesses, medical and psychiatric, have variable courses – waxing and waning of symptoms, variations in course of experience and social functioning, relatively unexplained variation in response to medication and other treatment. Whereas studies of symptomatology, prevalence, onset, and illness behavior have received primary attention from cross-cultural researchers, the schizophrenia data suggest the urgency of social and cultural research on the *course* of illness. Various hypotheses are currently being investigated. Nancy Waxler (1977, 1979) has argued for some years that culture has its primary effect on psychotic illness through definition of the condition – as spirit possession, as biological defect, as personality disorder – which in turn influences social response and expectations, and that these together account in large measure for differences in outcome. Others have argued that family emotional climate – *expressed emotion* toward the sick individual by primary family members – plays a significant role in the course of schizophrenia (Karno, Jenkins, De La Selva, Santana, Telles, Lopez, and Mintz 1987; Leff, Wig, Badi, Menon, Kuipers, Korten, Ernberg, Day, Sartorius, and Jablensky 1990; Jenkins 1991). Warner (1985) has made a strong case for the role of political economy; in particular, he argues that the level of involvement of a society or social group in capitalist labor and industrial employment predicts the extent to which disability is associated with employment and thus provides a mechanism by which variations in the economy influence disability, chronicity, and thus illness course.

Research in this area requires extreme methodological sophistication and an attention to measurement anthropologists have not usually given. But standard epidemiological studies have been relatively unavailing in accounting for the sources of variance discovered. One of the key opportunities for anthropological research is thus the investigation of the relations between lived experience, macrosocial arrangements, cultural forms, and family relationships, on the one hand, and course of illness on the other.

Finally, we must study psychopathology as "socially and historically produced." And here I refer not simply to analyses of the social distribution of psychiatric illness, nor to much of the recent "critical" literature in medical anthropology, nor even to work as sophisticated as that of Warner (1985) on the political economy of schizophrenia, important as that is. I rather point to the enormous difficulty of writing about *historicized* experience, of demonstrating how political and economic structures are embodied in experience every bit as much as early family experience and biology are, and of portraying these issues in our ethnographic and interpretive accounts.

In conclusion, I return to Sapir's call for efforts "to discover what maladjustment means in the remoter cultures." I do not believe the paradigm shift in psychiatry makes collaborative research with clinicians and epidemiologists impossible or even less plausible. In many ways it offers substantial advantages over previous paradigms. Anthropological research on psychopathology should, of course, be combined with the "person-centered" research called for by LeVine and others; it should be an integral part of our studies of indigenous concepts of the person, life-span, self, behavior, and mental functioning, both normal and deviant; and it should be combined with our renewed interest in case studies. The new paradigm, however, provides a spate of hypotheses and claims to be tested, rejected, or revised. It offers new specificity to our debates about universality. It suggests new questions about symptom formation and illness experience, about vulnerability, protective features of society, and triggering events leading to the onset of illness. And it suggests that one of the most profound roles of cultural and social forces may be in their effects on course of illness – on the promotion of positive prognosis or the development of chronicity. My own predilection is to formulate these issues in terms of interpretive studies, combining phenomenological, hermeneutic, and narrative analyses to investigate the role of culture in psychopathology. However, the challenge is not to develop a single theoretical paradigm, but to take advantage of current opportunities to develop a renewed psychiatric anthropology and cross-cultural psychiatry.

NOTES

1 Feminist historical studies have been especially important to our understanding of some aspects of this history. For example, see Showalter 1985.
2 Allan Young has been conducting particularly interesting anthropological research on PTSD, which is to date largely unpublished. See Young 1988.
3 Although not investigating the construction of diagnostic categories through prototypical narratives, Mattingly (1989) develops an interesting analysis of the role of prototypical narratives in clinical practice, focusing on the work of occupational therapists.
4 This paragraph reflects the cogent comments of Geoff White on the original draft of this paper.
5 The research was carried out along with Peter Guarnaccia, who was supported by an NIMH post-doctoral fellowship from Harvard's Training Program in Clinically Relevant Medical Anthropology (MH 18006), and Brad Christo, a graduate student. The research was supported by a Milton Fund Small Grant from Harvard Medical School.

6 For an overall review of the role of culture in shaping psychiatric conditions, see Kleinman 1988. For a recent review of the role of culture in depressive illness, see Jenkins, Kleinman and Good 1990; cf. Kleinman and Good 1985. Mezzich and von Cranach, 1988, provide a collection of essays from the World Psychiatric Association Section of Nomenclature and Classification that illustrates how issues of national and cultural differences in classification are being discussed by psychiatric professionals involved in developing an international psychiatric nosology.

7 Preliminary results of the WHO Collaborative Study on the Determinants of Outcome of Severe Mental Disorders are to be found in Sartorius, Jablensky, Korten, Ernberg, Anker, Cooper, and Day 1986. A full report is forthcoming shortly as a special issue of the journal *Psychological Medicine*. For further discussion, see Kleinman 1988: 47–48.

REFERENCES

American Psychiatric Association (APA). 1980. *Diagnostic and Statistical Manual of Mental Disorders* (3rd edn). Washington, DC: Author

Aronson, T. A. 1987. Is Panic Disorder a Distinct Diagnostic Entity? A Critical Review of the Borders of a Syndrome. *Journal of Nervous and Mental Disease* 175: 584–94

Ash, P. 1949. The Reliability of Psychiatric Diagnosis. *Journal of Abnormal and Social Psychology* 44: 272–276

Beck, A. T. 1976. *Cognitive Therapy and the Emotional Disorders*. New York: International Universities Press

Beck, A. T. and G. Emery. 1985. *Anxiety Disorders and Phobias: A Cognitive Perspective*. New York: Basic Books

Blashfield, R. K. 1984. *The Classification of Psychopathology: Neo-Kraepelinian and Quantitative Approaches*. New York: Plenum Press

Brandt, A. M. 1985. *No Magic Bullet: A Social History of Venereal Disease in the United States Since 1980*. Oxford: Oxford University Press

Chapman, J. 1966. The Early Symptoms of Schizophrenia. *British Journal of Psychiatry* 112: 225–251

Cooper, J., R. E. Kendall, and B. J. Gurland. 1972. *Psychiatric Diagnoses in New York and London: A Comparative Study of Mental Hospital Admissions*. London: Oxford University Press

Corin, E. 1990. Facts and Meaning in Psychiatry: An Anthropological Approach to the Lifeworld of Schizophrenics. *Culture, Medicine and Psychiatry* 14(2): 153–188

Darnell, R. 1986. Personality and Culture: The Fate of the Sapirian Alternative. In G. W. Stocking, ed., *Malinowski, Rivers, Benedict and Others: Essays on Culture and Personality* (pp. 156–183). Madison: University of Wisconsin Press

Ebigbo, P. O. 1982. Development of a Culture Specific (Nigeria) Screening Scale of Somatic Complaints Indicating Psychiatric Disturbance. *Culture, Medicine and Psychiatry*, 6: 29–43

Eisenberg, L. 1986. Mindlessness and Brainlessness in Psychiatry. *British Journal of Psychiatry* 148: 497–508

Foucault, M. 1966. *Madness and Civilization*. New York: Mentor

Gilbert, G. N. and M. Mulkay. 1984. *Opening Pandora's Box: A Sociological Analysis of Scientists' Discourse*. Cambridge: Cambridge University Press

Good, B. J. 1993. *Medicine, Rationality and Experience: An Anthropological Perspective*. The 1990 Lewis Henry Morgan Lectures. Cambridge University Press

Good, B. J. and M. J. D. Good. 1985. The Interpretation of Iranian Depressive Illness and Dysphoric Affect. In A. Kleinman and B. Good, eds., *Culture and Depression* (pp. 369–428). Berkeley: University of California Press

1986. The Cultural Context of Diagnosis and Therapy: A View from Medical Anthropology. In M. Miranda and H. Kitano, eds., *Mental Health Research and Practice in Minority Communities* (pp. 1–27). Washington, DC: U.S. Department of Health and Human Services

Good, B. and A. Kleinman. 1985. Culture and Anxiety: Cross-Cultural Evidence for the Patterning of Anxiety Disorders. In A. H. Tuma and J. Maser, eds., *Anxiety and the Anxiety Disorders* (pp. 297–324). Hillsdale, NJ: Lawrence Erlbaum

Guarnaccia, P. J. et al. (1989). The Multiple Meanings of Ataques de Nervios in the Latino Community. *Medical Anthropology* 11: 47–63

Guarnaccia, P. J., B. J. Good, and A. Kleinman. 1990. Culture and Psychopathology in Latin American Cultures. *The American Journal of Psychiatry* 11: 1,449–1,456

Guarnaccia, P. J., M. Rubio-Stipec, and G. Canino. 1989. Ataques de Nervios in the Puerto Rican Diagnostic Interview Schedule: The Impact of Cultural Categories on Psychiatric Epidemiology. *Culture, Medicine and Psychiatry* 13(3): 275–295

Jackson, S. 1986. *Melancholia and Depression: From Hippocratic Times to Modern Times*. New Haven: Yale University Press

Jenkins, J. H. 1988. Ethnopsychiatric Interpretations of Schizophrenic Illness: The Problem of *Nervios* Within Mexican-American Families. *Culture, Medicine and Psychiatry* 12(3): 301–329

1991. Anthropology, Expressed Emotion, and Schyzophrenia. *Ethos* 19: 387–431

Jenkins, J. H., A. Kleinman, and B. J. Good. 1990. Cross-Cultural Studies of Depression. In J. Becker and A. Kleinman, eds., *Advances in Mood Disorders*. Hillsdale, NJ: Lawrence Erlbaum

Karno, M., J. H. Jenkins, A. De La Selva, F. Santana, C. Telles, S. Lopez, and J. Mintz. 1987. Expressed Emotion and Schizophrenic Outcome Among Mexican-American Families. *Journal of Nervous and Mental Disease* 175: 143–151

Klein, D. F. 1980. Anxiety Reconceptualized. *Comprehensive Psychiatry* 21: 411–427

Kleinman, A. 1986. *Social Origins of Distress and Disease: Depression, Neurasthenia and Pain in Modern China*. New Haven: Yale University Press

1988. *Rethinking Psychiatry: From Cultural Category to Personal Experience*. New York: Free Press

Kleinman, A. and B. Good, eds. 1985. *Culture and Depression: Studies in the Anthropology and Cross-Cultural Psychiatry of Affect and Disorder*. Berkeley: University of California Press

Klerman, G. L. 1978. The Evolution of a Scientific Nosology. In J. C. Shershow, ed., *Schizophrenia: Science and Practice*. Cambridge, MA: Harvard University Press

1985. Controversies in Research on Psychopathology of Anxiety and Anxiety Disorders. In A. H. Tuma and J. Maser, eds., *Anxiety and the Anxiety Disorders* (pp. 775–782). Hillsdale, NJ: Lawrence Erlbaum

Leff, J., N. N. Wig, H. Bedi, D. K. Menon, L. Kuipers, A. Korten, G. Ernberg, R. Day, N. Sartorius, and A. Jablensky. 1990. Relatives' Expressed Emotion and the Course of Schizophrenia in Chandigarh: A Two-Year Follow-Up of a First-Contact Sample. *British Journal of Psychiatry* 156: 351–356

Leighton, A., T. Lambo, C. Hughes, D. Leighton, J. Murphy, and D. Mecklin. 1963. *Psychiatric Disorder Among the Yoruba*. Ithaca, NY: Cornell University Press

Lienhardt, G. 1961. *Divinity and Experience*. Oxford: Clarendon Press

Lin, T. Y., ed. 1989. *Neurasthenia in Asian Cultures*. Special volume of *Culture, Medicine and Psychiatry* 13(2)

Lock, M. 1990. On Being Ethnic: The Politics of Breaking and Making Identity in Canada, or, *Nevra* on Sunday. *Culture, Medicine and Psychiatry* 14(2): 237–254

Mattingly, C. F. 1989. *Thinking with Stories: Story and Experience in Clinical Practice*. Ph.D. Dissertation, Department of Urban Studies and Planning and the Anthropology/Archeology Program, Massachusetts Institute of Technology

Mezzich, J. E. and M. von Cranach, eds. 1988. *International Classification in Psychiatry*. Cambridge: Cambridge University Press

Reynolds, D. 1976. *Morita Psychotherapy*. Berkeley: University of California Press

Russell, J. 1989. Anxiety Disorders in Japan: A Review of the Japanese Literature on Shinkeishitsu and Taijinkyofusho. *Culture, Medicine and Psychiatry* 13(4): 391–403

Sapir, E. 1966. Cultural Anthropology and Psychiatry. In D. G. Mandelbaum, ed., *Culture, Language and Personality: Selected Essays*. Berkeley: University of California Press (originally published in 1932)

Sartorius, N., A. Jablensky, A. Korten, G. Ernberg, M. Anker, J. E. Cooper, and R. Day. 1986. *Early Manifestations and First-Contact Incidence of Schizophrenia in Different Cultures: A Preliminary Report on the Initial Evaluation Phase of the WHO Collaborative Study on Determinants of Outcome of Severe Mental Disorders. Psychological Medicine* 16: 909–928

Sheehan, D. V. 1982. Current Concepts in Psychiatry: Panic Attacks and Phobias. *New England Journal of Medicine* 307: 156–158

1983. *The Anxiety Disease*. New York: Charles Scribner's Sons

Showalter, E. 1985. *The Female Malady: Women, Madness, and English Culture, 1830–1980*. New York: Pantheon

Shweder, R. A. and R. A. D'Andrade. 1980. The Systematic Distortion Hypothesis. In R. Shweder, ed. *Fallible Judgement in Behavioral Research*. San Francisco: Jossey-Bass

Spitzer, R. L. and J. L. Fleiss. 1974. A Reanalysis of the Reliability of Psychiatric Diagnosis. *British Journal of Psychiatry* 125: 341–347

Strauss, J. S. and S. E. Estroff. 1989. *Subjective Experiences of Schizophrenia and Related Disorders*. Special issue of Schizophrenia Bulletin 15(2): 177–346

Tuma, A. H. and J. Maser, eds. 1985. *Anxiety and the Anxiety Disorders*. Hillsdale, NJ: Lawrence Erlbaum

Ward, C. H., A. T. Beck, M. Mendelson, J. E. Mock, and J. K. Erbaugh. 1962. The Psychiatric Nomenclature. *Archives of General Psychiatry* 7: 198–205

Warner, R. 1985. *Recovery from Schizophrenia: Psychiatry and Political Economy*. London: Routledge & Kegan Paul

Waxler, N. 1977. Is Mental Illness Cured in Traditional Societies? A Theoretical Analysis. *Culture, Medicine and Psychiatry* 1: 233–253

1979. Is Outcome for Schizophrenia Better in Nonindustrial Societies? The Case of Sri Lanka. *Journal of Nervous and Mental Diseases* 167: 144–158

Weissman, M. and G. Klerman. 1978. Epidemiology of Mental Disorders. *Archives of General Psychiatry* 35: 705–712

World Health Organization. 1979. *Schizophrenia: An International Follow-Up Study*. Chichester: John Wiley and Sons

Young, A. 1980. The Discourse on Stress and the Reproduction of Conventional Knowledge. *Social Science and Medicine* 14B: 133–146

1988. A Description of How Ideology Shapes Knowledge of a Disorder (Posttraumatic Stress Disorder). Manuscript presented at the Wenner-Gren Conference, "Analysis in Medical Anthropology," Lisbon, Portugal, March 5–13, 1988

10 A prologue to a psychiatric anthropology

Robert I. Levy

This chapter was stimulated by an invitation to comment on a paper of Byron Good's delivered at the 1987 meeting of the American Anthropological Association.[1] I came to anthropology from a first career in psychiatry via an interest in the "social" and "transcultural" psychiatry of the 1950s and 1960s. What follows is a reflection of my experience of mid-century American psychiatry, my response to some of the pioneering literature on comparative psychiatry, and my studies of some people and their problems in exotic places.

Contemporary anthropology has peculiar problems. It has an unsure sense of its identity, a lack of agreement on its central problems, on its relevant methods, and on the location of its boundaries. This is at best a stimulus to creativity but entails various heavy costs, particularly for cumulating understandings among us. One of the several symptoms of what psychiatrists might call our "borderline disciplinary personality" is an awed inability to deal in a mature fashion with our neighboring disciplines – for psychological anthropology in its classical form such seemingly self-assured neighbors as cognitive and general psychology, psychiatry, and psychoanalysis, and, to a much lesser degree, ethology, biology, and evolutionary theory. We tend to be naive about the contemporary certainties proffered by those neighbors and unable to deal with their tropes, metaphors, and shifting truths with the kind of sophistication that would make them useful for our own purposes – assuming of course that we knew what our own purposes might be. As anthropology is a compulsive borrower of other people's theories, having little central theory of its own, these are inescapable problems.

There are, of course, two possible directions of influence between us and the neighbors – their uses of our property and ours of theirs. Our usefulness and relevance was at its height, such as it was, in the 1940s and 1950s when the pious "in our culture (at least)" frequently qualified statements in some selected neighboring fields. But we are in latter days generally disappointed in our hopes for relevance. When we offer ourselves to their purposes, as Byron Good suggests we do for psychiatry elsewhere in this book, we may loan our ideas, our communities, and ourselves as technicians to the other enterprise, give them some more and a wider range of cases, and sensitize them to a few more parameters within which their models may or may not hold. Speaking of psychiatry, as I am here, the comparative phenomena to be so examined may bear on comparative ethnopsychiatry – that is local diagnoses, nosologies, and treatment – or, of more interest to most present-day psychiatrists, comparative aspects of what disease-model proponents would take to be the disease-in-itself – data on forms of disorder, on incidence and prevalence,[2] on the characteristics of the people "at risk," on the course of the disease, and so on. We may call such uses of us "anthropological psychiatry" or "anthropologically informed psychiatry." Obviously such enterprises are far from trivial. But I am arguing that a proper "psychiatric anthropology" (that is, our use of them) is, or should be, something else. A psychiatric anthropology should illuminate the problems of anthropology. It should investigate which aspects of local ethnopsychiatry and of local "mental problems" are sensitive to the particular aspects of history and community which concern us as well as the complementary problem as to which aspects of community processes may generate particular ethnopsychiatries and which aspects may be *pathogenic* in some regular and theoretically interesting ways.

Psychiatric anthropology would encompass Western psychiatry as one of its cases. To do so may make us a bit more sophisticated in our responses to that psychiatry. Western psychiatry in its medical search for hard, fact-like, organismically rooted "disorders" and "syndromes" – elegant terms for the "diseases" of yesteryear – moves erratically from one set of convictions to another ("paradigm shifts") motivated (it usually turns out in hindsight) to a large degree by failures in its claims to therapeutic power as well as by great ideological and moral pressures from the larger society. Over the decades everything having to do with treatment and conception in Western psychiatry drifts and oscillates. Different clumps of phenomena become variously visible and paradigmatic in support of one or another intellectual and ideological mood. The "congenital psychopathic inferiors" of my youth have disappeared along with neurasthenia, psychasthenia, and a host of mellifluous Greek-named nosological entities, all going the way of seventeenth-century "Tarantism," an "organic excitement and dancing mania" caused by the bite of a tarantula. With each lurch they, the psychiatrists, put their research money, medical-school appointments, and faith elsewhere. They mess around somewhere else or return to an old field of inquiry with new tools. In so doing they very often turn up fragments of therapeutic usefulness, of clinical importance. But therapeutic usefulness is the most limited warrant for the larger intellectual usefulness and profundity of their current models. Such shifting, always-renewed hopes make the world seem open again for discouraged medical practitioners and researchers; they relieve the depressive disease of the profession, so to speak. The "tremendous sense of excitement and energy" at the 1983 National Institute of Mental Health Conference on Anxiety and Anxiety Disorders, the "feeling of enormous progress," noted by Good (in the conference paper on which his chapter in this book is based) is a fine example. In the course of the resulting institutional high no one of the profession's members will welcome or in fact pay much attention to the kind of anthropological critiques proposed by Good as one of our possible contributions to psychiatry. We will only annoy them during such manic phases and they will properly ignore us. We must wait until they are in despair again for even the possibility of a serious hearing.

Psychiatry's forms and the phenomena it decides to attend to are dictated not only by its changing sociocultural contexts and internal dialectical discontents but by its disciplinary *purposes*. What are to be taken as symptoms, signs, disease, and pathogenic processes differ within psychiatry itself according to whether the theoretical frame is psychodynamic, genetic, infectious, endocrinological, familial, or social. Which is to suggest that the symptoms, signs, etc., of significance for the purposes of a psychiatric anthropology may not necessarily be the same as those gathered together in such compendia as the *Diagnostic and Statistical Manual* of the American Psychiatric Association. The phenomena of interest to an anthropological inquiry will be different in some respects from the ones which one or another Western nosology has carved out for its purposes. At the very least the importance of various syndromes for the two purposes will prove very different. The categories proposed for investigation in comparative psychiatry may be more than irrelevant, they may be misleading for the purposes of a psychiatric anthropology.

But, with all due caution, we still need to take medical psychiatry very seriously for people probably do tend to fall apart everywhere in roughly similar ways. Our awareness of the constructive powers of culture and symbols makes us suspicious of the pejorative uses of "illness," whether locally defined or externally discriminated, and we are thus natural partisans of "deviancy theory," sensitive to the imperious and seemingly unconstrained power of naming and categorization for social ordering and control. The choice as to whether to consider problematic behavior as locally conceived "deviance" or, instead, as "pathological" from the point of view of some transcultural calculus tends to be made by different and often quite antagonistic theorists. Awareness that every group, including Western folk and scientific category makers, uses pejorative classifications for social control has led to those radical positions in anthropology, sociology and the anti-psychiatry of the 1960s and 1970s that claimed that ascriptions of pathology are everywhere *only* manipulative stigmatizations. This is a polar ideology to that behind proposals about the predominantly culture-free usefulness of medical, universal models of pathology and their covert implications about the limits of culture. But short of such extreme and generally emotionally supercharged positions the opposition and forced choice between either "deviance" or "pathology" is not logically necessary. The two approaches in any given setting can be logically distinguished, and their interrelations studied.

If one wishes to use the idea of "pathology" then it is necessary to agree on criteria. We may begin with the once-familiar tactic of agreeing to agree more or less rigorously on some idea of minimal functional requirements for various social, cultural, and psychological "institutions," beginning with such obvious sociocultural matters as the production and distribution of food, defense against external dangers, the education of children to carry on the life of the community, and proceeding to such presently more obscure issues as the creation of the conditions for such sorts of mental operations as adequately functioning self and identity, effective cognition or, for that matter, sanity itself, and then agreeing that if such requirements are not fulfilled the institution or function is somehow "pathological," that it does not work as it should. Criteria for pathology, in short, require ideas of function and system – which some anthropologists reject. Some conception of *levels* is also useful, including ecological, social, cultural, psychological, and biological ones. Pathology can be considered at each distinct level, an approach which calls for an investigation of the exact *mechanisms* of the interaction of various levels. In this approach a disturbance at one level may "cause" a disturbance at another, it may be *pathogenic*, generating disturbances elsewhere. The pathologies of social order, for example, may induce individual pathologies, and, vice versa, private pathologies generating disturbances in community life.

Once we have some agreement on transcultural criteria for "pathology" then we can distinguish *local theories of deviancy* from analytically discerned local *pathology*, pathology which may or may not be consciously recognized within a community. We can then study the relation of such local theories in themselves to the recognition and denial, and to the production and shaping of such analytically discriminated "pathologies." How, that is, does local theory of deviancy respond to and affect, for better or worse, local pathology.[3]

We will find that whatever we take to be the particular mental pathologies that are responses to disorders at some other level – or which may, in fact, be the cost of particular (or universal) forms of *order* at such levels – will be differently distributed in a population. Perhaps everyone or most people may be affected. Perhaps only some special category of individuals is, as Public Health practitioners would put it, "at risk." If those individuals are sufficiently isolated, their disturbance may keep the culture as a whole "healthy" in itself, in analogy to the way the walled-off infection in a boil may allow the rest of the body to remain healthy. It is essential to try to distinguish two sorts of symptoms or signs of disorder: those which are the direct manifestation of some breakdown, and those which are the attempts, often costly in themselves, to contain or heal the breakdown. This is the difference between the life-threatening wound and the protective but disfiguring scar; between an individual's raw anxiety and his or her anxiety-binding psychological "defense mechanism," or the difference between starvation and cannibalism. We can call these "symptoms of breakdown" and "symptoms of defense." The symptoms of defense may do their work so well that the disorder is contained. In such cases one might infer pathology in a community even without obvious disorder through the presence of marked rigidity and of costly social defenses erected, consciously or not, against the production of or the effects of individual disorders. (This is analogous to the psychoanalytic conception that rigid aspects of "character" in individuals represent the binding of anxiety in the form of a *structure*, a move in the development of psychoanalytic theory which expanded the conception of "symptom.")

What should be of interest about local deviancy theory beyond its interaction with local pathology would be its comparative aspects, the contrasts and agreements of such theory in different communities. How are patterns of definition of disorder related to local conditions of life, to different technologies, scale, kinds of community order, degree of modernization and the like? As to investigations of *agreement* among various local systems of definition of deviance, we would gain some sense of the limits of tolerance in *any* community, of the limits of culture to mystify recalcitrant facts. I suspect, for example, that most, perhaps all, societies have necessarily a category of "craziness" which reflects, like our legal "insanity," the understanding that some people in the group are not capable of being affected by ordinary moral pressures nor by local healing practices. Such people are – like young children, the physically ill, and the very aged – not *competent*, to take the other, more coherent deviant roles that each society offers. In this respect, to anticipate a bit and to use Western language, there is a polar and widely recognized contrast between the "insane" (the incompetent deviant) and the "hysterical" (the highly competent deviant).

For the purpose of this prologue to a psychiatric anthropology we can begin with a consideration of the kinds of personal disorder which might be anthropologically interesting and then turn to aspects of community form which may be associated with personal disorder. I will note here some illustrative possibilities, possibilities which would be supported, amended, or discarded by a cumulative and up-to-date survey of the literature bearing on comparative phenomena and by further research.

(1) There seem to be some psychopathologies which characterize extensive social disorder anywhere in space and time, and others which seem to be the characteristic implications of particular types of sociocultural order. Extensive disorder, anomie, seems to be very generally associated with "unbound anxiety" and its consequences for individuals. "Unbound anxiety" means not only that people are chronically afraid because the sociocultural order is not working properly for them, but also that sociocultural devices for dealing with that fear, for "binding" it, are inadequate. The consequence is anxiety and its physiological concomitants – sleep disturbances, gastrointestinal disturbances, dry mouths, and various other vegetative nervous-system discomforts and, probably, greater vulnerability to many kinds of diseases.

(2) There is a group of psychosocial problems which may be considered as intermediate between the extreme breakdown symptoms of a highly disordered community and the ordered defensive symptoms of a viable order. These are those attempts at the management of anxiety and other unpleasant feeling which are very costly in themselves, a miscellaneous set of attempts at self treatment and tension-reducing behaviors – including the uses of alcohol and drugs, and various forms of violence against self and other, which are recognized as social problems, and which clearly show dramatic sociocultural variation among different communities and among segments of complex communities. "Alcoholism," for example, with its greatly different frequencies among different ethnic groups (prior to their dedifferentiating modernization) suggests the various mixtures of socioculturally differing quantities of stress in interaction with a complex field of values, types of social order, and prevalent psychological structures which make the pathological use of alcohol ("alcoholism") more or less likely.

(3) For obsessively taxonomic purposes one might differentiate a class of those transitional and unstable healing events which are not "social problems," costly in the same way as alcoholism and drug use. Calling them "pathological" is more contentious, a matter of taste. These events

and movements are often attempts to deal with, to contain, to "heal" more costly ones. Cults and new religions in their early and wilder stages are examples here – the Hare Krishna movement, Pentecostalism, Cargo Cults, American Indian Revitalization Cults are familiar examples.

(4) A next stage in a tentative classification of problems in terms of the dialogue and relative balance between breakdown and defence would be those "cures" which are stable in their outcomes and limited in their costs, no more costly than those other social institutions which workers in the Freudian tradition have convincingly argued to be anxiety binding, culturally constituted defenses for individuals. Local healing practices (including modern psychotherapies) are located here, therapies which are often complexly integrative both for their ostensive clients and for those clients' families and larger communities.

In most communities, as was the case in the early days of Western psychoanalysis, its precursors and rivals, there is, in fact, a close cooperation between healer and patient, which requires subtle, socially and culturally integrated cooperation on both their parts. The clients of native healers – as did the patients of turn-of-the century and early-twentieth-century Western healers – represent the kinds of "mental disorders" that anthropologists most frequently encounter in their studies.[4] These are the "dissociated states," which are the basis for the common and intimately interactive experience of native curers and patients, and which are an important local warrant for the reality of the supernatural. These, and some closely related phenomena, constitute the "hysteria" of Western diagnosis. Hysteria in the strong sense of the word – what used to be called Grand Hysteria – consists of states and actions seemingly alien to the "normal" self of an individual, but having in themselves *person-like characteristics*. They are "dissociated" actions and states characterized by motivations, goals, and intentions.[5] Such phenomena are very common in *certain kinds of communities*, in fact the very communities with which anthropology used to be primarily concerned, and tend to disappear in modern, particularly modern urban, communities.

"Certain kinds of communities" introduces the complementary question of a psychiatric anthropology. Thus, to anticipate later remarks, we might ask what would the sociocultural conditions be which would entail the possibility or probability of such dissociative states. It seems plausible, judging by the social distribution of such states and our studies of such cases in traditional communities, that they arise where there is a clearly agreed upon but quantitatively limited set of cultural schemata which make a circumscribed range of experience discussable, knowable, and easy to remember. *What* is doing the knowing, remembering, and so on, is the kind of coherently defined "self" that is generated under such conditions. Such management of a carefully specified knowable reality leaves a remainder of ineffable experience which is to a large extent organized as a "coherently unknowable," systematically unconscious. Aspects of self and mind regulated beyond the borders of agreed upon, proper, ordinary discourse become "ego alien."

In these communities there is, as part of their cultural coherence, a set of conventions and interpretations for the expression of the aspects of experience (usually as "possession") which such cultural and personal orders deny. "Hysteria" may, in short, well be the paradigmatic psychological condition found in ordered cultures whose order is the characteristic cognitive and moral agreement and pressures of relatively homogeneous, traditional communities.[6] Modernity seems to weaken the conditions for generating this kind of mind.

This implies that "hysteria" in traditional communities is not particularly (or at all) pathological,[7] whatever the distress which motivates people to make use of it, and whatever its personal costs might possibly be. I think that under those conditions where it is a common culturally generated mode of experience and action it is adaptive, no more (or less) pathological than other coping and adaptive devices, a function of competence not its lack. It is, as I have asserted above, a kind of polar opposite to "craziness."

(5) We may note in passing another category of recent *Diagnostic and Statistical Manuals* of the American Psychiatric Association, "psychosexual disorders." These include a very wide range of behaviors which are not ego-alien symptoms for individuals, but "ego-syntonic" aspects of their "character," "personality," or "self," which are taken by someone or other to be problematic, but which as the shifting conceptions of some at least of the "psychosexual disorders" in recent decades clearly show, are very unstably and variously assigned to "pathology," "deviance," or to "normality." Aspects of psychosexual disorder, particularly various kinds of deviation from conventional expectations about gender, vary greatly in different settings. For "problematic" sexuality and gender it is clear that pre-modern societies, at least, define and delimit deviant sexual role-playing in clear ways, recruit some people into such roles, and keep others out. This profoundly affects the "phenotypic" form of sexual expression, as well as the relation of the various underlying biological, culturally produced, and idiosyncratic factors which are the personal precursors in the formation of socially defined gender, to consciousness, repression, personality, and action.

Modern psychiatry and its precursors has always made an uneasy distinction between "minor" and "major" mental disorders (with much recent obsession with the ambiguous disorders which are "borderline" between the two sorts). "Minor disorders" blend, uneasily for many psychiatrists, with the realm of values, of everyday social contol, of shifting styles of disease. They seem, that is, closer to "culture" in some way. The major mental disorders, on the other hand, are clearly (by definition) more disturbing to everyone concerned, seem to be closer to other kinds of "diseases" physicians are familiar with, more related to measurable biological dysfunction, and, perhaps, less variable in occurrence throughout time and space – although their diagnostic categories and criteria have varied over time and, for that matter, among contemporary psychiatrists in different modern, presumably equally scientific, countries. The three major categories of major mental illness are the severe or "major" affective or mood disorder, "schizophrenic disorders" and "organic brain syndromes." All of these can be treated as aspects of a psychiatric anthropology.

(1) One of the first Western syndromes whose variation in incidence, prevalence, and form among social classes and different societies was noted in the earlier studies in social psychiatry was "mood disorder," particularly depression. Depression was held to vary in its form, frequency, and course in contrasting social and cultural conditions. As Anthony Marsella and his colleagues put it in a recent review (Marsella, Sartorius, Jablensky, and Fenton 1985: 306), results of a range of studies "indicate the experience and expression of depression varies across ethnocultural boundaries. Reviewers concur that feelings of guilt, self-deprecation, suicidal ideas, and feelings of despair are often rare or absent among non-European populations, whereas somatic and quasi-somatic symptoms, including disturbances of sleep, appetite, energy, body sensation, and motor functioning, are more common." This phrasing tacitly accepts a medical model. Instead of claiming that there are two different disorders whose presence is powerfully affected by sociocultural forms, it seems to imply that *only* the "experience and expression of depression" varies. This "depression" is, in such phrasing, the deep, significant, biological, pan-human condition whose surface manifestations vary with different sociocultural forms of life.

Kleinman and Good in their introduction to the same book, taking note of the same contrasts in depressive phenomena, suggest a somewhat different view.

In few societies of the world is depression associated with overwhelming guilt and feelings of sinfulness, as it often is in the Judeo-Christian West. Because such differences are found in the symptoms associated with depressive illness, determination of whether one is studying the same illness across societies is essentially problematic. There is no blood test for depression. If there were one, it would indicate some physiological disorder, but not the fundamentally social illness we call depression. (p. 4)[8]

Kleinman and Kleinman in their chapter in the book (Marsella, Sartorius, Jablensky, and Fenton 1985) disentangle themselves from the medical model in speaking simply of "social sources of human misery," and suggest specific conditions they hold to be significant for depression in China, namely local human contexts of power that distribute resources unequally. They discriminate a *microdepressogenic* system – that is, local contexts and forms of personal relations generating misery-producing action – in contrast to that system's larger economic, social, and political *macrodepressogenic* contexts.

Such analyses imply that aspects of the production of depression (whatever biological correlates may be involved) are not just the problem of living in *any* society at all, nor in any disordered society, but the problems produced by *specific* pathogenic conditions which are more prevalent in certain *kinds* of societies. Depression seems to be the product of certain kinds of order, and this may be true for all of the major mental illnesses. Kleinman and Kleinman seem to suggest that for their Chinese subjects the forms and prevalence of depression have something to do with a perception of inequitable resource distribution in an otherwise coherent moral order of a certain kind, an order which fosters motives, goals, and warrants for self-esteem of a certain kind, and which then does not operate correctly.

(2) The prototypical mental pathology, the very archetype of craziness, is the mental disorder, or family of disorders, which has come to be called "schizophrenia" (or "the schizophrenic disorders"). These are the behaviors which are recognized everywhere, apparently, as "crazy" (or "psychotic"), which put their victims in a category by themselves, on the one hand unable to become reintegrated through moral pressures and the creative use of dissociated behavior, while, on the other, not disturbed in the everywhere-recognized and quite different manner of amentia, senility, head injury, toxic delirium, and the like. The schizophrenias seem to exist in recognizable forms everywhere that there are enough people among whom to find them. But they clearly vary in what are called (to some degree exactly because they vary) "surface" features, and they vary strongly, according to some claims, in course and outcome among different communities and, thus, in prevalence, the amounts of recognizable disease which accumulate in a population. Schizophrenia is clearly "organic," in this case "genetic," with very high correlations among identical twins even when reared separately. But note (the datum which is of most interest for our particular purposes) that, according to recent

reports, in some 35 percent or more of such cases one member of the pair of identical twins (the other of whom has been diagnosed as schizophrenic) does *not* get clinically recognizable schizophrenia – even under what are from our perspective very similar sociocultural conditions. Something in his or her environment ameliorates, and/or something in his ill-fated sibling's environment aggravates the outcome. What then can and do different kinds of communities make of that genetic form, the genotype, which *under certain conditions* tends to produce one of the "schizophrenias," an organic disease, as the phenotypical outcome? That is a properly non-borrowed question, which seems to be profoundly relevant to sociocultural processes. If, by the way, the "proto-schizophrenic" genotype *is* universal, a concomitant of just being human, this is (anthropologically) curious in itself. If the genotype only leads to schizophrenia under certain ultimately specifiable conditions, can we, as anthropologists, reinterpret its phenotypic significance in some evolutionary and/or adaptive way. Does *this* fact of universality (if that is what it is) in itself illuminate sociocultural processes? The questions to be asked by us must be anthropological ones, not narrowly medical ones.

(3) It is, ironically, the most clearly and grossly "organic" diseases, those resulting from gross damage to the nervous system, which vary most clearly from culture to culture, which are most evidently and directly culturally determined. The availability of narcotic substances and the cultural and sub-cultural definitions of their permissible uses, the kinds of toxins and brain-threatening actions (e.g., pearl diving, working in the sun) vary sharply in different cultural, social, environmental, and economic situations.

We have been considering problems and disorders as possible pathways into a psychiatric anthropology. We can, alternatively, invert our approach to ask, as we did for hysteria, whether there are specific aspects, clusters of aspects, or kinds of sociocultural environments that are significant for the production or prevention of some features of or kinds of personal disorders. This direction of inquiry would take us beyond the search for phenomena illustrating variations in frequency and quantity, form and course of disorders, matters which are relatively concrete and "ethnographic." A search for pathogenic contexts, their historical and environmental causes, and the mechanisms by which they induce disorder in individuals, is an enterprise which must be based on informed but tentative speculations as to what might be the sorts of sociocultural/psychological transactions relevant to problems in the formation and actions of individuals.

Significant sociocultural variables for the extent and kind of individual disorder might include, among much else, such matters as the extent of sociocultural disorganization, the amount and organization of internal and contextual complexity, sociocultural forms affecting "individuality," the contexts of identity formation, and structures of external and internal sanctions.

We have argued that sociocultural disorganization leads to anxiety and its consequences, which may be bound or defended against in various ways depending on available cultural resources. In contrast various kinds and aspects of organization have their own virtues and their own costs for individuals. We have suggested that specific patterns of organization may influence depression. Let us look at some other heterogeneous aspects of sociocultural organization to suggest the shape of other possibilities.

How much do individuals in a given community have to know and understand, and, very significantly, how is that knowledge culturally organized? The quantity and ordering of information that an individual must know in order to be competent may differentially affect memory, the difficulty of computation and of adequate orientation and have consequences for the confusion, disorientation, and incompetence produced by any given degree of organic cortical deficit or of emotionally produced cognitive overload. A clinical impression, whether responsible or not, illustrates the problem of organization. I have heard it asserted by some Chinese child psychiatrists that the reading disabilities so common in the United States are almost unknown among native readers of Chinese, who must, nevertheless, master thousands of characters. This suggests that the complex context-determined calculus that determines which phoneme an English letter or complex of letters represents is the kind of organization which may overload some nervous system in a way that simple lists, no matter how extensive, may not. One might expect analogues for other sorts of breakdown in the relative difficulties of different communities' ways of organizing other aspects of the cultural knowledge that must be mastered by individuals.

Related to the quantity and the organization of knowledge is the question of the *consistency* of local systems of definition, particularly those bearing on culturally sensitive core aspects of people in a community – definitions of self, of other, of proper and improper action, of thinkable and unthinkable thoughts. Such consistency or its absence should have implications for self and its pathologies, for the nature of the unconscious, for the structure of psychodynamic defenses, for the possibility and usefulness of dissociation.

The amount of knowledge an individual must control is related to the larger problem of comparative "individuality." How are knowledge, competence for various tasks, moral responsibility, identity, and so on *distributed*? How much lies in relatively isolated individuals; how much is based in the various corporate groups to which an individual belongs? Differences here would suggest differences in various kinds of loads on individuals, and, reasonably, different ways they might break down.

Related to the differential concentration of tasks and functions in individuals are the community's values and forms of learning affecting individuals' independency versus dependency, autonomy versus interdependency, self-control versus yielding to the control of other people and to ego-alien pressures within their own minds. These balances will also shape breakdown in rather complex ways. I have argued that such variables have something to do with comparative quantities of "alcoholism" in different groups (Levy, 1973: chapter 12). Related to forms of individuality, autonomy, and so forth, in ways that cannot be reduced to easy formulas, are comparative differences in external and internal sanctions in different communities. Local patterns of guilt, shame, fear about the consequences of wrong doing, culturally supported direction of blame – toward self or toward others, or some particular category of others – and thus of the kind of actions to be taken to rectify matters and/or avoid such sanctions, are intimately associated with forms and kinds of pathology. Suicide or murder, paranoia – blaming others – or self-contempt, depression, or anger, are options which one would suppose to be profoundly influenced by local patterns of sanctions.

A different issue from the nature of "individuality," is the nature of "identity" in various groups. This problem, and particularly its sociocultural and clinical aspects, was defined and extensively considered in the writings, much of them anthropologically informed, of Erik Erikson. The dysfunctions of identity – problems in the development and synthesis of its "internal psychological" components and the "external" components in an individual's society – lead to a range of "psychopathological" problems.

An aspect of cultural complexity which differs from the internal complexity of a group is the complexity which has to do with its relations with neighboring groups. The contrast between the context of traditional Polynesian and Melanesian communities suggests that the cultural and psychological implications of isolation (or of having neighbors of highly similar culture) are significantly different from those of having neighbors of considerably differing culture and language. I suspect that such contrasts have implications for personal complexity, for self concept, for possibilities of blaming and projecting, for cognition, for the tasks and mechanisms of repression, all of which in turn presumably affect the nature of local disorder.

In order to make use of psychiatry for its own purposes anthropology has to naturalize the medical model. That model is a quest for *powerful* operations, it looks for aspects of disorder, like the tubercle bacillus, which are necessary, but which turn out never to be sufficient to generate tuberculosis, aspects which exist in *all* cases and which can be manipulated to eradicate the disorder. This quest for power encourages a reduction to the organic. It manipulates its model of disorder so that those people who have the "necessary factor" but do *not* have the disease may be said to have the "latent" disease, or the disease in a distorted or "aborted" form, a "*forme fruste*." Such conventions skew the investigation of sociocultural pathology of mind, for they tend to emphasize the kinds and dimensions of disorder which are the least relevant to sociocultural forms, making sociocultural phenomena ancillary, relatively trivial, or irrelevant.

Psychiatric anthropology needs its own center, and its own theory. It has to be comparative, so that it can take into full account the interesting things which do *not* occur in certain kinds of places as well as the things which do, and so that it can use comparison and contrast to suggest explanations. And it will, in keeping with our vision of people in communities, communities in turn differentially embedded in history and spatial context, be an investigation of patterns and fields and complex states, not of simplified objects such as diseases.

NOTES

1 A very few passages in this chapter are adapted from my article "The Quest for Mind in Different Times and Different Places" (Levy 1989).
2 The difference between the "incidence" of anything and its "prevalence" is of considerable anthropological importance. "Incidence," the number of new "cases" of something within a population of a certain size during a designated period of time, is an index of the *generation* of the phenomena. "Prevalence," the total number of cases in a population at a certain period of time, indicates the preservation and *accumulation* of the phenomena in a population. If, say, community A and community B "produce" the same number of lepers (thus having the same incidence) but community B exiles them as soon as they are discovered, the prevalence of lepers in the two communities is very different. Incidence and prevalence are indexes of two different aspects of, for our present purposes, sociocultural processes.
3 A mirror question is the effect of locally prevalent pathologies on local concepts of pathology and deviance. George Devereux (1980) suggested that the prevalent psychopathologies of a group are "model pathologies" which on the one hand reflect the particular psychological organization of "normal" people in the group, and on the other tend to mold a variety of other problematic behaviours into forms made culturally familiar by the "model pathologies."
4 I am referring here to healers and healing in relatively integrated communities.

Healing and healers and their patients in disordered communities (or segments of communities) have other tasks and characteristics.

5 Such person-like symptoms must be distinguished from the symptoms of breakdown of, say, schizophrenia or epilepsy, conditions where the disorders of integration or control are the most prominent signs, and where motives and goals are not primarily relevant.

6 I think that most of the so-called "culture-specific mental disorders" are dissociative patterns of this kind, which engage competent, albeit unhappy, people in creative attempts to further or reintegrate their personal and community orders.

7 Hysteria, dissociative, and conversion reactions, at the same time as they were becoming less common, have come to seem more pathological in our times, perhaps because they are seen as "regressive" and "innocent" holdouts against aspects of communication and cognition favored by our new order, and because they occur among a particular class of the "least culturally advanced" of that order.

8 For the medically minded the finding of a blood test for depression would indicate not a *correlate* of the "fundamentally social illness," but something closer to that illness's true essence and cause.

REFERENCES

Devereux, George. 1980. *Basic Problems of Ethnopsychiatry*. Chicago: University of Chicago Press

Levy, Robert I. 1973. *Tahitians*. Chicago: University of Chicago Press

1989. The Quest for Mind in Different Times and Different Places. In Andrew Barnes and Peter Stearns, eds., *Social History and Issues in Human Consciousness*. New York: New York University Press

Marsella, Anthony, Norman Sartorius, Assen Jablensky, and Fred Fenton. 1985. In Arthur Kleinman and Byron Good, eds., *Culture and Depression*. Berkeley: University of California Press

11 Hungry bodies, medicine, and the state: toward a critical psychological anthropology

Nancy Scheper-Hughes

This chapter does not pretend to be, nor to offer, a comprehensive or definitive statement on "critical psychological anthropology," nor will it present a method specific to itself. Rather, it poses the opening question: if there is to be a critical, indeed a radical, alternative to "conventional" psychological anthropology what form(s) might it take? And what is to be implied, after all, in the term "critical"?

I am motivated in part by a certain dis-ease, a malaise concerning the field of psychological anthropology which seems to have departed from its roots as a bridging discipline between the fragmented human sciences: between *biology* (and the biomedical sciences) on the one hand with its Cartesian legacy and its reified notions of the mechanistic (and universal) "body," and *psychology*, with its equally mechanistic and reified notions of "mind," on the other; and between both of these and social anthropology with its focus on society and the collectivity – the "social body," if you will. Meanwhile, the once-holistic discipline of anthropology itself no longer even pretends to an integration among its classic and bridging subdivisions so that biology and culture, history (writ large) and ethnology have seceded from the union and now "liberated" each is free to pursue its own form of reductionism.

Furthermore, as psychological anthropology becomes increasingly cognitive and formalistic in orientation, the field strikes me as alarmingly "disembodied" so that any integrated notion of the "mindful body" (see Scheper-Hughes and Lock 1987) has begun to fade, leaving, like the Cheshire cat, just the traces of a quizzical smile. Perusing the contemporary literature in psychological anthropology gives me the eerie feeling of being in a world rather like the one inhabited by some of the patients in Oliver Sacks' (1985) clinical practice – people with strange neurological deficits, like the woman who found herself utterly lacking in her "proprioceptive" sense, so that she had lost the "feel" of her own body, although she remained consciously analytical about the fact that "it" was there and that it impinged upon her "self."

In part, then, this chapter might be seen as an attempt to return psychological anthropology "to its senses." Hence, my focus on a *specific* ethnographic instance, the experience and meanings of hunger to a population of sugarcane-cutters in the plantation zone of Northeast Brazil. It is drawn from a larger ethnographic study (see Scheper-Hughes 1991) of the sugar plantation town of Bom Jesus da Mata in the state of Pernambuco, viewed from the point of view of the rural workers who inhabit a large hillside shantytown of more than 5,000 residents, the Alto do Cruzeiro, on the margins of Bom Jesus da Mata. The study begins in 1964 (when I first lived and worked in the shantytown as a health worker and community activist) and spans a period of twenty-five years following four periods of anthropological fieldwork (1982–1989).

My analysis is grounded in ethnography rather than in a critical review of the literature because I believe that it is in the practice of ethnography that the vitality of anthropology resides. In fact, there is no specific tradition or literature in "critical psychological anthropology" to draw on, such as there is for critical psychiatry or critical medical anthropology. Critical psychological anthropology as a specific theoretical orientation has yet to be invented. There is within psychological anthropology no well-developed discourse on power relations as these are embedded in specific social and economic formations, and one is struck by the alarming a-politicality of a field that purports to understand individuals in nature, in culture, and in society.

How did it happen that the theoretical concerns of psychological anthropology became so far removed from the practical concerns of real people? To what extent has psychological anthropology lost its moorings and grown out of touch with the world it seeks to understand and to explain? So, for another part, this contribution may be seen as a subdisciplinary "call to arms."

I begin by identifying a domain that, to paraphrase Wittgenstein (1969), is so much before our eyes (especially the so-called Third World) today that its very routineness and "familiarity" allows us to fail to notice it or to grant it any theoretical or abstract significance. I refer to the experience of chronic hunger as a primary motivating force in human life.

The taboo against hunger

When the Brazilian nutritionist Josué de Castro first published his classic book, *The Geography of Hunger* (1952), he framed his discussion of worldwide patterns of starvation and undernutrition as the breaking of a long-standing and implicit scientific taboo. Hunger, he wrote, was a well-kept secret about modern human existence, so that of all the calamities "that have repeatedly devastated the world ... it is hunger which is the least studied and discussed, least understood in its causes and effects" (1952: 5). In short, hunger was a base and vulgar instinct from which science had averted its gaze.

But even as the Brazilian nutritionist was writing these lines (in the first Brazilian edition) they were already negated in the flood of biomedical and clinical studies that appeared in the wake of World War II. These were fueled by an almost obsessive need to document in minute detail, to quantify every physical and psychological horror suffered by those interned in German concentration camps, abandoned in the Warsaw ghetto, and victimized by the famine that struck Holland in 1945. Of these perhaps the most detailed scientific examination of the effects of starvation on body and mind was the experimental study initiated in 1944 by Keys, Brozek, and their colleagues (Brozek 1950; Keys, Brozek, Henschel, Mickelsen, and Taylor 1950) in the cavernous underworld of the University of Minnesota's Sports Stadium with thirty-two volunteers recruited from alternative-service conscientious objectors.

What de Castro might have said, but what he failed to note, was that the attention of biomedical scientists to the subject of hunger had to wait until *white* Europeans began to suffer from the same conditions that had long afflicted black and brown peoples in many parts of the world (including the southern part of the United States). The ravaged face of hunger was a shocking novelty to the Allied Forces who liberated the Nazi camp of Bergen-Belsen on April 12, 1945, but it was a common reality during periods of drought and famine in the Brazilian Northeast where there are, even today, many hunger victims, most of them very young, who die alone, unattended, and anonymously.

One might have expected anthropologists to turn *their* attention to some consideration of hunger in non-white and non-Western contexts, but up through the period of de Castro's work only three well-known monographs dealt in any great detail with hunger: two by Audrey Richards (1932, 1939) on the Bantu and Bemba peoples of Northern Rhodesia, and Alan Holmberg's (1950) study of hunger-anxiety among the Siriono Indians of eastern Bolivia. Yet even these pioneering works in the anthropology of hunger are disappointing. Ultimately, they are more concerned with documenting the culture and social structure of the people studied than in documenting their hunger. A few psychological anthropologists, during the brief preeminence of culture and personality studies (1940s to 1960s), paid some attention to the experience of hunger, but they focused primarily on breast-deprivation and weaning problems in infants and small children, events which often had no reference to food scarcity in the larger society. I am thinking, in particular, of Cora DuBois' (1941, 1944) studies of the Alorese to whom DuBois attributed a suspicious and almost paranoid temperament due to the traumatic weaning and systematic underfeeding of children there. Dorothy Shack (1969) and William Shack (1971), however, explored both the psychological and the social dimensions of the hunger-anxiety and food scarcity in Gurage children and adults in Ethiopia.

Since the 1970s hunger and food practices have become of greater interest to anthropologists, who could be described as falling into two interpretive camps: bioecological and symbolic. Among the ecologists, including the cultural materialists, like Marvin Harris (1977), the bioevolutionists like William Stini (1971, 1975), and the medical ecologists like Claire Cassidy (1982, 1987), child malnutrition and chronic hunger tend to be viewed within a broad framework of biosocial adaptiveness. William Stini (1975), for example, has argued, based on his study of human growth and development in an impoverished Colombian population, that small size or "stunting" is adaptive there because it allows a greater number of adults to survive on less food in a context of chronic scarcity of food resources (see also Pelto and Pelto 1989). In these studies hunger is recognized, but its brutal effects on human lives may be subordinated to larger demographic or "ecological" issues.

Among social and symbolic anthropologists, owing to the influence of French and British versions of structuralism (see Lévi-Strauss 1964, 1965; Douglas 1970; Tambiah 1969), food, food taboos, and hunger tend to be understood as symbolic categories used in organizing social relations, ordering experience, or expressing or mediating contradictions. In this interpretive tradition, food is less good to eat than it is "good to think"; it is a language rich in symbolic content. Food (as well as hunger) serves as a medium for complicated social transactions, as individuals and social groups use food to control others, to establish and maintain sexual relations, to avoid or to initiate conflict, or to express some aspect of cultural identity.

The preference of cultural anthropologists for elegant homologies and their turning away, we might say, from the plain facts of hunger as a lived experience that consigns millions of Third-World people to an early grave is perhaps a manifestation of the "anxious taboo" against the study of hunger to which de Castro has alluded. Perhaps hunger *as* hunger – a frightening human affliction – is simply "not good to think" for anthropologists who, if they think of hunger and famine at all, prefer to think of them as symbols and metaphors, or as contributing positively to long-term adaption.

In order to avoid the pitfalls of both materialist and symbolic reductionisms, I will ground the following analysis of *Nordestino* Brazilian hunger within a conceptual framework that allows for an understanding of the body as individually and collectively experienced, as socially represented in various symbolic and metaphorical idioms, and as subject to regulation, discipline, and control by larger political and economic processes, an insight fundamental to European critical theory. Lock and I (1987) have referred to this as the relations among the "three bodies": the body politic, the body social, and the not-unrelated, self-conscious, more or less alienated, individual attribution of meanings to the individual body in different cultures.

Applying this framework to an analysis of *hunger* among the people of the Alto, I will now descend rapidly into the thicket of ethnographic description, beginning with the immediately perceived and "common-sense world." In taking the role of the "negative intellectual" and subjecting this practical reality to critical or oppositional questioning, I hope to arrive at a different interpretation and one that will allow, in Gramscian (1987: 90–92) terms, "good sense" to dislodge "common sense." I begin with the immediate experience of hunger in the Northeast of Brazil.

Delírio de Fome – the madness of hunger

During the summer of the drought of 1965 I was drawn one day by curiosity to the jail cell of a young woman from an outlying rural area who had just been apprehended for the murder of her infant son and her year-old daughter. The infant had been smothered, while the little girl had been hacked with a machete. Rosa, the mother, became for a brief period a central attraction in Bom Jesus, as both rich and poor passed by her barred window that opened to a side street in order to rain down invectives on her head: "animal," she was called, "unnatural creature," "shameless woman." Face-to-face with the withdrawn and timid slip of a girl (she seemed barely a teenager), I made myself bold enough to ask the obvious: "Why did you do it?" She replied as she must have for the hundredth time, "To stop them from crying for milk." After a pause she added (to her own defense), *Bichinhos não sente nada* – little critters have no feelings.

When I related the story later that day to Nailza de Arruda, with whom I was then sharing a tiny, mud-walled hut on the steep cliff path they call the "Segunda Travessa de Bernardo Viera" on the Alto do Cruzeiro, Nailza shook her head and commented sadly: "It was the *delírio*, the 'madness' of hunger." Nailza had seen many good people commit violent and shameful acts when driven to the brink by hunger-madness. I remembered her words but considered them, at the time, another example of the *Nordestino* imagination – vivid, dramatic, extravagant. Like the others who congregated to taunt Rosa I, too, felt that she was something of an "unnatural creature," rather than a creature of "nature." I soon had reason to reconsider.

Early one afternoon a small woman, whose patient, impassive face I did not immediately recognize, stood at my door with a small bundle in her arms. She unwrapped the clean sugar sacking to show a child of perhaps a year old whose limbs were wasted, leaving what seemed a large head attached to sticks. He was alive but very still, though his eyes stared out intently and without blinking. Seeing that the child's condition was precarious, I rushed with him to the local hospital of Bom Jesus, leaving his mother behind with Nailza for company. As a *visitadora*, a community health worker, I had the right to intern children such as these, but Dr. Tito frowned his disapproval. "It's too late for this one," he said, leaving me with an untrained practical nurse as together the two of us tried to find a single usable vein in which to insert an intravenous tube. The once-passive child threw its remaining energy into a fight against the needle, a reasonable enough response in a terrified and sick-to-death child. But this fight was just the beginning of an hour-long "delirium" during which the child went rigid, seemed to buckle, and then, finally, became wild, growling and snapping at our hands, until, thankfully, he died. The cause of death penciled into the head nurse's copybook, the only record of hospitalized cases, read: "Malnutrition, third degree; acute dehydration." I was tempted to add: *delírio de fome*, the madness of hunger.

In the context of this discussion the "madness" of hunger participates in various and sometimes ironical meanings, but its plainest one derives from the writings and folklore documenting the history of famine and drought in the Brazilian Northeast. The *delírio de fome* refers, in this context, to the frightening end point reached in starvation. References to the madness of hunger can be found as early as the sixteenth century in the diaries and other records left by Portuguese, Dutch, and French navigators, who documented the raving madness caused by hunger aboard ship on the seemingly endless voyages to and from Brazil.

Josué de Castro (1969: 56–57) cites the following reference to hunger-madness from Jean De Léry's *Histoire d'un voyage fait en la terre du Bresil* written in 1558 by a French Huguenot shoemaker who made the voyage to Brazil in the 1540s. De Léry wrote:

> The food ran out completely at the beginning of May and two sailors died of hunger madness . . . during such outright starvation the body becomes exhausted, nature swoons, and the senses are alienated, the spirit fades away, and this not only makes people ferocious but provokes a kind of madness, justifying the common saying that someone is "going mad from hunger."

In its early, historical context, *delírio de fome* can be taken to signify the unfettered, the primary experience of hunger. *Delírio de fome* is hunger before it was understood by the medical academy as "protein-calorie" or "protein-energy" malnutrition. *Delírio de fome* represents the subjective voice, the immediate experience, of hunger. It is the voice that emerges in the biting words of an angry *favelado*, Carolina Maria de Jesus (1962: 52), who writes in her celebrated diary, *Child of the Dark*: "When I am hungry I want to eat one politician, hang another and burn a third." And it is the rage that provoked young Rosa to destroy her year-old daughter and her infant son.

Nervous hunger

At first in Bom Jesus one's ear is jarred by the frequent juxtapositions of the idioms of *fome*, hunger, and *nervos*, nervousness, in the everyday conversation of the people of the Alto. Hunger and deprivation have set the people of the shantytown of Alto do Cruzeiro on edge. Hunger has made them lean, irritable and "nervous." Their lives are marked by a free-floating, ontological, existential insecurity. Life itself is a scarce commodity. There is not, and it is almost inconceivable that there could ever be, "enough" to satisfy basic wants and needs. Perhaps this is what George Foster (1965) meant to imply in his notion of "the limited good."

If food and sex are idioms through which the people of the Alto reflect on their social condition as "*os pobres*" (poor people), nerves and nervousness provide an idiom through which they reflect on hunger and hunger-anxiety, with consequences that are at once unintended and far-reaching. The prototypical "limited" good on the Alto do Cruzeiro is food, and nervous-hunger is the prototypical form of "nervos," "nervoso", or "*doença de nervos*" (nervous sickness), an expansive and polysemic folk syndrome. Those who suffer deprivation are not surprisingly nervous and insecure. Reflecting on their social condition, the squatters refer to themselves as "weak," "shaky," "irritable," "off-balance," and paralyzed, without a leg to stand on. These metaphors used so often in the everyday conversations of Alto people also mimic the physiological symptoms of hunger. There is an exchange of meanings, images, representations between the individual physical and the collective social bodies.

Here I explore the process through which a population, only recently incorporated into the biomedical health-care system, becomes prey to the "medicalization", indeed psychologization, of their basic needs. The folk syndrome *nervos* (a rich folk-conceptual scheme for describing the relations among mind, body, and social body) is gradually "appropriated" by clinical biomedicine and changed (and reified) into something else. The madness, the *delírio de fome*, once understood as a terrifying end point in the course of starvation, is transformed into a "psychological" problem that requires medication, tranquilizers in particular. In this way hunger is isolated and denied, and a discourse on "sickness" comes to replace a more radical discourse on hunger.

The medicalization of hunger and, even worse, of infant malnutrition in the clinics, pharmacies, and political chambers of Bom Jesus da Mata, represents a macabre performance of distorted institutional and political relations. I am suggesting, with insights from Foucault (1975) and Ivan Illich (1976), the usefulness to the state of the proliferation of "sick" bodies and sickness metaphors for an unstable, nervous system, individual and social (see Taussig 1989). And so, the hungry people of Bom Jesus da Mata come to believe that they desperately need what is given to them, and to forget that what they need most is what they are so cleverly denied.

But there is more to the story than bad faith and false consciousness. Bad faith obscures the extent to which doctors are themselves unwittingly drafted as agents of the social consensus, while false consciousness obscures the subversive uses to which *nervoso* is put in registering the refusal of rural workers to accept, at face value, the logic and the terms of their abuse at the "foot" of the sugar cane. And so, my analysis must be taken as incomplete and contradictory, like reality itself.

Critical consciousness

Insofar as I am engaged here in an ongoing work of praxis – theory derived in the context of political practice – the themes I am addressing did not arise in a social vacuum. Rather, they emerged within open and often chaotic discussions of the weekly general meeting, the *assembléia geral* of the Union for the Progress of Cruzeiro Hill (UPAC), the local squatters' association and "ecclesiastical base community" (CEB) of the shantytown. The "method" of the Brazilian base community movement is derived from Paulo Freire's (1970) "*conciêntização*," radical political action based on critical reflection. The method begins at the "base," ground level, with a ruthless questioning of the immediately perceived and the "practically" true, the given, experiential world. This reality is then subjected to deconstruction, and to critical, oppositional, and "negative" questioning. What is revealed and what is concealed in our given, commonsense perceptions of reality? Paradoxes are proposed. Whose interests are being served? Whose needs are being ignored?

The Freire method is open and dialogic. Any member of the community can suggest "keywords" or generative themes for critical reflection, discussion, and clarification, including such words as: *fome* (hunger), *nervos* (nervousness), *susto* (fright), *a mingua* (scarcity), or *jeito* (a knack, a way out of a jam, a means, a solution). And so, part of this analysis was derived in this public and contested manner at open UPAC meetings with the residents of the Alto. Out of the ensuing dialogue – at least in theory – emerges a critical form of practice. The Freire method can also be applied to the way in which "scientific" hypotheses are launched and tested in the process and the practice of "traditional" anthropological fieldwork.

The essential insight, derived from European critical theory, is that the given world or the "commonsense reality" may be false, illusory, and oppressive. It is an insight shared with all contemporary critical epistemologies including modern psychoanalysis, feminism and Marxism. All variants of modern critical theory work at the essential task of stripping away the surface forms of reality in order to expose concealed and buried truths. Their aim then, is to "speak truth" to power and domination, both in individuals and submerged social groups or classes. They are reflexive rather than objective epistemologies.

Critical theories differ radically in their epistemology from positivist theories derived from the natural sciences. All theories in the "natural" sciences presuppose an "objective" structure of reality knowable by minds that are likewise understood as sharing a uniform cognitive structure. Critical theories assert the subjectivity of knowable phenomena and propose "reflection" as a valid category and method of discovery. In this paper I am using the term "objectify" in a somewhat different way, to show how medicine falsely objectifies patients and their afflictions by reducing them to reified biomedical diagnostic categories. The objectivity of science and of medicine is always a phantom objectivity, a mask that conceals more than it reveals. (See also M. Taussig 1980.)

At the heart of all critical theories and methods is a critique of ideology and power. Ideologies (whether political, economic, or religious) can mystify reality, obscure relations of power and domination, and prevent people from grasping their situation in the world. Specific forms of consciousness may be called ideological when they are invoked to sustain or legitimate particular institutions or social practices. When these institutional arrangements reproduce inequality, domination, and human suffering, the aims of critical theory are broadly emancipatory.

The process of liberation is complicated, however, by the unreflexive complicity and identification of people with the very ideologies and practices that are their own undoing. Here is where Antonio Gramsci's notion of hegemony is useful. Gramsci (1971, 1987) recognized that the dominant classes exercised power both directly and forcefully through the state, and also indirectly by merging with the civil society and by identifying their own class-based interests with broad cultural ideas and aims, making them appear indistinguishable from each other.

Increasingly in modern bureaucratic states technicians and professionals – laboratory scientists, geneticists, doctors, psychologists, teachers, social workers, sociologists, criminologists and so forth – come to play the role of "traditional intellectuals" in sustaining "commonsense" definitions of reality through their highly specialized and validating forms of discourse. Gramsci anticipated Foucault (see Foucault 1972) in his understanding of the diffuse power circuits in modern states and of the role of "expert" forms of power/knowledge in sustaining the "commonsense" order of things. In the context of this discussion, doctors occupy the pivotal role of "traditional" intellectuals whose function is, in part, to fail to see the secret indignation of the hungry poor expressed in their inchoate folk idiom of "*nervos*." But anthropologists, too, often play the role of the "traditional" intellectual in their unconscious collusions with hegemonic interpretations of social reality fostered by powerful local interests.

Hence, my analysis is addressed to multiple audiences: to my *companheiros* in UPAC, as a tool for discussion, reflection, and clarification of thought as a prelude to collective action. Second, it is addressed to my anthropological colleagues. As social scientists (and not social revolutionaries) critical practice implies an epistemological struggle in which the contested domain is anthropology itself. The struggle concerns the way that knowledge is generated, the class interests that it serves, and the challenge to make our discipline more relevant and non-oppressive to the people we study. Finally, it is addressed to clinical practitioners as a challenge to reintegrate the social and political dimension in their practice so as to put themselves squarely on the side of human suffering.

Metaphors to die by

Nervos, *nervoso*, or *doença de nervos* is a large and expansive folk-diagnostic category of distress. It is, along with such related conditions as *fraqueza* (weakness) and *loucura* (madness), literally seething with meanings (some of them contradictory) that need to be unraveled and decoded for what the terms reveal as well as for what they may conceal. In fact, *nervos* is a common illness found among poor and marginalized people in many parts of the world, but especially in the Mediterranean and in Latin America. *Nervos* is viewed as a flexible folk idiom of distress having its probable origins in Greek humoral pathology. The phenomenon has been the subject of extensive inquiries by medical and psychological anthropologists who have tended toward psychological and symbolic interpretations. Often *nervos* is described as the somatization of emotional stress originating in domestic or work relations. Gender conflicts (Davis 1983), status deprivation (Low 1981), and marital tensions and suppressed rage (Lock and Dunk 1987) have been suspected in the etymology of *nervos, nervios, nevra*, or "bad nerves", depending on locality. In all, *nervos* is a broad folk syndrome (hardly culturally specific) under which can sometimes fall other common folk afflictions such as *pasmo* or *susto* (magical fright), *mau olhado* (evil eye).

What all of these ills have in common is a core set of symptoms. All are "wasting" sicknesses, gravely debilitating, sometimes chronic, that leave the victim weak, shaky, dizzy and disoriented, tired and confused, sad and depressed or alternating between periods of agitated elation and sudden, uncontrollable rage. It is curious that in the vast and for the most part uninspiring literature on *nervos*, there is no mention of the correspondence between the symptoms of *nervos* and the physiological effects of hunger. While I would not want to make the mistake of simply equating the two – conceptually and symbolically, at least, they are quite distinct in the minds of the people of the Alto – nor to suggest that in stripping away the cultural layers that surround a diagnosis of *nervos* one will *always* find the primary, existential, subjective experience of hunger, the *delírio de fome*, at its base, nor does it seem likely that what I am about to describe is completely unique to Northeast Brazil.

On the Alto do Cruzeiro today *nervos* is a primary idiom through which hunger and hunger-anxiety (as well as many other ills and afflictions) are expressed. People are more likely today to describe their misery in terms of *nervos* than in terms of hunger. They will say, "I couldn't sleep all night and I woke up crying and shaking with *nervos*" before they will say, "I went to bed hungry and miserable." Sleep disorders are frequent in a population raised from early childhood with the mandate to go to bed early when they are hungry. People on the Alto "sleep-off" hunger the way we sometimes "sleep-off" a bad drunk.

But it was not always so. There was a time, even at the start of the politically repressive years of the mid 1960s, when the people of the Alto spoke freely of fainting from hunger. Today one hears of people fainting from "weakness" or nerves, a presumed personal deficiency. There was a time, not long ago, when the people of the Alto understood nervousness (and rage) as a primary symptom of hunger, as the *delírio de fome*. Today, and since the right-wing military coup of 1964, hunger is a disallowed discourse in the shantytowns of Northeast Brazil and has been replaced in large part by the medicalized, metaphorized discourse on "nervousness."

"It doesn't help [*não adianta*] to complain of hunger," offered Seu Manoel, a cane-cutter of the Alto. "The *Nordestino* should be accustomed to hunger by now." Today the only "madness" of hunger is the delirium that allows a hungry people to fail to see in their wasted and tremulous limbs the signs of their body's slow starvation, and to attribute to themselves a chronic feebleness of body and mind.

Deconstructing popular idioms

In her celebrated diary, the Brazilian shantytown rag-picker Carolina Maria de Jesus (1962) recorded that she once complained to the director of the large public school where her children battled unsuccessfully to learn the rudiments of the alphabet, that she was constantly "nervous" and that there were many days she thought of killing herself. The school principal admonished Carolina to be "calm" for the sake of her children. Carolina replied that she was nervous *because* of them: "I told her that there were days when I had nothing to feed my children" (1962: 92). The clarity of Carolina's vision stands apart; she is one of Gramsci's (1987: 92) "organic intellectuals" speaking eloquently on behalf of her class. Most individuals trapped by poverty in a cycle of sickness, hunger, worry, and despair, are less aware, less critically reflective about their lives, lives that are, as one woman of the Alto put it, "too painful to think about." It is hardly surprising, then, that attempts to elicit discussions about *nervos*, *fraqueza*, and *fome* so often resulted in fuzzy, inconsistent, and contradictory interpretations. In the popular consciousness folk and biomedical idioms of illness are juxtaposed producing considerable ambiguity and confusion that contributes to the medicalization of hunger.

Through the idiom of *nervos* rural migrants, only recently "integrated" into the urban world of clinics, pharmacies, and hospitals, are able to express a great deal of their suffering. *Nervos* is an explanation for tiredness, weakness, irritability, the shakes, headaches, angers and resentments, grief, parasitic infections – *and* hunger. Here I am exploring the correspondences between *nervos* and hunger. But I do not want to suggest that *nervos* can be reduced to hunger alone, or that *nervoso* is an exclusively poor or working-class phenomenon. *Nervos* is an elastic and polysemic phenomenon that can be invoked by a frustrated middle class to express its dashed expectations in the wake of the decanonized "Economic Miracle," by the urban working class to express their condition of relative powerlessness (see Duarte 1986; Costa 1989; Cavalcanti 1986), *and* by an impoverished class of displaced sugarcane-cutters and their families to express their hunger.

In this particular context, the relevant question to be asked is, how did these people of the Alto come to see themselves primarily as nervous and only secondarily as hungry? How is it that the mortally tired cane-cutters and washerwomen define themselves as weak rather than as exploited? Worse, when overwork and exploitation *are* recognized, how in the world did these get reinterpreted as an illness, *nervos de trabalhar muito* (overwork nerves), for which the appropriate cure is a tonic, vitamin A, or a sugar injection? Finally, how did it happen that chronically hungry people will "eat" medicines while going without food? As one woman commented on the choice between buying food or purchasing a tranquilizer for a "nervous" family member: *Ou se come, ou se faz outra coisa* – Either you can eat, or you can do something else [with your money]. That something is, more often than not, a trip to the pharmacy to purchase a tonic or tranquilizer.

So I decided, finally, to challenge my friends on their *nervos* and their *fraqueza*. During a small meeting of UPAC with the leaders and several activist women of the Alto present, I made the suggestion: "Why don't we do some *conciêntização* about *nervos*. People say they are nervous and weak, but a lot of what is called *nervos* looks like hunger to me. It is the *nervousness* of hunger."

The women shook their heads: "No, *you're* confused," they insisted. "*Nervos* is one thing, and *fome* [hunger] is another." Beatrice tried to explain:

"Hunger is like this. A person arrives at market almost crazy, with a stomach ache, shaking and nervous, and then she sees spots and bright lights in front of her eyes, and a buzzing in her ears. The next thing she faints from hunger. *Nervos* is something else. It comes from weakness or from worries and perturbations in the head. You can't sleep, your heart pounds, your hands begin to shake and then your legs. You can have a headache. Finally, your legs get soft. They can't hold you up anymore, and so you fall over, you pass out."

"And the weakness, where does that come from?"

"That's because we are just like that, poor and weak."

"And hungry?"

"Yes, we are hungry, too . . . and sick."

"So weakness, hunger and *nervos* are sometimes the same thing?"

"No, they are very different."

"You'll have to explain it better."

Irene rushed in to rescue Beatrice: "*Fome* starts in your belly and it rises up to your head and makes you dizzy and disoriented, without balance. If you eat something, you feel better right away. The trembling stops. *Nervos* begins in your head and it can travel anywhere in the body – to your heart or to your liver or to your legs."

Biu interjected: "When I suffer a *crise de nervos*, it gives me an *agonia* in my heart. It can give a person a fit. It can paralyze you, so you can't walk."

"Yes, *nervos* can even kill you," continued Beatrice.

"Do men suffer from *nervos*?"

Zefinha replied: "Here on the Alto a lot of men suffer from nerves. They have heart palpitations, headaches, no appetite, and tiredness. Poor things, some even have trouble walking up the Alto. Some get agitated, and wild, and try to beat their wife or children."

"What's the difference between 'weakness' and nerves?"

Biu answered: "*Fraqueza* comes from inside a person, from their own organism. Some people are born weak like that. They can't take much in life. Everything affects them strongly because their body isn't well organized. Every little thing that happens makes them sick. Then there is the weakness that comes from anemia in the blood, or from parasites, or from ameba, or from tired lungs."

"Is there a treatment for *fraqueza*?"

Zefinha replied: "You can drink a strong *vitamina caseira* [a home-made vitamin 'tonic'] made from 'Nescau' [a Nestlé's powdered milk 'fortifier'] pineapple, apples, and beets. If you drink that once a day, it will strengthen the blood."

"So then hunger *weakens* the blood?" I forged on.

An elderly woman drew upon the wisdom and authority of her years to try to make things clear: "If you have weak blood, you will suffer weakness in the head as well. The veins of the body are connected everywhere and so are the nerves. The nerves in our hands and feet are the same ones in our head. If you eat poorly you can't be strong; it will affect the blood and the whole organism of the body. So, not enough food leads to *fraqueza*, naturally!"

Later, João Mariano, the socialist political advisor to UPAC, who had been puzzling over the riddle of *nervos*, *fome*, and *fraqueza* since the community meeting when the topic was first brought up for discussion, suggested that I visit two men of the Alto, Seu Tomás and Severino Francisco, both sugarcane-cutters who fell sick with *nervos*. "Maybe it is 'nervous-hunger,' as you say," my friend offered.

Severino Francisco, the proud owner of the tiny *Barbaria Unisex* on the Rua de Cruz of the Alto do Cruzeiro, looked considerably older than his thirty-five years. He invited me to step inside his shop although there was barely room for the barber and his client, seated on a sturdy kitchen chair in front of a fragment of what was once a much larger mirror. He was expecting me, and we speak to each other through the mirror, so that Severino can observe his work and maintain eye contact with me at the same time.

Until the age of twenty Severino was a man "of health and of strength" on the Alto do Cruzeiro. He began cutting cane with his father when he was a boy of eight years. His only schooling was a year of alphabetization in the local grade school. He worked in the cane, without stop, until his illness began with stomach aches, tiredness, and general malaise. He lost his appetite, and with his empty stomach, he suffered from the dry heaves. He lost his "taste" for food, and he now lives on coffee. Gradually his legs became weak and soft; they "collapsed" under him. He thinks perhaps he may have burst a vein. Or maybe he became sick from working in the cold rain while his body was heated up from the exertion of his labor. Or perhaps he hurt himself by lifting too many stalks of cut cane. In any event, it got so bad that he had to quit working in the fields, and then he began his frustrating search for a true cure.

"What have the doctors told you?", I ask, knowing already from João Mariano that Severino has been to every clinic in Bom Jesus as well as to hospitals in Recife.

"They don't know anything. They never told me what was wrong. They never operated on me. They just kept sending me home with *remédios* for my heart, for my blood, for my liver, for my nerves. Believe me, *só vivo de remédio*, I live on medications."

Once, during a *crise de nervos*, a nervous attack, he began to vomit blood, and he was carried by ambulance to a hospital in Recife where he "really started going down hill." The nurses told his wife that there was no hope for him, and so she returned to Bom Jesus and the next day she sent for his body with a rented funeral car. But when the car arrived, the nurses exclaimed: "He got lucky; he escaped!" (i.e., he escaped death).

"But to tell you the truth, I don't know if I was lucky or not," Severino continued, "because I never did get better. Even today only a part of me is alive. I have no strength; my legs have no 'force' in them. All I have left are my hands [and he waved them gracefully in the air over the head of his young client]. My hands are as strong and as steady as a rock; the miserable *nervos* never got to them!

"At first I had no way of making a living. What does a cane-cutter know beside his machete and his *foice* [sharp hoe]? I'm a donkey; I can't even read the sign outside my shop! And without a diagnosis and disability papers signed by the doctors, I can't get any benefits. Those bastards [i.e., the doctors] denied me what I had coming to me after all those years in the cane! So, here I am today, a cane cutter cutting *hair* instead. As if this were any kind of work for a real man! And with all this, I barely make enough to feed my wife and children. The *caçula* [the last born] cries for milk all the time, but I have to deny her, because out of the little *besteiria* that I earn I have to put something aside every week for my medicines. The pharmacy won't let me buy them on credit. And like I told you, I live on medications. Would you call this a life?"

Later, at the home of Seu Tomás, age thirty-two, the young man apologized for not being able to get up out of his hammock to greet me. He explained that he had been sick for two years, unable to work in the sugarcane, his work from the age of nine years.

"What exactly is your problem?" I asked.

"A weakness in my lungs, and tiredness. I have a coldness in my head, pains in my stomach, and a paralysis in my legs. There are days when my legs start to tremble and they can't hold up my body. I also have dizziness and fainting spells."

"Do you eat regular meals?"

"In this house it's a case of eat when you can, and when you can't try to sleep until the next day."

I suspect that the paralysis of which Severino, Tomás, and so many other Alto residents complain is part physical (hunger-weakness) and part metaphor. Men like Tomás are paralyzed within a stagnant semi-feudal plantation economy that treats them as superfluous. The weakness of which these men complain is as much social structural as physical, for they are trapped in a "weak" position.

A healthy, vigorous person does not give a thought to the acts of breathing, seeing, walking. These come without thinking and they go without saying. And yet *these* men (and women) have been made exquisitely aware and self-conscious of "automatic" bodily functions. This is a population that has had the wind knocked out of them, who have lost their balance, who seem to have had the chair pulled out from under their legs. And so they describe themselves as breathless, wobbly, disoriented, embarrassed, and unsure of their gait. How has this come about?

The psychiatrist Erwin Strauss (1966) provides us with a clue. Some years ago he wrote about patients in his practice who could "no longer master the seemingly banal arts of standing and walking. They [were] not paralyzed, but under certain conditions, they could not, or felt as if they could not, keep themselves upright. They tremble and quiver. Incomprehensible terror takes away their strength" (p. 137). Strauss analyzed his patients' existential dilemmas in terms of language. He notes that the expression, to be upright, carries two connotations. It means, first of all, to be mobile, independent, free. It also means to be honest, just, and to "stand by" one's deepest convictions. His patients had been morally compromised in some way.

In the Brazilian instance I would point to another connotation of "upright posture" in asking what is the difference between "standing up" to someone or something and "lying down," sinking, yielding, succumbing, giving up? In the cases of Severino Francisco and Seu Tomás, the language of the body is the language of defeat. Yet, their "failure of nerve" is understandable. The cards have been unfairly stacked against them, and one wishes, one hopes for more than a chemical solution to their problems.

Embodied lives, somatic culture

How are we to make sense of *nervos*? Are the Nordestino cane-cutters suffering, in addition to everything else, from a kind of metaphorical delirium that clouds and obscures their vision? Or, can we best understand *nervos* as an alternative form of embodiment, or body praxis?

Embodiment concerns the ways that people come to "inhabit" their bodies, so that these become in every sense of the term "habituated." This is a play on Marcel Mauss' (1950: 97–123) original meaning of "habitus" (a term later appropriated by Bourdieu 1977) by which Mauss meant all the acquired habits and somatic tactics that represent the "cultural arts" of using and being-in-the body and in the world. From the phenomenological perspective, all the mundane activities of working, eating, grooming, resting and sleeping, having sex, getting sick, and getting well are forms of body praxis and expressive of dynamic social, cultural, and political relations.

When I refer to the "somatic culture" of the displaced and marginalized sugarcane workers of the Alto do Cruzeiro, I mean to imply that theirs is a social class and culture that privileges the body and that instructs them in a close attention to the physical senses and to the language of the body as expressed through physical symptoms. Here I am following the lead of the French phenomenologist, Luc Boltanski (1984), who in his brilliant monograph, *As Classes Sociais e O Corpo*, argues that somatic thinking and practice is commonly found among the working and popular classes who extract their basic subsistence from physical labor. He notes the tendency of the poor and working classes in France to communicate with and through the body so that, by contrast, the body praxis of the bourgeois and technical classes may appear alienated and impoverished. In the middle classes personal and social distress is expressed psychologically rather than through a bodily idiom, and the language of the body is silenced and denied. This, incidentally, is viewed as *normative* behavior in biomedicine and psychiatry.

Among the agricultural wage laborers living on the hillside shantytown of Alto do Cruzeiro, who sell their labor for as little as a dollar a day, socioeconomic and political contradictions often take shape in the "natural" contradictions of sick and afflicted bodies. In addition to the expectable epidemics of parasitic and other infectious diseases, there are the more unpredictable explosions of chaotic and unruly symptoms, whose causes do not readily materialize under the microscope. I am referring to symptoms like those associated with *nervos*, the trembling, fainting and seizures, and paralysis of limbs, symptoms that disrespect and that breach mind and body, the individual and social bodies. These nervous attacks appear to be in part coded metaphors through which the workers express their politically dangerous and therefore unacceptable condition of chronic hunger, and in part acts of defiance and dissent, graphically registering the afflicted one's absolute refusal to endure what is, in fact, unendurable and their protest against the demand to work, meaning always in this context, the availability for physical exploitation and abuse at the foot of the sugarcane.

The "positive" expression of their somatic culture is to be found in these workers' love of physical activity, their concern with using their bodies (which are understood as a source of power, action, and movement) fully and intensely. The beautiful body is for all age groups and both sexes the strong, unblemished, carefully groomed and perfumed body. Countless times I have been asked to photograph a starvation baby, but only after the mother washed the child, arranged a ribbon in its sparse hair, and dusted a sweet-smelling talcum over its neck and shoulders. The toddler would be arranged so that her bloated belly and spindly, emaciated legs would not show.

The "negative" expression of their somatic culture concerns the tendency of these exploited and exhausted workers to blame their situation, their daily problems of basic survival, on bodies (their own) that have seemingly collapsed, given way on them. Insofar as they describe their body in terms of its immediate "use" value, it may be described as "good and strong" or as "worthless." A man will slap at his wasted limbs (as though they were detachable appendages from the self) and say that they are now completely "useless." A woman will pull at her breast and a man will clutch his genitals and declare them "finished," "used up" or "sucked dry." They describe organs that are "full of water" or "full of pus," and others that are "*apodrecem por dentro*," rotting away from within. "Here," said Dona Irene, "put your ear to my belly. Can you hear that nasty army of critters, those *ameba* chomping away at my liver-loaf?"

The phenomenology of *nervos* is complex[1] and it entails an understanding of the cultural representations of the individual body, its internal and external geography that links organs to each other, and individual bodies to the social body, and the larger moral economy that governs relations among the social classes. Rather than a torrent of indiscriminate sensations and symptoms, *nervos* is a somewhat inchoate and oblique, but nonetheless critical, reflection by the poor on their bodies and on their relationship to work and to the social relations of production that have sapped their force and their vitality, leaving them dizzy, unbalanced, and without a leg to stand on. But *nervos* can also be seen as the "double," the second and "social" illness that has gathered around the primary experience (and symptoms) of chronic hunger, a hunger that has made them irritable and depressed, angry and tired, "paralyzed" them so that they sense their legs giving way beneath the weight of their affliction.

On the one hand *nervos* seems to speak to a profound form of mind–body alienation, a collective delusion such that the sick-poor of the Alto can, like Severino Francisco, fall into a mood of self-blaming that is painful to witness, angrily calling himself a worthless *rato de mato* (forest rat), *inutilizado*, useless, a zero. On the other hand, the discourse on *nervos* speaks obliquely to the structural "weaknesses" of the social, economic, and moral order. The idiom of *nervos* (and perhaps this is the key) allows hungry, irritable, and angry Nordestinos, just now emerging from more than twenty years of militarism, political oppression, and the torture and disappearance of those who would dare to criticize the social political system, a "safe" way to express and to register their discontent. The recent history of the persecution of the Ligas Camponesas (the Peasant Leagues) in Pernambuco has impressed upon the rural worker the dangerous political reality in which he lives. If it is dangerous to engage in political protest (and it is) and if it is, as Biu suggests, pointless to *reclamar com Deus*, to argue with God (and it would seem so), then hungry and frustrated people are left with the possibility of transforming angry and nervous hunger into an illness, covertly expressing their disallowed feelings and sensations through the idiom of *nervos*, now cast as a "mental" problem.

When people do so, the health-care system, the pharmaceutical industry, commerce, and the political machinery of the community are fully prepared to back them up in their unhappy – and anything but free – "choice" of symptoms.

Medicine and bad faith

The modern state, Brazil at this conjuncture, this transition from brutal military politics toward more democratic forms, is faced with a serious dilemma: what to do with the explosive problem of poverty, hunger, indigency among its marginals, such as the former squatters inhabiting the Alto do Cruzeiro today. The modern bureaucratic state becomes more concerned with "organizing" rather than "punishing" people's collective needs. At this juncture the role that medical professionals can play as "traditional intellectuals" in reinterpreting and reorganizing people's needs is crucial.

Modern medicine has transformative qualities as doctors, nurses, pharmacists, and other health professionals contribute to the process through which more and more forms of human discontent are filtered through ever-expanding categories of sickness which are then treated, if not "cured," pharmaceutically. While the medicalization of life (and its social and political consequences) has long been understood as a feature of advanced industrial societies, medical anthropologists have been slow to explore the process and the effects of "medicalization" in those parts of the world where it is happening for the first time. Here I am trying to show how medicalization first begins to capture the imagination of a people who, until quite recently, interpreted their lives and their afflictions, and who experienced their bodies, in radically different ways.

Except in rare instances (and the history of psychiatry and the control of epidemics supplies most of these instances), medicine does not act on people coercively, but rather through the subtle transformation of everyday knowledge and practice concerning the body. By the time people start lining up in clinics and waiting long hours for three-minute consultations and a prescription, it is not because they have been "forced" to do so, and once inside those clinics they do not have the doctor's social and medical views thrust upon them. They go because to a great extent they have already come to share those same views (see Frankenberg 1988: 327). This is how hegemony operates and why one encounters such resistance in attempting to challenge notions and relationships that are now part of the shared commonsense world.

The expansion of clinical medicine in rural Pernambuco in the past three decades has been phenomenal and exponential. By 1982 the small, local hospital was greatly expanded to include a general medical clinic and a large maternity ward where almost all poor women now give birth. Today there are more than a dozen modern pharmacies in Bom Jesus, each well stocked with domestic and imported drugs. I was able to purchase, over the counter and without a prescription, both Depo-Provera (the controversial day-after contraceptive that was banned in the United States) and Prolixin, the long-acting antipsychotic injection. Meanwhile, the number of private doctors and clinics increased tenfold.

In 1989 there was another quantum leap as the *município* installed its first local Secretary of Health who now supervised a whole system of municipal clinics. The original centralized municipal health post had gone through a process of fission, now radiating out into a circuit of more than a dozen smaller "miniposts," as they were called, one for each poor neighborhood and for most rural villas within the *município*. Health posts were opened up in store-fronts, in schools, in Protestant and Catholic chapels, in the back of shops and bars, wherever any small space could be found. Most clinics had only a table and chair, a small supply of basic first-aid and injection materials, and a prescription pad. The medical care dispensed was primitive, but the social, political, and psychological impact of the "extension" of the medical "project" was enormous. From "centralized" to "capillary", the diffusion of medicine, or at least some semblance or "ruse" of it, was accomplished.

Central to the medical project was the transformation in the popular idioms and interpretations of human suffering which passed from a theological or an ethnomedical to a medicalized discourse. The traditional folk idiom, *nervoso*, is taken as one instance in the transformative process. It created a crevice, a space for the insertion of medical thinking and practice into the everyday experience of people's lives. It served as a vehicle for the medicalization (and domestication) of people's angry and "wild" unmet needs.

Why are people so easily fooled and mystified by medicine? Because the people of the Alto do Cruzeiro suffer, truly suffer from headaches, tremors, weakness, tiredness, irritability, angry weeping, and other symptoms of nervous hunger, they naturally look to their healers, and to doctors, pharmacists, as well as to political bosses and patrons in Bom Jesus for an answer to their afflictions. Sickness is recognized as a "crisis," manifesting itself dramatically and brutally, visiting itself on the body with a vengeance. Likewise, medical therapy is understood as a rapid, violent, and immediate assault on the ailing body, symbolized in the injection, intravenous *sôro*, the extraction of teeth, and the surgical removal of organs.

The people of the Alto look for strong, powerfully acting medications, drugs that will reinvigorate the body, "animate" the senses, and "fortify the bones." And so, they line up in clinics, in drug stores, in the mayor's office, in the municipal dispensary and they ask for *remédios*: "strong," powerful drugs to transform them into lively and healthy bodies, to reclaim the strength and the vitality they describe as having "lost." And they do not leave until they get these magical, potent drugs: antibiotics, painkillers, vitamins, tonics, "nerve pills," tranquilizers, and sleeping pills. And they get them, if they are "lucky," even without paying for them.

Although doctor and patient sometimes used the same words in communicating with each other, each was almost completely ignorant of the other's often very specific meanings. And neither particularly respected the other. "Doctors don't know anything about my illness," the patients complain with great frequency. "These people 'enjoy' being sick," retaliates Dr. Luíz, "Being sick makes the 'little people' feel important, valuable, long-suffering. They are terrific actors."

Because the poor have come to invest drugs with such magical efficacy, it is all too easy for their faith to be subverted and used against them. If hunger cannot be satisfied, it can at least be tranquilized, so that medicine, even more than religion, comes to actualize the Marxist platitude on the drugging of the masses. But the physicians working in the public hospital and clinics of Bom Jesus da Mata cannot be held solely responsible for the drug fetishes of the local populace. Doctors do not control the flood of harmful pharmaceuticals coming into their country from the United States, Germany, and Switzerland (see Silverman, 1976), nor are they responsible for the relatively free circulation of what should be restricted drugs through small pharmacies which occupy so strategic a position in both small towns and large cities of Brazil today. Nonetheless, physicians do participate in the irrational "drugging" of a sick-hungry population either because they have themselves fallen under the spell of the latest drug propaganda, or because they are, as one clinic doctor described himself, "totally demoralized" by the functions they perform and the political interests they serve in the small community.

The link between *nervos* and hunger is perhaps nowhere more poignantly illustrated than in the case of a young single mother of a nine-month-old baby presented as suffering from a kind of "*nervoso infantil*". The mother complained that her small, listless, and extremely anemic little girl was "irritable" and "fussy" and that she cried all through the night, annoying other family members, especially the child's grandmother. The old woman was the economic mainstay of a large household with many dependent children and several unemployed adults. The old woman had to rise each morning before dawn and walk a great distance to the ceramic factory where she worked. The perpetually fussy and crying toddler kept her awake and she had threatened to put her daughter and child out if she couldn't get the child to be quiet at night. The mother requested something that would calm the "nervous" child and make her sleep. The herbal teas, recommended by a local *curandeira*, had not worked.

Throughout the brief interview the little girl hid her head in her mother's shoulder and whined in a pitiful manner. She was an unattractive child: pale and thin, unhappy, insecure, and both physically and socially underdeveloped. Dr. Luíz gave the mother a broadly disapproving look and shook his head saying that he was a principled doctor and would not prescribe sleeping pills to a child under the age of four years. Instead he wrote the distraught young woman a prescription for vitamins that she was told to pick up at the *prefeitura*. As on many other occasions the doctor failed to acknowledge the mother's very real distress and the child's gross state of undernutrition for which the vitamins were merely an insult. That the child was "nervous-hungry" goes without saying, just as the causes of death on the burial certificates for the 200 to 300 children registered each year at the *cartório civil* of Bom Jesus da Mata go "without saying." In this way the reality of hunger can remain a fiercely guarded community secret. And so, there is a consequent failure to see what should be right before one's eyes, and an evasion of responsibility and accountability. In all, there is a dissociation from reality, a kind of collective psychosis.

Jean-Paul Sartre's (1956) *Being and Nothingness* contains a brilliant existential analysis of "bad faith" in the ways that people pretend to themselves and to others that they are not really involved in or responsible for what they are doing or for the consequences of their actions. In this Brazilian instance the "bad faith" is collective and it exists on many levels: among the doctors and pharmacists who allow their knowledge and their skills to be abused; among the politicians and power brokers who want to represent themselves as community servants and benefactors while, on another level, they know full well what they are doing; and among the sick-poor themselves who, even while they are critical of the medical mistreatment they receive, continue to hold out for a medical solution to their social dilemmas and their political and economic troubles. In effect we have a situation, similar to the one described by Pierre Bourdieu (1977: 173), where no one wants to betray "the best-kept and the worst-kept secret (one that everyone must keep) [so as not to break] the law of silence which guarantees the complicity of collective bad faith."

The medicalization of hunger is, in the final analysis, symptomatic of a "nervous system," individual and social. Hunger has made the people of the Alto lean, "nervous," and desperate. Sometimes it has made them violent. Such nervousness has in the past, under the idiom of the *delírio de fome* exploded into a rage that contributed to the many "primitive" rebellions in the backlands of Pernambuco, Ceará, and Paraíba during the last two centuries (see da Cunha 1904; Almeida 1937; Bastide 1964).

Into this potentially explosive situation, doctors, nurses, pharmacists, and the first few timid psychologists to appear on the landscape, are recruited in an effort to domesticate and pacify an angry-hungry population. It is an uneasy alliance, however, and I do not mean to suggest that Bom Jesus does not have its share of social critics among the ranks of both doctors and patients. As I suggested earlier, this analysis developed over time and within the process of political engagement with the members of a base community movement. To date, however, their analysis is rudimentary and inchoate with respect to differentiating hunger from sickness and the need for food from the need for medication. And so they speak of being "*enganado*" (fooled) by doctors and politicians, but they are not quite sure just how they are being deceived.

Despite their intuitive understandings that something is amiss, the people of the Alto remain perplexed about the social and political nature of *nervos*. They have not grasped how their own folk idiom has been appropriated by clinic physicians and used against them. Meanwhile, the doctors of Bom Jesus da Mata do not appreciate that when the poor people of the Alto complain of "nervousness" they are not expressing quite the same neurotic symptoms as one of Dr. Freud's Viennese patients. They might be best advised to return to the basics of their medicine and to attend to the primary symptoms of their patients' wasted bodies and thereby treat as well their tormented minds and frayed emotions.

For the people of the Alto one answer lies in subjecting *nervos* to oppositional and critical thinking within the context of their base community meetings so as to denaturalize the concept, to render it somewhat strange, exotic, and anything other than commonsensical. In this way the common sense can be replaced by "good" sense (see Gramsci 1957: 90–93), thereby allowing a new discourse (or an older one), a discourse on angry hunger, to contest the one on nervousness.

The irony has not been lost that it is the odd fellow anthropologist, indeed, who would argue against medicine working with and through a popular folk idiom, in this case *nervos*. There is also an irony in calling on physicians to return to the material "basics" of their practice, to treat the "hungry body" and so the "nervous mind" will follow, a seemingly blatant example of Cartesian thinking. All this would seem to situate me on the side of Susan Sontag (1979) arguing that bodies and diseases be de-metaphorized and treated for what they (presumably) *really* are: plain and "natural" things. Strip away the ragged metaphor of *nervos* and you will find the bare skeleton of hunger shivering under its mantle. But my argument is not, like Sontag's, against the "poetics" of illness, for hunger and thirst are no more "objects" and "things" than are any other aspect of human relations. Hunger and thirst are mindful as well as embodied states and they come trailing their own metaphorical meanings and symbolic associations. Blessed are those, after all, who hunger (and thirst) after justice. So, perhaps, I am arguing for the substitution of one set of metaphors for another. If so, that would not make me unhappy.

I began by considering *nervos* as the "double," as the second reality that coalesces around the cultural images, meanings, and metaphors that attach to particularly dreaded diseases and conditions, in this case hunger. The original ailment comes to assume a second nature, a double superimposed on the primary symptoms. These "doubles" can be seen as creative attempts by people to grapple with and to explain the meaning of suffering. The idiom of *nervos*, at the very least, provides an agitated, nervous, and hungry population with a less dangerous idiom through which to address their pain and to register their refusal. Although through the idiom of *nervos* the terror and violence of hunger is socialized and domesticated and its social origins concealed, *nervos* also contains within it the possibilities for critical reflection. "My illness is really just my own life," says Sebastiana. And Carolina de Jesus reached a similar conclusion: "My sickness is both physical and moral."

The sufferers of *nervos* have two possibilities: they can be open and responsive to the covert language of the organs, recognizing in their trembling hands and "paralyzed" legs the language of suffering and protest, defiance, and resistance. Or, they can silence it, cut it off by surrendering more and more of their consciousness and pain to the technical domain of medicine where suffering is transformed into a "disease" to be treated with an injection, a "nerve" pill, a soporific. Once safely medicated, however, the scream of protest and refusal is silenced, and the desperate message in the bottle is forever lost.

NOTE

This chapter was written while the author was a fellow at the National Humanities Center. I am grateful to the National Endowment for the Humanities for financial support. I first presented this topic as an invited paper for the Society for Psychological Anthropology's organized colloquium at the 1987 meetings of the American Anthropological Association in Chicago. An expanded version of the AAA paper, "The Madness of Hunger: Sickness, Delirium, and Human Needs," was published in *Culture, Medicine and Psychiatry* 12(4) (December 1988): 429–458. Since that time I have returned to Brazil for two subsequent field expeditions. This chapter is drawn from portions of chapters 4 and 5 from my book, *Death Without Weeping: The Violence of Everyday Life in Brazil* (1992), and is published with the permission of the University of California Press.

1 Brazilian social scientists have studied the phenomenon of *nervos* from a variety of theoretical and practical perspectives. To date Luiz Fernando Duarte's *Da Vida Nervosa* (1986) is the definitive study. A graduate student of Duarte's, Marina D. Cardosos, has written an excellent Master's thesis, empirically based, on the psychiatric treatment of *nervos* in community clinics in Rio de Janeiro: "Médicos e Clinetela: Sobre a Asistencia Psiquiatrica a Coletividade," 1987, Anthropology, Federal University of Rio de Janeiro, Museu Nacional. The book *Psicanalise e Contexto Cultural* by Juarandir Freire Costa (1989) contains relevant sections on dilemmas concerning the psychoanalytic analysis and treatment of *doença dos nervos*. Helinilda Cavalcanti (1986) raised some initial questions about the relationship of hunger to nervousness which I have taken up here.

REFERENCES

Almeida, J. A. 1937. *Paraiba e Seus Problemas* (2nd edn). Porto Alegre: Livraria do Globo, Barcellos e Bertaso

Bastide, R. 1964. *Brasil, Terra de Contrastes*. São Paulo: Difusao Europia do Livro

Boltanski, L. 1984. *As Classes Sociais e O Corpo*. Translated from the French by A. Marchado. Rio de Janeiro: Ediçoes Graal

Bourdieu, P. 1977. *Outline of a Theory of Practice*. Cambridge: Cambridge University Press

Brozek, J. 1950. Psychology of Human Starvation. *Scientific Monthly* 70(4): 270–274

Cavalcanti, H. 1986. O delìrio de fome. *Estudos Sociais* 2(2): 461–472

Cassidy, C. M. 1982. Protein Energy Malnutrition as a Culture-Bound Syndrome. *Culture, Medicine and Psychiatry* 6: 325–345

1987. World-View Conflict and Toddler Malnutrition. In N. Scheper-Hughes, ed., *Child Survival* (pp. 293–324). Dordrecht: D. Reidel

Costa, J. F. 1989. *Psicanalise e Contexto Cultural*. Rio de Janeiro: Editora Campus

da Cunha, E. 1904. *Os Sertoes*. Rio de Janeiro: Livraria Francisco Alves

Davis, D. 1983. *Blood and Nerves*. Memorial University of Newfoundland: Institute of Social and Economic Research

de Castro, J. 1952. *The Geography of Hunger*. Boston: Little, Brown

1969. *Death in the Northeast*. New York: Vintage

de Jesus, Carolina Maria. 1962. *Child of the Dark*. New York: Dutton. (Translation of 1960 *Quarto de Despejo*. Rio de Janeiro: Livraria Francisco Alves)

De Léry, J. 1558. *Histoire d'un voyage fait en la terre du Bresil*. Cited by J. de Castro (1969: 56)

Douglas, M. 1970. *Natural Symbols*. New York: Vintage

Duarte, L. F. 1986. *Da Vida Nervosa*. Rio de Janeiro: Jorge Zahar, Editora Vozes

DuBois, C. 1941. Food and Hunger in Alor. In L. Spier, A. T. Hallowell, and S. S. Newman eds., *Language, Culture and Personality* (pp. 272–281). Menasha, WI: Spier Memorial Fund

1944. *The People of Alor: A Social-Psychological Study of an East Indian Island*. Minneapolis: University of Minnesota Press

Foster, G. 1965. Peasant Society and the Image of the Limited Good. *American Anthropologist* 67(2): 293–315 (April)

Foucault, M. 1972. *The Archeology of Knowledge*. Translated by A. M. Sheridan Smith. New York: Harper Colophon

1975. *The Birth of the Clinic: An Archeology of Medical Perception*. New York: Vintage

Frankenberg, R. 1988. Gramsci, Culture and Medical Anthropology. *Medical Anthropology Quarterly* 2(4): 324–337

Freire, P. 1970. *Pedagogy of the Oppressed*. New York: Seabury

Geuss, R. 1981. *The Idea of Critical Theory: Habermas and the Frankfort School*. Cambridge: Cambridge University Press

Gramsci, A. 1957. *The Modern Prince and Other Writings*. New York: International Publishers

1971. *Selections from the Prison Notebooks*. Edited and translated by Q. Hoare and G. N. Smith. London: Lawrence and Wishart

Harris, M. 1977. *Cannibals and Kings: The Origins of Culture*. New York: Vintage

Holmberg, A. R. 1950. *Nomads of the Long Bow: The Siriono of Eastern Bolivia*. Washington, DC: United States Government Printing Office

Illich, I. 1976. *Medical Nemesis*. New York: Random House
Keys, A., B. Brozek, A. Henschel, O. Mickelsen, and H. Taylor. 1950. *The Biology of Human Starvation*. 2 vols. Minneapolis: University of Minnesota Press
Lévi-Strauss, C. 1964. *Mythologiques I: The Raw and the Cooked*. New York: Harper & Row
1965. The Culinary Triangle. *Partisan Review* 33: 586–95
Lock, M. and P. Dunk. 1987. My Nerves are Broken: The Communication of Suffering in a Greek Canadian Community. In D. Corburn *et al.* eds., *Health in Canadian Society*. Toronto: Fitzhenry and Whiteside
Low, S. 1981. The Meaning of *Nervos*. *Culture, Medicine and Psychiatry* 5: 350–357
Mauss, M. 1950. The Notion of Body Techniques. In his *Sociology and Psychology: Essays* (pp. 97–123). London: Routledge and Kegan Paul
Pelto, G. and P. Pelto, eds. 1989. Small but Healthy Symposium Papers. *Human Organization* 48(1)
Richards, A. 1932. *Hunger and Work in a Savage Tribe*. London: Routledge and Sons
1939. *Lands, Labour, and Diet in Northern Rhodesia*. London: Oxford University Press
Sacks, O. 1985. *The Man who Mistook his Wife for a Hat and Other Clinical Tales*. New York: Summit Books
Sartre, J.-P. 1956. *Being and Nothingness*. London: Methuen
Scheper-Hughes, Nancy. 1991. *Death without Weeping: The Violence of Everyday Life in Brazil*. Berkeley and Los Angeles: University of California Press
Scheper-Hughes, N. M. and M. Lock. 1987. The Mindful Body: A Prolegomenon to Future Work in Medical Anthropology. *Medical Anthropology Quarterly* 1(1): 6–41
Shack, D. 1969. Nutritional Processes and Personality Development Among the Gurage in Ethiopia. *Ethnology* 8: 292–300
Shack, W. 1971. Hunger, Anxiety, and Ritual: Deprivation and Spirit Possession among the Gurage of Ethiopia. *Man* N.S., 6: 30–43
Silverman, M. 1976. *The Drugging of the Americas*. Berkeley and Los Angeles: University of California Press
Sontag, S. 1979. *Illness as Metaphor*. New York: Farrar, Strauss, and Giroux
Stini, W. 1971. Evolutionary Implications of Changing Nutritional Patterns in Human Populations. *American Anthropologist* 73, 1,019
1975. *Ecology and Human Adaptation*. Dubuque, IA: W. C. Brown
Strauss, E. 1966. Upright Posture. In *Phenomenological Psychology: The Selected Papers of Erwin Strauss* (pp. 137–165). New York: Basic Books
Tambiah, S. J. 1969. Animals are Good to Think and Good to Prohibit. *Ethnology* 8: 423–59
Taussig, M. 1980. Reification and the Consciousness of the Patient. *Social Science and Medicine* 14B: 3–13
1989. The Nervous System. In L. Green, ed., "The Anthropology of Illness", special issue of the *Kroeber Society Papers* (nos. 69–70), pp. 32–61
Wittgenstein, L. 1969. *On Certainty*, ed. G. E. M. Anscombe and G. von Wright. New York: Harper and Row

Part V

Psychoanalytic approaches

12 Is psychoanalysis relevant for anthropology?

Katherine P. Ewing

Introduction

Many anthropologists cringe when they hear the word "psychoanalysis." Even those who focus on phenomena such as the "self" or "emotions" may carefully differentiate their object of study, "culture," from anything that they construe as the domain of psychology. This almost visceral rejection is usually justified by reference to the misappropriation of the object of anthropological study by psychoanalysts beginning with Freud and perhaps best epitomized by his phantasy about the evolution of society in *Totem and Taboo* (1950). Cultural relativists reject Freud's claims for the universality of the Oedipus complex, accepting on hearsay (and misinterpreting) Malinowski's 1927 counterclaim (1955) as the definitive last word, despite the glaring flaws in Malinowski's argument that have been effectively pointed out by Spiro (1982). With the rise of interpretive approaches in anthropology, Freud's biological-drive theory, based on a reification of motivation as mechanical forces and counterforces, also strikes many as outdated and irrelevant. But Freud's theorizing about the origins of society and the functioning of the mind occurred at a time when the founding fathers of social science, such as Durkheim, were themselves developing some rather remarkable theories about the origins and functioning of various social institutions. Fortunately, we do not today reject all of Durkheim because of his "alka seltzer" theory of the origins of ritual in a state of collective effervescence (Durkheim 1965).[1] Durkheim produced a complex, not entirely consistent, body of theory that subsequent thinkers have elaborated, modified, and extended in many different directions, so that it continues to undergird anthropological theorizing today. But within the disciplines of anthropology and sociology, there has been little careful working and reworking of Freud's equally complex body of theory and data, despite the profound, even revolutionary impact of Freud's work on modern culture more broadly.

Though the study of Freud has never been central to the discipline, it was only with the development of interpretive anthropologies in the 1960s and 1970s that a nearly impenetrable barrier developed between the study of culture and the study of the psyche.[2] Such a barrier had not previously existed either in American cultural studies or even in British-inspired functionalist studies of social organization.[3] This barrier was firmly set in place for a generation of anthropologists by Clifford Geertz. In his seminal formulations of the anthropological project, Geertz argued that only phenomena which were public and shared should be considered the proper object of interpretation (see Geertz 1973a: 12–13). Adopting this perspective, many cultural anthropologists assumed that "psychological" meant private, and they rejected as irrelevant anything psychoanalytic or even more broadly psychological. This stance locked them into stereotypes about psychoanalytic research. It has also obscured anthropologists' recognition that Freud's insights are one of the sources of their own understandings about symbolic processes. Several of the anthropologists who have played a major role in shaping the discipline were seriously influenced by Freud. Victor Turner and Lévi-Strauss, for instance, imported basic analytic tools of psychoanalysis into mainstream anthropology twenty-five years ago, but they did so while simultaneously criticizing Freud or denying his direct relevance to their work, thus obscuring their debt to psychoanalytic theory. Hence, the influence of Freud has gone virtually unrecognized, and developments in the field of psychoanalysis are regarded as marginal or irrelevant.

As anthropologists become increasingly concerned with how their relationships with informants shape the production of the ethnographic text, however, the concepts and theories developed by psychoanalysts grow even more relevant to the discipline. But misapprehensions impede anthropologists' abilities to make wise use of these psychoanalytic concepts. These prejudices cut the field off from the diverse strands within Freud's corpus of research and writing, several of which are developing in new directions as the discipline of psychoanalysis evolves (see Cohler, this book). Anthropologists, for instance, have only recently become aware of some of the logical and practical difficulties surrounding the research technique of "participant observation." Anthropological self-consciousness about the issue, imbedded as it typically is in an antipsychological project, has given rise to a spate of self-reflective texts that often substitute introspection bordering on self-indulgent reminiscence for accurate insight into the effects of the interviewer on the research.[4] In contrast, psychoanalysts have devoted considerable attention to problems of participant observation,[5] since the perspectives developed by psychoanalysts are based on close observation of the relationship that develops between themselves and another in a controlled setting.

Anthropologists, I argue, would benefit from a knowledge of psychoanalytic observations made in this type of relationship.

The metaphor of depth

The unwillingness of anthropologists even to consider the possibility that the discipline of psychoanalysis might have anything to say to them is fostered by the unfortunate metaphor of "depth" (see Crapanzano, this book), as in the designation of psychoanalysis as "depth psychology." This was an image used by Freud, who saw himself conducting an "archaeology" of the mind. The idea that psychoanalysts are somehow getting at information that is inexpressibly deep inside people's heads is the primary justification for the demarcation between the anthropologist's and psychologist's object of study. Associated with the idea of depth is the assumption that these underlying, hidden, inner phenomena are not directly observable – that they are private and mysterious. Hence, the colorful image of the cave recurs in anthropological writings about psychological issues.

Victor Turner, for instance, used the image of the cave in his influential paper "Symbols in Ndembu Ritual" (1969). In this extended metaphor, anthropology basks in the light of day, while psychoanalysts wrestle in the dark interior: "At one end of the symbol's spectrum of meanings we encounter the individual psychologist and the social psychologist, and even beyond them (if one may make a friendly tilt at an envied friend), brandishing his Medusa's head, the psychoanalyst, ready to turn to stone the foolhardy interloper into his caverns of terminology" (1967: 46). Of course, it is not the terminology that is the cavern, but the depths of the psyche itself. Turner continued: "We shudder back thankfully into the light of social day. Here the significant elements of a symbol's meaning are related to what it does and what is done to it by and for whom."

Given what I am arguing is Geertz's role in the banishment of the psyche from anthropological discourse, it is ironic that Geertz himself seemed to be struggling against the same metaphor of the cave in his effort to establish symbols and interpretation as a legitimate object of anthropological study when he argued:

> To undertake the study of cultural activity – activity in which symbolism forms the positive content – is thus not to abandon social analysis for a Platonic cave of shadows, to enter into a mentalistic world of introspective psychology ... Cultural acts, the construction, apprehension, and utilization of symbolic forms, are social events like any other; they are as public as marriage and as observable as agriculture. (1973b: 91)

In this rhetorical move, Geertz rescued symbols from the depths of the cave, leaving psychology to languish behind, devoid, presumably, not only of light but also of symbols, a step even more radical than Turner's. Geertz thus used, almost in passing, the image of "depth," constituting the psyche as something private and not directly observable, understandable only through some kind of mysterious nonsymbolic empathy. This image carries with it the absurd implication that all communications understood by others are only cultural and reveal nothing of psychological or idiosyncratic processes. Geertz relied on this image of the psyche to construct a firm barrier dividing anthropology from psychology, the study of culture from the study of the individual and the mind.

Geertz then proceeded to appropriate for anthropology the "self," the subject matter of psychology and particularly of modern psychoanalysis (1983). He even defined his goal as "understanding the form and pressure of, to use the dangerous word one more time, natives' inner lives." He described the process of attaining this understanding as more like grasping a proverb or reading a poem and contrasted it with achieving communion, which is presumably a nonsymbolic process (1983: 70). One can only infer that he was here alluding to, and rejecting, the "empathy" which psychoanalysts claim to establish with their patients.

Geertz's strategy of equating symbols, culture, the public arena, and communication has become a central paradigm in anthropology. Taking off from this interpretive paradigm, anthropologists have gradually moved toward the analysis of increasingly psychological-looking phenomena, while continuing to declare that what they were looking at was purely "cultural" and had nothing to do with psychology. Subsequent researchers are moving to claim some of what Geertz ruled out of bounds in his establishment of the appropriate object of anthropological study. In particular, Geertz firmly, if casually, ruled out the relevance of the fieldworker and his or her relationship with the informant for the effort of grasping the informant's subjective experience: "Whatever accurate or half-accurate sense one gets of what one's informants are 'really like' comes not from the experience of [the] acceptance [of us as people worth talking to] as such, which is part of one's own biography, not of theirs, but from the ability to construe their modes of expression, what I would call their symbolic systems, which such an acceptance allows one to work toward developing" (Geertz 1983: 70).

Intellectual descendants of Geertz, in contrast, now consider their own biographies a relevant aspect of the anthropological object. Rabinow, for instance, included himself in his descriptions of his Moroccan field experience. Retaining Geertz's barrier, however, he carefully claimed to be rejecting consideration of anything "psychological" (though he failed to specify what the "psychological" might include):

> I define the problem of hermeneutics ... as "the comprehension of self by the detour of the comprehension of the other." It is vital to stress that this is not psychology of any sort, despite the definite psychological overtones in certain passages. The self being discussed is perfectly public, it is neither the purely cerebral cogito of the Cartesians, nor the deep psychological self of the Freudians. Rather it is the culturally mediated and historically situated self which finds itself in a continuously changing world of meaning. (Rabinow 1977: 5–6)

What is this psychological self that Geertz and Rainbow and many others avoid like the snakes of Medusa? On the basis of these passages, in which the metaphor of depth is explicit, it can be inferred that the self which is the object of psychological (and, perhaps worse from an anthropological perspective, psychoanalytic) study, is characterized mostly by negatives: it is not public, not symbolic, not historical, not cultural – it never sees the light of day. It can only be discerned by some mysterious process that contrasts with Geertz's strategy for discovering the cultural "self": "In short, accounts of other peoples' subjectivities can be built up without recourse to pretensions to more-than-normal capacities for ego-effacement and fellow-feeling" (Geertz 1983: 70). The anthropologists' version of this psychological self, I am arguing, bears little relationship to what psychoanalysts actually psychoanalyze in their clinical practice or write about in their scholarly publications.

Is there any justification for Geertz's move? Does it coincide with the way in which psychoanalysts delimit their object of study? Is the psyche somehow nonsymbolic and noncultural, according to psychoanalytic models? Yes and no.

Freud's pre-symbolic psyche versus culture

One strand of Freud's thought, which has unfortunately been developed into perhaps the most visible point of juncture between psychoanalysis and anthropology, *does* posit a precultural, nonsymbolic self that is somehow "deep," hidden, and inaccessible except by indirect methods of observation. In the classical psychoanalytic model, espoused by Jones in his debate with Malinowski, culture and social structure were reduced to a set of defense mechanisms against sexual drives and aggressive impulses (see Malinowski 1955). Sex and aggression, in the form of the Oedipus complex, were assumed to be at the core of all conflict, and specific cultural forms such as matriliny were explained as strategies for resolving or defending against this conflict. The goal of early psychoanalytic studies of culture was to uncover the fundamental drives underlying cultural forms. Anthropologists, unimpressed with such studies, found little to enlighten them in the terminology of drive psychology, with its depiction of the driving force of the psyche as a timeless cauldron of aggressive and libidinal (oral, anal, and phallic) impulses untouched by culture. Furthermore, they correctly denounced in these psychoanalytic studies of whole societies the confusion of cultural forms such as myth with individual psychological issues.

Though Freud's notion of the id, depicted as a timeless cauldron of untamed impulses, the seat of primary process thinking, bears some or considerable resemblance to the anthropological depiction of the self of psychology, it is a caricature of psychoanalysis to suggest that the uncovering of such an entity is all that the discipline has to offer anthropologists. The tripartite model of the mind, of which the id is a part, is actually only one of Freud's several models. There are analysts, in fact, who would argue that it is the least useful for current research (see Cohler, this book). Unfortunately, the *Journal of Psychoanalytic Anthropology*, until its recent demise, continued to publish a surfeit of articles claiming to uncover manifestations of a sexual drive behind every cultural form – a project far from the cutting edge of current psychoanalysis.

The cultural psyche

Today many psychoanalysts have themselves moved away from a dichotomous drive model, in which the goal of interpretation is simply to remove defenses in order to uncover repressed conflicts fueled by a-cultural drives. With the development of ego psychology came a direct focus on the defensive process itself and, eventually, a focus on the role of the ego or self in organizing its perceptual world, including the conflicting goals and concerns that constitute one's identity (see, for example, Erikson 1963; Hartmann 1958). Some recent theorists, particularly the self psychologists (see Kohut 1977), have eliminated drives from their models altogether, focusing instead on motive and a model of the self which is interpersonally (and, I would add, culturally) constituted, and then internalized. In these models, the psyche is essentially a culturally shaped entity.

This view has important implications for our understanding and characterization of motivation and intrapsychic conflict. Individuals have a variety of aims which are often inconsistent. Though from the perspective of a drive model, it may be possible to distill aims to their biological or cultural essence, what the psychoanalyst actually does in a clinical setting is to examine conflicts among symbolically (and thus culturally) organized aims as they are experienced, defended against, disguised, and otherwise managed by the analysand (see Gedo 1973). Actors are concerned with simultaneously expressing and concealing their motives as they interact with others. Psychoanalysts have developed a wealth of techniques for uncovering the strategies that individuals use to conceal their motives (even from themselves), as well as their strategies for managing and resolving conflict. In the psychotherapeutic process, the psychoanalytically oriented psychotherapist focuses on the multiple layers of significance that are embedded in every communication (see Labov and Fanshel 1977).

It is possible to observe how people handle conflict using Freudian concepts like defense without reducing those conflicts to nonobservable fundamental forces driving human beings. As anthropologists, we can see that humans are constantly beset by conflict, particularly when we shift from the analysis of culture as a coherent entity to the interpretation of cultural scenarios for action in specific contexts. Individuals operate in terms of multiple frames of reference that are often inconsistent (Ewing 1990a, 1990b; see also D'Andrade 1987, for another perspective on this issue), and these inconsistencies are frequently (though not always) a source of conflict.

Freud's influence on Lévi-Strauss and Turner

My view of the usefulness of psychoanalysis for studying conflict among culturally specified goals actually has its roots in the work of Lévi-Strauss and V. Turner, both central figures in the development of mainstream anthropology. Despite Turner's warnings of the dangers of "Medusa's cave," it is precisely Turner, along with Lévi-Strauss, who was successful in importing key elements of psychoanalytic thought into the analysis of culture and social processes. Their forays into Freud were acceptable to anthropologists, and even inspiring, precisely because they focused on conflicts and contradictions within the sociocultural order itself, instead of positing a core conflict between culture on the one hand and a-cultural instincts on the other. They then adapted Freud's interpretive insights into the properties of symbols, as exemplified in *The Interpretation of Dreams* (1965), for their own purposes. The properties of symbols recognized by Freud, such as condensation and displacement, as well as the frequently found overt and covert sexual content, could be understood as vehicles for expressing and resolving social conflict. They drew on Freud's insights into the symbolic expression and resolution of conflict to help them explain the cultural transformations and social processes that evolve from these sociocultural conflicts.

Lévi-Strauss's overt textual dialogue with Freud was one that equated Freud with the primitive. In "The Sorcerer and His Magic" (1967a) and in "The Effectiveness of Symbols" (1967b) Lévi-Strauss likened psychoanalytic clinical technique to the shamanistic cure and to the native healer's recitation of a myth. In "The Structural Study of Myth," he labeled Freud's theory of the Oedipus complex as simply one more variant of the Oedipus myth, to be understood along with the rest by means of structuralist analysis (1967c). In these discussions of Freud, Lévi-Strauss did highlight a useful perspective on Freudian theory by linking the Freudian therapeutic process to the reorganization of thought in terms of culturally generated symbols, but what he did not make explicit were the ways in which he had borrowed some of his own strategies for analyzing myths from Freud.

Basically, what Lévi-Strauss drew from Freud was a way of moving from static approaches to the interpretation of symbols, in which equivalences are merely identified, to a way of getting at symbolic processes. Specifically, the idea of taking all the variants of a myth as equally valid has its equivalent in Freud's approach to dream interpretation, in which multiple free associations to a dream are elicited, and the question of which are "real" associations is declared meaningless. The characteristics of mythological time which Lévi-Strauss identified are like Freud's descriptions of primary process thought. Lévi-Strauss's concept of the "mediation" of opposites has its parallel in Freud's elaboration of the ways in which condensation operates in dreams to unite disparate thoughts. Freud differentiated several types of condensation, all of which share characteristics of Lévi-Strauss's concept of mediation.[6] For example, Freud's idea of the "collective image" synthesizes a number of contradictory characteristics into a single image (Freud 1965: 327), as does Lévi-Strauss's concept of the mediator.

Lévi-Strauss, like Freud, broke apart the linear sequence of the narrative, seeking meaning in the relations among distinct elements – uncovering a hidden grammar, which in turn points to a hidden meaning. Just as for Freud, this hidden meaning is a conflict or contradiction. Though Lévi-Strauss drew an explicit analogy between his method and Saussure's, his procedure was actually close to Freud's approach to the interpretation of dreams, looking at bundles of relations that are repeated several times over in the surface imagery of the myth or dream. Lévi-Strauss identified the therapeutic process initiated by Freud as one of the cultural transformation and ordering of disrupted inner experience. Further, he suggested that the unconscious, far from being a cauldron of biological impulses, as Freud had assumed, is instead the capacity for generating symbolic thought. Like Freud's id, it is pre-cultural, but unlike the id, it is contentless.

Lévi-Strauss's approach to the study of myths is ultimately as reductive as Freud's, pointing to a single dimension of experience as the cause of the generation of a myth. Typically, Lévi-Strauss discovered an intellectual problem linked to social organization as the "meaning" of myth, as in his analysis of Oedipus-like myths: the problem of autochthony versus bisexual reproduction; or, the problem of finding a mediation between life and death. But Lévi-Strauss did succeed in introducing many anthropologists to the problem or possibility of interpretation and enriched the repertoire of tools available for the analysis of cultural forms.

Turner struggled to reconcile Durkheim and Freud in his theory of symbols as he articulated it in *The Forest of Symbols* (1967). His concept of multivocality was a way of reconciling the Durkheimian interpretation of religious symbols, that they "really" represent society, with the Freudian notion that they "really" represent unconscious psychological forces. Though asserting that the anthropologist and psychoanalyst had separate domains, and caricaturing the psychoanalyst with his "Medusa's cave" metaphor, he nevertheless borrowed many of his theoretical concepts from Freud. As Turner himself put it in 1978, he "rediscovered" Freud's *The Interpretation of Dreams* about two years into his fieldwork (Turner 1978: 573). Thus, more than a decade after the publication of *The Forest of Symbols*, Turner acknowledged Freud as the inspiration for several of his major theoretical contributions. But in *The Forest of Symbols* itself, Turner suppressed this debt to Freud. The paper "Symbols in Ndembu Ritual," where Turner's debt to *The Interpretation of Dreams* is particularly evident, does not include Freud in the list of references.

The concept of multivocality, which is central to "Symbols in Ndembu Ritual," was inspired by Freud's recognition that dream images are "overdetermined" (Freud 1965: 318). For Turner, a symbol represented both unconscious, biologically based drives and images (the "sensory pole") and cultural ideals linked to the organizing principles of a society (the "ideological pole"). Turner's recognition that what people say they are doing and what people actually do with their religious symbols do not necessarily coincide was also inspired by Freud. This is an observational technique that has its parallel in Freud's recognition of the phenomenon of "acting out," in which a patient performs actions of which he is unaware in a psychotherapeutic setting. Freud recognized these activities as direct expressions of intrapsychic conflict. In a parallel interpretation, Turner suggested that unacknowledged acts which the anthropologist observes in a ritual setting can be an important source of data about sociocultural processes. This is a parallel which Turner, however, did not make explicit.

Victor Turner thus used Freud's ideas in two distinct ways. Most obviously, he argued that ritual symbols are powerful because they conjoin sensory and ideological poles in a single image. But he also identified the ways in which conflicts among inconsistent sociocultural principles are managed, often covertly, in ritual activity. He, therefore, displaced the locus of conflict. No longer is the conflict between the cultural and the biological, the ego and the id, the ideological and the sensory, the symbolic and the nonsymbolic – the ideological and the sensory poles are working together to enhance the power of ritual symbols. Rather, the conflict is between symbols, within the sociocultural order itself. This insight is particularly relevant to anthropologists now working to develop models that, instead of assuming the coherence of culture as a *system* of symbols and meanings, highlight inconsistencies and conflict (see, for example, Boon 1986; Strauss 1990).

Observing the ethnographer

Anthropologists have not only questioned the coherence of the cultures they study – they have also questioned the coherence and even the validity of the ethnographies by which they represent these cultures. Traditionally, anthropologists based many of their ethnographic models on public statements made by informants. These statements were taken at face value with little awareness of the ways in which both context and implicit aspects of the relationship between informant and anthropologist shape what is communicated. Much has changed recently, however, with the deconstructionist movement that has swept across anthropology. This movement has generated a self-consciousness about anthropology's past as a manifestation of colonial power and has led to a preoccupation with the act of text production. One of the chief concerns has been the power the ethnographer wields over the informant through the act of objectifying him in the ethnography. A reaction to this concern has been to deconstruct the ethnography, or to strive somehow to allow one's informants' voices to be heard directly, either through the text, or in the act of text production.

But it is precisely in this project of self-observation that anthropologists have had few guidelines for transcending their own self-criticisms. I would like to illustrate the anthropologist's inexperience at self-observation with a text that was one of the earlier self-conscious efforts to expose the relationship between anthropologist and informant, Dwyer's *Moroccan Dialogues* (1982). Dwyer tried to avoid the privileged position of author by presenting what are virtually transcripts of dialogue, hoping by this device to right the imbalance of power inherent in the ethnographic relationship. But the result was essentially an evasion of ethnography and interpretation. In Dwyer's effort to give the other voice, he suggested concrete strategies for reproducing dialogue, such as preserving the timing of the dialogue. Strategies such as this were intended to make the text more transparent so that the reader could perceive the other for oneself. But this type of strategy is based on the erroneous assumption that meaning resides in words that can be captured and transcribed. With respect to timing, for example, who knows how to interpret a pause? Pauses are usually charged with meaning, but even when pauses are heard in a tape recording, they are difficult to interpret. Yet the participants in a dialogue are often able to interpret such a pause, based on a variety of other cues, of which they are mostly unaware on a conscious level. Ultimately, the interpretation, which shapes one's response to the subsequent utterance, is based on one's immediate, intuitive assessment of the pause. The reader must rely on the anthropologist for that interpretation.

In justifying his approach to ethnography, Dwyer advocated that we listen to the "challenges to the self" that the other may voice in dialogue. I would agree with this project. In fact, this is an issue that psychoanalysts are particularly sensitive to in the development of the clinical psychoanalytic relationship. "Transference" and "countertransference" are two of the concepts which Freud and later psychoanalysts have developed to articulate aspects of this interactive phenomenon. Dwyer made his own suggestions for how to go about hearing these challenges to the self, but his suggestions strike me as ways to reinforce barriers to communication while assuaging one's conscience. Specifically, Dwyer advocated a constantly vigilant self-criticism so that one is not only aware of the metaphors in terms of which one's relationship with one's informant is implicitly defined (i.e., doctor–patient, parent–child, friends, etc.), but seeks to foster only certain ideologically acceptable metaphors and to squelch other, unacceptable ones.

From a clinical psychoanalytic point of view, self-criticism is not the route to knowledge of self and other, but is rather a form of censorship that itself should be observed. The goal of the psychoanalyst in the psychoanalytic process is to be observant and non-critical of all reactions, because even the disvalued ones (especially the disvalued ones) can serve as guides for interpreting the interaction between anthropologist and informant.[7] For example, the psychoanalyst may find himself disliking a patient. Following Dwyer's model, one might say to oneself, "I'm not supposed to feel that" and suppress the reaction. In contrast, the psychoanalyst (ideally) will notice his own reaction, become aware of his own specific behaviors that may be communicating his dislike to the patient, and reflect upon the sources of this countertransference reaction. He will identify to himself the components of his own history and stereotypes that he associates with this particular reaction of dislike. He will then strive to disentangle his personal history from the actions of the patient that tend to stimulate such a reaction in others. The premise here is that the patient's actions are shaped by transferences and tend to recur in real-life contexts as well, causing difficulties in the patient's other relationships. To the patient, he will communicate only what he thinks will be a therapeutically effective interpretation. This communication will draw upon the insights which the analyst has achieved from reflecting upon his own history, without necessarily communicating that history to the patient.

What would undoubtedly disturb most anthropologists about this example is the obvious power imbalance between the psychoanalyst and patient. The relationship between the anthropologist and informant is, in many respects, quite different and more complex. But it is precisely this issue of power that is so problematic for anthropologists concerned about the practice of fieldwork and the writing of ethnography. Anthropologists tend to be uncomfortable in their role as representatives of a dominant society and have embraced Bakhtin's argument that there is no neutral or privileged position from which to represent the language of another (1984). Prescriptions such as Dwyer's are efforts to change this imbalance of power by forcibly changing metaphors – an ideological change at best. Overt metaphors may be censored, but this censorship does not alter the socially conditioned relationship. As in the psychotherapeutic relationship, a power imbalance is predefined through both the culturally articulated and implicit images of the relationship between their respective societies on the one hand and, on the other hand, the fact that it is the anthropologist who represents the informant and his society to others. This relationship will continue to express itself in covert ways if it is simply suppressed. The informant may attribute power to the anthropologist just as the patient does to the psychoanalyst. Yet anthropologists have traditionally regarded themselves as detached observers, claiming for themselves the impossible status of "participant–observer." Now aware of the impossibility of simultaneously participating and observing, anthropologists are finally struggling with issues of power and involvement, often taking the nihilistic stance that since participation is unavoidable, observation is, therefore, not possible.

I cannot suggest that psychoanalysis has a fully satisfactory answer to this problem, but anthropologists might find a useful strategy for ethically managing issues of involvement and power imbalances by considering the way in which psychoanalysts deal with power in the psychoanalytic relationship. The psychoanalytic situation is a highly structured one in which an initial power imbalance is clearly established through the cultural image of the doctor–patient relationship which the analysand brings to the relationship. The analyst sets clear limits which reinforce this image and carefully delimit the scope of the relationship. Paradoxically, however, the psychoanalyst regards himself as a detached observer for whom any "interested" reactions are treated as transference and countertransference. Within this explicit context, the two participants explore (among other things) how the analysand constructs power relationships. One of the psychoanalyst's primary strategies is to observe the kinds of reactions ("countertransferences" in the broadest sense) the analysand's behavior stimulates in the psychoanalyst. The goal is to help the analysand become aware of the images of self and other that arise during the course of the interaction and to observe how he uses these images to shape and define the relationship. In other words, psychoanalysts use the status difference between analyst and patient as a projective screen on which the patient gradually learns to recognize the ways in which he traps himself in a subordinate position. The analysis is successful when the patient comes to experience the psychoanalyst as an equal who has no actual power over him in the social world.

The psychoanalyst's strategy is to use the paradox, the tension between participation and observation, as a tool for accomplishing a therapeutic goal. But here the analogy between the psychoanalyst and the anthropologist apparently breaks down. Anthropologists do not have a therapeutic goal. Or do they? It would seem that the concern for giving the other "voice" in anthropological discourse, manifested in a variety of forms in experimental ethnography, is actually a therapeutic concern or perhaps a fear of having any impact on the life of one's informants. Some anthropologists claim to be providing their informants with an identity that they can claim as their own in the international community of discourse – hence, the recourse to transcripts of dialogue and the like. Alternatively, such a retreat may be an effort to sabotage the ability of one's informants to use the anthropologist's account as a tool in the real world. Many ethnic groups in a number of countries have already used ethnographic accounts to help them articulate and demonstrate their identities in political discourse. Transcripts, with their obvious inconsistencies and their individually identifiable sources, would seem to be less amenable to this type of appropriation.[8] Harvey in his critique of postmodernism has concisely stated the problem: "While [postmodernism] opens up a radical prospect by acknowledging the authenticity of other voices, [it] immediately shuts off those other voices from access to more universal sources of power by ghettoizing them with an opaque otherness, the specificity of this or that language game" (Harvey 1989: 117).

Anthropologists are correct in recognizing that it is not possible to observe another society without somehow participating in it. Freud had a similar realization when he and his colleague Breuer set out to conduct psychotherapy with hypnotism and found that the cure somehow had more to do with the patient's emotional attachment to the physician than it did with the technique of hypnotism itself. Breuer was horrified by his patient's emotional attachment to him and abandoned the treatment precipitously. Freud went on to develop the theories and techniques of psychoanalysis. Psychoanalytic technique is essentially the process of observing one's own participation in dialogue with another. Anthropologists still have much to learn about how to use their own reactions as an observational tool. They need to move beyond a Breuer-type reaction of flight from participant observation or its opposite, a self-confessional mode reminiscent of the patient new to psychotherapy, who can't restrain himself from talking about his sessions with all his friends.

Conclusion

Interpretation in psychoanalysis is still an "art," since the source of many of the psychoanalyst's insights remains intuitive. It was this ostensibly private source of knowledge which Geertz rejected as a foundation for the anthropological project of the interpretation of symbols. But the difference, I would argue, is merely one of degree. Geertz's interpretations themselves tend to be based on highly intuitive leaps ultimately grounded in the personal "experience" of fieldwork (Clifford 1988: 38). He then supports his interpretation with a careful selection and juxtaposition of diverse data. The interpretations of the psychoanalyst begin with the self-observation of one's reactions to the analysand. These self-observations are then followed by an attention to specific nonverbal cues, including timing, word choice, sequencing, etc., that reveal the pragmatic intentions of the analysand. These cues are as public as the communications which Geertz observed in his research, and they enable the psychoanalyst to confirm an intuitively formulated hypothesis.

As Geertz pointed out, symbols are not mysterious, unobservable entities locked inside of people's heads, but rather the stuff of everyday communication (1973a). Though as anthropologists we cannot truly know how another experiences the world, we can examine closely how others actively respond to and communicate that experience. Even those symbols that represent what we think to be our "innermost" or "deepest" selves and motives are manifested, at least indirectly, in the social world.

We do not have to venture inside the Medusa's cave of primordial drives, since even our biological drives become the stuff of pragmatic negotiation and rhetoric. Conflict and inconsistency, regardless of their ultimate sources, are always experienced in cultural terms and can be observed in these terms.

Geertz's interpretive project is intimately linked to his stance of cultural relativism, which is antithetical to Freud's drive-based universalism. But it is not necessary that we adopt a stance of pure cultural relativism as the only alternative to a Freudian drive model. Rather, we can observe how individuals use cultural symbols and articulate their experience through those symbols. One difficulty with the relativist interpretive stance has been that anthropologists, when stepping into the "hermeneutic circle," have been constrained by the interpretive worlds they set out to explicate. Cultural descriptions in this tradition tend to be static and monolithic, with no place for the creative contributions of the individual or even the social group in shaping the history of a culture. But when we recognize that for individuals in any society, interpretive frames are never all-encompassing and that alternative "realities" are often juxtaposed (see Ewing 1990a), the anthropological project shifts to one of examining informants' interpretive *strategies* in a social world of conflict and inconsistencies. Though specific strategies may themselves be culturally shaped, components of a distinctive pragmatic style, we should expect to find that, for the most part, the pragmatic use of symbols can be understood in more universal human terms.

This was the type of project which Turner and Lévi-Strauss were engaged in when they drew on the resources to be found in Freud's work. Lévi-Strauss identified the unconscious as a fundamental, human capacity for generating symbols. Turner recognized that the Ndembu managed social inconsistencies with symbolic processes analogous to the process recognized by Freud in the production of dreams. It is perhaps unfortunate that Turner and Lévi-Strauss did not make explicit the extent of their debt to Freudian thought. As a result, the reductive psychoanalytic project of finding nothing but biological impulses behind every symbolic form continues to give psychoanalysis a bad name among anthropologists, though it is the aspect of psychoanalysis that has actually had the least impact on anthropology as a discipline. Such issues become increasingly relevant to anthropologists as they expose to scrutiny the relationship between anthropologist and informant, including the roles of both in constructing the anthropological text. Given this current concern with the contextualization of meaning, the barrier between culture and the psyche that Geertz felt it necessary to stress has become a serious obstacle to the understanding of cultural processes.

NOTES

The ideas in this chapter were originally presented as a discussion of Robert Paul's paper "Psychoanalysis and Anthropology for the Eighties," as part of the Symposium on Psychological Anthropology: Appraisal and Prospectus, at the Annual Meeting of the American Anthropological Association in Philadelphia, December 6, 1986. I would like to thank Robert Paul for the inspiration that his paper provided, as well as Geoffrey White, Claudia Strauss, and Catherine Lutz for their suggestions and comments on earlier drafts of the chapter.

1 My thanks to John MacAloon (personal communication) for this characterization of Durkheim's concept of collective effervescence.

2 During this period, the popularity of culture and personality studies waned, and many of those who had dabbled in psychoanalytic approaches (for example, David Schneider) renounced their interest in this area of research. Nevertheless, a few scholars, perhaps most notably (or at least most vociferously) Spiro, as well as others such as Paul and Peacock, retained a commitment to the study of psychological issues while engaging in the debates stimulated by interpretive approaches to the study of culture (see Spiro 1987).

3 Anthropologists continue to frame their rejection of Freud and psychoanalysis within the terms of the Malinowski–Jones debate about the universality of the Oedipus complex, assuming that to assert the primacy of culture in shaping interpersonal relationships within the family means rejecting Freud and even psychology more generally. The lesson not usually taken from this debate is that Malinowski was inspired and challenged by Freud's insights and found them highly relevant to his anthropological project. Also see Fortes (1987), for an illustration of the extent to which at least some of these British scholars were open to issues raised by psychoanalytic theory.

4 See Dwyer (1982) for one of the earliest examples of this genre.

5 Devereux has demonstrated how important an anthropologist's awareness of his own "countertransferences" is in understanding the significance of an interaction with one's informants in the field (1968). He focuses particularly on issues of "transference" and "countertransference." These are psychoanalytic terms for the unconscious, unexamined emotional expectations and assumptions that the analysand and psychoanalyst project onto each other, thus shaping the relationship to conform to, and repeat, childhood experience.

6 Kracke has independently noted the similarities between aspects of primary process thought in Freud's theory and the transformation that the elements of a myth undergo according to Lévi-Strauss (see Kracke 1987: 38–39).

7 Though this interpretive process may be a goal in psychoanalytic clinical practice, it is admittedly difficult for a scholar from another discipline to discern this process from a chance encounter with the corpus of psychoanalytic writings. Most texts produced within the psychoanalytic tradition tend to reduce the rich texture of the psychoanalytic process to an objectified, diagnostic summary. Psychoanalysts have themselves become aware of this issue and have begun to produce more interpretive case studies (see, for example, Gedo 1979). Anthropologists have also played a significant role in articulating this gap in psychoanalytic discourse (Crapanzano 1981). In particular, Crapanzano's work has been important in linking the concept of transference and

countertransference in psychoanalysis with the linguistic concept of pragmatics as it has been developed in anthropology by Silverstein (1976), distinguishing the pragmatic functions from the referential content of utterances in dialogue. Crapanzano has made and developed the argument that both anthropologists and psychoanalysts are guilty of reducing dialogue to a single text that obscures the intentions of the participants. He has himself sought to create an interpretive text in which the multiple intentions of the participants in dialogue are represented as they emerge, including their efforts to "center" the interaction around specific images (Crapanzano, this book).

8 We can see a close analogy to the anthropologist's concern in one of Freud's patients whom he dubbed the "Wolf-Man." The patient recognized himself in Freud's well-publicized case history and spent much of the remainder of his life as an emotional (and financial) dependent of Freud and other members of the psychoanalytic community. This man's clinical identity as "Wolf-Man" became the basis of his relationships with others in the social world. This is precisely the type of problem that anthropologists face when their informants read their books. One reaction among anthropologists to this possibility has been to become more confessional themselves, thus apparently placing informant and anthropologist on equal footing. But this does not resolve the problem.

REFERENCES

Bakhtin, M. 1984. *Problems of Dostoevsky's Poetics*. Trans. C. Emerson. Minneapolis: University of Minnesota Press

Boon, J. 1986. Symbols, Sylphs, and Siwa: Allegorical Machineries in the Text of Balinese Culture. In V. Turner and E. Bruner, eds., *The Anthropology of Experience* (pp. 239–260). Urbana: University of Illinois Press

Clifford, J. 1988. *The Predicament of Culture: Twentieth-Century Ethnography, Literature, and Art*. Cambridge, MA.: Harvard University Press

Crapanzano, V. 1981. Text, Transference, and Indexicality. *Ethos* 9(2): 122–148

D'Andrade, R. 1987. Anthropological Theory: Where Did It Go? (How Can We Get It Back?) Unpublished manuscript

Devereux, G. 1968. *From Anxiety to Method in the Behavioral Sciences*. The Hague: Mouton

Durkheim, E. 1965. *The Elementary Forms of the Religious Life*. New York: The Free Press

Dwyer, K. 1982. *Moroccan Dialogues: Anthropology in Question*. Baltimore: Johns Hopkins University Press

Erikson, E. 1963. *Childhood and Society*. New York: W. W. Norton and Company

Ewing, K. 1990a. The Illusion of Wholeness: "Culture," "Self," and the Experience of Inconsistency. *Ethos* 18(3): 251–278

1990b. Confrontations with Cultural Inconsistency: How Pakistani Muslims Make Sense of, or at Least Get By in, a World of Multiple Realities. Unpublished manuscript

Fortes, M. 1987. *Religion, Morality and the Person: Essays on Tallensi Religion*, ed. J. Goody. Cambridge: Cambridge University Press

Freud, S. 1950. *Totem and Taboo*. Trans. J. Strachey. New York: W. W. Norton and Co

1965. *The Interpretation of Dreams*. Trans. J. Strachey. New York: Avon Books
Gedo, J. 1973. *Models of the Mind: A Psychoanalytic Theory*. Chicago: University of Chicago Press
1979. *Beyond Interpretation: Toward a Revised Theory for Psychoanalysis*. New York: International Universities Press
Geertz, C. 1973a. Thick Description: Toward an Interpretive Theory of Culture. In *The Interpretation of Cultures* (pp. 3–30). New York: Basic Books
1973b. "Religion as a Cultural System." In *The Interpretation of Cultures* (pp. 87–125). New York: Basic Books
1983. "From the Native's Point of View": On the Nature of Anthropological Understanding. In *Local Knowledge: Further Essays in Interpretive Anthropology* (pp. 55–70). New York: Basic Books
Hartmann, H. 1958. *Ego Psychology and the Problem of Adaptation*. New York: International Universities Press
Harvey, David. 1989. *The Condition of Postmodernity*. Oxford: Basil Blackwell
Kohut, H. 1977. *The Restoration of the Self*. New York: International Universities Press
Kracke, W. 1987. Myths in Dreams, Thought in Images: An Amazonian Contribution to the Psychoanalytic Theory of Primary Process. In B. Tedlock, ed., *Dreaming: Anthropological and Psychological Perspectives*. Cambridge: Cambridge University Press
Labov, W. and Fanshel, D. 1977. *Therapeutic Discourse: Psychotherapy as Conversation*. New York: Academic Press
Lévi-Strauss, C. 1967a. The Sorcerer and His Magic. In *Structural Anthropology* (pp. 161–180). New York: Doubleday
1967b. The Effectiveness of Symbols. In *Structural Anthropology* (pp. 181–201). New York: Doubleday
1967c. The Structural Study of Myth. In *Structural Anthropology* (pp. 202–228). New York: Doubleday
Malinowski, B. 1955. *Sex and Repression in Savage Society*. New York: New American Library, Inc. (Meridian Books) (originally published in 1927)
Rabinow, P. 1977. *Reflections on Fieldwork in Morocco*. Berkeley: University of California Press
Silverstein, M. 1976. Shifters, Linguistic Categories, and Cultural Description. In K. Basso and H. Selby, eds., *Meaning in Anthropology* (pp. 11–55). Albuquerque: University of New Mexico Press
Spiro, M. 1982. *Oedipus in the Trobriands*. Chicago: University of Chicago Press
1987. *Culture and Human Nature: Theoretical Papers of Melford E. Spiro*, ed., B. Kilborne and L. Langness. Chicago: University of Chicago Press
Strauss, C. 1990. Who Gets Ahead? Cognitive Responses to Heteroglossia in American Political Culture. *American Ethnologist* 17(2): 312–328
Turner, V. 1967. Symbols in Ndembu Ritual. In *The Forest of Symbols: Aspects of Ndembu Ritual* (pp. 19–47). Ithaca: Cornell University Press
1978. Encounter with Freud: The Making of a Comparative Symbologist. In G. Spindler, ed., *The Making of Psychological Anthropology*. Berkeley: University of California Press

13 Intent and meaning in psychoanalysis and cultural study

Bertram J. Cohler

> Cultural ideas and ideals, manifested in their narrative form as myths, pervade the innermost experience of the self. One cannot therefore speak of an "earlier" or "deeper" layer of the self beyond cultural reach. As a "depth psychology" psychoanalysis dives deep but in the same waters in which the cultural river too flows. (Kakar 1989: 361)

Psychoanalysis and anthropology share concern with determination of wish and intent, and rely upon study of lives over time as the means for understanding the significance of meaning. Culture provides the matrix of meanings which serves as the basis for the life story as enacted within the psychoanalytic situation. Further, these two human-science disciplines rely upon the relationship between two persons as the experiential foundations providing understanding of meaning. Recent contributions by LeVine (1982), Briggs (1987), Crapanzano (1980), Kracke (1981, 1987), Herdt (1987b), Ewing (1987), and others, have documented the value of the reflexive approach characteristic of clinical psychoanalysis for cultural study, focusing on the experience-near study of the relationship between ethnographer and informant.

Much of the misunderstanding regarding the significance of psychoanalysis for cultural study may be attributed to the confusion between the experience-distant metapsychology, reflecting Freud's scientistic world view, and the clinical theory, focusing on meaning, and arising from this psychoanalytic study (Klein 1976; Cohler 1987; Galatzer-Levy and Cohler 1989). Indeed, it is Freud's distinctive approach to the study of subjectivity, rather than his scientific world-view, which has had particular impact upon twentieth-century study in the human sciences and the arts. The significance of this distinctively psychoanalytic concern with subjectivity for cultural study has been further enhanced through recent contributions which have highlighted issues of self and maintenance of continuing coherence or personal integrity over time. Over the past two decades, there has been reconsideration of the human-science approach within psychoanalysis itself (e.g. Kohut 1971; Schafer 1983; Cohler 1988). This extension of findings based on an experience-near clinical theory is particularly consonant with recent developments in sociology and anthropology, also concerned with the study of meaning, providing the foundation for a new human-studies discipline.

Culture and the construction of wish and intent

The contribution of the human-science approach to the study of wish and intent within the context of shared meanings, or culture, becomes especially relevant when viewed in the context of reports from psychoanalysts working in other cultures, such as Kakar (1982, 1985, 1989) and Doi (1973, 1989), who suggest that the significance of particular modes of enactment in the relationship between analyst and analysand must be understood in terms of culturally expectable modes for experiencing self and others. Study of self, and the developmental line of psychological integrity within other cultures, may clarify the significance of this new approach. Ramanujan's (1988) portrayal of the sources and resolution of a depressive episode in an Indian villager, using Marriott's (1980) concept of fluidity in the Hindu concept of the person, shows the significance of understanding variation in cultural construction of self for the study of development and intervention across the course of life.

Shared domains of psychoanalytic and cultural study

Psychoanalysis as an interpretive or human-science approach must be differentiated from the experience-distant metapsychology, or Freud's scientific world-view, which has often, and incorrectly, been assumed to represent the contribution of psychoanalysis to the study of culture. The human-science approach is represented by the clinical psychoanalytic interview, based on Freud's clinical experience, emerging both from his early collaboration with Breuer, and his continuing introspective efforts, in the years following his father's death, which culminated in recognition of the impact of unacceptable wishes upon mentation and conduct (Sadow, Gedo, Miller, Pollock, Sabshin, and Schlessinger 1968; Gedo 1976; Anzieu 1986). This view of the psychoanalytic process is distinctive both in its differentiation from a natural-science account of psychoanalytic inquiry, and also in its particular concern with reflexive inquiry, in which the relationship between two persons, including either informant and ethnographer, or analysand and analyst, becomes both the means through which intentions are enacted, and also evidence or text for studying lives over time in the consulting room or in culture (Ricoeur 1971, 1977; Freeman 1985a).

Relying upon empathy, or vicarious introspection (e.g. Levy 1985), analyst and analysand jointly focus on the analysand's experience of their relationship as a means for constructing a presently inclusive account of the analysand's narrative of the course of life, including hopes and fears for the future. As Schafer (1981) has argued, the psychoanalytic interview may be understood as an effort to construct a narrative which provides a relatively more flexible and adaptive account, leading to enhanced sense of personal integration, than that existing prior to the analytic collaboration. Further, as Ricoeur (1971) and Freeman (1985a) have both noted, while it is possible to gain increased understanding through the continuing relationship between analyst and analysand, or between ethnographer and informant, once the interview is concluded, this relationship becomes a text to be studied using interpretive perspectives also founded in empathic understanding (Moraitis 1985; Pletsch 1987).

First efforts to apply this empathic perspective underlying clinical psychoanalytic study of meaning and intention to ethnographic inquiry have been reported by Riesman (1977), Kracke (1981, 1987), Briggs (1970), Ewing (1987) and, particularly, Crapanzano (1980). Psychoanalytically trained ethnographers have observed that the same evenly hovering attention, vicarious introspection, and sensitivity to the process of enactment which characterizes the clinical psychoanalytic interview also characterizes interviews with informants. Kracke (1981) has shown the significance of the method of the clinical psychoanalytic interview for ethnographic study in his discussion of mourning in Kagwahiv culture. Using dreams and free associations, Kracke shows how he was able to facilitate resolution of mourning in a householder belonging to an Amazon Indian informant who had recently experienced the death through illness of his young son.

Use of the empathic method, characteristic of the clinical psychoanalytic interview, permitted Kracke to appreciate the pain of this loss, and to use Jovenil's feelings of anger and sadness regarding Kracke's imminent departure, reenacted in the interview situation, in terms of long-standing feelings of guilt, now focused around the death of his informant's son. These guilt feelings, in turn, were based on childhood violation of sexual taboos distinctive of the informant's culture. Informed by his psychoanalytic perspective, Kracke recognized a parallel feeling of guilt on his own part that he had not done enough to assist the child to recover from the illness, which he was able to relate to experiences in his own life. This self-inquiry permitted Kracke to maintain an empathic stance, and permitted interpretation and working through these feelings through a series of clinically informed ethnographic interviews. These interviews fostered resolution of feelings of presumed personal responsibility connected with loss in a culture which ordinarily provides little opportunity for expressing feelings of grief.[1]

Lives as texts: from interview to study of the life history

A similar problem is posed both for clinical and ethnographic inquiry as relationship is transformed into transcript. Ricoeur (1971, 1977) and Freeman (1985a) have noted that, within the interview situation, it is possible to make inquiry, clarify possible areas of confusion or misunderstanding, and, in general, to explicate meanings emerging within the clinical or ethnographic interview. However, once a particular session or interview has ended, relationship becomes transcript. Subsequent effort to understand meanings within either the clinical or ethnographic situation must take place between text and interpreter (Freeman, 1985b). At least to some extent, the interpreter of the text places himself/herself in a position similar to that of the analyst in the initial encounter. Further, as both Briggs (1970, 1987) and Kracke (1981) have observed, experiences subsequent to gathering field material, such as personal psychoanalysis, may alter the manner in which the transcript is read. Interpretation of a text changes over time, a consequence both of the changing perspectives of the interpreter, and larger socio-historical changes and changes in the theory itself. For example, Kohut (1979) presents two quite different interpretations of an analysand's dream reflecting emergent understanding of psychopathology and treatment of disorders of the self.

This focus on lives as texts, and texts of lives, has led to caution regarding both decontextualization and substitution of text analysis for first-person encounters through field work (Kracke and Herdt 1987; Ewing 1987; Geertz 1988). Just as more generally in the study of criticism, there is concern with issues of authoritorial or cultural intent. Hirsch (1976) has argued that, regardless of subsequent interpretations, the author does have a purpose in writing; that purpose must not be subverted by subsequent study. Problems presented by the study of cultures are not unlike that of the author's intent. Lives are studied within the complex context of culture, and subsequent study either of the text of ethnographic inquiry or the psychoanalytic interview must preserve recognition of context, including that of ethnographer and informant or analyst and analysand. Understood as a statement of method regarding life-history materials obtained from both the psychoanalytic interview and field work, the interpretive perspective raises important questions regarding methods of study in the human sciences. The interpretive perspective points to the importance of understanding ethnographic inquiry as an open system in which analysis of texts from interviews as diverse as psychoanalytic process, and inquiry with informants in ethnographic study, is continually open to new interpretations based on continuing scholarly study and emerging theoretical perspectives.

There is the additional problem, even assuming the use of empathic understanding in the study of texts, that the nature of the questions asked changes over time. When contrasted with the sophisticated understanding of text and relationship reflected in recent psychoanalytic inquiry across cultures, earlier efforts such as that of Kardiner (1939), Kardiner, Linton, DuBois, and West (1945) or DuBois (1944) seem naive. We are less concerned today with issues of modal personality or collective character than at the time of Kardiner's seminars at Columbia University. Just as it is possible to obtain a transcript which is able to anticipate developments within the discipline it is impossible to obtain information which can be understood apart from any particular interpretation which is brought to the text. For psychoanalytic and ethnographic interview alike, successive readings of the text provide successive readings as a function of both personal and intellectual orientation of the investigator.

This interpretive domain of psychoanalytic study emerging within the past decade (Crapanzano 1980; Obeyesekere 1981, 1990; Kracke 1987), focusing on meanings, provides a promising integrative approach for psychoanalytic and cultural study without the reductionist, deterministic approaches which have so long characterized psychoanalytic contributions to the study of culture. As a consequence of changing perspectives in human science study more generally, it has been possible to clarify the nature of psychoanalytic contributions to human science inquiry. Detailed study of the origins of psychoanalysis has fostered this inquiry, clarifying Freud's worldview, and distinguishing between proximal contributions founded on study of lives over time, and that logically derived from means other than experience-near, process-oriented, clinical psychoanalytic inquiry.

Clinical theory, nuclear neurosis, and culture

Observing that clinical psychoanalytic intervention was effective in eliminating the conversion symptoms of the hysteric, and the ruminations of the obsessional analysand, Freud (1895, 1990) suggested that the curative effect in psychoanalysis was realized through the reenactment of wishes transferred on to the person of the physician from the presently remembered personal past. These wishes, originating in early childhood, are a consequence of the necessary control of sexuality within the family circle, and lead to the formation of an infantile neurosis in which anxiety and its accompanying mode of protection against the underlying wish, leading to formation of symptoms, is said to be equivalent to that of the adult psychoneurosis (Nagera 1966; A. Freud 1971). Some form of socially constructed control upon realization of sexual satisfaction within the family is among the few universals within culture (Wallace 1983). The particular form in which this control, and accompanying psychological conflict, is expressed within the West, at least since the Enlightenment (Aries 1962), is governed by two particular factors: the attribution of particular psychological fragility to early childhood, and the conflict between parental intimacy and provision of child care.

Just as reflected in Rousseau's (1762) portrayal in *Emile*, Freud assumed that children may be overwhelmed by the sexual wishes arising from care-taking and other aspects of life within the family circle. Children experience conflicting loving and hating wishes as inconsistent with sense of self. As a consequence both of shared abhorrence of these wishes, and efforts to maintain personal integrity, these wishes are kept out of awareness. However, these wishes continue to demand satisfaction in such disguised form as psychoneurotic symptoms and, within the psychoanalytic situation, are expressed as the transference neurosis. Resolution of the experimental or transference neurosis is equivalent to the resolution of the infantile neurosis.

Primal scene, nuclear neurosis, and variation in family structure

There are two aspects of this account regarding the origins and resolution of the nuclear neurosis within Western culture, focused on the child's conflicting wishes regarding both parents, which are significant more generally for cultural study. The first concerns the role of childhood in the construction of the life history, while the second concerns the concept of enactment as a means for studying these developmental narratives. Accounts of childhood, including place of childhood in the course of life, vary across cultures. It is possible to study these narratives through enactments or attribution of particular wishes and sentiments to others, particularly contexts such as the psychoanalytic or ethnographic interview in which the observer is not connected with the analysand or the informant's daily life within the family circle or at work.

Much of Freud's own study concerned those enactments issuing out of the bourgeois Western family, emphasizing both enhanced concern for the sensitivities of childhood, and the tension between parental intimacy and provision of child care. Indeed, Freud's (1909a, 1909b, 1910) careful study of childhood within the family provides perhaps the most detailed ethnography presently available regarding the bourgeois family of Western Europe in the late nineteenth century. At the same time, it must be emphasized that there is marked cultural variation both in representation of childhood and in the place of the parental relationship within the family circle. Our own culture is distinctive in the concern which is expressed regarding the potentially harmful impact of potentially overwhelming sexual stimulation for the child's present and future personality development. As Aries (1962) has shown, this concern has emerged since the Enlightenment, and is well reflected both in Rousseau's (1962) account of child care and education in *Emile* and in Wolff's (1988) account of child abuse in Vienna at the end of the nineteenth century.

The fact of separate sleeping arrangements of parents and children in our own culture, symbolizing the special intimacy between parents, plays a particularly important role in the evolution of the nuclear conflict. While it is widely believed that such separate sleeping arrangements assist in reducing access to such harmful stimulation, they also become the focus of the child's curiosity and the source of intrinsic, developmentally appropriate phantasies regarding parental sexual activities termed the "primal scene" (Shapiro 1977, 1981). First discussed in a letter to Fliess (March 10, 1987) as a scene remembered from early childhood, the concept of primal phantasy was elaborated in the classic Wolf-Man case, in which features of a critical dream become a screen for presumed memories of parental intercourse.

Freud maintained that, in any event, the reality of witnessing parental intercourse is significant because it resonates with inherent, primal, phantasies founded on desires emanating from early childhood. Missing in the discussion of the infantile neurosis, reenacted by the "Wolf-Man" across the adult years, is the cultural context of the Wolf-Man's childhood experience. A child of a great Russian noble family, the expected relationship between parents and children may have already been variant from that of bourgeois European society. As Kakar (1985) has observed:

> since in most Indian homes parents and children sleep and in fact live in one room, the opportunities for the child to witness parental coitus are common. The sexual excitement caused by these occasions, since often repeated, becomes integrated and is normally not a source of intolerable disturbance. In other words, the primal scene, in being a long-running play, is not the momentous event is appears in the analyses of Western middle-class patients with their very different living conditions, notions of privacy and the mystification around the "parental bedroom."

Where parental relationships are differently constructed, and where expectable sleeping arrangements are quite different from European bourgeois culture, as in Caudill and Plath's (1966) discussion of the middle-class Japanese family and, most significantly, where expectations of intimate relationships between the parental couple are differently constructed from that of the West, the content of the child's phantasy life will also be different.[2] For example, if there are multiple woman caretakers, or groups of lateral relatives as among members of the mother's age grade, phantasies may center not just on a particular caretaker, but on a group of persons such as women of mother's generation. Further, it is possible that children will make different attributions regarding parental intimacies than those of children in our own culture who are believed to focus on the pleasurable aspects of these intimacies which are denied to them.

Much of the debate subsequent to the publication of Freud's discussion of the nuclear neurosis, such as "Totem and Taboo" (1912–1913), and the Wolf-Man case, concerned Freud's assumption of the universality of the Western family without sufficient consideration of the impact of variation in family structure upon the child's experience of himself/herself in relation to parents. From Jones' (1924a, 1924b) original defense of Freud's essays, to Malinowski's critique, and more recent discussions of this issue (Spiro 1982), the fundamental issue which has been debated concerns the universality not of phantasies about oneself in relation to parents, but of a particular constellation defined by rivalry with the same-sex parent in competition for the sexual favors of the opposite-sex parent.[3] Fox (1967) notes the significance of descent rules as limits set on the nature of the child's phantasy constructions of relations within the family, observing that: "the incidence of incest taboos is different in different unilineal systems [and they] are human inventions with origins in time and ... are a response to deep feelings about mothers, sisters, sex, and power" (p. 175).

Fox carefully avoids questions regarding the origins of these deep feelings. Anne Parsons (1964) carefully unpacks the Malinowski–Jones debate, noting that Jones insisted only that infantile sexuality exists, and that Malinowski insisted that family structures vary across cultures, and that the nature and scope of the family romance varies with meanings attributed to relations within a complex extended-family system. The biological facts are not sufficient to explain the origins and course of the resolution of the particular family romance engendered within any particular culture. Jones used biology in the same manner as had originally been represented by Freud's metapsychology – as a psychological analogy to presumed biological processes. It is only necessary to point out, in addition, that every known culture, including the Nayar of South India (Moore 1988), has patterned relationships known as a family. There is no known culture in which it is routinely permissible for family members to obtain sexual gratification and reproduce the family unit within the confines of the biological nuclear family consisting of biological progenitors and offspring.

Finally, in every known society, the mother is the principal caretaker, and her physical ministrations have consequences, including the child's experience of physical or bodily sensations, excitations, and diffuse feelings of pleasure. Anne Parsons' (1964) paper summarizes the debate and points in the direction of a new understanding of the nuclear neurosis. For example, Parsons shows that the Madonna complex reflects the conflict posed within the Western family system between women's femininity and sexuality. Parsons shows that understanding of "intimate dynamics"' of kinship, or meanings attributed to relationships, is requisite for decoding the nuclear conflict shown by a particular culture.

Recognizing that sexual wishes are inevitably evoked within the family, there is marked cultural variation in the manner in which possible tensions associated with the expression of these wishes may be resolved. For example, Anne Parsons (1964) portrays the Madonna complex in the European and American family; problems of seeing women as both sexual and maternal in our culture are closely connected with the origins of Christianity, and the concept of the "Holy Family," in which the mother is able to provide complete love and care in a manner in which her sexuality, and with it, inevitable feelings of envy and jealousy, may be absent. The relationship with the maternal caretaker is an important area for study but, as in the Trobriands, early experience of the importance accorded to other relations within the family, such as mother's brother, as well as the tie to father, all become elements of the family romance forming the basis of the nuclear conflict observed within that culture. Psychoanalysis calls attention to the fact that children experience wishes and desires in the context of the care which they receive, while ethnography calls attention to possible sources of variation in provision of this care.

Spiro (1979, 1982) criticizes Malinowski both for simplistic attention to mother's brother rather than to study of the male biological progenitor as the presumed source of jealousy, as well as the failure to appreciate the intensity of the wishes evoked in the child. However, he is less appreciative of the importance of Malinowski's caution that meaning systems, encoded in particular social structures, are critically important in the nature of the child's construction of subjectivity. As Anne Parsons (1964) emphasizes, account must be made of the child's awareness of the importance of mother's brother in Trobriand culture, and of the intense preoccupation with the brother–sister relationship, overvalued to an extent far beyond that within Western culture. It is not the case that the nuclear phantasy refers in all cultures to the triadic mother–father–child tie so characteristic of bourgeois Western society.

Spiro's trenchant critique of Malinowski's (1927) imputation of a displacement of the boy's aggressive wishes from father to mother's brother cannot be faulted. Undoubtedly, within Trobriand culture, as elsewhere in culture, experiences of early childhood, including awareness of pleasurable stimulation inevitably arising in the course of maternal care-taking of young children, foster emergence of wishes which, at the same time are defined as socially reprehensible and personally unacceptable. The intensity of these wishes varies with the number of caretakers, and the emerging relationship between child and caretaker. One extreme is represented by the Western bourgeois family, in which parental sexual intimacy is emphasized in opposition to the children's relationship with care-takers. The Madonna complex (A. Parsons 1964) describes one Western variation based on this triadic conflict. Alternative solutions may be found in other cultures, such as those in which many female care-takers are available to the child.

Problems in expression of diffuse pleasurable wishes stimulated both by care-taking, and developmentally appropriate phantasies about rivalries in the realization and resolution of conflict related to a particular family romance, are present in all cultures. The nuclear conflict derived from a particular family romance, experienced within the particular context of particular family structure requires more detailed study of the kind begun by Anne Parsons (1964), and reviewed most recently by Kakar (1985) and Kracke (1987). The problem is that Spiro also adopts Freud's solution, based on Freud's self-analysis, for the family romance and resulting family romance in the West, together with Freud's scientific worldview, as a more universal solution. Spiro assumes that, across cultures, the biological mother and father are constructed according to Western meaning systems, and that definition of care-taking, sexuality, and rivalry within the family is defined in the same manner as within the bourgeois West. The question is what particular family romance may be characteristic within a particular culture.[4]

Cultures other than our own may pay relatively little attention to such elements of the nuclear neurosis in the bourgeois West as the primal scene. There has been little developmental observation of children's experience of the tie between their parents, phantasies about the parents' exclusive relationship, or parental sexuality. Even castration anxiety has been little studied apart from clinical reports. Indeed, it is ironic that there has been relatively little systematic clinical and observational study of such issues as the child's emerging understanding of gender, and age-related changes in the children's experience of their own body.

First efforts regarding such study within our own culture have been reported by Parens, Pollock, Stern, and Kramer (1976), and Roiphe and Galenson (1981) in anecdotal study. Marriott's (1980) study of meanings attributed to the body and bodily fluids among Hindu adults attests to the importance of such cultural differences in the conception of the body. Kakar's (1989) account of the role of the mother-goddess in traditional Hindi society as an influence upon the boy's experience of self and relationship to mother further illustrates the significance of culturally determined meanings for development of gender identity across the course of life. Reports by Herdt (1981, 1987a) and Gregor (1985) regarding the anxiety reported by men in two different cultures (Highland New Guinea and the Amazon) concerning men's production of semen and the role of women as a source of pollution, further attest to the importance of understanding gender and sexuality in the context of culture. However, apart from such pioneering study as that of the LeVines and their colleagues working on the Guisii, there has been little study of variations in the child's body self as a function of symbolic context.

It is critical that systematic observational study be carried out in the context of particular cultures, focusing not only on such socialization factors as nature of parental ties, concepts of children's emotions, and management of children's expression of bodily curiosity and sexual wishes, but also regarding children's accompanying phantasies reciprocally stimulated or enhanced by these socialization practices. The concept of incest taboo suggests that there *are* wishes whose explicit expression must be censored through the counterforce of society, resulting in compromise formations, and suitably disguised expression of these wishes through dreams, artistic productions, neurotic symptoms, and "transference-like" situations such as the ethnographic interview.

The father–son relationship and the "negative" element of the nuclear neurosis

The myth of Oedipus, as portrayed in Sophocles' tragedy, used by Freud as an analogy in portraying the child's experience within the Western bourgeois family circle (later viewed as the defining characteristic of the nuclear conflict), reifies both myth and psychological development. Indeed, the term "Oedipus complex" (Freud 1910) fails to account for some of the most interesting characteristics of the myth itself. Kanzer (1964) notes that Homer's initial account of the myth of Oedipus did not include the sphinx, nor was Oedipus blinded or exiled as a consequence of his incestuous activities. Rudnytsky (1987) suggests that, just as later with Freud, Sophocles expressed his own concerns in the particular manner in which he portrayed the myth in the tragedy which he wrote (Rudnytsky shows that Freud was preoccupied with Sophocles at a time which well predates his self-analysis and saw in the riddle of the sphinx the hero's capacity to unlock the secrets of nature). Further, often forgotten in classic discussions of the myth as used in psychoanalysis, is the original basis of the myth, including Laius' homosexual attack on another king's son, for whom he was supposed to serve as a mentor, resulting in the curse which caused Laius to demand that his own son be killed.

Ross (1982, 1984) and Weiss (1985) have called attention to Laius' actions as a cultural construction of the "darker side of fatherhood." Ross calls attention to the destructive aspect implicit in the father–son tie, including Laius' terror that the prophecy would be realized. In each case, fathers had not been sensitive to their sons, and parents had not been able to maintain a parenting alliance (Cohen and Weissman, 1984), in the best interests of their child. As Kohut (1977) has noted, it is this abandonment, leading to an enfeebled sense of self, which may be most striking in Sophocles' tragedy.

Representing yet another means for resolving tensions of sexuality within the family, father–son incest, and the regression to a passive or negative position as sexual object for father as a means for forestalling presumed castration, the homosexual tie has quite different meanings across cultures. (Indeed, there is continuing concern regarding the extent to which Freud's initial portrayal of the onset and resolution of the nuclear neurosis is equivalent among men and women within our own culture.) As Herdt (1981, 1987a) has shown, fellatio activities accompanying the transition to manhood are viewed as essential for later masculinity: among the Sambia, a reservoir of semen is viewed as essential in neutralizing the devastating impact of women upon men. Attribution of particular power or control to women must be neutralized, through semen which provides an inoculation of heightened masculinity. This tension between men and women is portrayed by Ross (1984/1988) as a constellation of paternal conflicts, described as the "Laius motif." Fear of women among men appears to have been significant in classical Greek culture, just as among people of Melanesia and, in Gregor's (1985) account, Amazon Basin groups as well.

From an interpretive perspective, as Kanzer (1964), Pollock (1983), and Weiss (1985) have all noted, and consistent more generally with understanding of the narrative perspective (Cohler 1987), each generation within each culture retells myths in the manner most appropriately suited for that time. It is less that the veneer of culture as a cover for drive or instinctual forces is greater now than in the past, as Freud (1912–1913) has suggested, than that historical and cultural forces shift over time. This is but another reason why the concept of family romance underlying the nuclear neurosis of a particular culture is more central than the particular cast of the conflict as portrayed by the myth of Oedipus within the West.

Self and foundations of intersubjectivity: implications for cultural study

The experience-near realm of study within psychoanalysis highlighted in the work of Winnicott, Kohut, and others, has been portrayed as the intersubjective realm. Atwood and Stolorow (1984) observe that inclusion of the different worlds of observer and observed within a common frame of reference provides a unique opportunity for psychoanalytic study of social life and provides a bridge between the intrapersonal and the interpersonal. Stern (1985, 1989b) further notes that the effort to share experiences regarding events and things (reflected in joint maintenance of attention, shared wishes or intents and "interaffectivity") represents an essential task of development which leads to emergence of the capacity for relatedness over the first year of life. Realization of enhanced intersubjectivity not only facilitates psychological development, but also is essential as the foundation of empathy or the capacity for social understanding which is reflected both in normative study and the psychoanalytic process.

Based on both developmental study and clinical observation, Stern (1985, 1989a) posits that the child's "subjective experience of the observable event" (1985: 119) results from the unique life-experiences of each partner in the relationship. Starting at birth, and experienced by the baby as short-lived episodes of assistance with regulation and attunement, by the second half of the first year of life, care-taker and child have fashioned a relationship based on reciprocally shared intents and feelings. Attunement permits the baby to match own state with that of others, providing the foundation both for the subsequent capacity to use care provided by others and to offer this care to another.

Stern's study of the development of intersubjectivity is consistent with Winnicott's (1953, 1960) observation that children create an intermediate, transitional, space between self and care-taker which, over time, increases the child's capacity for self-regulation. Stern's study is also consistent with the formulations of psychological development posited by Kohut and his colleagues, suggesting that infants experience the care-taker regulation of their inner states in the same manner in which they experience self-regulation (Cohler 1980). Stern describes a matrix of reciprocity enhancing self-regulation which is concerned less with the child–care-taker tie than with the child's *experience* of the relationship and its connection with the capacity for self-regulation, vitality, and creativity (e.g. Stechler and Kaplan 1980).

Kohut (1971, 1974, 1977) maintains that psychoanalysis represents a mode of study using the method of empathy, of vicarious introspection, which may be contrasted with the experience-distant mode of experimental laboratory study. In the experience-near mode, the observer uses own psychological processes in understanding the other from *within* the field of observation which necessarily constitutes observer and observed. In the experience-distant mode, this method is ruled out as inappropriate in favor of a perspective from without this relationship. As Kohut (1975/1978) has suggested, the issue is not whether these observations are subsequently transformed into counted data but the perspective of the observer.

Theorists such as Winnicott (1953) and Kohut (1971, 1979, 1984) have shown the importance of an experience-near observational perspective for the study of intersubjectivity, leading to increased understanding regarding the source of sense of personal integrity, the capacity for solace or self-soothing, and for the origins of disorders of self and integrity across the course of life. The concept of the transitional object, or function of care-taking useful in attaining a sense of solace which can be provided for self (Winnicott 1953), has proven useful in cultural study as well (Herdt 1987b; Dahl 1988). Kohut (1971, 1977, 1984) has extended this concept to study of a variety of enactments other than those reflecting vicissitudes of the family, in the psychoanalytic situation.

Much of this recent concern with self and personal integration has been a result of empathically informed clinical study, and is based on a model of psychological development which assumes continuing tension between valuation on self-reliance and psychological autonomy in our own culture and the reality of continuing interdependence across the course of life (Cohler and Stott 1987). Reconsideration of psychological development has emphasized the significance of factors in addition to psychic conflict which may be important in understanding particular experience of self and others (Winnicott 1953; Kohut 1971, 1977, 1985; Stern 1985, 1989a, 1989b).

Winnicott's (1953, 1960) developmental studies have led to increased understanding of the manner in which the young child constructs care-taking on the basis of an "intermediate zone" between mother and self. Idealizing "transference-like" reactions leads persons to feel an increased sense of vigor and integrity as a result of being in the presence of an admired and acknowledging other person. Mirroring enactments lead to enhanced sense of integrity and integration arises from efforts to merge with and seek confirmation of worth from the other: admiration of the other enhances sense of confidence and worth.[5]

Winnicott and Kohut both recognize that attributes of care-takers, including their reliability and capacity to be with the child at times of distress, contribute to the child's emerging experience both of the reliability of others and of a cohesive self. At the same time, the focus is less on the time and space relationship with the care-taker than upon the child's *experience* of this relationship as "good enough" for that child (Winnicott 1953), which is reflected in variations in the extent to which the child is able to encounter the world in a hopeful, joyous, and spontaneous manner, endowed with a sense of confidence and competence.[6]

Intersubjectivity, maintenance of personal integrity, and cultural study

As contrasted with enactments arising from particular resolutions of the family romance, which may be somewhat culture bound, enactments reflecting increased concern with self and personal integrity may have somewhat greater generality. Even granting that concern with personal integration and maintenance of a coherent and integrated life story may uniquely reflect Western post-modern society (Cohler 1988), concern with a sense of continuity of experience and feelings of depletion and lack of self worth may be more general. However, both resolution of this issue, and the particular manner in which such concerns are expressed, may appear quite different in cultures in which life takes place within complex corporate family groups.

Rudolph and Rudolph (1978) show the significance of the extended family group for the maintenance of morale in the diary of an Indian nobleman. This study of the experience of self in relation to others in cultures other than our own shows the importance of understanding intersubjectivity in terms of both personally and culturally constructed meanings. Their observations are supported by Kakar's (1982, 1985) accounts of the sources of psychological healing practices in Indian psychiatry. The particular manner in which concerns regarding self integrity are expressed varies with understanding of the relationship of person and family across the course of life and across cultures (Cohler and Stott 1987; Cohler and Galatzer-Levy 1990; Galatzer-Levy and Cohler, in press). Additional detailed study of the relationship between enthnographer and informant may provide understanding of yet additional enactments beyond those observed in the West.

While much of Kohut's formulation is implicit in Crapanzano's (1980) report of his work with his Moroccan informant Tuhami, the first explicit study of these transferences reflecting the search for self integrity has been reported by Kracke (1981) in his work with his Kagwahiv informant mourning a recent loss of a child. At the same time, as Kakar (1989) has cautioned, the very assumption of the manner in which others are experienced as sources of solace and support may vary across cultures. The concept of self-object, as presently used in Western psychoanalysis, may be just as subject to particular experiences within the western bourgeois family as the concept of nuclear neurosis. Cultures respond in quite different ways in assigning meanings regarding the child's intents, and have quite different ideals of childrearing. The child's experience of care-taking, including possible deficits in realization of personal integrity, is also culturally constructed. Indeed, the experience of self is formed within a matrix of shared meanings of person (Marriott 1980). Indian culture, emphasizing a self which is inherently corporate or collective in its origins, leads to a quite different experience of care-taking and family ties than is present within our own culture (Kakar 1985, 1989).

Conclusion

The concept of the nuclear neurosis, arising from wishes experienced toward other members of the family, may be among the most significant contributions of psychoanalysis to anthropology. Initially fashioned by Freud in the process of his self-analysis following his father's death, Rudnytsky's (1987) review of Freud's long-standing and intense involvement with Sophocles' tragedy of Oedipus Rex suggests that Freud viewed the tragedy as a metaphoric statement regarding means for overcoming riddles of (human) nature through self scrutiny. Oedipus' solution of the riddle of the sphinx provided Freud's initial fascination with the tragedy. Only following his father's death in 1896 did Freud begin to fasten on the later part of the play, seeing in Oedipus' challenge to Laius, and his entanglement with Jocasta, a dramatic enactment of every boy's wishes within the intimate family.

Over time, for reasons more relevant to psychoanalytic politics than to psychoanalysis as a human science, Freud emphasized the concept of the "Oedipus complex" which reified a range of family experiences. Much of subsequent study of the place of psychoanalysis in the study of culture focused on this too-often reified concept of the Oedipus complex, particularly as portrayed in Freud's (1912–1913) problematic essay "Totem and Taboo," rather than his larger contribution to the study of wish and intent (Wallace 1983). Further, most of this subsequent study of the contribution of psychoanalysis to the study of culture has not sufficiently reflected observations concerning lives over time which has emerged with the widening scope of psychoanalysis. Schafer (1981), Kohut (1971, 1977), and others, have shown that concerns with maintenance of a life history experienced as coherent or "followable," personal integrity or self, including the psychological significance of others in maintaining the experience of cohesion over time, may be as prominent as issues of competition and rivalry in understanding intention across the course of life.

Further, even when considering the place of nuclear conflict in psychological development, it is important to recognize that problems in the resolution of desires within the family are inevitable in all cultures. The particular family romance, and the nuclear neurosis which is derivative of efforts to solve the family romance in ways which are socially and personally acceptable, must be understood within the family structure within any particular culture. The family romance, and resulting nuclear neurosis portrayed in such classic cases as those reported by Freud (1909b), or Bornstein (1935), must be understood within the context of the bourgeois Western family, in which the relationship between the two parents, understood as biological progenitors, is necessarily opposed to the relationship between parents and child. The fact of the child's existence is evidence of parental sexual activity and intimacy from which the child is necessarily excluded.

This exclusive parental relationship is accentuated both by nuclear-family residence patterns, by the separate sleeping arrangements of parents and children, and by the conflict between caring for children and spending time apart from children. The child in the bourgeois Western family sees that his parents have particular meaning to each other, apart from his relationship to them although the child may also take comfort from the close bond between the parents when it is not placed before the best interests of the child (Goldstein, A. Freud, and Solnit 1979). At least within the bourgeois Western family, the tension which is implicit in parental pairing (Bion 1961), and the competition which is instilled within the parental family, is assumed to affect the child's own emerging wishes over the years of early childhood. In other cultures, with a larger, extended family system, marked by patrilocal residence, such as among Hindi culture in India, or in which the mother and children are in a kinship group different from that of the father, as among the matrilineal Trobrianders, the nature of the family romance, and the ensuing nuclear neurosis, may be expressed in somewhat different ways.

Meaning systems within particular cultures provide the symbols which the child uses in constructing a nuclear neurosis of a particular sort. The particular sources of conflict and fear may differ across cultures, just as the symbols used to express this anxiety differ. However, the universality of the barrier on the expression of sexuality within the primary family unit ensures that the nuclear conflict must be evoked and resolved, and also that this resolution is only partial, leading to additional compromise formations, including symptoms of psychological distress, dreams, and artistic productions, together with enactment in such relationships as ethnographer and informant.

It is assumed that we can portray a finite number of structural characteristics along which the family romance might vary. Indeed, a first systematic effort may be the cataloguing of these cultural variations, and then observation of the child within cultures systemically varying on particular dimensions. Concern with the origins and course of phantasies derived from the family romance, forming the content of the nuclear neurosis, must be observed through an experience-near rather than experience-distant perspective. Even within our own culture, there are few studies reporting the child's experience of self in relation to parents, as recounted in story, drawing, and reenacted relationships with a psychoanalytically trained interviewer. There has been relatively little study of elements presumed in much cross-cultural study, including the child's discovery of bodily pleasure, attribution of meaning accompanying the child's discovery of gender, and response to variation in care-taking. This systematic study of the child's phantasy world, or experience of others, viewed in connection with other cultural variation, is a prelude to being able to understand the manner in which wish and intention derived from childhood continue to influence adult intentions and conduct. The clinical theory of psychoanalysis may be useful in fostering new means for understanding the significance of culture for personal experience, and the means by which personal experience elaborates on those meanings encompassed by culture, including those encoded as relations within the family.

NOTES

This chapter is a revision of a paper presented at the Annual Meeting, American Anthropological Association, Phoenix, Arizona, November, 1988 and, in revised form, at the Chicago Psychoanalytic Society, September, 1989. Discussions, over more than a decade, with colleagues, both students and staff, in the common-year course, Self, Society, and Culture (Social Sciences II) at the University of Chicago helped make this chapter possible. I am particularly indebted to Kim Marriott for his monumental reformulation of psychology and culture, and to the cultural psychology faculty of the Committee on Human Development, the University of Chicago, particularly Gil Herdt, Rick Shweder, and Sudhir Kakar, for discussing these issues with me. Mark Busse read the manuscript and noted deficiencies and points of confusion in my discussion of culture. The continuing encouragement of the faculty of the Institute for Psychoanalysis for study of the mutual contributions of psychoanalysis and the human sciences greatly facilitated this chapter.

1 Kracke's discussion also shows the value of Freud's formulation of psychic conflict based on repression of socially unacceptable wishes of early childhood, reenacted symbolically in violation of kinship taboos in early adolescence, as the basis of adult personal distress.
2 Significantly, while Caudill and Plath (1966) demonstrate that the close sleeping arrangements of the Japanese family reflect continuing closeness, sleeping is separated from sexuality, little discussed in this paper. Karlstrom (personal communication) has reported that the parental couple leaves the sleeping area for another place in the house where they have privacy during sexual intimacies. Often, in the small-scale, non-literate cultures reported in traditional ethnographic study, there is greater proximity to the natural surround, permitting the parental couple to seek privacy out of doors. To date, there has been little comparative study of the manner in which parental intimacies are experienced by family members, including young children.
3 These discussions have often overlooked the distinction between positive and negative Oedipal constellations, gender differences in the experience of these feelings toward parents, and the fact that these factors are, themselves a reflection of particular symbolic constructions.
4 Offenkrantz and Tobin (1978) have suggested that preoccupation with the primal scene may be observed among adults within our own culture in such disguised ways as the research process within psychoanalysis itself. For example, the analyst's own unresolved elements of the nuclear neurosis leads to undue concern with the analysand's private life and, more generally, research in the human sciences. Extending Offenkrantz and Tobin's formulation, it is likely that ethnographers raised in other cultures where issues related to the primal scene are differently expressed and resolved, will reflect these earlier life experiences in their present response within the culture being studied and, more generally, in mode of approach to human-science inquiry.
5 Kohut refers to the experience-near use of others as a means of realizing continuing sense of continuity and integrity across the course of life as "self-object" ties which may be expressed as mirroring, idealizing, and twinship transference like enactments in the clinical (and, presumably, ethnographic) setting (Kracke 1981). Stern (1985) prefers the term "evoked companions" in portraying the continued psychological experience of others over time, while Galatzer-Levy and Cohler (in press) prefer the term "evoked other."
6 Much of this work avoids the tortured explanations of traditional psychoanalytic accounts of the child's tie to care-takers, and is less concerned with issues of "outside," "inside," and mechanistic construction of psychological representations of the time/space world, than with the child's continuing use of others first experienced as an attribute of the child's own capacity for self-soothing, and later understood as persons in their own right (Winnicott 1960; Cohler 1980).

REFERENCES

Anzieu, D. 1986. *Freud's Self analysis*. Trans. P. Graham. London: The Hogarth Press

Aries, P. 1962. *Centuries of Childhood: A Social History of Family Life*. Trans. R. Baldwick. New York: Random House–Vintage Books

Atwood, G. and R. Stolorow. 1984. *Structures of Subjectivity: Explorations in Psychoanalytic Phenomenology*. Hillsdale, NJ: The Analytic Press
Berkowitz, L. and T. Brunner. 1966. *Sophocles, Oedipus Tyrannus: Norton Critical Edition*. New York: Norton
Bettelheim, B. 1967. *The Empty Fortress*. New York: Free Press–Macmillan
Bion, W. 1961. *Experiences in Groups, and Other Papers*. New York: Basic Books
Bornstein, S. 1935. A Child Analysis. *Psychoanalytic Quarterly* 4: 190–210
Briggs, J. 1970. *Never in Anger: Portrait of an Eskimo Family*. Cambridge, MA: Harvard University Press
1987. In Search of Emotional Meaning. *Ethos* 15, 8–15
Caudill, W. and D. Plath. 1966. Who Sleeps by Whom? Parent-Child Involvement in Urban Japanese Families. *Psychiatry* 29: 344–366
Cohen, R. and S. Weissman. 1984. The Parenting Alliance. In R. Cohen, B. Cohler, and S. Weissman, eds., *Parenthood: A Psychodynamic Perspective* (pp. 33–49). New York: The Guilford Press
Cohler, B. 1980. Developmental Perspectives on the Psychology of the Self. In A. Goldberg, ed. *Advances in Self-Psychology* (pp. 69–115). New York: International Universities Press
1987. Approaches to the Study of Development in Psychiatric Education. In S. H. Weissman and R. J. Thurnblad, eds. *The Role of Psychoanalysis in Psychiatric Education: Past, Present and Future* (pp. 225–269). Madison, CT: International Universities Press. Emotions and Behavior Monographs Number 7
1988. The Human Studies and the Life History. *Social Service Review* 62: 552–576
Cohler, B. and R. Galatzer-Levy. 1990. Self, Meaning and Morale across the Second Half of Life. In R. Nimeroff and C. Calarusso, eds. *Frontiers of Adult Development* (pp. 214–269). New York: Basic Books
Cohler, B. and F. Stott. 1987. Separation, Interdependence and Social Relations across the Second Half of Life. In J. Bloom-Feshbach and S. Bloom-Feshbach, eds. *The Psychology of Separation and Loss* (pp. 165–204). San Francisco: Jossey-Bass
Crapanzano, V. 1980. *Tuhami: Portrait of a Moroccan*. Chicago: The University of Chicago Press
Dahl, E. K. 1988. Anthropological Perspectives on the Origins of Transitional Phenomena. In P. C. Horton, H. Gewirtz, and K. J. Kreutter, eds. *The Solace Paradigm: An Eclectic Search for Psychological Immunity* (pp. 301–320). New York: International Universities Press
Doi, T. 1973. *The Anatomy of Dependence*. Tokyo Kodansha International Publishers
1989. The Concept of *Amae* and its Psychoanalytic Implications, *International Review of Psychoanalysis* 16: 349–254
DuBois, C. 1944. *The People of Alor: A Social-Psychological Study of an East Indian Island*. Minneapolis: University of Minnesota Press
Ewing, K. 1987. Clinical Psychoanalysis as an Ethnographic Tool. *Ethos* 15: 16–39
Fox, R. 1967. "Totem and Taboo" Reconsidered. In E. R. Leach, ed., *The Tavis-*

tock Structural Study of Myth and Totemism (pp. 161–178). London: Tavistock

Freeman, M. 1985a. Paul Ricoeur on Interpretation: The Model of the Text and the Idea of Development, *Human Development* 28: 296–312.

1985b. Psychoanalytic Narration and the Problem of Historical Knowledge. *Psychoanalysis and Contemporary Thought* 8: 133–182

Freud, A. 1971. The Infantile Neurosis: Genetic and Dynamic Considerations. *Psychoanalytic Study of the Child* 26: 79–91

Freud, S. 1895/1966. Project for a Scientific Psychology. In J. Strachey, ed. and trans., *The Standard Edition of the Complete Psychological Works of Sigmund Freud* (vol. I, pp. 295–387). London: Hogarth Press

Freud, S. 1900/1958. The Interpretation of Dreams. In *Standard Edition of the Complete Psychological Works of Sigmund Freud* (pp. 4–5). London: Hogarth Press

1909a/1955. Analysis of a Phobia in a Five-Year old Boy. In *Standard Edition of the Complete Psychological Works of Sigmund Freud* (vol. X, pp. 5–147). London: The Hogarth Press

1909b/1959. Family Romances. In *Standard Edition of the Complete Psychological Works of Sigmund Freud* (vol. IX, pp. 235–244). London: The Hogarth Press

1910/1957. Five Lectures on Psychoanalysis. The Clark Lectures. In *Standard Edition of the Complete Psychological Works of Sigmund Freud* (vol. XI, pp. 9–58). London: The Hogarth Press

1912–1913/1955. Totem and Taboo: Some Points of Agreement Between the Mental Lives of Savages and Neurotics. In *Standard Edition of the Complete Psychological Works of Sigmund Freud* (vol. XIII, pp. 1–161). London: The Hogarth Press

1914–1918/1955. From the History of an Infantile Neurosis. In *Standard Edition of the Complete Psychological Works of Sigmund Freud* (vol. XVII, pp. 7–122). London: The Hogarth Press

Galatzer-Levy, R. and B. Cohler. 1989. The Developmental Psychology of the Self and the Changing World View of Psychoanalysis. *The Annual For Psychoanalysis.*

In press. *The Essential Other*. New York: Basic Books

Gedo, J. 1976. Freud's Self Analysis and his Scientific Ideas. In J. Gedo and G. Pollock, eds. *Freud: The Fusion of Science and Humanism, the Intellectual History of Psychoanalysis* (pp. 286–306). New York: International Universities Press. Psychological Issues Monographs 34/35

1984. *Psychoanalysis and its Discontents.* New York: Guildford Press

Geertz, C. 1973. Person, Time, and Conduct in Bali. In C. Geertz, *The Interpretation of Cultures* (pp. 360–411). New York: Basic Books (originally published in 1966)

1988. *Works and Lives.* Stanford, CA: Stanford University Press

Gill, M. 1976. Metapsychology is not Psychology. In M. Gill and P. Holzman, eds. *Psychology versus Metapsychology: Psychoanalysis Essays in Memory of George S. Klein* (pp. 71–105). New York: International Universities Press. Psychological Issues Monograph 36

Goldstein, J., A. Freud, and A. Solnit. 1979. *Beyond the Best Interests of the Child.* Rev. Edn. New York: Basic Books

Gregor, T. 1985. *Anxious Pleasures: The Sexual Lives of the Amazonian People.* Chicago: University of Chicago Press

Herdt, G. 1981. *Guardians of the Flutes.* New York: McGraw-Hill

1987a. *Sambia: Ritual and Gender in New Guinea.* New York: Holt, Rinehart and Winston

1987b. Transitional objects in Sambia initiation. *Ethos* 15: 40–57

Hirsch, E. D., Jr. 1976. *The Aims of Interpretation.* Chicago: University of Chicago Press

Horton, P. 1981. *Solace – The Missing Dimension in Psychiatry.* Chicago: University of Chicago Press

Jones, E. 1924a/1951. Psychoanalysis and Anthropology. In E. Jones, *Essays in Applied Anthropology* (vol. II, pp. 114–144): *Essays in Folklore, Anthropology, and Religion*

1924b/1951. Mother-Right and the Sexual Ignorance of Savages. In E. Jones, *Essays in Applied Anthropology* (vol. II, pp. 145–173): *Essays in Folklore, Anthropology, and Religion*

Kakar, S. 1982. *Shamans, Mystics, and Doctors.* New York: Knopf

1985. Psychoanalysis and Non-Western Cultures. *International Review of Psychoanalysis* 12: 441–448

1989. The Maternal-Feminine in Indian Psychoanalysis. *International Review of Psychoanalysis* 16: 355–362

Kanzer, M. 1964. On Interpreting the Oedipus Plays. *Psychoanalytic Study of Society* 3: 26–38

Kardiner, A. 1939. *The Individual and His Society: The Psychodynamics of Primitive Social Organization.* New York: Columbia University Press

Kardiner, A., R. Linton, C. Du Bois, and J. West. 1945. *The Psychological Frontiers of Society.* New York: Columbia University Press

Klein, G. 1976. *Psychoanalytic Theory: An Exploration of Essentials.* New York: International Universities Press

Kohut, H. 1971. *The Analysis of the Self.* New York: International Universities Press Psychoanalytic Study of the Child Series, Monograph 1

1974. Introspection, Empathy, and Psychoanalysis: An Examination between Mode of Observation and Theory. In P. Ornstein, ed., *The Search for the Self: Selected Writings of Heinz Kohut, 1950–1978* (vol. I, pp. 205–232). Madison, CT: International Universities Press (originally published in 1959)

1975/1978. The Psychoanalyst in the Community of Scholars. In P. Ornstein, ed., *The Search for the Self: Selected Writings of Heinz Kohut, 1950–1978* (vol. II, pp. 685–724). New York: International Universities Press

1977. *The Restoration of the Self.* New York: International Universities Press

1979. The Two analyses of Mr. Z. *International Journal of Psychoanalysis* 60: 3–27

1984. *How Does Analysis Cure?* Chicago: University of Chicago Press

1985. Self Psychology and the Sciences of Man. In C. Strozier, ed., *Self-Psychology and the Humanities: Reflections of a New Psychoanalytic Approach by Heinz Kohut* (pp. 73–94). New York: Norton, (originally published in 1978)

Kracke, W. 1981. Kagwahiv Mourning: Dreams of a Bereaved Father. *Ethos* 9: 258–275

1987. Encounter with Other Cultures: Psychological and Epistemological Aspects. *Ethos* 15: 58–82

Kracke, W. and G. Herdt. 1987. Introduction: Interpretation in Psychoanalytic Anthropology. *Ethos* 15: 3–8

LeVine, R. 1982. *Culture, Behavior and Personality*. Revised Edition. First edn. 1973. Chicago: Aldine Publishing Company

LeVine, S. 1981. Dreams of the Informant about the Researcher: Some Difficulties Inherent in the Research Relationship. *Ethos* 9: 276–293

Levy, S. 1985. Empathy and Psychoanalytic Technique. *Journal of the American Psychoanalytic Association* 33: 353–378

Malinowski, B. 1955. *Sex and Repression in Savage Society*. New York: New American Library, originally published in 1927

1967. *A Diary in the Strict Sense of the Term*. London: Routledge and Kegan Paul

Marriott, McK. 1980. The Open Hindu Person and Interpersonal Fluidity. Paper presented at annual meetings, Association for Asian Studies, Washington, DC

Moore, M. 1988. Symbol and Meaning in Nayar Marriage Ritual. *American Ethnologist* 15, 254–273

Moraitis, G. 1985. A Psychoanalyst's Journey into a Historian's World: An Experiment in Collaboration. In S. Baron and C. Pletsch, eds., *Introspection in Biography: The Biographer's Quest for Self-Awareness* (pp. 69–106). Hillsdale, NJ: The Analytic Press

Nagera, H. 1966. *Early Childhood Disturbances, the Infantile Neurosis, and The Adulthood Disturbances*. New York: International Universities Press, Monograph Number 2, The Psychoanalytic Study of the Child Series

Obeyesekere, G. 1981. *Medusa's Hair: An Essay on Personal Symbols and Religious Experience*. Chicago: University of Chicago Press

1990. *The Work of Culture: Symbolic Transformation in Psychoanalysis and Anthropology*. Chicago: University of Chicago Press

Offenkrantz, W. and A. Tobin. 1978. Problems of the Therapeutic Alliance: Analysis with Simultaneous Therapeutic and Research Goals. *International Review of Psychoanalysis* 5: 217–230

Parens, H., L. Pollock, J. Stern, and S. Kramer. 1976. On the Girl's Entry into the Oedipus Complex. *Journal of the American Psychoanalytic Association* 24 Supp: 79–108

Parsons, A. 1964. Is the Oedipus Complex Universal? The Jones–Malinowski Debate Revisited and a South Italian "nuclear complex." In W. Muensterberger and S. Axelrad, eds., *The Psychoanalytic Study of Society* (vol. II, pp. 278–328). New York: International Universities Press

Parsons, T. 1949. The Social Structure of the Family. In R. Anshen, ed., *The Family: Its Function and Destiny* (p. 190). New York: Harper and Row

Pletsch, C. 1987. On the Autobiographical Life of Nietzsche. In G. Moraitis and G. Pollock, eds., *Psychoanalytic Studies of Biography* (pp. 405–434). New York: International Universities Press

Pollock, G. 1983. Oedipus: The Myth, the Developmental Stage, the Universal Theme, the Conflict and Complex. In G. H. Pollock and J. M. Ross, eds., *The Oedipus Papers* (pp. 339–371). Madison, CT: International Universities Press

Ramanujan, A. K. 1988. Psychiatry in an Indian Village. Unpublished manuscript, Department of Psychiatry, University of Illinois, Chicago

Ricoeur, P. 1971. The Model of the Text: Meaningful Action Considered as a Text. *Social Research* 38: 559–562

1977. The Question of Proof in Freud's Scientific Writings. *Journal of the American Psychoanalytic Association* 25: 835–873

1979/1981. The Function of Narrative. In J. B. Thompson, ed., *Paul Ricoeur: Hermeneutics and the Human Sciences* (pp. 274–296). Cambridge: Cambridge University Press

1983. *Time and Narrative*. Vol. I. Trans. J. McLaughlin and D. Pellauer. Chicago: University of Chicago Press

Riesman, P. 1977. *Freedom in Fulani Social Life: An Introspective Ethnography*. Chicago: University of Chicago Press

Roiphe, H. and E. Galenson. 1981. *Infantile Origins of Sexual Identity*. New York: International Universities Press

Ross, J. M. 1982. Oedipus Revisited: Laius and the "Laius Complex." *Psychoanalytic Study of the Child* 37: 167–200

1984/1988. The Darker Side of Fatherhood: Clinical and Developmental Ramifications of the "Laius Motif." In G. H. Pollock and J. M. Ross, eds., *The Oedipus Papers* (pp. 389–417). Madison, CT: International Universities Press

Rousseau, J.-J. 1762/1969. *Emile or On Education*. Trans. A. Bloom. New York: Basic Books

Rudnytsky, P. 1987. *Freud and Oedipus*. New York: Columbia University Press

Rudolph, S. and L. Rudolph. 1978. Rajput Adulthood: Reflections on the Amar Singh Diary. In E. Erikson, ed., *Adulthood* (pp. 149–172). New York: Norton

Sadow, L., J. Gedo, J. Miller, G. Pollock, M. Sabshin, and N. Schlessinger. 1968. The Process of Hypothesis Change in Three Psychoanalytic Concepts. In J. Gedo and G. Pollock, eds., *Freud: The Fusion of Science and Humanism, The Intellectual History of Psychoanalysis* (pp. 257–285). New York: International Universities Press. Psychological Issues Monographs 34–35

Samuels, A. 1986. The Image of the Parents in Bed. In A. Samuels, ed., *The Father: Contemporary Jungian Perspectives* (pp. 111–134). New York: New York University Press

Schafer, R. 1981. *Narrative Actions in Psychoanalysis*. Worcester, MA: Clark University Press, Volume XIV of the Heinz Werner Lecture Series

1983. *The Analytic Attitude*. New York: Basic Books

Shapiro, T. 1977. Oedipal Distortions in Severe Character Pathologies: Developmental and Theoretical Considerations. *Psychoanalytic Quarterly* 46: 559–579

1981. On the Quest for the Origins of Conflict, *Psychoanalytic Quarterly* 50: 1–21

Spiro, M. 1965. Religious Systems as Culturally Constituted Defense Mechanisms. In M. Spiro, ed., *Context and Meaning in Cultural Anthropology: Essays in Honor of A. I. Hallowell* (pp. 100–113). New York: Free Press–Macmillan

1979. Whatever Happened to the Id? *American Anthropologist* 81: 5–13

1982. *Oedipus in the Trobriands*. Chicago: University of Chicago Press

Stechler, G. and S. Kaplan. 1980. The Development of the Self. *Psychoanalytic Study of the Self* 35: 85–105

Stern, D. 1985. *The Interpersonal World of the Infant*. New York: Basic Books

1989a. The Representation of Relational Patterns: Developmental Considerations. In I. A. Sameroff and R. Emde, eds., *Relationship Disturbances in Early Childhood: A Developmental Approach* (pp. 52–68). New York: Basic Books

1989b. Developmental Prerequisites for the Sense of a Narrated Self. In A. Cooper, P. Kernberg, and E. Person, eds., *Psychoanalysis: Toward the Second Century* (pp. 168–180). New Haven, CT: Yale University Press

Tambiah, S. 1969/1985. Animals are Good to Think and Good to Prohibit. In S. Tambiah, *Culture, Thought and Social Actions: An Anthropological Perspective* (pp. 169–211). Cambridge, MA: Harvard University Press

Wallace, E. R., IV. 1983. *Freud and Anthropology: A History and Reappraisal*. New York: International Universities Press, Psychological Issues Monograph 55

Weiss, S. 1985/1988. How Culture Influences the Interpretation of the Oedipus Myth. In G. H. Pollock and J. M. Ross, eds., *The Oedipus Papers* (pp. 373–385). Madison, CT: International Universities Press

Winnicott, D. W. 1953. Transitional Objects and Transitional Phenomena. In D. W. Winnicott, *Collected Papers: Through Paediatrics to Psycho-Analysis* (pp. 229–242). New York: Basic Books

1960. The Theory of the Parent–Infant Relationship. *International Journal of Psychoanalysis* 41: 585–595

Wolff, L. 1988. *Postcards from the End of the World: Child Abuse in Freud's Vienna*. New York: Athenaeum

14 Some thoughts on hermeneutics and psychoanalytic anthropology

Vincent Crapanzano

Let me begin with the juxtaposition of our two disciplines: anthropology and psychoanalysis.[1] Though both anthropology and psychoanalysis are considered to be part of the sciences of man, and therein differentiated on the basis of their purview, they differ less in terms of their purviews than in terms of their structure as disciplines.[2] Psychoanalysis has what can be called a theological structure. It has a privileged body of texts – the Freudian corpus – that determine its parameters, ground its practice (whether understood as therapy or research), and give full stop to what might otherwise be an infinite interpretive regress. There are also secondary and tertiary texts of varying authority that may elaborate the primary corpus (within limits that are never so fully elaborated as to avoid some negotiation) but ultimate intra- and extra-textual authority lies with the primary texts. Too great a deviation from what is deemed to be the content or meaning of these primary texts can and usually does lead to denunciation, heresy, and excommunication. There are institutions that support the structure of the discipline by providing initiatory procedures, standards of membership, channels of publication, a tribunal, and, as in the case of the expulsion of Jacques Lacan from the International Association of Psycho-Analysis on the grounds that his Institute did not provide appropriate training for its candidates, procedures for excommunication.[3] Heretical groups have tended to replicate this institutional structure, and rarely have ecumenical movements succeeded in mending breaches. The closed structure of the discipline has, with some success, been masked by the adoption of a broader, open-ended progressivist ideology that is shared with other contemporary sciences.

By contrast, anthropology seems chaotic. There is no central text (though there have been frequent attempts to privilege some texts – those of Boas, Malinowski, Radcliffe-Brown – to establish a canon). Indeed, there is little agreement on the subject matter of the discipline and on its parameters. Witness all the debate about the four-field approach.[4] Anthropological practice is restricted, at least symbolically, to field work. What anthropologists do most of the time, namely teach, is ignored. The nature of field work itself, exalted to have become the ultimate hallmark of the discipline, is left vague. It is labeled "participant observation" – a term so devoid of content by now as to be simply tautological – and characterized, if at all, by anguished banalities that lay stress on its contradictory, its oxymoronic status. Without a central, authoritative text or even an arbitrary tribunal, interpretation is always uncertain. To be sure, reference is made to the canon, but as there is little agreement about the canon, such reference is rhetorical and does little to ease interpretive uncertainty. Or, particularly in the subfields of the discipline, like psychological anthropology, reference is often made to authoritative texts, like those of Freud, in other, possibly "theological" disciplines. As the subfields do not share the cultural and institutional features of these other disciplines, they can only partially (particularly in as relativistic a discipline as anthropology) receive hermeneutical succor. A second tendency has been to borrow crudely positivistic, methodological strategies from the hard sciences, but such borrowings have so severely limited the range of investigation that only the most diehard proponents of this strategy – those willing to dismiss just about everything to that nasty category (whatever it may mean) of epiphenomena – have persisted in this direction.

Institutionally too anthropology is loose. There are no hard-and-fast initiatory procedures; standards of membership are ethical rather than theoretical. There is no tribunal and no procedures for excommunication other than for ethical reasons. There are, of course, numerous channels of publication. Under these circumstances there can be no heresies, officially at least, though there has been a proliferation of associations, that, to my knowledge, are not exclusive. Indeed, they relate to one another like the shrines of ancient Greece. It is in this context that the field of psychoanalytic, and a good deal of culture and personality, anthropology has to be understood.

In the last few years, there has been a turn in both anthropology and psychoanalysis toward interpretation – a turn that has been critically questioned by many practitioners in both fields. According to this view, both disciplines are not, and cannot be evaluated in terms of, the hard sciences. Rather they have to be understood as exercises in interpretation. I use the word "exercises" in order to stress not always explicit or even desired results of this interpretive turn: an emphasis on process or strategy – the exercise – of interpretation and the recognition, however reluctant, that even in the most fundamentalistic of hermeneutical systems, there is no final interpretation, though there may be authoritative interpretations. (The authority of such interpretations is external to the interpretive strategy itself.) If they have no extrinsic goals such as, for example, cure –

goals that can be somehow measured or evaluated – the exercises of interpretation risk becoming in an art-for-art's-sake sort of way interpretation for interpretation's sake. At best they become exemplary and programmatic; at worst, attestations of the interpreter's virtuosity (Crapanzano 1986). Interpretation, more correctly "interpretation," can – and has – become a bridge between anthropology and psychoanalysis.

The interpretive turn in anthropology and psychoanalysis has deep roots in Western thought, extending back to Aristotle's *Peri Hermeneias*, in which Aristotle dealt with the grammaticality of predication, but it is not until the Renaissance, with the rediscovery of classical learning, and the Reformation, with the reevaluation of Holy Writ, that hermeneutics, the science of interpretation, comes into being.[5] (I should add a third, important source of hermeneutics: the renewed interest in Roman law in twelfth-century Italy.) As Hans Georg Gadamer (1975) has noted, all three sources of modern hermeneutics begin with the awareness of a *gap* between the object to be interpreted – one of Cicero's orations, a book of the Old Testament, or the Code of Justinian – and the cultural assumptions of the interpreter. The gap can be understood in temporal or spatial terms, that is, historically or ethnographically. It results from an opacity – an intransigence – in the object to be understood, which can no longer be taken for granted. It is in Heidegger's (1962) terms (though not necessarily as Heidegger meant them) no longer *zu-handen* (ready-at-hand) but *vor-handen* (present-to-hand). "The modes of consciousness, obtrusiveness, and obstinacy all have the function of bringing to the fore the characteristics of presence-at-hand in what is ready-at-hand" (Heidegger 1962: 104). It is the intransigence of the object to be understood that problematizes the worldview of the interpreter, creating a peculiar sense of time ("historical"), a peculiar sense of space ("ethnographic") and a peculiar relationship, which some theorists of interpretation have likened to dialogue. (These theorists stress, romantically, the mutuality, the continuity, the open-ended understanding, the merging of horizons of the interpretive dialogue at the expense of its conventionality, its discontinuity, its closed understanding, its creating opposing horizons. They fail to recognize the way in which their understanding of the dialogue defends against an existential, a perceptual solitude. Jean Genet [1958: 26] has likened this solitude to *royauté secrète, incommunicabilité profonde mais connaissance plus ou moins obscure d'une inattaquable singularité*. The anthropologist's solitude should not be reduced simply to a by-product of the cross-cultural encounter.) The "historic," the "ethnographic," and the "dialogical" mediate – or, better perhaps, *justify* in the printing sense of the world – the interpretive gap.

Through its confrontation with the opaque, the intransigent, the obtuse, interpretation – that is, meaningful, courageous, interpretation – always threatens the interpreter's complacency by problematizing his world. (Relativism is one mode of problematizing.) *And* with this threat comes a danger: a potential surrender to an authoritative, unquestioned position that incorporates the intransigent in an interpretation that does away with its intransigence arbitrarily, without even acknowledging its possibility. Examples of this surrender are legend in cross-cultural encounters: the assumption that they, those others, are just like us or, more often, that they are different (read: primitive, Black, Hopi, heathen, etc.). The rise of Protestant hermeneutics itself grew out of the Reformers' refusal to accept the Roman Church's authority in understanding Scripture. That authority rested on "a grandiose *petitio principii*" since the basis for Rome's interpretive authority was an interpretation of the very book to be interpreted – of those Biblical passages that were understood as a demonstration of how God had instituted the Holy Catholic Church with St. Peter and his successors as its authoritative interpreter (Burckhardt 1968). Early Protestant theologians stressed the principle of perspicuity (*perspicuitas*) and the self-sufficiency of Holy Writ. They laid the basis for an intrinsic interpretation that accepted no external worldly authority though, in pietistic circles, divine guidance, even through vocalization, was sought. Matthis Flacius Illyricus, one of the earliest of these Protestant hermeneuticists, argued in 1567 in his *Clavius Scripturae Sacrae* that Scripture had *not yet* been understood correctly and that true understanding did not – could not – proceed from external authority (Mueller-Vollmer 1985). It required careful linguistic and hermeneutical preparation.

The object of hermeneutical speculation has been the *text* and insofar as interpretive social and psychological sciences rest upon the hermeneutical tradition as filtered through Heidegger, Gadamer, and Paul Ricoeur, they have adopted, implicitly at least, a text metaphor. Culture, society, and psyche are all metaphorized as texts – texts to be read and interpreted. In anthropological circles the text metaphor has received its most explicit if uncritical expression in the writings of Clifford Geertz (1973: 452): "the culture of a people is an ensemble of texts." Without denying the illuminating capacity of the text metaphor – it has enabled many scholars to present, in often enlightening ways, aspects of culture that had to be ignored by those of a more positivist bent – it does require critical regard. We have to ask: why is the text metaphor so popular today? Why is any one of several understandings of "text" given to the text metaphor? For, obviously, there is more than one understanding of text.

I do not propose to answer these questions here. I only want to point out the need to raise them if a critically reflective anthropology, psychoanalysis, or psychoanalytic anthropology is to be established. I suggest, however, that the prevalent text metaphor in these disciplines can block critical self-questioning. The reduction of the human and its products to a text can produce political and ethical complacency. Put simply: if we are treating texts, we don't have to bother ourselves terribly about people. Text metaphors seem also to refract the very process that produces their tenor, literally the collecting of texts of one sort or another: that is, the reducing of complex multidimensional exchanges to simplified, highly conventional renditions – recordings, paraphrases, and other reports – of such exchanges that are, insofar as they are written, decontextualized and subject to ever greater decontextualizations. Descriptions of the circumstances in which such exchanges occur – of what Henry James (1984) called the medium – are also conventional and subject to similar chains of decontextualization and recontextualization.

More important, a text can be internally reflexive (as, for example, through the use of shifters and other meta-locutions [Jakobson, 1963]) and this "internal" reflexivity, read as critical self-reflection, can cover for the absence of an "external" vantage point of any sort necessary for such reflection. In other words, self-reflection occurring in a frame can hinder the questioning of the frame itself by creating the illusion of critical reflection. We find, for example, much self-reflection in psychoanalytic theory and therapy – the discussion of transference, of memory lapses, of slips of the tongue, of changes in style and tone, of accompanying emotion – and in anthropological studies of field work if not in the actual field encounter – discussions about *rapport* or, on rare occasions, discussions in the field with one's informants about the nature of the encounter (Dwyer 1982). Such discussions do not raise, however, the role, say, of psychoanalysis in Western political arrangements or of anthropology – of rapport – in some social context or another. Discussions of the hierarchical relationship between analyst and patient, even if they touch upon social and political implications of such hierarchical relations, are immediately incorporated into the psychoanalytic frame: why, asks the analyst, are you projecting *our* relationship onto the social? What are the transferential implications of such a political discussion? (There are moments when this incorporation can become downright obscene as, for example, in Argentina during the military dictatorship, when some analysts tried to reduce the fear of male authority of the victims of political torture to castration anxiety.[6]) In anthropology there are moments – the reinventing anthropology moments for which some of us, despite ourselves, suffer a sort of nostalgia in this conservatively complacent era – in which the social and the political implications of the field situation (and the relations that transpire therein) are brought up, alas, rather more conventionally (as self-indices: "I am appropriately liberal, leftist") than self-critically. But, in these examples, the significance of their discussion is not questioned. And certainly if such discussions occur in the field, they are immediately reduced (by the anthropologist at least) to data!

In contemporary hermeneutics, as I have noted, the dialogue has become an important metaphor for describing – indeed prescribing – the relationship between the interpreter and the text (Heidegger 1962; Gadamer 1975; Maranhao 1989). The relationship between the two should be like a dialogue, that is, a conversation that is ideally open ended, historically conscious, and continually questioning the prejudices and pre-understandings of the dialogue partners. *Dialogue* evokes the "mutually" lived experience of the oral encounter that is lost in the asymmetrically lived experience of textual interpretation. Here, Hermes, the messenger god and progenitor of interpretation, leads the dead, another of his tasks, not to Hades but from Hades to the quick world of the interpreter. Ironically, in the hermeneutically understood encounters of contemporary anthropology and psychoanalysis, the dialogue, having passed through the Stygian defiles of the text, is restored to its original context – the live, oral encounter between two or more conversationalists. This passage is not without peril. It may fail. The resurrected live encounter always bears the mark of its textualization. Its mutuality is dulled through the metaphor. A distance between speakers is created, at least interpretively, and, in such confessional modes as the anthropological memoir or less frequently that of the psychoanalyst, is described. The interlocutor is, as it were, dead. Speaker A is to Speaker B as Interpreter is to Text as Live is to Dead.[7] The dialogue model comes to resurrect that which has been declared by the power of an inappropriate metaphor dead all the time it was live and well. I speak of course of the patient – and the informant. No wonder Hermes was – and is – a trickster. Or am I now talking about Christ before Lazarus?

Distance, death, Hermes, and Christ aside – I cannot sustain this Nietzschean mode in the discourse prescribed here – there is an important consequence to the passage of the dialogue through the defiles of the text: an attitude toward language, toward communication, that ignores if it does not deny the pragmatic (the rhetorical or paralexical) dimensions of the lived encounter (Silverstein 1976, 1979). Insofar as a dialogue is an active exchange between two or more parties who are live and well, there is a continual, a responsive, negotiation of the reality of the encounter: how it is framed, how it is to be discussed, understood, and interpreted, and how the parties to it – and their relationship as both part of the reality, the context, and the creator of the reality, the context – are themselves to be constituted. Through the acceptance of the text metaphor and the model of the dialogue for its interpretation (at least as they have been articulated in today's hermeneutical thought) the pragmatic features are, pragmatically, by the very metaphor and model, drastically reduced. Culture, society, and psyche, so reduced, are to be understood in essentially referential terms; that is, in terms of that (at least through our granting agencies) fetishized commodity – data.

In traditional hermeneutics meaning has been generally understood in referential terms. Focus has been on the symbol – on that which stands for something else (even if, ideologically at least, in certain types of poetic discourse *that something else* is the symbol itself), and the task of interpretation is the discovery of what that something else is, or, in the case of polysemy, what those somethings-else are. In anthropology, interpretive strategies have been founded on intensional and extensional notions of symbolic significance, on indigenous exegesis, on system-, context-, and use-determined meaning. Often several different, inconsistent approaches have been used in a sort of hip-shooting way. We find, for example, that Victor Turner (1967: 50; Crapanzano 1984) approaches ritual symbols in three ways: (1) the exegetical (based on indigenous interpretations); (2) the operational (based on the way symbols are used); and (3) the positional (based on the relationship between symbols). In addition Turner (1967: 20) takes account of the iconic value of the symbol – its "external and observable characteristics" – and its context "largely worked out by the anthropologist" who, according to Turner (1967: 27), having once made the appropriate "structural analysis of society" "has no particular bias [!] and can observe the real [!] interconnections and conflicts between groups and persons, insofar as they receive ritual representation." Turner does not develop a hermeneutical theory that systematically relates these several approaches. He seems content with teasing out meaning intuitively. We have to recognize, however, that the anthropologist is never without his biases; that exegeses are directed to someone, the anthropologist, for example, and are determined in part at least by the exegete's image of *that someone*, what he desires of that someone, and what he perceives that someone to desire of him; that "use" is often more rhetorical than informational, more pragmatic than referential, and that referential – symbolic – glosses derived from "use" tend to conceal its rhetorical, its pragmatic function as well as their own rhetorical and pragmatic functions; that the systematicity of symbols, understood referentially, is problematic and determined by metapragmatic considerations that transcend their specific occurrence (e.g. in the interpreter's "dialogue" with them); and that icons (however realistically they may appear to picture objects and events "out there in reality") are also arbitrary, polysemic, and subject to both conscious and unconscious referential motivation. The white sap of the mudyi tree that Turner and the Ndembu make so much of resembles semen as well as milk! For other anthropologists, most notably Geertz (1973), the symbol is understood less in terms of denotation than in a presentational manner, making it difficult to determine for whom the symbol presents – the native, the anthropologist, or the reader.

In psychoanalysis, the dominant interpretive mode, delineated in Freud's *Interpretation of Dreams* (1967), is also referential.[8] The aim of psychoanalysis is to uncover the hidden meanings of dreams and other symbols that give masked expression to desires or their objects that are barred from consciousness. Through free-association, through the creating of a counter-text, the psychoanalyst is able, in ways that are not clearly spelled out, to discover those hidden symbolic referents. The correctness of interpretation, which arises out of the montage of text and counter-text, of dream and associations is justified (a) intuitively, (b) on, admittedly circular, theoretical grounds, and (c) in terms of therapeutic efficacy. Freud does admit, reluctantly perhaps, in his by now famous navel image the impossibility of fully unfathoming a dream's symbolism. More radically Lacan (1966) argues that symbolic referents are, inevitably, symbols themselves, for the object of desire, desire itself, is determined by symbolic – linguistic – processes. Despite Freud's reluctant and Lacan's playful admission of the impossibility of full symbolic disclosure, psychoanalysts tend to assume it.

In both anthropology and psychoanalysis interpretation is archaeological: the uncovering of what is below the surface. Its predominant metaphor is "depth."[9] "The 'deeper' the meaning the 'truer' the meaning." The deepest referents, particularly in psychoanalysis, are few in number. This reductive tendency is not corrected by an elaborated theory – and a methodology for a study – of symbolic hierarchy. In psychoanalysis and in anthropology at least where it assumes presentational symbols, symbolic interpretation, understood referentially, covers pragmatic processes that are not understood as such (Crapanzano 1981). In other words, referential symbolicity becomes the model for pragmatic processes when in fact it is not a model for such processes but a gloss – a metapragmatic statement cast in referential terms for the pragmatic processes.

In the remainder of this chapter, I will consider, superficially but hopefully in a suggestive way, how a hermeneutical approach sensitive to the pragmatic dimensions of an encounter can throw light on (a) the dynamics of such an encounter and (b) the translation of such dynamics – such pragmatic processes – into a referentially comfortable gloss. This gloss is usually not expressed in linguistic terms but, metaphorically, in psychological terms, and it is not understood as a gloss, a meta-statement of some sort, but as direct, primary-level description (Crapanzano 1992).

In *Text, Transference, and Indexicality* (1981) I suggested, through an examination of Freud's Case of Dora, that the interpretation of transference and counter-transference is based on the pragmatic features of therapeutic encounters. I pointed out how switches between personal pronouns (the formal and informal second-person pronouns, for example, *Sie* and *du*) and between terms of reference for significant figures such as Dora's father were used to create a complicity – an "understanding" – between the analyst and patient. The use of *Papa* and *Vater* (whether with a *deiner* or an *Ihrer*) affected pragmatically the relationship, the transferences, between Freud and Dora. I noted that the language used to describe the transference, in terms, say, of father figures, was in fact metapragmatic and that *that* metapragmatic language was masked by the metaphorical extension of the metareferential (in Freud's terms, the metapsychological) language used to describe the referentiality of symbols.

Put so succinctly the argument is, I am afraid, a bit opaque. Let me elaborate my position through another example. To the extent that anthropologists and other social scientists have accepted a role model for describing social transactions, they have, I believe, accepted an overly simplified model that may give conceptual elegance to their descriptions but does not do justice to the "play" that occurs in the transactions themselves. Although role theorists have recognized that people may, and usually do, have more than one role and that these roles are often in conflict – in the office romance, for example – they do not have an adequate way of conceptualizing the play over time among these multiple roles, which are rarely articulated as such. I doubt if role play reaches awareness most of the time, and, if it does, then it does so retrospectively or in highly calculated ways. Roles are constantly being negotiated, pragmatically played up and down. Think of a job interview between a man and a woman where despite the objectivity "required" by the occasion, gender plays an important part in the interaction and in the typifications that occur in it. Think of the mild (or heavy) flirtation, of expressions of seriousness, of attestations of expertise, of leadership, of the ability to follow instructions, etc. – all of which occur simultaneously or seriatim within an "event" that is condensed (labeled) as a single event, the job interview, with one party to it understood simply as the applicant and the other as the employer.

Freud's discussion of transference alerts us, in a very special context, to the interdependent play of multiple, articulated, quasi-articulated, unarticulated, and inarticulatable role modalities in any transaction.[10] The constituted role of doctor and patient, pragmatically marked and remarked, permits the play, the indulgence, of acting out other roles (understood, here, conventionally, in terms of the individual participant's biography). If we look carefully at the transactions between a doctor and the patient, we see that despite the intensity of the transference, the "doctor" and the "patient" are always there, as it were, behind the scene. Indeed, they enter into the defenses and counter-defenses of the two. One moment the patient plays daughter, for example, and the next, perhaps having gone too far, eliciting too intolerable a "paternal" response from the analyst, becomes patient, eliciting a more distant, a more professional response. Given the fact that exchanges such as these occur on many registers at once, these several "roles" may be played simultaneously.

We always have to be cautious "countertransferentially" about labeling relations, for such labeling tends to detemporalize and essentialize the on-going pragmatic play of any transaction. There is, it would seem, in any social transaction, an attempt to negotiate (not explicitly) a common understanding of what is transpiring: that is, an attempt to determine metapragmatically how the transaction will be referentially read – named, paraphrased, and interpreted. A single event, image, or theoretical construct, some sort of verbal nucleus or point of concentration, takes on central importance. It gives a certain coherence, an order, to what would otherwise be a random, a meaningless sequence of expressions. Centering, as I (1991) call this process, is both recursive and procursive. It gives meaning and order to those utterances that preceded it – they become prefigurements – and it will give meaning and order to those utterances that will follow it, its entailments. Centering stops narrative time, at least the narrative display of meaning. Time past folds forward; time future folds backward – into the center from which meaning and order spring. Examples of centering in the literature of psychoanalysis would include the wolf dream in Freud's Case of Wolf-Man, the rat punishment in the Case of Rat-Man (Crapanzano 1983), and the alleged seduction of Dora by Herr K. Childhood seductions, traumatic events, conversion experiences, important dreams can all become major centers of ongoing conversations. In anthropological field work we also have such centering events. In my relations with a Moroccan tilemaker, Tuhami, I (1980) tried, without much success, to find a "center" that would somehow enable me to summarize Tuhami's character, our relationship, or my own position. A South African friend's comment on waiting enabled me to articulate a dimension of white South African life I had not appreciated before (Crapanzano 1985). Such experiences are a bit like epiphanies or those "glimpses" of reality Henry James

(1984b) writes about that give the novelist his story. They are not articulate centers, and most of the time we are not particularly aware of them as centers.

What is characteristic of such centering images and events is that they become expository centers in the accounts we give of what transpired. Freud describes Wolf-Man's neurosis through the dream, Rat-Man's obsession through the Turkish punishment, Dora's hysteria through the seduction ... At both the interactional and the discursive level these centers orient interpretation, facilitate the incorporation of what happened into broader interpretive schema, and freeze the relationship among the participants in the interaction. Insofar as these centers are understood only symbolically, they conceal the centering process that gave rise to them. They give to the interaction, the discourse – and the vision of reality that interaction presumes – an illusory fixity. This fixity may comfort those who find intolerable a Heraclitean view of the world – one that stresses change and resists closure – but the Parmenidean solace it offers is not without cost, for it precludes understanding of the pragmatic, the rhetorical, dimensions of social engagement, ultimately of the creative, the non-creative and the destructive.

The critical attention traditional hermeneutics gives to the prejudices and preunderstandings, the historical and cultural biases, with which it approaches events, objects, and texts, does not prevent it from supporting – confirming – that which is centered and the ideological implications of that centering activity; for, by focusing on the referential significance of the center, the center's constitutive function is masked. Such an interpretive strategy conforms to the marked propensity, at least in the West among speakers of Indo-European languages, to essentialize the pragmatic *Gestalten* of exchanges, to detemporalize perduring transactions, to permit, in often morally and politically compromising ways, decontextualizations and recontextualizations, and to perpetuate thereby cultural and psychological pictures – texts, we might say – that do not threaten the complacency with which we have come to accept notions of otherness. We have then to question the most fundamental epistemological assumptions of our social, cultural, and psychological understandings – and this I take to be the mission, so often obscured in scientistic and hermeneutical preoccupations, of anthropology.

NOTES

1 The reader will find some of the arguments in this chapter developed in my book *Hermes' Dilemma and Hamlet's Desire* (1992), particularly in the Introduction and in the chapters entitled "Talking (about) Psychoanalysis," first published in volume 12 (1989) of *Psychoanalysis and Contemporary Thought*,

and "On Dialogue," first published in Tullio Maranhao's *The Interpretation of Dialogue* (1989).

2 There are very important differences between the two disciplines with respect to their relative positions and evaluations within larger socioeconomic arrangements that I cannot treat in this chapter. Anthropologists are, for example, usually attached to some sort of academic or research organization and are subject to all of the constraints – and freedoms – that come with institutional affiliation. Psychoanalysts have for the most part less "consuming" institutional affiliations. Anthropologists are salaried, and like most academics, receive lower wages than other professionals with whom they are, at least symbolically, equated. Psychoanalysts, most often in private practice, receive a remuneration that is more commensurate with the professionals with whom they are associated though they have a somewhat ambiguous status within the medical establishment. (Anthropologists also have a somewhat ambiguous status within university circles.) Despite the claims of applied anthropology, anthropologists are generally considered to be researchers and teachers while psychoanalysts, despite their research claims, are considered to be therapists and have all the "privileges" that relate to this status. Anthropologists are evaluated in terms of the quality of their research, their publications, and the status of the institution to which they are affiliated. The esteem of a psychoanalyst is less institutionally bound and is usually a matter of "reputation," the criteria for which are vague.

3 For a discussion of Lacan's expulsion from the International Association of Psycho-Analysis, see the *International Journal of Psycho-Analysis* 35 (1954): 267–278, and 37 (1956): 122.

4 All the debate about the four-field approach to anthropology has to be seen in a larger context than it has been so far. Just as cultural anthropology is beginning to break out of the chrysalis it has created for itself and engage in live intellectual debate with disciplines outside the social and psychological sciences – with history, literary criticism, philosophy, art, and literature – and may even be having an influence on these "exotic" disciplines, one suddenly hears talk of anthropology losing its identity, its core, its heart. Is intellectual debate, is intellectual influence, so frightening? Must disciplinary boundaries be so impervious? More important, what is the relationship between this retrenchment and the conservative political climate in which we find ourselves?

5 For a history of hermeneutics see Gadamer (1975) and Mueller-Vollmer (1985), who includes an extensive bibliography.

6 I do not deny that "an unresolved Oedipal conflict" can govern a victim's response to torture and its aftermath. What I find objectionable is the fact that infantile phantasms are given interpretive priority over political reality and can thus facilitate a complacency before, if not an actual denial of, that political reality. So long as psychoanalysis fails to question its own praxis, so long as it does not attempt to integrate social and political reality into its theoretical perspective (and not simply incorporate it), it lends itself to the political and social misuse of the sort that has been seen in Argentina and to a lesser extent in Brazil. For at least one important discussion of psychoanalytic understanding and political reality (by a psychoanalyst) see Parin 1978. Parin (p. 33) writes: "Die Aussage, dass ein politisches Engagement *nichts anderes* sei

als der Versuch, persönliche Konflickte zu lösen, ist ebenso unsinnig wie jene andere, dass die Beteiligung an einer politischen Bewegung aus rein objektiven oder rationalen Motiven ohne die Mobilisierung individueller Konflickte zustände kommen könnte."

7 Put another way, the field or therapeutic encounter which consists of exchanges between partners who refer to one another by I and you, that is, by indexical, first- and second-person personal pronouns, is transformed into exchanges described minimally by one anaphoric pronoun – a he, a she, or a they – for the informant or patient or by two such pronouns, one for the informant or patient and the other for the ethnographer or therapist (that is, if the ethnographer or therapist resists even more impersonal, though perhaps more authoritative, passive locutions). Under normal circumstances there can be no dialogue between an I and a he or she or they, or between he's, she's or they's.

8 This referential bias in psychoanalysis is also found in the psychoanalytic anthropology. See White's discussion, in this book, of Melford Spiro's work.

9 The metaphor of depth is related to the notion of origin. The deeper one probes, so the argument goes, the closer to an origin one comes. Depth so understood, like origin, is a distinctly romantic preoccupation (de Man 1979).

10 I am not suggesting that there is a transferential dimension to all social transactions. I believe "transference" and "countertransference" should be restricted to psychoanalytic and other psychotherapeutic encounters where identity play has been granted a conventional freedom of expression whose very conventionality is barred from consideration. Rather I want to stress the fact that in all social encounters, including the psychoanalytic and the psychotherapeutic, there is always a pragmatic negotiation of identity that is rarely subject to immediate reflection and discussion. Psychoanalysis differs from other such encounters in that it promotes reflection and discussion, but as in other encounters, it does not question the way in which the pragmatic features of the encounter are to be discussed.

REFERENCES

Burckhardt, Sigurd. 1968. Notes on the Theory of Intrinsic Interpretation. In *Shakespearean Meaning* (pp. 285–313). Princeton: Princeton University Press

Crapanzano, Vincent. 1980. *Tuhami: Portrait of a Moroccan*. Chicago: University of Chicago Press

1981. Text, Transference, and Indexicality. *Ethos* 9:122–148

1983. Einige Bemerkungen über Symbole und das denken in Sinnbildern. In H. P. Duerr, ed., *Sehnsucht nach dem Ursprung* (pp. 71–81). Frankfurt am Main: Syndikat

1984. Review of Victor Turner's *From Ritual to Theater* (April 27, p. 473). *The Times Literary Supplement*

1985. *Waiting: The Whites of South Africa*. New York: Random House

1986. Hermes' Dilemma: The Masking of Subversion in Ethnographic Description. In J. Clifford and G. E. Marcus, eds., *Writing Culture: The Poetics and Politics of Ethnography* (pp. 51–76). Berkeley: University of California Press

1992. *Hermes' Dilemma and Hamlet's Desire: Essays in the Epistemology of Interpretation*. Cambridge, MA: Harvard University Press

de Man, Paul, 1979. *Allegories of Reading*. New Haven: Yale University Press
Dwyer, Kevin. 1982. *Moroccan Dialogues: Anthropology in Question*. Baltimore: Johns Hopkins University Press
Freud, Sigmund. 1967. *The Interpretation of Dreams*. London: George Allen & Unwin Ltd
Gadamer, Hans-Georg. 1975. *Truth and Method*. New York: Seabury
Geertz, Clifford. 1973. *The Interpretation of Cultures*. New York: Basic Books
Genet, Jean 1958. *L'Atelier d'Alberto Giacometti*. Décines, Isère: L'Arbalète
Heidegger, Martin. 1962. *Being and Time*. Oxford: Basil Blackwell
Jakobson, Roman. 1963. Les Embrayeurs, les catégories verbales et le verbe russe. In *Essais de linguistique générale* (pp. 176–196). Paris: Editions de Minuit
James, Henry. 1984a. The Lesson of Balzac. In *Literary Criticism: French Writers, Other European Writers, The Prefaces to the New York Edition* (pp. 115–139). New York: The Library of America
1984b. The Art of Fiction. *Literary Criticism: Essays on Literature, American Writers, English Writers* (pp. 44–65). New York: The Library of America
Lacan, Jacques. 1966. *Ecrits*. Paris: Seuil
Maranhao, Tullio, ed. 1989. *The Interpretation of Dialogue*. Chicago: University of Chicago Press
Mueller-Vollmer, Kurt. 1985. Introduction. In *The Hermeneutic Reader* (pp. 1–53). New York: Continuum
Parin, Paul. 1978. Freiheit und Unabhängigkeit; Zur Psychoanalyse des politischen Engagements. *Der Widerspruch im Subjekt: Ethnopsychoanalytische Studien* (pp. 20–33). Frankfurt am Main: Syndikat
Silverstein, Michael. 1976. Shifters, Linguistic Categories and Cultural Description. In K. Basso and H. Selby, eds., *Meaning in Anthropology* (pp. 11–55). Albuquerque: University of New Mexico Press
1979. Language Structure and Linguistic Ideology. In P. Clyne, W. Hanks, and C. Hofbauer, eds., *The Elements: A Parasession on Linguistic Units and Levels* (pp. 193–247). Chicago: Chicago Linguistic Society
Turner, Victor. 1967. *The Forest of Symbols*. Ithaca, New York: Cornell University Press

Part VI

Disciplinary perspectives

15 Polarity and plurality: Franz Boas as psychological anthropologist

George W. Stocking, Jr.

Although the matter of his original disciplinary identity is somewhat problematic, it could be argued that before Franz Boas became an anthropologist, he was a psychologist: six of his first ten publications were on topics in Fechnerian psychophysics (Andrews 1943: 67). His first regular academic appointment, at Clark University between 1889 and 1892, was in a Department of Psychology, and when he came to Columbia in 1896 as a lecturer in physical anthropology, it was initially in another such department (Lesser 1968). Although he published few explicitly psychological articles after those first six, what is arguably his single most important piece, "On Alternating Sounds" (1889), as well as most of his major generalizing anthropological statements, may be regarded as essays in comparative psychology. And when he returned to Clark for that university's twentieth anniversary celebration in 1909 – at which Sigmund Freud, in a series of morning lectures, gave the first authoritative account of "The Origin and Development of Psychoanalysis" to American audiences (Hale 1971, pp. 3–5) – Boas spoke on "Psychological Problems in Anthropology." Throughout this period, there is evidence that he maintained contact with a number of different strands of psychological thought – displaying some degree of familiarity with the work of Herbart, Fechner, Wundt, Lazarus and Steinthal, Dilthey, Tarde, James, Baldwin, and Freud.

Yet if I may judge from the sampling on my own shelves, Franz Boas has been given rather short shrift in histories of "The Making of Psychological Anthropology." Generally, he lurks behind the historical scenes, as a "remote intellectual ancestor" of the present elder generation (Spindler 1978: xxiii), or as the teacher of the founding generation of Sapir, Benedict, and Mead. Although in that latter capacity his "psychological interests are well known" (Spiro 1972: 578), they are not systematically discussed, but briefly referred to in the context of his critique of the idea that there are significant cognitive differences between primitive and civilized peoples (Bock 1980: 28–29). Even my own earlier work in this area focused on the relation of his critique of racial mental differences to the development of the culture concept (Stocking 1968). The present chapter is thus a first approximation of a more systematic treatment of Boas as psychological anthropologist.[1]

In all the major statements Boas made about the aims of his anthropological work prior to 1911, psychology was given a central place. Disputing Otis Mason in 1887 about the principles governing the classification of ethnological specimens in museum collections, he argued that the goal of ethnology was to study ethnological and anthropological phenomena "in their historical development and geographical distribution, and in their physiological and psychological foundation" (1887a: 63). A year later, he regarded the discovery of the laws "of the development of the human spirit [*geist*]" as "the greatest aim of our science" (1888: 636–637). In 1901, he spoke of "the study of the mind of man" in its "infinite variety of form" as "one of the chief aims of anthropology" (1901: 1). In reviewing "The History of Anthropology" in 1904, he discussed "psychological anthropology" and "biological anthropology" as the two main branches of the discipline (p. 32); in a general overview three years later, he divided the "researches carried on by anthropologists" into the same two categories (1907: 270). In contrast to its position today – rising above the mass of modern adjectival anthropologies, but not usually granted parity with the traditional "four fields" within the disciplinary core – "psychological anthropology" was for Boas one of anthropology's "two large branches of investigation" (1907: 270). And in terms of his own interests, it was clearly the predominant one.

Underlying Boas' "psychological anthropology" – and all of his anthropological thought – was a set of epistemological and psychological assumptions he articulated at the very beginning of his career in the essay on "The Study of Geography" – an essay whose far-reaching significance is better marked by its place at the very end of *Race, Language and Culture* than by the "Miscellaneous" heading under which Boas included it (1940: 639–47). In his own formulation of the characteristic Germanic distinction between the *Natur*- and the *Geisteswissenshaften*, Boas there defined a series of oppositions that ran through all his work. On the one hand, there was the physicist, who analyzed phenomena having an objective unity in the real world, so that by systematic arrangement and comparison of their component elements he might deduce the laws that governed them. On the other hand, there was the cosmographer, who studied phenomena whose connection "seems to be subjective, originating in the mind of the observer"; refusing to break that subjectively constituted whole into elements, the cosmographer sought rather "to penetrate into its secrets until every feature is plain and clear" in order to achieve not law but "a thorough understanding." Despite the ontological instability implied by the subjective psychological grounding of its object matter, the "study of phenomena for their own sake [was] equal in value to the deduction of laws." Indeed, from another point of view, there was a sense in which Boas might be said to have privileged subjective psychological grounding as opposed to "objective reality" – since he insisted that the choice between the physical and the cosmographic (or historical) approaches could only be "a confession of the answerer as to which is dearer to him." Each method originated "in a different desire of the human mind" – the one based on the aesthetic/logical and the other on the affective impulse. Whether one preferred "to recognize the individuality in the totality, or the totality in the individuality" was thus entirely a matter of "personal feeling" (1887b).

As I have argued elsewhere, Boas' own personal feelings about the physical and the historical methods were somewhat ambivalent and complicated (Stocking 1974b). His first important theoretical statement was an anti-comparativist proclamation that "in ethnology all is individuality" (1887a: 66): although the "outward appearance" of two ethnological phenomena might seem the same, it was only on the basis of an historical study of their "immanent qualities" that one might legitimately establish groupings for the comparative derivation of "laws." And while he long gave lip-service to the ultimate goal of deriving such laws of cultural development, the overall trajectory of his anthropological thought was toward increasing doubt of the possibility of establishing valid categories for the comparison of cultural phenomena, and a consequently growing skepticism as to the possibility of establishing significant laws in the cultural realm. On the other hand, he approached historical reconstruction and psychological analysis by methods more in the spirit of the physicist's elementaristic analysis than the cosmographer's holistic understanding. In short, in Boas the relationship between the two approaches tended to be less one of complementarity than one of mutual inhibition – leading Robert Redfield later to observe that "he does not write histories, and he does not prepare scientific systems" (as quoted in Stocking 1974b: 13).

The same dualism of approach can be seen in the development of Boas' "psychological anthropology." There is much in Boas that can be read as reflecting the influence of Moritz Lazarus and Heymann Steinthal, who in 1860 founded the *Zeitschrift fur Völkerpsychologie und Sprachwissenschaft*, and whose thinking on the *Völksgeist* was elaborated in terms of assumptions about "apperception" derived from the psychological thought of Johann Gottfried Herbart (Kalmar 1987). But although Boas seems from the beginning to have accepted Herbartian assumptions, the reflection of Lazarus and Steinthal's thinking about the *Völksgeist* was later and more diffusely manifest – with no specific acknowledgment of debt. Despite this current of holistic interest in the *geist* or "genius of a people," much of Boas' psychology (like his history) was predominantly "isolative" rather than "embracive" in method and assumption, if not in spirit.

In the first instance, Boas' psychology was that of Gustav Fechner: a "psycho-physics" that proceeded by the measurement of specific sensations in individual subjects, in order to unite mental and physical phenomena within a framework of deterministic laws of universal generality (Marshall 1982). It is true that Boas' most important contribution in this tradition tended to make such generalization problematic, inasmuch as he insisted on the fundamental subjectivity of some of our perceptions of external reality. Drawing on the Herbartian tradition, Boas argued that sound stimuli produced by a native speaker of one language and heard for the first time by a native speaker of another were not directly perceived, but "apperceived" and classified in terms of their similarity to the sound categories of the hearer's language. What had been called "alternating sounds" and taken as indicators of the fluctuating, unstable character of primitive speech were actually "alternating perceptions" on the part of the European observer (1889). Although in the past I have argued that this article foreshadows "much of Boas' later criticism of late nineteenth century racial thought" and "a great deal of modern anthropological thought on 'culture'" (1968: 159), for present purposes I would emphasize rather its embeddedness in Fechnerian psycho-physics. While the effect of his argument was to relativize perception, it did so in terms of psychological "laws" governing the "differential threshold" for the perception of stimuli by individuals. In Boas' dualistic vision of scientific knowing, psychology still stood with physics in the realm of objective entities, of analysis, and of law – rather than in that of subjective entities, holism, and understanding.

Thus it was that in 1888, in his first general discussion of "The Aims of Ethnology," Boas distinguished two such aims: first, "the critical analysis of the characteristics of each people" (p. 629), and second, the discovery of the "laws governing the life of peoples" (p. 634). However, it must be noted that Boas spoke of the former more culturally specific inquiry as *Kulturgeschichte*. It was the latter more comparative inquiry, that he called *Völkerpsychologie* – using as his exemplar not Lazarus and Steinthal, but Adolph Bastian. Its goal was defined not in terms of the "genius" of particular peoples, but the "general laws" of "the development of the human *geist*," conceived in broadly evolutionary terms (p. 636). The psychological contrasts that concerned Boas were structured by the polarity of progress from the primitive to the civilized, from the *naturvölker* to the *kulturvölker*, whose modes of "thinking and feeling" were strikingly different.

When Boas next turned again to problems of psychological anthropology in 1894, in the lecture on "Human Faculty as Determined by Race," it was in terms of this same fundamental polarity. By this time, however, he had begun to develop the systematic criticism of evolutionary assumption which we associate with his more mature thought, and his argument was directed toward reducing the opposition, by showing that the psychological traits usually attributed to "primitive people" – impulsiveness, improvidence, and the lack of concentration or originality – were products either of the distorting circumstances of prior ethnographic observation, or of the "differing valuation of motives" (p. 236), or of the role of "unconscious and conscious imitation" – which, as Tarde had demonstrated, affected civilized no less than primitive society (p. 239). Boas still did not rule out the possibility that differences might be found "in the more complicated psychological phenomena" between the "lower and higher races." But although he saw some possibilities in the work of Francis Galton on the inheritance of mental ability, he expressed doubt that a method could be found to "separate in a satisfactory manner the social and the hereditary features" (p. 239). And for this reason, he specifically eschewed the attempt to discuss the psychological character of specific groups – among whom he instanced the Jews, the Gypsies, the French, the Irish, the Bushmen, and the Lapps.

After offering a more fully elaborated critique of "The Limitations of the Comparative Method of Anthropology" in 1896, Boas turned again to the problem of "The Mind of Primitive Man" in 1901. He did so in the explicit context of discussions he had held with the psychologist Livingston Farrand who, in addition to being Boas' departmental associate at Columbia, was also a co-worker of James McKeen Cattell, one of the leading figures in American psychology. Indeed, Boas found it "impossible to say what share" his own or Farrand's suggestions had in the development of his argument (p. 1). Boas distinguished between the laws of the "organization of the mind" (which had to do with perception, association, and the manner in which stimuli produced both actions and emotions) and "the character of individual experience that is subjected to the action of these laws" (p. 2). In explicating the latter, Boas appealed to "one of the fundamental laws of psychology" (which he might have found discussed in William James' discussion of habit [1890, chapter 4]), "that the repetition of mental processes increases the facility with which these processes are performed, and decreases the degree of consciousness that accompanies them" (p. 2). In this context, Boas went on to discuss three fundamental psychological processes – the "faculty of forming abstract ideas," the "power to inhibit impulses," and the "power of choosing between perceptions and actions according to their value" – from the point of view first of the organization of the mind and then of "the influence of the contents of the mind upon the formation of thoughts and actions" (pp. 4–6). Arguing that the apparent deficiency of primitive man in the "power of logical interpretations of perception" was due to "the character of the ideas with which the new perception associates itself," he suggested that the role of such traditional matter in governing individual interpretations was almost as powerful "in our own community" (p. 7). In discussing the influence of tradition on action, Boas drew on the evidence of food habits, table manners, and fashion to argue that the more frequently an action was performed, the more unconscious it became, and the greater was the emotional value attached to its performance. In this context, Boas concluded by suggesting that

> It is somewhat difficult for us to recognize that the value which we attribute to our own civilization is due to the fact that . . . it has been controlling all our actions since the time of our birth; but it is certainly conceivable that there may be other civilizations, based perhaps on different traditions and on a different equilibrium of emotion and reason, which are of no less value than ours, although it may be impossible for us to appreciate their values without having grown up under their influence. (1901: 11)

Although Boas still treated emotion and reason as opposite poles of a single continuum, the passage nevertheless evidences a shift since 1894 from polarity to plurality – from the opposition of *naturvölker* and *kulturvölker* to the variety of civilization*s*.

This tension – between the polarity of emotion/reason and the variety of cultural traditions – was still manifest when Boas turned in 1904 to the psychological analysis of "Some Traits of Primitive Culture." His focus was still on "the typical differences that do exist between the modes of thought and action characteristic of primitive society and of civilized society" – more specifically, on "the general lack of differentiation of mental activities" among primitives (1904b: 243). To explain it, he developed further his previous argument about habit and emotion. Any departure from traditional behavior that had become automatic and unconscious precipitated a "reflex action" of emotional antagonism, which was greater the more unconscious and automatic the behavior had become. This "dissonance with the habitual" elicited a "rationalistic explanation" of the opposition to change, and this reasoning "must necessarily be based on the ideas which rise into consciousness as a break in the established custom occurs; in other words, our rationalistic explanation will depend on the character of the associated ideas" (pp. 245–246). Because these could change in time, they might have no relationship to the origin of the custom – which might be the result of conscious mental processes, but might also have developed unconsciously, like the morphological categories of language. In primitive cultures, the tendency was for a variety of predominantly emotional and social associations to collect around particular customs, and for their rationalistic explanations to be related to their "general views of the constitution of the world" (p. 249). In "our own culture," the range of associations was likely to be narrower, and more instrumentally rational, "because, on the whole, the rationalistic tendencies of our times have eliminated many of the lines of association." Even so, there were "a thousand activities and modes of thought that constitute our daily life" which had no special claim to rationality. Nor could we "remodel, without serious emotional resistance, any of the fundamental lines of thought and action which are determined by our early education, and which form the subconscious basis of all our activities" (p. 254). Although the argument was carried on largely in terms of polarity, the implicit movement was still toward plurality; significantly, it was in the opening of this essay that Boas spoke for the first time of the "diversity of cultures that furnish the material with which the mind operates" (p. 252).

Boas' movement from polarity to plurality is evident also in his changing representation of *Völkerpsychologie*. In discussing the place of "psychological anthropology" in "The History of Anthropology" in 1904, he specifically contrasted "individual psychology" with *Völkerpsychologie*, which dealt "with those psychic actions which take place in each individual as a social unit," and which he seemed to assimilate to "social psychology" – mentioning as exemplars Steinthal, Wundt, Baldwin, Tarde, and Stoll, and suggesting that "the relation of 'folk-psychology' to individual psychology" had not yet "been elucidated satisfactorily" (1904a: 31). While he did not explicitly refer to *Völkerpsychologie* in his general consideration of "Anthropology" three years later, he did discuss Bastian's thought, emphasizing now not the similarity of evolutionary development, but rather Bastian's typological approach (which he associated also with Dilthey) to the "fundamental forms" of human thought (1907: 276). But whereas Bastian had felt that the origin of these "elementary ideas" was beyond empirical investigation, Boas suggested that the "analytic study" of the languages of primitive tribes was revealing "categories of thought" that had developed entirely unconsciously, and which he expected would correspond to "the variety of philosophical systems" (p. 279). Plurality, however, was still in tension with the polarity of emotion and reason: although he spoke of alternative "lines of progress which do not happen to be in accord with the dominant ideas of our times," he did so in the context of insisting on the "differences between our civilization and another type in which perhaps less stress is laid upon the rationalistic side of our mental activities and more upon the emotional side" (p. 281).

The parallelism between the origin of linguistic and cultural categories was reasserted in somewhat stronger terms in the introduction to the *Handbook of American Indian Languages*, which was written in 1908. Echoing themes from the article "On Alternating Sounds," Boas suggested that "an extended classification of experiences must underlie all speech" (1911: 20). And in the same way that "concepts and groups of perceptions are classified by a single term, relations between perceptions are also classified" – by a "grouping of sense impressions and of concepts which is not in any sense of the term voluntary" (pp. 63–64). It seemed to Boas that ethnic phenomena, including "fundamental religious notions" might have a similar origin; but whatever their ultimate origin, many of our cultural categories "develop at present in the individual and in the whole people entirely subconsciously" – and were, as we have already indicated, only later subject to rationalizing processes of secondary explanation (p. 65).

The same argument (including a portion of the same language), was incorporated into Boas' culminating statement on "Psychological Problems in Anthropology." And indeed a striking aspect of this piece (in view of its presentation at the same meeting Freud spoke) is its systematic elaboration of the unconscious origin of psychic phenomena. Suggesting that "anthropological investigations carried on from this point of view offer[ed] a fruitful field of inquiry" (1909: 249), Boas went on to argue that "the classification of concepts, the types of association, and the resistance to change of automatic acts" all developed unconsciously, and that "secondary explanation" – "one of the most important anthropological phenomena" – was "hardly less common in our society than in primitive societies" (p. 253).

In making this argument, however, Boas began to apply to psychological anthropology the skepticism of comparative generalization that increasingly characterized his anthropology as a whole. By implication, he now criticized Bastian's interpretation of "elementary ideas" on the grounds that "anthropological phenomena, which are in outward appearances alike, are, psychological speaking, entirely distinct, and that consequently psychological laws can not be deduced from them" (p. 246). Equally significant was the fact that Boas cast his whole discussion in an individualistic frame. Without referring to *Völkerpsychologie*, and distinguishing his inquiry from a "crowd psychology based largely on the data of social psychology in a wider sense," he emphasized that what concerned him was "man as an individual member of society" – "the influence of the society of which he is a member" as manifest in "the habits of action and thought of the individual" (p. 244).

Having defined anthropology in terms that gave half its domain to "psychological anthropology," and having offered a statement about the fundamental problems of that field, Boas had little of a general nature to say about psychological anthropology during the last three decades of his career. In discussing "The Methods of Ethnology" in 1920, he commented approvingly of Freud, insofar as he had argued that "the social behavior of man depends to a great extent upon the earliest habits which are established before the time when connected memory begins ... [and which] do not rise to consciousness." But he doubted that "the theory of the influence of suppressed desires" would be universally applicable, and cautioned against "the crude transfer of a novel, one-sided method of psychological investigation of the individual to social phenomena ... subject to influences that are not at all comparable to those that control the psychology of the individual" (pp. 288–289). The same essay clearly evidenced a shift then going on in Boas' anthropology from historical reconstruction to the "study of the dynamic changes in society that may be observed at the present time" – an inquiry for which the "problem of the relation of the individual to society" was critically important (p. 284).

That problem provided the leitmotif of Boas' later generalizing statements on psychological issues in anthropology. But in discussing what he now referred to as "social psychology," Boas consistently emphasized the human individual as the focal point of inquiry. Thus in 1930, in a general consideration of "Some Problems of Methodology in the Social Sciences," he argued that "the problems of the social sciences ... relate to forms of reactions of individuals, singly and in groups, to outer stimuli, to their interactions among themselves, and to the social forms produced by these processess" (p. 260). The study of the "dynamics of social life" could be understood "only on the basis of the reaction of the individual to the culture in which he lives and of his influence upon society" (p. 268). Or, as he suggested in discussing "The Aims of Anthropological Research" in 1932, "it seems a vain effort to search for sociological laws disregarding what should be called social psychology, namely, the reaction of the individual to culture" (pp. 258–259).

Boas' focus on the human individual may have been in part a reaction to the influence of more sociological and scientistic currents associated with functional social anthropology. However, it is worth noting that he showed a similarly cautious attitude in regard to the culture and personality movement that emerged after 1920 in the work of several of his students. Although by 1930 by spoke of "the integration of culture'" as one of the major problems facing anthropology, he felt that it depended on a prior attempt to understand the "dynamics" of the interrelation of the various aspects of culture (p. 268). In his customarily cautious fashion, Boas insisted that "integration is not often so complete that all contradictory elements are eliminated," and "that the degree of integration is not always the same" (p. 256). When in 1938 he edited a volume on *General Anthropology*, there was no chapter on "culture and personality"; Ruth Benedict was assigned the chapter on "Religion," and Margaret Mead and Edward Sapir were not included among the contributors. Boas, however, did himself discuss the culture and personality movement in his own concluding chapter on "Methods of Research." Although suggesting that "each culture is a whole, and its form has a dynamic force which determines the behavior of the mass of individuals," he qualified this by immediately adding "it is only from their thoughts and acts, [and] from the products of their actions, that we derive the concept of culture" (p. 673). Granting that "it seems most desirable and worthwhile to understand each culture as a whole and to define its character," he expressed doubt that "it is possible to give a picture of the culture which is at the same time a picture of a personality" (pp. 680–681). "No matter how strongly a community may be controlled by dominating thoughts, they do not influence the behavior of the same individual at all times in the same ways, and different individuals also react to them each in his own way" (p. 681). In this context, Boas argued that "most attempts to characterize the social life of peoples are hampered by the lack of uniform behavior of all individuals, by the diversity of social activities, and by the subjective interest of the student, which is challenged by the contrast between the observed behavior and his own accustomed attitudes" (p. 683). Granting that "the wider the scope of a leading motive of culture, the more it will appear as characteristic of the whole culture," he cautioned lest we "be deceived into believing that it will give us an exhaustive picture of all the sides of culture" (p. 684).

The fact that Boas instanced this problem by pointing to the danger of overlooking the "amiable qualities" of life among the Indians of the Northwest Coast of America (p. 685) makes clear enough whose work he had in mind, and serves perhaps to explicate the final line of Boas' introduction to *Patterns of Culture*: "the extreme cases selected by the author make clear the importance of the problem" (Benedict 1934: xiii). This was not the first time that one of his students picked up a theme in Boas' thought and carried it further than the mutually inhibiting polar tendencies of the master's intellectual predisposition would allow – although in the case of aspiring alpha males like Kroeber and Sapir, it led on several occasions to Oedipal unpleasantness rather than muted grandparental skepticism. Boas' own thinking about the relationship of the individual and culture was in fact much closer to that of Edward Sapir (Darnell 1986; Handler 1986). Caught between reason (which would have drawn him away from Benedict toward Sapir) and emotion (which impelled him in the other direction), Boas may simply have preferred to distance himself from developments in psychological anthropology. Be that as it may, what was once half of the discipline went unmentioned in the definition of "anthropology" that he offered as preface to the textbook of 1938.

Despite his evident distancing from the culture and personality movement which in the 1930s became for a time the distinctive incarnation of "psychological anthropology," Boas' role in the development of that broader tendency cannot be minimized. His infusion of the Germanic interest in the "genius of peoples" reinforced and generalized an orientation that was already foreshadowed in earlier American anthropology (as far back as Schoolcraft); his critique of evolutionary racialism laid the basis for a cultural interpretation of psychological differences. Following up various threads of his interest, his students were instrumental in establishing the culture and personality movement. Some of the methodological and theoretical reservations he had about that movement foreshadowed more recent tendencies in what is once again often called "psychological anthropology" (cf. Stocking 1986).

NOTE

This chapter is frankly an occasional piece. When I was originally asked to speak at the symposium, I agreed to discuss the somewhat broader topic of "Boasian Assumption and Psychological Anthropology." That topic began to seem unmanageable in the time available, and I retreated to something that could be approached through the close reading of a small number of texts: the present text is unchanged save for the addition of a concluding paragraph. But since I have argued elsewhere that much of twentieth-century American anthropology developed along several lines implicit in the basic assumptions of Boas' own viewpoint (1974b, 1976), this analysis may perhaps serve as a template for discussing the broader topic, many aspects of which are also considered in a book that I recently edited (1986). The implicit argument about the polarity of reason (civilization)/emotion (culture) should perhaps be read in the context of a similar polarity in Boas' political involvement (Stocking 1979).

REFERENCES

Andrews, Helen and others. 1943. Bibliography of Franz Boas. *American Anthropological Association Memoir* no. 61, pp. 68–119

Benedict, Ruth. 1934. *Patterns of Culture*. New York: Houghton Mifflin & Co.

Boas, Franz. 1887a. The Principles of Ethnological Classification. As reprinted in Stocking, 1974a (pp. 61–66)

1887b. The Study of Geography. In Boas, 1940, (pp. 639–647)
1888. The Aims of Ethnology. In Boas, 1940 (pp. 626–638)
1889. On Alternating Sounds. In Stocking, 1974a (pp. 72–76)
1894. Human Faculty as Determined by Race. In Stocking, 1974a (pp. 221–242)
1896. The Limitations of the Comparative Method of Anthropology. In Boas, 1940 (pp. 270–280)
1901. The Mind of Primitive Man. *Journal of American Folklore* 14, 1–11
1904a. The History of Anthropology. In Stocking, 1974a (pp. 23–35)
1904b. Some Traits of Primitive Culture. *Journal of American Folklore* 17, 243–254
1907. Anthropology. In Stocking, 1974a (pp. 167–181)
1909. Psychological Problems in Anthropology. In Stocking, 1974a (pp. 243–254)
1911. Introduction. *Handbook of American Indian Languages, Part I.* Bulletin 40, Bureau of American Ethnology. Washington: Government Printing Office
1920. The Methods of Ethnology. In Boas, 1940 (pp. 281–289)
1930. Some Problems of Methodology in the Social Sciences. In Boas, 1940 (pp. 260–269)
1932. The Aims of Anthropological Research. In Boas, 1940, (pp. 243–259)
ed. 1938. *General Anthropology*. Boston: D. C. Heath & Co.
1940. *Race, Language and Culture*. New York: Macmillan

Bock, P. K. 1980. *Continuities in Psychological Anthropology: An Historical Introduction.* San Francisco: W. H. Freeman & Co.

Darnell, Regna. 1986. Personality and Culture: The Fate of the Sapirian Alternative. In Stocking, ed., 1986 (pp. 156–183)

Hale, Nathan. 1971. *Freud and the Americans: The Beginnings of Psychoanalysis in the United States, 1876–1917.* New York: Oxford University Press

Handler, Richard. 1986. Vigorous Male and Aspiring Female: Poetry, Personality, and Culture in Edward Sapir and Ruth Benedict. In Stocking, ed. 1986 (pp. 127–155)

James, William. 1890. *The Principles of Psychology*. 2 vols. (reprinted. New York: Dover, 1950)

Kalmar, Ivan. 1987. The *Völkerpsychologie* of Lazarus and Steinthal and the Modern Concept of Culture. *Journal of the History of Ideas* 48: 671–690

Lesser, Alexander. 1968. Franz Boas. *International Encyclopedia of the Social Sciences*. New York: Macmillan

Marshall, Marilyn. 1982. Physics, Metaphysics, and Fechner's Psychophysics. In W. R. Woodward and M. G. Ash, eds., *The Problematic Science: Psychology in Nineteenth-Century Thought*, pp. 65–87. New York: Praeger

Spindler, George, ed. 1978. *The Making of Psychological Anthropology*. Berkeley: University of California Press

Spiro, Melford. 1972. An Overview and a Suggested Reorientation. In F. L. Hsu, ed., *Psychological Anthropology* (pp. 573–608). Cambridge, MA: Schenckman Publishing Co. (originally published in 1961)

Stocking, G. W. Jr. 1968. *Race, Culture and Evolution: Essays in the History of Anthropology*. New York: Free Press
1974a. *The Shaping of American Anthropology, 1883–1911: A Franz Boas Reader*. New York: Basic Books

1974b. The Basic Assumptions of Boasian Anthropology. In Stocking, 1974a (pp. 1–20)
1976. Ideas and Institutions in American Anthropology: Thoughts Toward a History of the Interwar Years, in Stocking, ed., *Selected Papers from the American Anthropologist, 1921–1945* (pp. 1–53) Washington, DC: American Anthropological Association
1979. Anthropology as Kulturkampf: Science and Politics in the career of Franz Boas. In Walter Goldschmidt, ed., *The Uses of Anthropology* (pp. 33–50). Washington, DC: American Anthropological Association
ed. 1986. *"Malinowski, Rivers, Benedict and Others": Essays on Culture and Personality. History of Anthropology*, vol. IV. Madison: University of Wisconsin Press

16 Anthropology and psychology: an unrequited relationship

Theodore Schwartz

In this chapter I will contend that anthropology has not had the impact it should on mainstream psychology considering the claims that psychological anthropology makes or should make. I will qualify this assertion later in considering remaining limitations in some "best-case" psychologies. Where we have been neglected or ignored, I will try to identify failings on both sides including our own neglect of academic, mainstream psychology.

Anthropological knowledge of the evolution, nature, forms, and role of culture implicates a set of claims concerning the constitution of human nature and of the bases of human behavior that should not be ignored and yet are largely ignored in mainstream academic psychology, psychoanalysis, and psychiatry. The consequence is an incomplete and misconceived psychology that undershoots its mark – fully human nature. If psychology has failed to accept both the challenge and the resource of anthropological knowledge, we must look for the fault on both sides. Though we began together in the quest for human nature, there has been a mutual estrangement – an inter-paradigmatic misunderstanding. I will contend, nevertheless, that obscured by this estrangement, a major convergence is taking place in some areas (I have in mind cognitive science and the psychology of culture) but perhaps not in some others that we most take for granted (I have in mind psychoanalysis and psychiatry).

The incompleteness thesis

What are these claims of anthropology? They derive from the centrality of culture for the understanding of human nature and psychology. Culture, including language, is the primary human adaptation. Culture consists of the derivatives of experience, more or less organized, learned or created by the individuals of a population, including those images or encodements and their interpretations (meanings) transmitted from past generations, from contemporaries, or formed by individuals themselves. More will be said below concerning the nature of culture. The study of culture and of cultures, at its locus in individuals and populations, is the main task of anthropology.

The incompleteness thesis asserts that human nature is radically incomplete if taken in its biological component including the generic psychological consequences of that biology. The existence of a normal, living human body and brain, does not guarantee characteristically human behavior. That brain and body, if they are to manifest human behavior, must physically incorporate an enculturative structure derived from participation in any human culture. The enculturative structure is as important as the nervous system that enables it. A brain and the enculturative structure that informs and implements it, together with a trained and habituated body, constitute a complete human being possessing not only a set of functions and capacities but a specific content. Although the brain makes culture possible and basic perceptual, cognitive, and affective functions are intrinsic in a general sense, there is no evidence of which I am aware for any inborn representational or ideational content. Culture not only supplies this content but it implements and extends the very capacities that give rise to it. Culture is necessary for the constitution of the human intellect or mind, conscious and unconscious, and to the affective-cognitive fullness, differentiation, and subtlety of human experience, the derivatives of which, in turn, extend culture. Human psychological processes not seen in this context, are, to an important degree, not seen.

The acquisition of culture and enculturative specificity are consequences of the incompleteness thesis. It follows from the incompleteness thesis that culture must be acquired by each individual both in interaction with others, through mediated and direct experience of its environment, and through internal process and production working on and within the enculturative structure. The term "acquisition" is too passive in connotation, but it should be clear in discussion that the process contains self-selective and creative aspects as well as the acquisition of a transmitted "inheritance" (Schwartz 1981).

Brain and body alone do not ensure a human nature. A human life in interaction with, not generalized, but specifically enculturated others results in the build-up of an enculturative structure in each individual. Call this enculturative structure what one will – mazeway, idioverse, or personality – for a population, it is the distributive unit and locus of culture. Aside from our more abstract, aggregate views of culture, we are relatively ignorant of culture at its locus which needs to be approached through the psychology of culture and the ethnography of the individual.

Every process studied by psychology has, for human beings, its place, adaptive function, and to some considerable extent, its means, in culture.

To study memory, for example, and to ignore the fact that it is the primary repository of culture, is to ignore its human context and function and the adaptive circumstance in which it took its human form. Human memory, for example, functions extremely well on culturally encoded, meaningful – which is to say, culturally embedded material, and very poorly otherwise – on nonsense syllables or random digits, for example. Similarly, learning theory that is not directed at enculturation is empty and misdirected, missing the point of human learning. It is not the case that it does not matter what is being learned or in what context. But although culture supplies much of the content of human consciousness, the claims of psychological anthropology do not permit regarding culture as "mere" content. Not only would this mean a failure to understand the constitutive role of content but it fails to comprehend the contribution of culture to psychological processes and structures in the cultural implementation of human personality and intellect.

The incompleteness thesis means also that human nature is open, not finally fixed or determinate. Human nature, taken as self completing with its acquired cultural component that interpenetrates the rest, is open in several ways: first, in the individual it is open to culture in the lifelong process of enculturation. The development of individuals, as well as the form and products of psychological processes, are not entirely endogenous but are available from the a-priori and ambient stock of culture. Culture is the missing factor in the perennial discussions of mind and body. Second, culture is, in any given state of that culture, underspecified. It does not predetermine all thought, feeling, and value, partly because culture is underspecified, variable, and subject to revision. Culture is both the means, a constituent, and the object of cognition. Third, it is open to culture change which may intersect or merge with the enculturative process. Fourth, for populations and for the human species, human nature is open to cultural evolution in the course of which, psychological processes and structures may show continuing or new emergent properties. Individuals experience and embody the typological transitions which we call evolutionary change. Transitional phenomena may endure for generations or may never be resolved, providing one source of the dynamics of culture, of human experience and diversity. Given the place of culture in human nature, I find it unthinkable that the human personality and intellect should not themselves be transformed in the process of cultural evolution. Failure to recognize or to derive fully the implications of the cultural evolutionary context is, perhaps, anthropology's own "creationism."

Although I focus on culture, I am not speaking of disembodied, eviscerated, or castrated human beings who are mere carriers of culture.

Culture is ontologically superorganic only in the sense that it is not transmitted genetically and in the Boasian sense that cultural variation among populations is not a function of their biological variation. Kroeber's superorganic is perspectival, a matter of ethnographic distance or abstraction, not ontological. Leslie White's striking phrase, "A constant cannot explain a variable," was used to argue that human psychology, the constant of psychic unity, cannot explain cultural variation. The incompleteness thesis offers another view of the relationship. Human nature is not a constant. It is not apart from culture. It cannot fully explain culture which is included among its contributory sources. White's formulation seems identical to the argument against racial determinism but its objective was to separate human nature taken as biology – misnamed "psychology," from an ontologically independent culture. Given the incompleteness thesis and the self-completion of human nature in culture and given that culture has continued to evolve since the advent of *Homo sapiens*, then human nature must be considered to have evolved along with its cultural constituent.

On our part, since early in this century, anthropology has responded to psychology. Initially it looked for variation at the biopsychological level, much as we measured skulls and classified the human spectrum of skin color. It has been one of anthropology's principal responsibilities to respond to recurrent claims for racial determination of traits and capacities with the demonstration that cultural, not biological variation accounts for differences in behavior among human populations. It is a matter that cannot be put behind us as long as the racial determinism is asserted, increasingly garbed in the data and complex statistical forms of contemporary behavioral science. Nor can such claims be dismissed out of hand – rather, it is a continuing responsibility of both anthropology and psychology to disprove them. Most psychologists, however, do not proceed from the refutation of racial determinism to an interest in culture.

"Best-case" psychologies

Now I must offer qualifications that might seem so extensive that some may feel they invalidate the assertion with which I began. Then I will turn to explanation of the character of the relationship between the two fields, and finally, I will offer some remedies.

It is obvious that anthropology has had an effect on some eminent psychologists, psychoanalysts, and psychiatrists. There are fields of cross-cultural psychology, transcultural psychiatry, and psychoanalytic anthropology that complement and overlap with psychological anthropology. There is a considerable roster of *émigrés* and fellow travellers whose work is almost wholly interdisciplinary. In various universities discussion and collaboration between the disciplines has taken place episodically. One thinks of Harvard, Yale, Columbia, Chicago, UCLA, and others. There are psychologists who have taken their research to the field: Bartlett (1932), Greenfield and Bruner (1969), Cole, Gay, Glick, and Sharp 1971, 1974) among others in psychology; in psychiatry one thinks of Alexander and Dorothea Leighton (1949 among others), or among the *émigrés* from psychiatry to anthropology, Robert Levy (1973); in psychoanalysis such as Róheim (1950 among others), and Erikson (1963). So close is our relation to the latter field that there has been a good deal of crossing and passing. One thinks of how much we owe to analysts such as Kardiner and Erikson and of a considerable roster of anthropologists qualified in both fields such as Devereux, DeVos, and Spiro. With so much traffic, how can I maintain that there has been little impact on mainstream psychology, psychoanalysis, and psychiatry? It is obvious from a Groucho Marxist point of view that anyone who would join our club either wasn't or is no longer mainstream psychology. In any case they may have joined us in being ignored.

Those who bridge both fields may have varying agendas. Some wish to see all cultures as psychologically equivalent. This may have two quite different philosophical bases. One position that might be termed "relativistic universalism" extends the antiracial argument to all potential differences, cultural or psychological – perhaps because any significant difference may be taken as invidious by those being compared or used by others to justify domination or exploitation. The other position might be called "non-relativistic universalism." This position is committed to a particular view of universal human nature and the belief that it provides the commensurability needed if moral judgment is to be possible. Some but not all psychoanalytically oriented anthropologists may be in this position. In contrast to the universalistic, one might coin the term differentialistic – expecting and accepting significant cultural differences. For the non-evolutionary relativist, the expected differences are particularistic and unsystematic. In its non-relativistic form, the significant differences are typological or evolutionary. I am inclined toward this latter position, which one might term "cultural evolutionary relativism" – relative, that is, to cultural evolutionary status. It accepts psychic unity at the genotypic but not at the phenotypic level. The evolutionary position does not accept the possible moral entailments of cultural difference that seem to be a basis for the other positions (Schwartz 1991).

The cross-cultural versus the cultural relevance of anthropology to psychology

It is difficult to document a negative proposition – that we have not had the impact on psychology that our claims, indicated above, would seem to demand. All of us have done extensive field work among psychologists, psychoanalysts, and psychiatrists. We should compare our results and perhaps conduct direct research with interviews aimed at exploring what psychologists know and understand about anthropology and culture.

There are degrees to which the two fields ignore or are ignorant of each other. Those psychologists who do work with human beings may fail entirely to see the relevance of culture. They believe themselves to be working at a biopsychological level of generic or universal human nature. They seek the shortest path to the universal and believe it to be available in any and all subjects. They may attempt to filter out culture, as in Piaget's quest for the "spontaneous." As psychological testers, they may claim to employ "culture-free," "culture-fair," or "cross-culturally valid" instruments, whereas anthropologists take the same tests or construct their own, to be culturally sensitive and therefore interesting probes of human psychology, from which culture is not separable. More commonly, however, psychologists accept that while everyone has culture, it is mainly relevant elsewhere where it produces certain exotic affects that anthropologists study. It is as if others have culture while we have human nature.

My own convictions were strengthened during some years that I served on the Social Science Research Council's Committee on the Social and Emotional Development of the Child. To my eminent psychological colleagues on that committee culture didn't seem to matter. I tried to show them that they were, in part, doing local ethnography but there was strong resistance, even irritation, at my perseveration on the cultural theme.

One psychologist, just as an example, who studied the "development of empathy in the child" suggested that the development of empathy may be furthered at one stage by play with animals. I asked if pulling the wings off bats or making a Jew's harp by impaling a beetle on a stick and humming across its vibrating wings, would help in the process. I was not simply using what Margaret Mead called the "Yes, but the Eskimo ... " approach. I want more than the acceptance of significant cross-cultural variation. I argued that the developmental processes they studied were not simply maturation, the unfolding of human nature, but were, in part, the child's acquisition of culture – a topic that I felt anthropologists and psychologists should approach together. The psychological study of any individual anywhere, even college sophomores, brings one into contact with culture at its locus, crucial to all human psychology, not to be ignored, filtered, or factored out because without it that individual would not be a psychological human being. *But even where the cross-cultural point is grasped, the cultural point is not.*

The study of cognition

I read at the Houston meetings some years ago, on "The Cognitive Status of the Symbol." My reading in both fields (cognitive psychology and symbolic anthropology) indicated that in the psychological literature including leading textbooks of cognitive psychology, the terms "symbol" and "culture" were infrequently mentioned or totally absent. This is supported by a survey of psychology texts reported recently in the *Anthropology Newsletter*. On our part, anthropologists writing about symbolism seemed unaware of or rarely made reference to work in cognitive psychology (Sperber being a conspicuous exception). In general, symbolic, and to a lesser extent psychological anthropologists do not seem to follow work in cognitive psychology. Cognitive anthropology is exceptional. It has extensive contacts with and awareness of academic psychology. Linguistics, ethnosemantics, and cognitive anthropology have made important contributions to cognitive psychology and the broader, interdisciplinary field, cognitive science. I am not sure that this contribution is recognized. There is reason to doubt that cognitive anthropologists have had an impact with respect to my argument that cognitive studies would be deeper if they understood their participation in the development of a psychology of culture.

Cognitive anthropology is well placed with respect to the current interests of psychology that converge toward anthropology but its relation to psychological anthropology is problematic. Cognition is a part of psychology but some cognitive anthropologists do not identify with psychological anthropology, seeing it rather as a separate field. The situation perhaps parallels the current separation of linguistics and cultural anthropology. I would conjecture that, like most psychologists, they identify psychological anthropology with its clinical and psychoanalytic foci and see themselves as dealing with harder, more manipulable models and methods. In my view, psychological anthropology should be coextensive with psychology. We narrow that extensiveness at the cost of our own provincialism and isolation. We need cognitive anthropology in psychological anthropology. What is required is the development of psychology-wide interests in both subfields. But to be psychology-wide in scope is not enough because psychology largely omits what should be, and I believe, will be one of its most important fields – the psychology of culture, a field in which we must take the initiative.

All of cultural anthropology studies cognition to the extent that we look at the content of memory, thought, categorization, the solving or not solving of problems. But what we do does not go far enough to have direct bearing on cognitive psychology. We are inclined to stop at descriptive formalisms or else to leave a product that is largely interpretive. We could do more, in any domain, to get closer to how the native to a culture actually thinks. In a kinship inquiry, for example, it is possible to observe or elicit indications about actual processing. Even a formalism that works, that can predict or match an informant's output in a way that is ethnosemantically revealing, is not, in itself, cognitive. It may be elegant, but actual processing may involve simplifying methods as well as complex, mixed strategies and considerable redundancy. There are uses for formal elicitation procedures but it may be more important that we extend our usual modes of elicitation more deeply into cognition – beyond the product into the process. It would provide the sort of material we need in the study of the psychology of culture.

There are areas under development in the field of cognitive science in which we should become involved. To mention only one, there is currently great interest in the study of artificial intelligence including the practical concern of modeling expert knowledge in various areas such as medical diagnosis or investment strategy, to make it available on computers to assist in human decision making. Some of what would interest us takes place before the computer is importantly involved – the bases of expertise, often intuitive, must be elicited and analyzed – certainly an ethnographic task. A great deal of thought is being given to representation of knowledge. In our hands this could be generalized nor need such representations be confined to affectless, secondary-process propositional forms. I would maintain, consistent with the "incompleteness thesis," that the expression "artificial intelligence" is a redundancy in terms. Human intelligence is always artificially, that is, artifactually extended through culture, language, and the evolutionary process of metageny (Schwartz 1991), including metacognition, whereby thought comprehends itself and proceeds accordingly. Anthropology clearly has a place in cognitive science.

Psychiatry

I believe that our impact on most of psychiatry has been quite limited in spite of our own long-term interest in questions of normality, pathology, and therapy. Anthropology is accorded some interest when the patient is ethnic or distant or when they report themselves possessed or hexed. Culture is also seen as relevant for some exotic and picturesque syndromes. I read a paper a while back which I gave the title, "Why does everyone else have ethnopsychoses whereas we have the real thing?" In anthropology we subscribe to a Lyellian uniformitarianism. We speak of the health, pathology, or disorder of enculturated, and therefore human, beings. We have not made our point in psychiatry until it is understood that any disorder, whether developmental or disruptive, and to whatever extent organic, involves in cause or expression, the enculturative structure of the individual. There have been exacting studies of language aphasias dealing with the effects of brain lesions on differential language functions but this is not extended beyond language to the rest of culture which is also represented and supported in the brain. Are there cultural aphasias? Are there enculturative disorders? (We have some indications from Luria [1972].) Regardless of etiology, the enculturative structure is always involved as much as it is in support of normal states and functioning. We should speak, perhaps, of "ethnormality" to understand the sustaining effect of culture as we find it in the individual from early acquisition to its possible attenuation or supportive persistence in aging. A combined clinical/life historical/ethnographic approach to the individual would be illuminating. The individual who is injured, diseased, developmentally malformed, stressed, conflicted, inadequate or disrupted in structure, function, or external relations, draws upon the culture, in himself or others or externally represented. That culture is deformed by the impairment and will, more or less successfully, be reformed or recast in a way that may alleviate suffering or enhance acceptability to himself and to others.

Psychoanalysis

For psychoanalysis the exchange is even more unbalanced. Psychoanalysis, and anthropology's attempt to extend it beyond its original cultural context, has been the main source of the field of psychological anthropology, though the field has also drawn, sporadically, from the main body of psychology which lies outside of psychoanalysis. With the exception of some individuals who came to practice both psychoanalysis and anthropology, the several varieties of psychoanalysis have accepted little in return from anthropology. From the outside and for many within anthropology, psychological anthropology is commonly identified with psychoanalytic anthropology, rather than seeing the latter as a subfield of the former. The process of conversion has been largely one-sided. Is it necessary that psychoanalysts must do field work in other cultures and that anthropologists must undergo psychoanalysis to work through their Oedipal residues, and if so, might not successful conversion diminish critical resistance? In my view selected aspects of psychoanalysis have enriched anthropology, but we in turn should be among its deepest critics and emendators.

We have learned much from psychoanalysis. It is a kind of learning theory, but unlike academic, formal learning theories, even social learning theory, psychoanalysis is a psychology with a thematic content, largely derived from purported universals of generic human biopsychological and developmental experience. It led us to the fundaments of experience in childhood and later formative phases. It made us aware of unconscious as well as conscious levels of experience and psychological structure. It led us to look for motives as well as functions in cultural forms. It was one of the several sources of our sensitivity to symbolism and provided a method for the interpretation of personal symbols by annotation with the informants' own "free" associations. It offered rich insights into symbolic, figurative discourse. Psychoanalysis focused our attention on the intimate relation of cognition and affect. It was rationalistic at the same time that it offered understandings of the irrational. It was a dynamic theory in that it centered on conflict between growth and fixation, between the wishes and needs of the child, parents, and siblings, between the biological, the learned, and the social as well as the internalized conflicts and defenses that mediated among the representations of these persons and forces. It required us to look at the manifestations of sex and aggression, pleasure and pain, life- and death-tending forces in human personality. It offered a theory of culture as at once the cause and the result of repression.

Psychoanalysis has continued to develop after Freud and we must also come to terms with these later developments. I personally get something from Alfred Adler (namely, the perception of the role of power in intergenerational relations) and little, if anything, from Carl Jung. I am resistant to the tendency in much post-Freudian psychoanalysis to load ever more fateful influence, astrology-like, on earliest, "pre-Oedipal" childhood. I find much value in Hartmann (1958), whose "Ego Psychology" provided a more clearly marked place in Freudian-derived psychoanalysis for the findings of academic and cognitive psychology and for adaptation to the world actually encountered by the individual. The "Self Psychology" of Kohut (1971) and others, would seem to offer common ground with the perennial interest of anthropologists in the Self (Róheim, 1921, Hallowell, 1974), though our interest is largely in the ethnography of the Self as culturally constituted. The pursuit of the Self has been weakened by vagueness of reference and by multiplication of intra-psychic entities. It becomes, in some sources, a super-agent, an integrative center, a repository of identity, its place in personality and its relations to Ego, problematic or undefined. I prefer to treat the Self prosaically as one domain, of great importance, among the many that segment our phenomenal fields – a domain of self-referential experience, knowledge, and belief. It is accessed by Ego – an envelope in which we place a variety of psychological functions and to which we assign various metaphors of contested possession and agency (Moore and Schwartz n.d.). To the extent that psychological anthropology identifies and is identified with psychoanalysis, we share its insularity. I would prefer to see psychoanalytic theory absorbed by psychology and a psychological anthropology which is truly psychology wide.

It should be clear from the remarks above on the contributions of psychoanalysis to anthropology, that although I advocate a thoroughgoing critique and revision of psychoanalysis and its place in anthropology and in psychology, I do not wish to throw out either the baby (though now a bearded one) or the bath. In this sweeping and hopefully, provocative, review, I will not be able to defend my criticisms or my characterizations of psychoanalytic anthropology, to which I know my most respected colleagues will take strong exception. I must simply state my misgivings about psychoanalytic anthropology and leave exceptions, qualifications, and documentation for a later time.

Although I have listed it as a virtue that psychoanalysis is a psychology with a thematic content, when it comes to its application to the explanation of cultures and their institutions (whether in their origins or persistence) or in the cultural roles of specific individuals in case studies, it seems to me that psychoanalysis offers a single script read over and over again regardless of the culture to which it is applied. The standard Oedipus complex, for example, is one of its most oft-told tales (though it is applied with less certainty to women). It was Malinowski (1955) and Kardiner (1939, 1945) who pressed anthropology's claims that culture produces real differences in human experience and its resultant personalities. They set the agenda, at least with respect to the consideration of psychoanalytic propositions, to expand our knowledge of human personality formation and variation, by examining its formation in a variety of different cultures, even though some common framework of human needs and development might apply across cultures. I believe their movement was in the right direction but did not go far enough. Malinowski and Kardiner accepted the psychoanalytic focus on childhood socialization and though they assigned culture a greater role, it operated primarily by shaping those institutions which impinged most directly on childhood and on child–parent relations. The direct impact of culture as an ideational environment with behavioral, motivational, and evaluative implications (and its internalization through enculturation) was neglected.

Psychoanalysis has defended itself against the anthropological critique that had attempted to open it to a wider range of formative situations shaped by culture. Psychoanalytically oriented anthropologists (with some exceptions) appear to have stepped back from the culturist critique and expansion of psychoanalysis to one that emphasizes a biologistic, generic human nature underlying the range of cultural variation that supports the original Freudian emphases.[1] Spiro's recent critique of Malinowski's *Sex and Repression* is of singular importance in the recent anthropological literature (Spiro 1982). It is the greatest challenge to the Malinowski–Kardiner agenda that has provided one of the main axes of psychological anthropology for some fifty years. It is presented as a refutation of a myth – the myth of the matrilineal complex as a culturally conditioned alternative to the Oedipus complex which Malinowski saw as a product of European-derived cultures. In a way somewhat reminiscent of Freeman's "refutation" of Mead's "myth" of Samoan character, which Freeman reports to be the opposite in virtually every respect from Mead's depiction, Spiro offers a close and relentless argument to the effect that not only do the Trobrianders have an Oedipus complex contrary to Malinowski's claim, but that it is even more extreme to the extent that the father, who despite matriliny occupies his usual place in the nuclear household and marital bed, is thoroughly repressed in various projective genre where an absence is more telling than a presence. Spiro argues that questions such as those of authority, paternal nurturance, ideology of descent, are irrelevant to Freud's concept of the requirements for the *ocurrence* of the Oedipus complex and may not, in any case, have had much bearing on the experience of the child (Spiro 1982: 5). The Oedipus complex (in the case of a male child) is thought to occur if the child has a mother (or female surrogate) who has a male consort (father or not) whom the child will perceive as a successful sexual rival for the mother. The Oedipus complex is then universal almost by definition. Spiro accepts the "complementary Oedipus complex" (the role of the parent toward the child, e.g., maternal seductiveness) as an amendment to Freud's perception of the complex. We should, perhaps, add to this the adult's use of the child as a projective screen upon which adult- or genito-centric thoughts and wishes are projected onto the child.

Spiro does, in the end, allow room for a variety of cultural factors to influence the *intensity* and *resolution* of the Oedipus complex and, therefore, its cultural consequences. This may leave us somewhere near where we started with the Malinowski–Kardiner agenda, as the outcome of the Oedipus complex is seen in psychoanalysis as having major culture-formative consequences. In any case, psychological anthropologists will agree that such matters as authority, kinship, power, nurturance, living and working arrangements, and ideation (cultural knowledge and beliefs) do shape human experience and its derivatives in personality and culture. Spiro's formidable argument raises a deeper question – just how much difference does cultural difference make? Perhaps it is resistance on my part, or that I am among the unanalyzed, or that it was an interest in culture that brought me into and sustains my interest in anthropology, but for me it remains that Malinowski and Kardiner were indicating the right direction to a more open and inclusive analysis of factors, including culture itself, contributing to human experience and a culturally variable nuclear complex of the personality. I would, as I have indicated above, go further than they did to give culture a more directly constitutive role. I would also avoid the assumption of a single or simple "nuclear" complex, simply "instantiated" in individuals and build psychological ethnographies from both ends at once, that is, the collective and the individual.

Though I think that an open approach would more adequately account for cultural variation in the effects of socialization, it will be apparent throughout this chapter that we would regard such an approach as decisively incomplete. As I have argued elsewhere (Schwartz 1981), I must distinguish socialization, which attunes or conditions certain propensities, from enculturation in which one learns the ideational content of a culture in childhood as throughout life. The constructs that make up this ideational content are not purely cognitive, though in their cognitive aspect they bear a variable implicative force, but are simultaneously motivational and evaluative, variably constraining or motivating behavior. This means we cannot make a simple division between socialization as affect and motive, on the one hand, and on the other hand, enculturation as cognitive, supplying cultural content. In this respect Kardiner's model, which made its contribution toward placing psychoanalysis in its cultural context, is excessively but not entirely lineal, proceeding from culture and environment to primary institutions impinging on childhood, to individual personality, to projective systems and secondary institutions. A more balanced circular chain of causality (indicating the internalization and use of projective systems by the individual) would have been an improvement but would still have neglected the overall ideational ambiance (which cannot be totally subsumed under projective systems) and its direct enculturation.

Have we pursued the more expansive program or have we stayed with the original Freudian dispensation? Psychoanalysis is still the only game in town when we look to psychological theories with specifically human content having some articulation with culture, but it should have been absorbed selectively into a broader psychology. As it stands, it offers us a method that is too powerful, too predictable, epistemologically elusive. It accounts for too much with too little. There is much truth to be culled from psychoanalysis but it is flawed in the same way here attributed to the rest of psychology. In effect, it takes culture as epiphenomenal, accounted for psychodynamically (and it does not seem to me to matter whether we are speaking of accounting for origins or persistences), and in so doing neglects the direct causal contribution of culture to personality formation. This statement requires extensive qualification beyond the scope of this essay (for a discussion that covers some of the qualifications to which I refer, see Kakar 1981: 183). In general and in effect, in psychoanalytically oriented anthropology, culture is taken as the thing to be explained. Psychodynamic trauma, disturbances, and defensive processes are the explanation. If it is said that culture is a historical product that develops independently of the psychodynamic uses to which it is put, it makes the fit between cultural content and psychodynamic demand appear to be serendipitous. I prefer to accept the Freudian proposition, developed by Kardiner, that some domains of culture may be psychodynamic precipitates, some not. Psychoanalytic anthropology tends to be reductionist to the near-biological level of generic psychology. It does allow that the individual utilizes culture, symbolic materials or institutionalized defense mechanisms in self-maintenance, restoration or transcendence of traumas and that society participates as a source of stress or conflict with biological or developmentally based needs. Although culture is seen as available to provide palliatives to personal conflicts, needs, losses, and anxieties, it is relatively neglected that culture creates worlds so premissed that it may be as much or more the source of such conflicts and anxieties as it is the cure.

In spite of such appearances of culture as a term on both sides of the equation (as *explanans* and *explanandum*), I would prefer a mix of determinants in which culture, in its a-priori and constitutive sense is given a direct and weightier role as an ideational (enculturative) factor and not only or mainly as a socializing environment in personality formation and in the generation of behavior. It would be comparably erroneous to the neglect or imbalances I have been discussing, for cultural analysis to neglect psychodynamic and motivational inputs to the mix of determinants. There are indications that a more comprehensive model is still developing, uniting the cultural and the psychodynamic without losing either in the other. We have had a century to come to terms with Freud, more than sixty years since Malinowski's *Sex and Repression*, a long acquaintance with a variety of neo-Freudian modifications, and we have before us many serious critiques and recent developments in psychoanalysis. Any work in this area that attempts to model the human psyche continues to be of great importance to us, though if it does it without us, that is, without our own hard-won understandings of the nature and contribution of culture and its psychology, they will have missed their mark. It is time for us to decide where we stand with respect to psychoanalysis, to maintain our critical and comparative role and to offer our own synthesis.

Cross-cultural use of psychological tests of cognition and personality

The notion is prevalent that the use of psychological tests cross-culturally has been discredited on the basis of demonstrated, unsolved problems of validation and interpretation. I refer to personality tests, often called "projective" tests, as well as to tests of intelligence and of cognitive skills. Numerous factors including cultural incommensurability, observer and situational effects are said to impair the plausibility of such tests.[2] Gardner Lindzey's critical review of cross-cultural personality testing, though not entirely negative, raises so many questions and doubts that they are often thought to be a definitive invalidation of such tests.[3] Kaplan called attention to the great variability among sets of Rorschach tests when compared across many cultures – some so sparse as to afford little material for analysis and interpretation; some extraordinarily rich in phantasy material. He suggested that the test varies because it is construed very differently in different cultures and that one must start by discovering what the test is to a particular population. A similar range of variation can be found within Euro-derived populations and the subject's construal of the test cannot always be separated from factors such as anxiety and defensiveness (Kaplan 1961: 302). In clinical psychology itself, personality and diagnostic testing still is used but does not command the interest or confidence that it did in the fifties and earlier. Similarly, the use of cognitive and intelligence testing in both anthropology and psychology have come into disrepute. Their validity within the range of internal variation in Western cultures has come under attack because they are said to be biased with respect to ethnicity and gender, and their application in education and employment, therefore, is discriminatory.

Yet in spite of these formidable deterrents, some psychological anthropologists, including myself, continue to use and to develop such tests and, hopefully, more sophisticated methods of analysis and interpretation. De Vos and Boyer have just published the first major work in this area to have appeared in decades (De Vos and Boyer 1989). Others, such as Suárez-Orozco offer vigorous defense and demonstration of their use, in his case, of the Thematic Apperception Test, to get at material possibly unavailable through more direct elicitation (Suárez-Orozco, in press and 1989). At least one study based on the Rorschach test, though reflecting an early, methodologically, statistically, and interpretatively unsophisticated horizon, is regarded as a classic, a milestone, and is widely cited even in texts that see little value in the use of such tests. I refer to Anthony Wallace's *Modal Personality of the Tuscarora Indians* (1952b), which, in spite of the above faults, building on the work of Hallowell (1956) and of Du Bois (1960), attempted to apply a psychological measure to determine actual variation and centrality in a population. Through their work the value and possibility of implementing psychological variables empirically, rather than inferring them from institutions and "projective systems," became an additional possibility in psychological anthropology. Without testing, which I regard simply as a specialized form of interview, a frame of elicitation, a whole class of research designs is precluded and we are left to interpretive methods the validity of which is less amenable to critical evaluation than the use of tests has been.

I cannot discuss here, nor do I dismiss, the specific issues raised by critics of cross-cultural testing. It is useless and misleading to speak of the tests as "culture-fair" and naive to do so simply because some may be minimally verbal, as Arthur Jenson argues in favor of such tests as the Raven Progressive Matrices Test (1980: 531). I regard the tests, instead, as culturally sensitive. The performance, described and analyzed fully, not simply taken as a score (such as IQ or a set of Rorschach scores) may provide material on thought or phantasy not otherwise available within a frame of elicitation that makes the results somewhat more comparable within the population, which can be characterized in its own norms, and more loosely, between populations. One does not take, as in the case of one of the main Rorschach systems, the employees of the Spiegel Mail Order Company, to provide a universally applicable set of norms, but only as representing themselves, as one subcultural sample. Without what would now be stupid assumptions, internal and external analysis and comparison can be informative. Some researchers, such as Cole and associates, in their African work, kept looking for more and more culturally familiar tests to overcome what could be interpreted as a deficit when standard tests were used. By this method one demonstrates eventually that people can do what they do, that is, they can do the familiar tasks that their culture requires of them.

I would argue that there is much to be learned from letting people respond to test situations with which they are not familiar and for which their culture does not prepare them specifically as long as one looks closely at what they do and compares them with each other. So, for example, a test of categorization of objects and their retrieval from memory produced more interesting results among unschooled adults than it did among the next generation of primary and high-school children who had been equipped with readymade categories and strategies (Schwartz, 1991). Anthropologists who have used projective tests such as the notorious Rorschach inkblots in other cultures are often captured by it, intrigued with the cultural specificity of the type and pattern of responses compared to other cultural groups. In 1953 when I first began testing in Manus, the tests we administered and, I am sure, almost any we might have devised, such as "Draw a line on a piece of paper" or "Tell me any ten words," would have differentiated the sea-faring Manus from their near, closely related, but ecologically, sharply differentiated horticultural neighbors (see also Edgerton 1971). In later studies when I was engaged in an ethnographic survey of the more than twenty cultural–linguistic groups of the Admiralty Islands, I used screening tests as simple indices of psychological variation, to be included among other structurable variables such as kinship, language, ecotype, etc. Whether we know what the variations indicate or not, there is a high likelihood that groups who strive for integrated whole percepts on the Rorschach test are psychologically significantly different from groups who readily give a lot of unarticulated small details and few whole responses. Beyond such demonstration of difference, it is up to us to discover what these differences mean psychologically and what they reflect or parallel in cultural differences and behavior. That we have largely turned away from psychological testing is, for me, a further indication of the general paucity of "normal science" in anthropology. With some important exceptions, encountering difficulty we turn aside to whatever is the latest trend or "hot" topic, leaving behind unresolved, undeveloped, but potentially valuable problems and methods. We cannot expect to find our methods readymade in psychology. Our needs are even more demanding than clinical usage. The use of computers now offers opportunities for pre-statistical pattern analysis of a wide variety of test protocols. This would be a good time to reexamine some of the things we have rather carelessly discarded along the way.

Communicating the concept of culture

Mainly I am concerned with the understanding and use made of the concept of culture. That understanding which may be responsible in part for the failure of psychologists to see the relevance of culture to their own preoccupation, probably runs along the following lines: that culture is a learned, historical formation; that culture is held in common by the members of a society; that culture is most commonly placed in a tripartite model as expounded by Talcott Parsons and others, in which culture is the ideational, symbolic sphere, including language; personality is seen largely as affective and motivational; and society consists of relations, statuses, roles, and institutions.

Although culture is acknowledged as subsuming language, psychology has given far more thought and work to language, often not mentioning the rest of culture including the message or meaning level of culture that is not reducible to its encoding in language forms. Most of the work on language acquisition or on language disorders, makes no mention of the rest of culture. Where psychology moves toward culture, it has tended to do so through language and through theorists such as Vygotsky rather than through the influence of anthropology. "Cognitive science", the newly emergent interdisciplinary field, is successor, reminiscent in its scope and pretensions, to the "General Systems Theory" of the forties and fifties. It may lead to rediscovery and, perhaps, to incorporation and further development of the theory and psychology of culture.

Much of the above construction of psychologists' views and use of "culture" applies to some of our "best–case" psychologists, such as Jerome Bruner and Michael Cole. Bruner's understanding of "culture" and his encounters with anthropologists are accessible to us through his intellectual autobiography, *In Search of Mind* (Bruner 1983). He had extensive interaction at Harvard with figures in our field such as Clyde Kluckhohn and John Whiting, and he reports discussions with Kroeber. He accepted that cultural variation may have important psychological concomitants and that Piagetian theories, in which he was absorbed for a considerable period, should be tested cross-culturally. This led to his work with Patricia Greenfield among the Wolof of Senegal (Greenfield and Bruner 1969). Yet he seems to be among those who accepted the cross-cultural but not the cultural point. He did not return for some time to an interest in culture, and then, through Vygotsky, Luria, and Austin, and largely confined to language.

The view of culture, even among cross-cultural psychologists, most often follows the outline given above. For most in the mainstream the concept of culture is there but it is the business of anthropologists. It is seen as vague, intractable, not subject to convenient observation or experimental manipulation. Certainly it is not for the fastidious or the scientifically rigorous. Or else it is seen as located elsewhere, not accessible to the experimenter or clinician unless there are "ethnic" subjects. Local culture is invisible, not just because of its sameness to one's own, but because we assume commonality by definition. If it is not shared by the members of some social designate, it is not culture. It is deviance, deprivation, disorder, or cultural incompetence. I will not be satisfied that the significance of culture in human nature is grasped until we have explored its implications fully for any individual and understand that the place of culture in human nature would be just as great if there were only one culture on earth.

A distributive and experience-processing model of culture

I believe that few psychologists are aware that alternatives have developed in anthropology to the generally accepted model of culture sketched above. Much remains to be done but the outlines of a model of culture can be indicated that may be more suitable ground on which the two fields can converge in the further exploration of human nature. It has a different sort of complexity from the Parsonian model, which was complicated enough.

It is an "experience-processing" model of culture that in some ways differs from the psychological notions of "information-processing" and "learning." The model also modifies the "superorganicism" of culture, rooting it in human experience and its stored or encoded derivatives. I called the alternative model a "distributive model of culture," designating a class of models of culture that take culture as distributed non-uniformly over a population (Schwartz 1962: 360–362; 1978a; 1978b; Mead and Schwartz 1960; Schwartz and Mead 1961). Distributive models of culture begin, as far as I am aware, with Edward Sapir (1932, 1938, also in Mandelbaum 1949). A distributive model was given a detailed exposition and rationale by Spiro (1951). Anthony Wallace developed the most well-known distributive model and the notion is largely identified with him (1952a and b, 1961). I would include Roberts (1951, 1964, 1987); Goodenough (1981); LeVine (1982); and Swartz (1982, 1991) among other theoretical contributors. In the 1970s and 1980s there has been very considerable interest in "intra-cultural variation" (Pelto and Pelto 1975; Boster 1987) as well as in "consensual models" (Romney, Weller, and Batchelder 1986, 1987; D'Andrade 1987) in part inspired by Roberts' earlier work. "Consensus" reverts to the idea of culture as shared knowledge, but as distributive models render commonality problematic, work that focuses on sharing has an important place among distributive models. There is intra-disciplinary variation among these models but I cannot expound on that here.

My own variant, proposed in Mead and Schwartz (1960) and generalized in an article, "Where is the Culture?" in 1978, may be taken as representative. It neither assumes nor excludes any degree of commonality among the members of a population but expects to find a complex structure of commonality. Culture is not confined to the structure of commonality, but includes all of the internalized derivatives of experience distributed among the members of a population. These derivatives are organized as the enculturative structure or idioverse of each individual, constituting the personality of that individual. (See Schwartz 1978a and 1989b for further exposition of this model.) It is an experience-processing model allowing for the full scope of human experience which notions such as "information" and "knowledge" do not, though they may be appropriate to a culture modeled after "trivial pursuits." It is a culture with an individualized texture but the individual is not the "pristine processor" of experience, recreating the world. It is populated with individuals who to a large extent process culturally informed experience in interaction with differentially enculturated adults, organizing and creating their own versions of culture employing a culture-acquisitional system amounting to their whole personalities. The internalized derivatives of experience are not purely cognitive – they are simultaneously cognitive-affective-evaluative mappings or representations of experience derived from the events of the life-history-thus-far. They are at once, to varying degrees motivational and representational, having some degree of behavior-determining force or compulsoriness. I can go no further in expounding such a model here. Its advantages as a common base for anthropology and psychology in studying culture in the individual as well as in its distributive loci in populations should be evident. It is nearer to reality, less the analytic entity than the more standard model.

The model is unified, in contrast to the tripartite model. Spiro's dichotoclastic article (1951) made the argument for a unified model, in which culture and personality are seen as derivatives from the same stream of experience, differentially internalized by individuals in interaction with specifically enculturated others.[4] My own model is quite similar and must be partly derivative. Spiro has since changed his mind. He returned to the tripartite model on the grounds, to oversimplify, that it is a more dynamic model. A dynamic model must have parts that can be in conflict from which change can be derived. Spiro's allows for conflict, for example, between the personality of the individual and the demands of society – a conflict that, it is argued, can generate cultural forms that may, for example, be understandable as defenses in a psychoanalytic sense. I do not dispute the utility in some contexts of the more established, tripartite theory. It would be possible, though not in this paper, to demonstrate a somewhat different dynamism of the experience-processing, distributive, unified model as well as its ability to accommodate established psychodynamics.

The trends in anthropology to which I have alluded bring us closer to psychology in an area that may be labelled the "psychology of culture." On its part psychology also indicates various moves toward dealing with larger, more significant units of behavior in more ecologically realistic contexts. There is much to be gained by insisting on our point – that the understanding of human nature is an understanding of the specifically enculturated human being.

The credibility and scientific status of psychological anthropology

The claims of which I speak are primarily at the conceptual level concerning the nature of the object (human nature) to which psychology and anthropology direct their studies. If these claims and their implications for research are not generally accepted, is it that we lack credibility – that we are not to be taken seriously? I think we do have a credibility problem of major proportions. We are in crisis to the point of being shaken in our belief in our own enterprise. The Mead–Freeman controversy brings it into the open but our epistemological *angst* has been growing, particularly in this decade. Psychologists who have doubted, dismissed, or simply ignored our claims, have still more reason to do so. The question of the credibility of our ethnographic reporting is not the only and possibly not the most important basis for our problem with psychology. In addition to deficiencies in the positions with which we are identified, is psychology's need to make the most of the subjects at hand and to believe that they have a direct and autonomous line to the universal. Our claims concerning the depth of cultural diversity are based on over a century of ethnographic documentation, which, even if deeply discounted, makes a denial of cultural depth, diversity, and cultural evolution as willfully irrational as a declaration that there is not a shred of evidence for biological evolution. We join in the discounting. I know that although I have done my best to describe and understand a particular culture, my knowledge is incomplete; I am partly wrong in ways of which I am still unaware; and my reports are subject to some complex and subtle biases. But they are a part of science in the sense that one has a concern for truth, a responsibility to reality which, of course, includes the people whose culture one studies. One does one's best methodologically and, finally, one submits one's data and interpretations to a critical community. Whatever meets these broad criteria is science, whether historiography, anthropology, or chemistry.

I am most concerned, however, by a different sort of self-discrediting which seems to be a trend in current anthropology, though it is not new nor are we the only discipline afflicted by it. It is in part a way of responding to the epistemological difficulties that we confront as human beings studying ourselves and other human beings across cultures (even within our own). It differs from the earlier phenomenological concerns of anthropologists such as Hallowell that lead us to seek the informant's view of his world (though our task does not end there). The trend to which I refer is the opposite of the quest to discover the world as it exists for others. It arrogates to itself the creation of that culture. It speaks of "constructing"[5], "inventing"[6], or "writing cultures" (Clifford and Marcus 1986). It represents anthropology as "story telling." One review of Mead–Freeman speaks of ethnographies in general as alternative myths among which we chose according to our preference for the values they support (Rappaport 1986). One could take all of this as simply the latest cant or fashionable import which changes every few years in anthropology, but it may reflect a deeper strain and division among us. Perhaps it is the shape of New Age Anthropology – self-preoccupied to the verge of a delusion of reference, "making one's own reality," exquisite self-consciousness, literary and moral pretentiousness, casting science as scientism, taking the world as word, relativistic in a way that celebrates every obstacle to knowledge without accounting for the fact of knowledge, exocentric and allo-rational (if not anti-rational) (Schwartz 1989a), spiritual in their belief in their own intuition and empathic understanding, engaged in the wistful magic of rendering the exotic familiar and the familiar exotic?

The model of culture suggested in this chapter as a suitable common base for anthropology and psychology is more complex than previous models but it does place Samoan culture in Samoans as their creation, not ours. The inverted perspective to which I refer above, confuses epistemology with ontology by confounding the ethnography with the culture. The error has prestigious antecedents in physics but is nonetheless erroneous. Confronted with the gap between the object and its representations, we can chose to develop appropriate scientific methods – doing our best better – or we can proclaim anthropology to be a genre of literature and literary criticism of the "life is but a text" variety.

It is possible that some partial reconciliation or illumination of difference could occur between neo-positivist or science-aspiring anthropology and interpretive, post-modernist anthropology around the question of the nature of interpretation (non-determinate explanation?) – how we arrive at and choose among alternative interpretations, as the most interpretivist among us must do. Interpretation is not a divide but a common ground for anthropology – given the complexity and emergent nature of culture and our own self-involvement, rarely if ever do we arrive at fully determinate explanation or selection among alternative theories. On what grounds do we select among interpretations and what claims are made for them about the world?

If my picture of the relation of anthropology and psychology is generally correct, our colleagues in other fields don't need to be told by us not to take our "story telling" seriously. We have knowledge and perspectives critical to the understanding of human nature. There have been Herculean efforts in bringing the diverse cultures of this planet under close observation and in the huge task of sorting, evaluating, and comprehending the data that have been accumulated. What we have done or are yet engaged in, in fact, is comparable to the task that biology now sets itself of mapping the entire human genome.

I have my own list of heroes who have followed one approach or another with passionate persistence in pursuit of a truth that comes in small increments. In this spirit, psychological anthropology can insist to our colleagues in psychology, whose object of research we share, that what we have learned of culture is not to be ignored – it is as essential a constituent of human nature as the human brain and body.

NOTES

1 Robert Paul in a recent survey of psychoanalytic anthropology also notes this trend (1989: 189).
2 See discussion in LeVine (1982).
3 But see Spain (1972), who tabulates a long list of "problems" but suggests that they may be soluble.
4 But see also Spiro (1961) for a reconsideration of this earlier model.
5 "Constructionism" is so prevalent, no specific citation is needed.
6 For example, Allen Johnson (1978: 8–9), citing Wagner (1975).

REFERENCES

Bartlett, F. C. 1932. *Remembering: A Study in Experimental and Social Psychology*. Cambridge: Cambridge University Press

Boster, James S. 1987. *Intracultural Variation*. Special Issue of *American Behavioral Scientist* 31(2)

Bruner, Jerome. 1983. *In Search of Mind: Essays in Autobiography*. New York: Harper and Row

Clifford, James and George E. Marcus. 1986. *Writing Culture: The Poetics and Politics of Ethnography*. School of American Research Advanced Seminar. Berkeley: University of California Press

Cole, M., J. Gay, J. A. Glick, and D. W. Sharp. 1971. *The Cultural Context of Learning and Thinking: An Exploration in Experimental Anthropology*. New York: Basic Books

Cole, M. and S. Scribner. 1974. *Culture and Thought: A Psychological Introduction*. New York: Wiley

D'Andrade, Roy G. 1987. Modal Responses and Cultural Expertise. In James S. Boster, ed., *Intracultural Variation, American Behavioral Scientist* 31(2)

De Vos, George A. and L. Bryce Boyer. 1989. *Symbolic Analysis Cross-Culturally: The Rorschach Test*. University of California Press

DuBois, Cora. 1960. *The People of Alor: A Social-Psychological Study of an East*

Indian Island. Minneapolis: University of Minnesota Press (originally published in 1944)

Edgerton, Robert. 1971. *The Individual in Cultural Adaptation: A Study of Four East African Peoples.* Berkeley: University of California Press

Erikson, Erik. 1963. *Childhood and Society.* New York: W. W. Norton and Co.

Goodenough, Ward H. 1981. *Culture, Language, and Society.* Addison-Wesley Module in Anthropology, no. 7

Greenfield, Patricia Marks and Jerome S. Bruner. 1969. Culture and Cognitive Growth. In David A. Goslin, ed., *Handbook of Socialization Theory and Research.* Chicago: Rand McNally

Hallowell, A. I. 1956. The Rorschach Technique in Personality and Culture Studies. In B. Klopfer, ed., *Developments in the Rorschach Technique*, vol. II, *Fields of Application.* Yonkers, NY: World Book Co.

1974. The Self and Its Behavioral Environment. In *Culture and Experience.* Philadelphia: University of Pennsylvania Press (originally published in 1954

Hartmann, H. 1958. *Ego Psychology and the Problem of Adaptation.* New York: International Universities Press

Jensen, Arthur R. 1980. *Bias in Mental Testing.* New York: The Free Press

Johnson, Allen W. 1978. *Quantification in Cultural Anthropology: An Introduction to Research Design.* Stanford: Stanford University Press

Kakar, Sudhir. 1981. *The Inner World: A Psycho-Analytic Study of Childhood and Society in India* (2nd edn). Oxford: Oxford University Press

Kaplan, Bert. 1961. Personality Study and Culture. In *Studying Personality Cross-Culturally.* Bert Kaplan, editor. New York: Harper & Row

Kardiner, A. 1939. *The Individual and His Society: The Psychodynamics of Primitive Social Organization.* New York: Columbia University Press

1945. *The Psychological Frontiers of Society.* New York: Columbia University Press

Kohut, H. 1971. *The Analysis of the Self.* New York: International Universities Press

Leighton, Alexander H. and Dorothea G. Leighton. 1949. Gregorio, the Hand Trembler: A Psychobiological Study of a Navaho Indian. *Papers of the Peabody Museum of American Archaeology and Ethnology, Harvard University*, 40(1)

LeVine, Robert. 1982. *Culture, Behavior, and Personality.* Revised edn. New York: Aldine

Levy, Robert. 1973. *The Tahitians: Mind and Experience in the Society Islands.* Chicago: University of Chicago Press

Lindzey, Gardner. 1961. *Projective Techniques and Cross-Cultural research.* New York: Appleton-Century-Crofts

Luria, A. R. 1972. *The Man with a Shattered World: The History of a Brain Wound.* Cambridge, MA: Harvard University Press

Malinowski, B. 1955. *Sex and Repression in Savage Society.* New York: Meridian (originally published in 1927)

Mandelbaum, David G. 1949. *Selected Writings of Edward Sapir in Language, Culture, and Personality.* Berkeley: University of California Press

Mead, Margaret and Theodore Schwartz. 1960. The Cult as a Condensed Social Process. In *Group Processes.* New York: Josiah Macy, Jr., Foundation

Moore, Carmella C. and Theodore Schwartz. n.d. The Self: Metacognician or Metacognition? Unpublished manuscript

Paul, Robert. 1989. Psychoanalytic Anthropology. *Annual Review of Anthropology*. Palo Alto, CA: Annual Reviews, Inc.

Pelto, P. J. and G. H. Pelto. 1975. Intra-Cultural Diversity: Some Theoretical Issues. *American Ethnologist* 2:1–19

Rappaport, Roy. 1986. Desecrating the Holy Woman: Derek Freeman's Attack on Margaret Mead. *American Scholar* summer issue

Roberts, J. M. 1951. Three Navaho Households: A Comparative Study in Small Group Culture. *Papers of the Peabody Museum of American Archaeology and Ethnology*, Harvard University 40(3)

1964. The Self Management of Cultures. In W. Goodenough, ed., *Explorations in Cultural Anthropology: Essays in Honor of George Peter Murdock*. New York: McGraw-Hill

1987. Within Culture Variation: A Retrospective Personal View. In James Boster, ed., Intracultural Variation. *American Behavioral Scientist*, 31(2)

Róheim, G. 1921. Das Selbst. *Imago* 7, 1–39; 142–179; 310–348; 453–504

1950. *Psychoanalysis and Anthropology*. New York: International Universities Press

Romney, A. K., S. C. Weller, and W. H. Batchelder. 1986. Culture as Consensus: A Theory of Culture and Informant Accuracy. *American Anthropologist* 88(2): 313–338

Sapir, Edward. 1932. Cultural Anthropology and Psychiatry. *Journal of Abnormal and Social Psychology* 27: 229–242. Also in Mandelbaum, 1949

1938. Why Cultural Anthropology Needs the Psychiatrist. *Psychiatry* 1: 7–12. Also in Mandelbaum, 1949

Schwartz, Theodore. 1962. The Paliau Movement in the Admiralty Islands, 1946–1954. *Anthropological Papers of the American Museum of Natural History*, no. 49

1978a. Where is the Culture? In George Spindler, ed., *The Making of Psychological Anthropology*. Berkeley: University of California Press

1978b. The Size and Shape of a Culture. In Fredrik Barth, ed., *Scale and Social Organization* (pp. 215–252). Oslo: Universitetsforlaget

1981. The Acquisition of Culture. *Ethos* 9(1), pp. 4–17

1989a. The Exocentric and Allo-rational in New Age Religion. Paper read at the 1989 meeting of the American Anthropological Association in Washington, DC

1989b. The Structure of National Cultures. In Peter Funke, ed., *Understanding the USA: A Cross-Cultural Perspective*. Tübingen: Gunter Narr Verlag

1991. Behavioral Evolution Beyond the Advent of Culture. In B. L. Boyer, ed., *The Psychoanalytic Study of Society*, vol. XVI, pp. 183–214. Essays in Honor of A. I. Hallowell. Hillsdale, NJ: Analytic Press

n.d. A Study of Cognitive Acculturation in Manus. Unpublished research

Schwartz, Theodore and Margaret Mead. 1961. Micro- and Macro-Cultural Models for Cultural Evolution. *Anthropological Linguistics* 3(1): 1–7. Also in Margaret Mead. 1964. *Continuities in Cultural Evolution*. New Haven: Yale University Press

Spain, David H. 1972. On the Use of Projective Tests for Research in Psychological Anthropology. In Francis L. K. Hsu, ed., *Psychological Anthropology* (pp. 267–308). New Edition. Cambridge, MA: Schenkman Publishing Company

Spiro, Melford E. 1951. Culture and Personality: The Natural History of a False Dichotomy. *Psychiatry* 14: 19–46

1961. An Overview and a Suggested Reorientation. In Francis L. K. Hsu, ed., *Psychological Anthropology: Approaches to Culture and Personality*. Homewood IL.: Dorsey

1982. *Oedipus in the Trobriands*. Chicago: University of Chicago Press

Suárez-Orozco, Marcelo M. 1989. Central American Refugees and U.S. High Schools: A Psychosocial Study of Motivation and Achievement. Stanford: Stanford University Press

1990. Speaking of the Unspeakable: Toward a Psychosocial Understanding of Responses to Terror. *Ethos* 18: 353–383

Swartz, Marc. 1982. Cultural Sharing and Cultural Theory: Some Results of a Study of the Nuclear Family in Five Societies. *American Anthropologist* 84: 314–338

1991. Aggressive Speech, Status, and Cultural Distribution Among the Swahili of Mombasa. In D. K. Jordan and M. J. Swartz, eds., *Personality and the Cultural Constitution of Society: Essays in Honor of M. E. Spiro*. Tuscaloosa: University of Alabama Press

Wagner, Roy. 1975. *The Invention of Culture*. Englewood Cliffs, NJ: Prentice-Hall

Wallace, A. F. C. 1952a. Individual Differences and Cultural Uniformities. *American Sociological Review* 17: 747–750

1952b. The Modal Personality of the Tuscarora Indians as Revealed by the Rorschach Test. *Bureau of American Ethnology Bulletin* 150

1961. *Culture and Personality*. New York: Random House

Index